The Economics and Regulation of Digitalisation

Turkey offers an interesting case study, both when it comes to the practice and the regulation of digitalization, as it combines a Western economic and legal system with an emerging country approach to digitalization. This co-edited volume examines the history, policies, economics, and various regulations of digitalization in Turkey.

The chapters provide a comprehensive overview of how digitalization has developed in Turkey and how digitalization has come to be regulated, inspired by EU legislation yet with a "Turkish touch". It explores the take up of digitalization by industry, society, and government, before delving into examples from FinTech and cryptocurrency, to social media and e-commerce, and yielding lessons for comparable emerging countries.

Covering all the relevant aspects of digitalization, this book will be of interest to academics and students, particularly to those with an interest in innovation, economics of digitalization, policy, and regulation.

Muzaffer Eroğlu is Assistant Professor at the University of Boğaziçi, Faculty of Law; he lectures on company law, corporate governance, sustainability, and competition law. He holds an LLB from Ankara University, an LLM from the University of Kent, and a PhD from Queen Mary, University of London. He carried out research as a visiting academic at the University of Oslo, the Max Planck Institutes for Comparative and International Private Law in Hamburg, the European Institute of Florence, and the University of Oxford. His academic research focuses on corporate governance, competition law, and regulation of network industries. He has several publications in the fields of company law, competition law, and network industries, in both English and Turkish.

Matthias Finger is Professor at the Istanbul Technical University (ITÜ), Faculty of Management. He holds a PhD in political science from the University of Geneva. He has been Assistant Professor at Syracuse University (New York), Associate Professor at Columbia University (New York), Professor of Management of Public Enterprises at the Swiss Federal Institute of Public Administration, and between 2002 and 2020, the Swiss Post Chair in Management of Network Industries at EPFL. Since 2010, he has been a part-time professor at the European University Institute (EUI) in Florence, Italy, where he directs the Florence School of Regulation's Transport Area (FSR-T). Since 2017, he has been a professor at the Faculty of Management at Istanbul Technical University (ITÜ), directing the Istanbul Center for Regulation (IC4R).

Emin Köksal is Associate Professor of Economics at Bahçeşehir University. He teaches managerial economics for MBA programs and industrial organization for the undergraduate program. He also teaches courses such as Platform Economics and Competition Policy in Digital Markets. He publishes extensively on competition and regulatory issues in telecommunications, energy, and platform industries. He has experience in platform business models, network neutrality regulations, and internet usage. He is the associate editor-in-chief of the journal *Competition and Regulation in Network Industries*. As an economic consultant, he has led economic analyses for antitrust cases and regulatory assessments.

RIOT!

Routledge Studies in Innovation, Organizations and Technology

Corporate Entrepreneurship and Innovation in Tourism and Hospitality
Global Post Covid-19 Recovery Strategies
Edited by Teresa Aguiar-Quintana, Jonathon Day and Francisca Rosa Álamo Vera

Grassroots Innovation
Discourse, Policy and Practice in the Global South
Hemant Kumar and Gautam Sharma

Business Models and Digital Technology Platforms
Implementation and Complexities for Digital Business
Krzysztof Bartczak

Artificial Intelligence, Co-Creation and Creativity
The New Frontier for Innovation
Edited by Francisco Tigre Moura

Knowledge Management, Leadership and Innovation in Digital Transformation
Navigating the Future of Organizations
Asha Thomas

Collaborating for Museum Innovation
Technological, Cultural and Organizational Innovation in Spanish Museums
Chuan Li

The Economics and Regulation of Digitalisation
The Case of Türkiye
Edited by Muzaffer Eroğlu, Matthias Finger and Emin Köksal

For more information about this series, please visit: www.routledge.com/Routledge-Studies-in-Innovation-Organizations-and-Technology/book-series/RIOT

The Economics and Regulation of Digitalisation

The Case of Türkiye

Edited by Muzaffer Eroğlu,
Matthias Finger and Emin Köksal

Routledge
Taylor & Francis Group
LONDON AND NEW YORK

First published 2025
by Routledge
4 Park Square, Milton Park, Abingdon, Oxon OX14 4RN

and by Routledge
605 Third Avenue, New York, NY 10158

Routledge is an imprint of the Taylor & Francis Group, an informa business

British Library Cataloguing-in-Publication Data
A catalogue record for this book is available from the British Library

Library of Congress Cataloging-in-Publication Data
Names: Eroğlu, Muzaffer, editor. | Finger, Matthias, editor. | Köksal, Emin, editor.
Title: The economics and regulation of digitalisation : the case of Türkiye / edited by Muzaffer Eroğlu, Matthias Finger, and Emin Köksal.
Description: Abingdon, Oxon [UK] ; New York, NY : Routledge, 2024. | Series: Routledge studies in innovation, organizations, and technology | Includes bibliographical references and index.
Identifiers: LCCN 2024031057 (print) | LCCN 2024031058 (ebook) | ISBN 9781032692333 (hardcover) | ISBN 9781032692470 (paperback) | ISBN 9781032692937 (ebook)
Subjects: LCSH: Digital media—Law and legislation—Turkey. | Digital media—Economic aspects—Turkey. | Information technology—Law and legislation—Turkey. | Computer networks—Law and legislation—Turkey.
Classification: LCC KKX80.C65 E36 2024 (print) | LCC KKX80.C65 (ebook) | DDC 343.56109/944—dc23/eng/20240714
LC record available at https://lccn.loc.gov/2024031057
LC ebook record available at https://lccn.loc.gov/2024031058

ISBN: 978-1-032-69233-3 (hbk)
ISBN: 978-1-032-69247-0 (pbk)
ISBN: 978-1-032-69293-7 (ebk)

DOI: 10.4324/9781032692937

Typeset in Sabon
by Apex CoVantage, LLC

Contents

Figures

Tables

Contributors

Aslı Ak is an associate at Balcıoğlu Selçuk Ardıyok Keki Attorney Partnership, Türkiye.

Muhammed Furkan Akıncı is an assistant professor at Boğaziçi University, Faculty of Law, Türkiye.

Şahin Ardıyok is a partner at Balcıoğlu Selçuk Ardıyok Keki Attorney Partnership, Türkiye.

Zeynep Ayata is an associate professor at Koç University, Faculty of Law, Türkiye.

Ozan Bakış is a professor at Bahçeşehir University, Türkiye.

Alparslan Bayraktar is the Minister of Energy and Natural Resources, Türkiye.

Pınar Çağlayan Aksoy is an associate professor at Bilkent University, Faculty of Law, Türkiye.

Cihan Doğan is a partner at CD Law Firm, Türkiye.

Hakan Erek is the regulation manager at Vodafone, Türkiye.

Çiçek Ersoy is an assistant professor at Istanbul Technical University, Türkiye.

Mehmet Bedii Kaya is an associate professor at Istanbul Bilgi University, Faculty of Law, Türkiye.

Harun Muratoğulları is an assistant professor at Boğaziçi University, Faculty of Law, Türkiye.

Fatma Davarcıoğlu Özaktaş is an associate professor at Abant İzzet Baysal University, Türkiye.

Fatih Cemil Özbuğday is a professor at Ankara Yıldırım Beyazıt University, Türkiye.

Kerem Cem Sanli is a professor at Istanbul Bilgi University, Faculty of Law, Türkiye.

Zeynep Şengören Özcan is a senior consultant at Balcıoğlu Selçuk Ardıyok Keki Attorney Partnership, Türkiye.

Beril Taşkin Kapusuzoğlu is an assistant professor at Boğaziçi University, Faculty of Law, Türkiye.

Hüseyin Taştan is a professor at Yıldız Technical University, Türkiye.

Foreword

Stakes are high when it comes to digitalization, as digitalization is a key factor for the competitiveness of any country in the global economy. Getting it right is indeed a complex matter: telecommunications infrastructures need to be put into place early on; digital literacy needs to be developed in parallel, digital services need to be offered both by the government and the private sector, and the corresponding regulations and regulatory authorities need to set the institutional framework for all this to be unfolding logically as well as to be societally useful.

In this edited volume by three renowned academics 14 chapters offer a thorough, sometimes critical but always constructive, description and analysis of the main facets of digitalization in Türkiye, starting with its foundational infrastructures, the main policies and regulations, along with the take-up of digitalization by government, industry, and society. The editors of this volume have done an excellent job gathering, for the first time, all these academics in the various Turkish Universities who have made digitalization their field of expertise. By doing so, the book offers a unique and comprehensive overview of how digitalization has emerged, evolved, and gradually become regulated in Türkiye. As such, it will without doubt become a valuable resource for many young researchers. Moreover, it will put Türkiye on the international map of digitalization, as in many areas, especially in e-government and e-health the country is clearly a forerunner.

Of course, not everything is rosy, as one would expect in an area of technological development where it is difficult to get things right from the start and without learning by doing. But, as the reader will see, Türkiye has chosen a pragmatic and to a certain extent unique approach, combining elements from the currently prevalent three global models of digitalization, that is, the American market-centric, the Chinese state-centric and the European citizen-centric models. This pragmatic approach and ultimately beneficial outcome may not have been fully planned, but was certainly made possible because, relatively early on, Türkiye has given itself a structure at the highest level – the so-called Digital Transformation Office – which has been instrumental in navigating all the pitfalls of digitalization.

Digitalization is of course an ongoing process, which is moreover still accelerating. And so are the regulatory challenges governments will continue to face. Already on the horizon are the potentially profound positive and negative impacts of artificial intelligence, impacts which will inevitably call for appropriate policies and regulations. I hope this book inspires and encourages the intellectually curious practitioners and practically minded academics who strive to keep pace with all these transformative impacts of digitalization on our economies, societies, and cultures.

Dr Alparslan Bayraktar
Minister of Energy and Natural Resources Türkiye

1 Setting the scene

Matthias Finger, Emin Köksal, and Muzaffer Eroğlu

Introduction

This book examines the history, policies, economics, and the various regulations of digitalization in Türkiye. Türkiye offers indeed a very interesting case study, as it combines a Western economic and legal system with an emerging country approach to regulating digitalization. The purpose of this introductory chapter is not to comment on the various regulatory policies and practices in matters of digitalization in Türkiye, as this will be done in much detail by the contributors. Rather, we want to set the scene for this edited volume. Indeed, digital technologies, enterprises, and industries have developed exponentially over the past approximately 50 years worldwide. Governments have mostly reacted to these profound and pervasive technological developments. First, they have tried to digitalize themselves, and subsequently, they have developed policies and regulations to simultaneously harness the potential of digitalization for their economies and their citizens, as well as to mitigate and address some of the perceived negative economic, societal, and sometimes even cultural effects of digitalization. But what exactly have governments done? What issues have they tried to address? How successful have they been? What has inspired them? Do their actions, policies, and regulations reflect underlying strategies or even visions? Those are the questions we will briefly touch upon in this first chapter.

Over the past few years, a clearer understanding of the various approaches to digitalization has slowly emerged among the small community of scholars that have been following digital policies and regulations systematically over time as we did and continue to do. However, there is still a lot of disagreement among scholars, and we do not pretend to be providing the scientific truth about the matter. Rather, we will offer our assessment of governments' reactions to digitalization by following a historical approach. Quite logically, the closer we get to today, the more personal our assessment will be. We will thus trace back the evolving relationship between government (as operator, policymaker, and regulator) and "digitalization" in the broad sense. We will do so in four distinct steps, thus reflecting the rapid advancements of digital technologies. More precisely, we will distinguish between a first step in

DOI: 10.4324/9781032692937-1

the 1970s with the so-called information society, a second step during the 1990s with the various efforts by governments for a digital public sector reform called "e-gov", a third step as of 2010 whereby governments became concerned by powerful global and private "digital platforms" and how to regulate them, and a fourth most recent step, reflecting a growing concern with "data" and their governance as of 2020. This last step is also paving the way for an ever more geopolitical approach to digitalization, a topic we will touch upon in the conclusion of this chapter. With these four steps, we think that we are able to capture the broader context of this evolving relationship between digitalization and government. However, before doing so, let us briefly explain the conceptual framework that underlies our approach to the matter.

Co-evolution between technology and institutions

We are grounding our approach in the framework of the co-evolution between technology and institutions. This approach states that there is a constant "back-and-forth", but never an equilibrium, between the evolution of technology on the one hand and the institutions (the rules) governing technology on the other hand (Finger et al., 2005; Crettenand & Finger, 2013). Figure 1.1 represents this approach graphically.

Figure 1.1 depicts technological developments along a timeline. This evolution is quantitative and incremental but can also be qualitative and disruptive. It is framed by rules: in the beginning of this technological evolution, rules are not specific to a particular technology, but they still apply and determine the technological trajectory even though they might not be appropriate. It is also important to note that the apparent absence of specific rules, from an institutional economics point of view, still sets incentives to behave

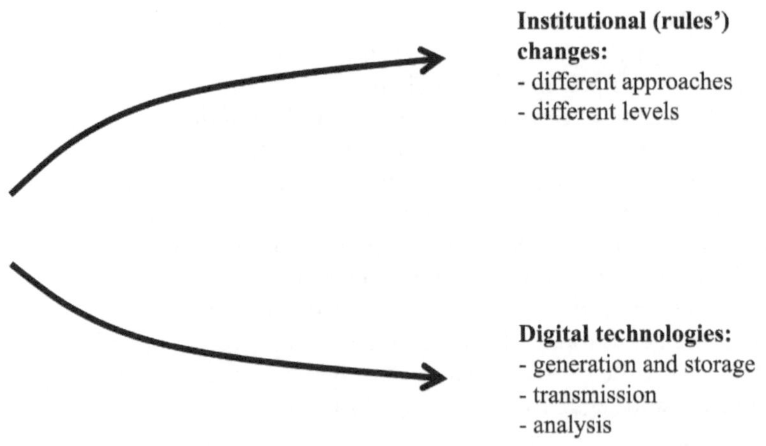

Figure 1.1 Co-evolution between technology and institutions.

and develop the technology in certain ways. As technology and institutions (rules) evolve, a corresponding industry emerges and evolves. Perhaps, the term "ecosystem" of stakeholders would be more adequate, as this ecosystem encompasses simultaneously technological (universities, science parks, early start-ups etc.), institutional (policymakers, regulators, financiers, industry standard-setting bodies, etc.), as well as economic actors (firms of different age and sizes, suppliers, consumers of different types).

Whereas this conceptualization can and is being broadly applied to all kinds of technologies, their trajectories, and their corresponding industries, we are applying it here to the specific case of digital technologies. In the case of digital technologies – a particularly pervasive and particularly rapidly evolving and qualitatively changing set of technologies – the institutional framework governing digitalization is mostly lagging, or in other words constantly trying to catch up. Figure 1.2 applies this co-evolution framework to digitalization.

On the technological side we observe the evolution in the areas of devices (computers, smartphones, smart meters, sensors, cameras, satellites, etc.) which become ever more powerful, often also always smaller and cheaper, generating ever more data and information of ever better quality, increasingly in real time. A similar evolution, at a little later stage, can also be observed in terms of data and information storage. This evolution is paralleled by equally rapidly developing technologies in the area of transmission, namely in telecommunications (fixed telephony, fiber, mobile data transmission, satellite transmission), whereby ever bigger amounts of data can be transmitted at ever more rapid speed and ever lower costs and this to the point of bidirectionality and real-time monitoring of everything. The so-far last stage in this development takes place in data treatment (including visualization) and analytics, up to the most recent developments in artificial intelligence

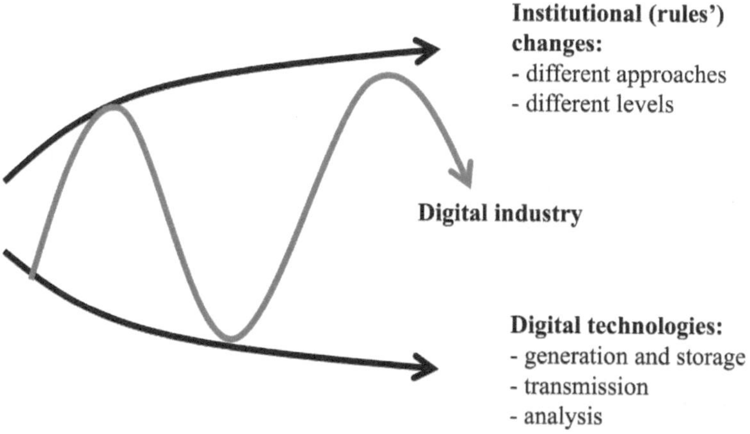

Figure 1.2 Co-evolution of technology and institutions in the case of digitalization.

(algorithms). Here, as well, ever more data can be analyzed ever more rapidly at ever lower costs, up to the point of real-time analysis.

On the institutional side, this technological evolution is accompanied, and to a certain extent steered, by policies and regulations (or the absence thereof). Noteworthy is the time lag between the technological developments on the one hand and the reactive policies and regulations on the other. For this chapter, we have structured these institutional developments, that is, more generally the ways governments react to them, in four stages, being fully aware that the last words have not yet been spoken in matters of digital policies and regulation (see concluding section of this chapter). We have labeled these four stages respectively "information society", "e-government", "platform regulation", and "data governance" and will now present and critically discuss each of these.

The 1970s: "Information Society"

The 1970s saw a qualitative jump in the development of what was then called Information and Communication Technologies (ICTs), in the areas of both telecommunications (networks, wireless communications) and computers (especially personalized computers and mostly software). These developments led people to envision, or rather to dream about, the economic and mainly societal potential of these technologies, best captured by the concept of the "information society". Because much of these technological developments were taking place in the United States, and more specifically in California, the interpretation of what one could do with these technologies was very much tainted by the countercultural (also called hippie) movement of the late 1960s. Of course, it is not the hippie movement that invented and developed these technologies but rather some technological universities (notably Stanford University) did, supported as they were by the US government (Department of Defense) as well as private investors (see O'Mara, 2019). The universities had also their countercultural student protests, and many of the individuals involved in the early stages of digital technology development adhered to countercultural ideas, leading to a unique blend of technological optimism and cultural and political idealism (Stewart Brand, Steve Jobs, Bill Gates, etc.) (Berlin, 2017).

There are several direct links between the countercultural movement's ideas and the *societal* or even *cultural* aspirations of the information society (see Turner, 2006). First, the countercultural movement wanted to break away from traditional and conservative American society and power structures. It thus opened up a space for creativity, experimentation, and innovation, including at a technological level. Silicon Valley and the greater San Francisco Bay area became the physical location where countercultural ideas, technological innovation, and venture capital would meet to develop new disruptive technologies, which became the foundation of the information society. Among these technologies, the PC (personal computer) and networked computing (later on the internet) turned out to be the symbols of individual creativity, sharing of information among equals beyond established media channels, and a more egalitarian society as a networked (potentially global) community. In summary, the countercultural movement of the 1960s, especially in California, provided a fertile ground for the emergence of the Information Society in the 1970s, fostering both technological innovation and the discourse supporting it. As a result of this profoundly libertarian movement, the information society became a very optimistic construct synonymous with the emergence of a new type of society (and economy) that would gradually replace the old so-called industrial society.

At an *economic* level, it is important to remember the oil crises of the 1970s. Consequently, the information society was said to be no longer driven by fossil fuels and extractionism but by information and knowledge as the new motors of economic growth. Just as the industrial revolution had replaced agricultural society, the ICT revolution was going to replace industrial society. Unlike traditional industrial societies, where the primary focus was on large-scale industrial manufacturing of tangible goods, the Information Society was now about the exchange of information among autonomous and decentralized yet interconnected actors across the globe, unleashing creativity and leading to innovation and a new type of economy and society (Castells, 1996, 1997, 1998). Just like farmers had been replaced by industrial workers, the latter were now going to be replaced by people who processed information and produced services, so-called information workers. New service sectors such as finance, insurance, education, and media would replace extractive industries, agriculture, and industrial production. Information was going to be the "new oil" that would fuel the economy. In short, thanks to the ICT revolution, industrial society was going to be replaced by a post-industrial society (Bell, 1976).

Policy and regulation were not part of the equation, as the underlying assumption of the information society was grounded in technological determinism, moreover a very optimistic version of it, so-called techno-optimism. Not only was industrial society inevitably going to be replaced by post-industrial society thanks to the ICTs and the internet, but moreover the post-industrial society was going to be "better", whereby "better" means freer, happier, and less hardworking people with more time for leisure, art, and social life. It is therefore not astonishing that political intervention and especially regulation were not needed, given that this all evolved in the "right" direction, a truly liberal if not libertarian view as inspired by the countercultural movement. Government should abstain from interfering in this "techno-libertarian" historical unfolding, which is exactly what the US government did. At best, government should join the movement toward better services, more satisfied citizens, that is, consumers of government services, provided by civil services as knowledge workers. And to a certain extent, this is what governments did, or rather tried to do, about 20 years later under the banner of e-government.

Given this optimistic and techno-deterministic view, criticism of the information society had a difficult time. At most, the concept was criticized for its lack of inclusiveness, whereby some could be left behind, unable to partake in this rosy future. Thus, concerns about a "digital divide" and "information inequality" were voiced (see van Dijk, 2019). However, quite paradoxically, digital technologies have enormously advanced since the 1970s, whereas the digital divide has rather been reduced. But, in a certain sense, this optimistic view about the ICTs is still around, though now mainly instrumentalized by BigTech. The techno-optimism of the 1970s prevents a more critical and also more realistic look at what the ICTs have done to society up to today.

The 1990s: e-gov or how to make government fit for the information society

"e-gov" for "e-government" is the attempt by governments worldwide to appropriate the information and communication technologies that have developed since the 1970s and, by doing so, enter the information society. To be clear, e-gov is not about policies and regulations about the ICTs; rather it is about making use of the ICTs, notable for its own reform efforts. And these efforts were – and actually still are – necessary, given the basically pre-industrial origin and functioning of the state and its public administration. Furthermore, public sector reform did not start with e-gov but with a broader movement called "New Public Management" (NPM). We will present NPM first and subsequently show how e-gov builds on it.

New public management

The NPM emerged in the 1980s and developed throughout the 1990s in Europe and the United States in response to globalization. NPM's main aim is to increase the efficiency and effectiveness of the public administration while simultaneously becoming more responsive vis-à-vis the citizens (Pollitt & Bouckaert, 2000). Globalization, especially economic globalization, had indeed made public sector reform necessary, as global trade grew rapidly with the end of the Cold War and governments and their public administrations had to become more competitive to attract capital, business, and especially qualified labor. In other words, the prevailing bureaucratic administrative model, stemming from the origins of the nation-state before the industrial revolution, had to be modernized.

The main idea of the NPM was to make the public administration work like a business: public administrators were to become (public) managers; they would be granted (some) managerial autonomy (decentralization of power) so that they would respond better, that is, more innovatively and more flexibly to the citizens' needs. Simultaneously, the citizens would be treated as "customers" of the services, whose quality would be monitored and constantly improved. Overall, the functioning of the public administration would become similar to the functioning of businesses in a service market (Osborne & Gaebler, 1993).

It is true that, at least to a certain extent, public administrations in the industrialized countries did become more cost-efficient, more performing, more transparent, more accountable and more customer-oriented as a result of the various NPM initiatives launched by their respective governments. However, bureaucracy was difficult to reduce, and performance measures and indicators rapidly added to the bureaucratic burden. It was also rapidly discovered that the marketization approach was in contradiction with the public service mandate of governments and the public interest more largely. Overall, it turned out that NPM was a too simplistic approach for the much more complex nature of public administration, which is, indeed, tasked with not only service delivery but also policymaking and regulation. In short, NPM did not manage to overcome the tension and perhaps fundamental contradiction between a commercial approach to service delivery and a political approach to governance of public affairs, thus leading to debatable results.

E-gov as the continuation of public sector reform

The emergence and rapid spread of the ICTs was therefore welcomed by the proponents of NPM as a new impetus for an increasingly exhausted NPM movement as of the 1990s (OECD, 2005). As such, e-gov became the continuation of the NPM movement of the 1980s pursuing basically the same objectives, namely (even more) efficiency, more decentralized decision-making, more innovation, more flexibility, and more customer focus (Finger, 2010). All this was made possible thanks to the introduction of computers, first mainframes and then PCs. But the term "e-gov" became mainly prominent in the 1990s when government started to use the internet as the interface with its citizen-customers, even though the internet was not used to its full potential but merely as a new way to deliver information (and often not even services) to its citizens. Later on (as of the 2010s), and namely with cloud computing and smartphones, public services delivery gained in accessibility and convenience.

E-gov has been adopted and implemented very differently across countries, owing to different factors among which political will, infrastructure development, and digital literacy are the most important ones (see Heeks, 1999). The most prominent success stories of e-gov implementation are generally said to be Estonia (where basically all public services are digitally available), Singapore (known for its easy digital access to services), and South Korea (particularly known for its national digital identity system which in turn opens the door to public services). As we will see in this book, also Türkiye can be considered a country where e-gov has been successfully implemented (e-devlet). Interestingly, the most successful adopters of e-gov are emerging countries.

Indeed, many industrialized countries have not been able to successfully roll out e-gov services and even less so to use the ICTs as a means to reform their public administrations. This is particularly the case in the United States, Germany, and Switzerland, where the federal system, along with concerns about privacy and security, has prevented a decisive, coherent, and coordinated approach to integrated digital (and other) services. Pahlka (2023), who was deputy chief technology officer under the Obama administration, has provided a very critical analysis of the failure of e-gov in the United States, which is said to result from excessive outsourcing as a result of a lack of internal digital expertise, compensated by "procedure fetish" in the procurement processes, as well as the fact that (outsourced) consultants respond to specifications and requirements rather than to needs. This same assessment is probably also valid for most of the countries where e-gov has failed. In short, the usage of the ICTs for improving public services and even more so for the digitalization of the public administration have, with a few exceptions, failed in large parts of the world.

The 2010s: platform regulation

The economic and with a certain delay also the societal implications of digitalization started to become visible worldwide only in the early 2000s with the extraordinary rise of the so-called digital platforms, most of them of American (Californian) origin. Of course, these platforms could emerge only because of the massive development of digital infrastructures earlier on in the areas of data generation, data transmission (via the internet), and data storage. The platforms' original contribution however lies in data analysis, allowing the platforms to exploit ever more powerful network effects. Best known are Amazon (which started in 1994), which at that time was selling only books, eBay (1995), Google Search (1998), Facebook (2004), Airbnb (2008), and Uber (2009), all of which are now dominating the markets they have so created. In this section, we will first present the inner workings of digital platforms and, by doing so, explain their rise to dominance. We will then discuss how governments have come to react (or not) to the rise of these digital platforms over the past 10–15 years.

The inner workings of digital platforms

It is important to have a clear understanding of what digital platforms are, how they function, the benefits and risks they entail, including their underlying business model (see Belleflamme & Peitz, 2021; Evans & Schmalensee, 2016; Knee, 2021; Parker et al., 2016). Indeed, digital platforms are not simply service providers like enterprises operating in the physical world, such as a retailer, a hotel, or a radio and television company. Rather, they are "intermediaries" that "mediate" between providers of physical services offerings on the one hand and the consumers of these services on the other hand. As such, they resemble postal and telecommunication service providers, which also service the so-called two-sided markets (Montero & Finger, 2021). The consequence is that both the physical provider and the consumer of the physical service become customers of the platform. A digital platform is, therefore, a commercial endeavor whose business is to identify, optimize, and maximize previously unexploited – or insufficiently exploited – network effects. This implies that the more connected users or "customers" a platform has, the greater the additional value or benefit of the network for everyone, a process which leads to monopolization, as was already the case in postal and telecom operators. For example, the more users connected to platforms like Facebook or eBay, the greater the value for newcomers to join such a network, something called "direct network effects". The more users make use of Google Search, the more attractive Google becomes as an advertising medium for other companies, a phenomenon called "indirect network effects". And the better a platform like UBER knows and serves its different types of customers (drivers and users) through data analysis, the better the quality of service for all customers, something Montero and Finger (2021) have labeled "algorithmic network effects". All these network effects combined lead to "platform power" and ultimately to monopolization (Moazed & Johnson, 2016; Nielsen & Ganter, 2022).

Digital platforms provide clear economic and other benefits to customers but also come with disadvantages. Positive aspects include easier access to physical services, innovative new services, increased competition among the underlying traditional physical services providers, and overall efficiency gains due to digitized coordination of fragmented actors. Conversely, the price of this development is a reduction in privacy due to the extensive collection of user data, as well as a tendency toward monopolization on a cross-border and potentially global level, reflected in the dependency of customers (users as well as service providers) upon the platforms, something called "Lock-in effects". This dependency is reflected in excessive profits but also in a power shift in favor of the platforms, a phenomenon Montero and Finger (2021) have labeled "platformization" of the underlying physical services providers.

Finally, it is very important to understand the business model of the digital platforms. This business model is based on the availability of, the access to, as well as the analysis of "data". Most and, especially, the most valuable of this data comes from the customers of the platforms themselves, which are usually provided voluntarily and free of charge. In reality, digital platforms are hardly involved in the production of their own services but primarily in better and, above all, more efficient coordination of the actors they serve but from which they extract all the valuable information to better serve them. This of course represents a very important contribution to the economy but also ties all the different customers to the platforms and ultimately serves the platforms' commercial interests as well as it leads to a winner-takes-all dynamics (monopolization).

Governments' reactions: regulating digital platforms

With digital platforms becoming ever more dominant and sometimes abusing their market power, the need for their regulation has become more and more obvious. This need has become recognized in many countries, starting with the European Union (EU). More recently, the United States as well has come to acknowledge that some of these digital platforms are abusing their market power. This need for regulating digital platforms is also recognized in Türkiye and will be discussed by some contributors to this volume. However, how exactly to regulate these platforms is not yet settled, neither in practice nor by academics (see Flew, 2021; Montero & Finger, 2021; Thomas, 2023). In this section, we will first highlight what currently seems to be the dominant approach to regulating digital platforms, after which we will argue for some more advanced regulatory policies in this matter that go beyond the currently prevailing approaches.

The currently dominant approach to regulating digital platforms in both the United States and the EU is grounded in competition theory and antitrust law. However, while antitrust seems to be so far the only approach in the United States, the EU does go beyond it. Indeed, the US regulatory efforts focus on ex post antitrust enforcement and are exclusively concerned with market power. In the United States, regulatory efforts often focus on antitrust enforcement by both the Federal Trade Commission (FTC) and the Department of Justice (DoJ) to address concerns related to the market power of major tech companies, typically by means of antitrust investigations and lawsuits for anti-competitive behavior. The EU has two instruments to deal with digital platforms: there is, on the one hand, the Digital Markets Act (DMA) of 2022 which targets large online platforms with significant market power, the so-called gatekeepers. It does so not with a typical competition regulation approach, since it imposes some ex ante conditions, namely the prohibition of self-preferencing and unfair conditions for users, as well as the obligation to grant access to certain data (see next section on "data governance") along with interoperability measures. The Digital Services Act (DSA) of 2022, on the other hand, focuses on content moderation and user rights and outlines certain responsibilities of platforms.

However, with Montero and Finger (2021), we do think that even the EU approach is still not sufficient, as antitrust law, even when applied in an ex ante manner, is not best suited to addressing market power that stems from highly powerful network effects. As we will argue in the next section on "data governance", powerful digital platforms should furthermore be obliged to make data portable, interoperable, more easily shareable as well as more openly accessible. As a matter of fact, we think that digital platforms must be regulated more explicitly in their role as intermediaries and not only in their role as service providers. Similar to other more traditional intermediaries, such as real estate agents, insurance agents, stock exchanges, or marriage brokers, digital platforms need to be made liable as well as accountable to their clients, providing neutral, objective, transparent, and non-discriminatory services at reasonable conditions. This should include greater transparency as well as a certain accountability when it comes to their algorithms.[1] Finally, platforms should be regulated so as to share some of their profits with the physical service providers they have "platformized", all things that are beyond the scope of current platform regulation in the EU and even more so in the United States.

Yet, doing so will require going beyond the currently still prevailing antitrust and competition regulation theory. Together with Montero and Finger (2021), we think that the regulation of digital platforms – which these authors call the "new network industries" – could and should be inspired by the regulation of the traditional network industries. In the next section on "data governance", we will see that at least the EU is as of recently thinking along similar lines, when envisaging a data layer, or more precisely "data spaces", as a new type of "infrastructure" to which access has to be granted to create more downstream competition.

The 2020s: data governance

While digital platforms and their regulation remain an ongoing concern among regulators, especially in the EU (e.g. Digital Services and Digital Markets Acts), the growing concern as of the late 2010s has become "data", or "big data", that is, the huge amounts of data that are being collected by the digital platforms from their users, as well as from the numerous devices connected to the internet, the so-called Internet of Things (IoT), as such data constitute the very foundation of their business model (Mayer-Schönberger & Cukier, 2013). Again, it is important to understand the nature and economics of data in a first section, before addressing the question of how to regulate them in the second section.

Understanding "Data" as an economic good

To recall, during the early days of digitalization in the 1970s, "data" and more often "information" were considered a public good that would be freely available and shared for the benefit of a coming information society. However, this philosophical and profoundly (techno-)optimistic view did not take into account the economic nature of data and information. In this section, we will therefore recall what has, since, become the accepted view among economists and scholars more generally (Montero & Finger, 2021; Shapiro & Varian, 1999).

Indeed, data and information can be used by multiple users without depleting or reducing their quality for others, a feature called "non-rivalrous consumption". However, their use can be easily restricted to a specific group of users. Obviously, when companies collect and make data usable, they generally prefer not to share it with third parties, treating the data, the resulting information, as well as the algorithms needed for their analysis as trade secrets and subject to copyright protection. This excludability in usage is referred to by economists as "excludability in consumption".

Goods (and services) possessing these characteristics – non-rivalry and excludability – are termed "club goods" or "toll goods". Typical club or toll goods include infrastructure goods, such as tool roads, thus establishing an economic and regulatory parallelism between data (spaces) and infrastructures (see later when it comes to their regulation). In the case of a club good, the actors controlling access to it can determine both the user circle (the "club") and the conditions for its use. Consequently, data and information usage become privately tradable. Data policy, in an abstract sense, thus involves decisions regarding the nature and extent of provisions for the exclusivity (and excludability) of data usage. For example, usage rights to data may remain solely with the companies, making their use privately tradable and generally not shared. Alternatively, companies may be interested, for strategic purposes, or they may be compelled by regulators, to provide data to a group (e.g. all active companies in a specific industry) or even make data publicly accessible. Thus, data policy essentially shapes the participant circle of the "data club".

Furthermore, it is also important to recall the digital value chain: as a matter of fact, the term "data" can refer to various forms of data – raw data, structured data, linked data, and evaluated or analyzed data – representing different forms of data usage. Digital value creation occurs along these different forms of "data". The value chain begins with data collection using digital technologies such as sensors, cameras, radio-frequency identifications (RFIDs), and other data collection technologies (raw data, value creation stage 1). In a second step, data is linked, connected, and structured to become information (value creation stage 2). The majority of what is referred to as "data" today is in fact essentially information, that is, already linked data. The evaluation and analysis of information and (raw) data lead, in a third step, to actionable knowledge, on the basis of which services can then be offered to customers (value creation stage 3). Such value creation takes place thanks to ever more powerful algorithms, trained thanks to ever more data and information (Evans et al., 2006; O'Neill, 2016).

This digital value creation chain is further complicated by the fact that it also involves a "feedback effect": at value creation stage 3, not only are services (in digital form) delivered to customers, but customers, in turn, provide "data" back to the service provider (ideally with their knowledge and consent). Customer "data" is often most valuable (e.g. movement data or purchase decisions), which means that it is knowledge and information rather than simply data. Interestingly, the business literature talks about "customer insights" rather than customer data. Based on such insights, service providers can improve and personalize their products and offerings, thereby increasing their efficiency. This flow of information back into the value creation chain is a typical feature of the digital market, which leads, as we have seen earlier, to powerful network effects and ultimately to monopolization, just like in the traditional network industries.

Regulating data as an "Infrastructure"

The earlier economic characteristics – data as a club or toll good on the one hand, along with the feedback effects in the value chain – need to be taken into account when it comes to the regulation of data and of the digital platforms. To be clear, the only efforts currently underway to regulate data can be found in the EU.[2] In this section, we will first outline these efforts by the EU and subsequently its underlying approach.

In 2023, the EU adopted two complementary acts about data regulation, namely the Data Act and the Data Governance Act. Their goal is not primarily to weaken the digital platforms, even though this might be a collateral outcome. Rather, the aim is to make data, especially data from industry, more generally available in so-called *data spaces*, so as to enable innovation, research, and development of new digital services, digital markets, and consequently economic growth across Europe. This should especially happen in these sectors or industries that are considered key to Europe's global competitiveness, such as manufacturing, energy, and agriculture. Moreover, the so-called high-value datasets should be facilitated, probably directly by the European Commission, in areas that are considered particularly strategic, such as research, government, and health care. Both acts introduce the concept of "data intermediaries", which are new entities that should facilitate data sharing between the relevant actors (businesses, universities, public authorities, etc.), while at the same time guaranteeing data protection,[3] data quality, security, interoperability, and therefore competitive access and ultimately competition. However, it is still not entirely clear what these entities are going to be: private? commercial? or simply virtual? In any case, these data intermediaries would then be regulated accordingly.

Still, the concept of data intermediaries does not (yet) align with the economic reality of "data" today (see earlier), as data is primarily in the hands of private (and often global) digital platforms (directly collected from their customers) and located in physical data centers and cloud servers, which are also privately operated and often located offshore. It seems to us that both "data spaces" and "data intermediaries" are analogous to the concept of infrastructures in the traditional network industries (see Montero & Finger, 2021). Just like the traditional physical infrastructures (such as an electricity grid, a road, or a rail infrastructure) these (virtual?) "data infrastructures" would have to be created by government (EU) regulatory intervention, just as was the case in the traditional infrastructures by way of unbundling rules, by which vertically integrated monopolies such as a railway or an electricity company were forced to institutionally separate ("unbundle") competitive services from monopolistic infrastructures.

Once unbundled or created, these (data) infrastructures could not only be considered toll or club goods (see earlier discussion) but could subsequently be regulated in the general economic interest by inspiration from the regulation of the traditional physical network industry infrastructures (access, non-discrimination, interoperability, etc.). And this, we think, is the regulatory model that the European Commission has in mind, not to mention the fact that the officers in charge of digitalization at the European Commission have previously been working in postal and telecommunications regulation. As a result, data utilization subsequently becomes possible thanks to regulated access to the respective data spaces, whereby such data spaces are a combination of technological standards and institutional interoperability rules and, more generally, environments (entities?) that enable (organize?) the collection, storage, processing, exchange, and use of data. They can range from large-scale clouds to specialized systems designed for specific types of data, such as scientific data or industrial data. Currently, the EU envisions nine such data spaces (see Data Act).

At this point, it is in our view premature to say whether and how these EU regulations will ultimately play out in reality. Still, the EU has outlined an alternative to the currently prevailing US and Chinese approaches to (not) regulating digitalization. By doing so, it has, to a certain extent, already triggered a global competition among models to regulate data, the internet, digital platforms, and digitalization more generally. We think that any country, including Türkiye, will ultimately have to position itself in respect to these models in the future.

The coming geopolitical digital order

Over the past 50 years, digital technologies, be they in data generation, transmission, storage or analysis, have not only substantially evolved but have become ever more powerful. This evolution, along with a very lax approach of governments to regulating digitalization, has led to big and powerful global and private digital platforms, in the beginning mostly American but later also Chinese ones. Governments have mostly been busy digitalizing themselves, often with mixed success. The originally very techno-optimistic view has over time given rise to skepticism and growing calls for regulatory intervention, especially when it comes to reigning in the global digital platforms and exerting control over data. Privacy, security, and sovereignty concerns are increasingly being voiced globally and not just in the global South. In short, digitalization has become a geopolitical topic, as witnessed by the most recent publications about "The Digital War" (Ma, 2021), "Data War" (Diagne, 2021), "Data Trafficking" (Kokas, 2023), "Data Cartels" (Lamdan, 2023), and "Cloud Empires" (Lehdonvirta, 2022).

The by far most insightful and most comprehensive book on the coming global geopolitical – that is, the new global "Digital Empires" – has been written by Columbia University Law Professor Anu Bradford (2023). In it, the author outlines in a highly systematic way how three so-called digital empires are emerging around the United States, China, and the EU, each with a very distinct approach to data, the internet, and digital platforms. While it is imaginable that some combinations between the three approaches are possible, no other country or union has come up with yet another coherent approach so far. The three models each define themselves in relationship to markets, government, and citizens. The *market-driven (techno-libertarian) approach,* as actively promoted by the US government within the United States and throughout the world, favors free speech, a free, that is, mostly unregulated internet and innovation by private (American) platform companies (Google, Amazon, Facebook, Apple, Microsoft), again resulting from a minimum of government intervention into digital markets and companies. Needless to say, in this US approach, citizens are also minimally protected, and competition regulation is also only minimally applied. While originally benefiting from Californian techno-optimism and active US government support, this model is clearly suffering from backlash and may not survive in the future (Wheeler, 2023).

The *state-driven (surveillance) approach* as actively promoted by the Chinese government aspires to technological dominance worldwide by instrumentalizing private Chinese companies (Alibaba, Huawei, Tencent, ByteDance, Didi, etc.). This approach uses data to exert social control at least in China as well as beyond its borders. Needless to say, citizens are also not very well protected, but companies are more regulated than in the United States, sometimes by taking inspiration from the EU. The *rights-driven (regulatory) approach* as actively promoted by the EU, also beyond its borders, heavily uses regulation of digital companies and data to promote simultaneously an EU-wide digital economy and fundamental rights of citizens. Not having their own global digital companies, the EU approach strongly regulates BigTech to more widely share some of the profits they generate and benefits they bring to the market and to society. However, at this point in history, it is not clear which of the two – the Chinese or the EU – approaches will prevail, nor is it certain whether any of the three approaches will actually prevail against the digital platforms themselves, be they from the United States or from China.

As the reader will see from the various contributions to our book, Türkiye is trying to find and hopefully assert its own way in a digital world that is increasingly global, private, and geopolitical. Our book therefore aims at illustrating the country's various policy and regulatory initiatives, actions and achievements in this context. It delves into the foundational elements – infrastructure development, policy landscape, and the growth of e-commerce – that are essential for digital economies and societies. It then examines how different industries in Türkiye are adopting ICTs and explores the broader digitalization of Turkish society through a digital society index. Also, it takes a critical look at the legal environment for digital markets within the Turkish constitution, focusing on economic freedom. It then dissects the regulations governing e-government services, data privacy, competition in the digital sphere, the rise of FinTech and cryptocurrencies, and the governance of social media platforms.

Outline of the chapters

This edited volume investigates the multidimensional landscape of regulation within the growing digital economy of Türkiye. With contributions from experts and scholars, the book offers a comprehensive exploration of the complex interplay between economic considerations and the regulatory framework that shapes Türkiye's digital transformation.

In Chapter 2, Hakan Erek delves into the critical issue of infrastructure development for the telecommunications industry in Türkiye. He examines the legal landscape of the industry, historical data regarding its evolution, and its present financial state. Erek emphasizes the restrictive nature of Türkiye's regulatory framework and its hindering effects on much-needed investment within the telecommunications sector. International benchmarks highlight that despite progress, Türkiye lags in fiber penetration and fiber connectivity for base stations compared to other G-20 nations. The chapter advocates for targeted public interventions to address these limitations and catalyze digital transformation.

Chapter 3, authored by Fatma Davarcıoğlu Özaktaş and Şahin Ardıyok, provides a historical overview and contemporary analysis of Türkiye's digitalization policies and legislation. The authors focus on Türkiye's efforts to enhance broadband internet infrastructure and the digitalization of government services. Özaktaş and Ardıyok argue that Türkiye has learned valuable lessons from past mistakes during privatization and liberalization processes. Moving forward, amending existing regulations and strategically designing policies around competitive market structures are presented as essential steps for creating an environment helpful to technological progress and innovation.

The development of e-commerce in Türkiye is the focus of Chapter 4, written by Zeynep Şengören Özcan and Aslı Ak. They explore the factors driving the remarkable growth of e-commerce, analyze consumer behavior, and discuss the role of key market players. The authors highlight the interplay between legal developments, such as competition, data protection, and consumer protection, and the continued expansion of the e-commerce sector in Türkiye.

Fatih Cemil Özbuğday, in Chapter 5, addresses the dynamics of foreign and Turkish digital platforms within Türkiye's digital economy. Using insightful case studies, Özbuğday investigates the influence of network externalities on platform competition and ownership structures. The findings illustrate that local platforms tend to dominate markets where network externalities are primarily confined within the country's borders. In contrast, global platforms leverage cross-country network externalities to compete effectively in a variety of sectors.

Chapter 6 by Hüseyin Taştan provides a comprehensive analysis of ICT adoption within Türkiye's manufacturing and service sectors. Taştan leverages data from Turkstat's and Eurostat's ICT surveys to benchmark Türkiye's digitalization against EU countries. This comparative approach sheds light on Türkiye's progress and highlights specific areas for future improvement. Insights from the chapter point to a need for focused strategies to address disparities in technology adoption across different industries and firm sizes.

Chapter 7, written by Emin Köksal and Ozan Bakış, introduces the innovative "Türkiye Digital Society Index" (TDSI). The TDSI provides a valuable metric for understanding the digitalization of Turkish society. Köksal and Bakış discuss the index's methodology and how it captures progress and disparities in connectivity, internet usage, and the uptake of digital public services in Türkiye. The TDSI serves as a powerful tool to guide policy interventions aimed at bridging digital divides across demographics and regions within Türkiye.

Chapter 8, written by Harun Muratoğulları, examines digital capitalism's constitutional challenges from the platform power perspective. Muratoğulları mainly focuses on the disruptive impact of private powers from the digital environment on the fundamental rights of individuals and the resulting normative counteractions. The chapter examines the responses of the Turkish constitutional ecosystem to the normative challenges of digital capitalism. The chapter explores whether the country's path to digital constitutionalism has unique characteristics in developing its own narrative in regulating digital markets.

The development of e-government services in Türkiye is the focus of Chapter 9, written by Beril Taşkın Kapusuzoğlu. She explores the legal and administrative aspects of regulating e-government services in Türkiye. Kopusuzoğlu provides a contextual analysis of e-government services and an emphasis on their global growth, a detailed outline of the legislative milestones in Türkiye's e-government journey, and finally, scrutinizes the institutions that oversee electronic government services in Türkiye.

Çiçek Ersoy, in Chapter 10, addresses the data protection and privacy laws in Turkey, especially from the point of Turkish Data Protection Act No. 6698, which entered into force on 7 April 2016 and related secondary legislation. Ersoy presents the legislative framework and legal sources for privacy and data protection and the implementation of newly amended law and dynamic by-laws of the Turkish Data Protection Authority. The chapter clearly defines the concept of data breach and the procedures and legal consequences for sanctions.

Chapter 11 by Zeynep Ayata analyses the new elements and tools in competition regulation and implementations to digital markets. Ayata provides a comprehensive scrutiny of the decisions of the Turkish Competition Council regarding digital platforms, the critical findings of sector inquiry reports, and the consequent developments of new policies in digital markets in Türkiye. The chapter also examines the proposed amendment to the Turkish Competition Act and draws parallels to the case law and sector inquiry reports in digital markets.

In Chapter 12, Kerem Cem Sanli and Cihan Doğan look into the essential characteristics of the digital platform regulation under Turkish law and focus mainly on the E-Commerce Law as it is currently in force. This chapter examines the economic rationales behind regulating digital platforms and the challenges associated with applying competition law to digital platforms. Finally, they demonstrate that the E-Commerce Law in Türkiye, unlike other similar regulations, sets forth several unorthodox obligations for digital platforms.

Chapter 13, authored by Pınar Çağlayan Aksoy, provides the effects analysis of opportunities and challenges of the transformation of traditional financial services by technological advancements, particularly the emergence of financial technology (FinTech) and distributed ledger technology (DLT) in Türkiye. She indicates that Türkiye is adapting its legal and regulatory framework to embrace the opportunities presented by FinTech and DLT while ensuring the safety and security of its financial system. Moreover, the chapter provides a comprehensive analysis of Türkiye's current regulatory framework regarding FinTech and crypto assets and presents projections about the future.

Mehmet Bedii Kaya and Muhammed Furkan Akıncı, in Chapter 14, presents a detailed examination of the evolving landscape of social media regulation in Türkiye, emphasizing the development of legal measures and their implications for both social media companies and individual users. They examine recent changes in social media law and the interactions between Internet Law and other regulatory frameworks and assess the roles of various regulatory bodies. This chapter situates Türkiye's approach to social media regulation within a broader context of seeking equilibrium between online freedom, societal welfare, and national security, mirroring global trends in digital governance.

Collectively, the chapters in this volume highlight the relationship between regulation, technology, and economic development in Türkiye. The authors offer valuable perspectives and evidence-based insights that can inform policymakers, industry leaders, and researchers seeking to maximize the benefits and mitigate the challenges posed by Türkiye's ongoing digital transformation. This book aims to spark further discourse and encourage continued research into this dynamic and critical area.

Notes

1 It appears that the EU's proposed Artificial Intelligence Act (AI Act, proposed in 2012) also includes provisions for a greater transparency of algorithms, in addition to prohibition and audits of certain AI applications.
2 And to a certain extent also in China (see next section on the coming global digital order).
3 In other words, ensuring compliance with GDPR, the European General Data Protection Regulation of 2016.

References

Bell, D. (1976). *The coming of post-industrial society: A venture in social forecasting*. London: Basic Books.
Belleflamme, P., & Peitz, M. (2021). *The economics of platforms: Concepts and strategy*. Cambridge: Cambridge University Press.
Berlin, L. (2017). *Troublemakers: Silicon Valley's coming of age*. New York: Simon and Schuster.
Bradford, A. (2023). *Digital empires: The global battle to regulate technology*. Oxford: Oxford University Press.

Castells, M. (1996, second edition, 2009). *The rise of the network society, the information age: Economy, society and culture* (Vol. 1). Malden, MA; Oxford, UK: Blackwell.

Castells, M. (1997, second edition, 2009). *The power of identity, the information age: Economy, society and culture* (Vol. 2). Malden, MA; Oxford, UK: Blackwell.

Castells, M. (1998, second edition, 2010). *End of millennium, the information age: Economy, society and culture* (Vol. 3). Malden, MA; Oxford, UK: Blackwell.

Crettenand, N., & Finger, M. (2013). The alignment between institutions and technologies in network industries. *Competition and Regulation in Network Industries, 14*(2), 106–129.

Diagne, C. O. (2021). *Data war: Le déclin des états et la disparition des nations.* Paris: Editions Muse.

Evans, D. S., Hagiu, A., & Schmalensee, R. (2006). *Invisible engines: How software platforms drive innovation and transform industries.* Cambridge, MA: MIT Press.

Evans, D. S., & Schmalensee, R. (2016). *Matchmakers: The new economics of multisided platforms.* Boston: Harvard Business Review Press.

Finger, M. (2010). What role for government in e-government? *Journal of E-Governance, 33*(4), 199–204.

Finger, M., Groenewegen, J., & Künneke, R. (2005). The quest for coherence between institutions and technologies in infrastructures. *Journal of Network Industries, 6*(4), 227–260.

Flew, T. (2021). *Regulating platforms.* London: Polity Press.

Heeks, R. (1999). *Reinventing government in the information age: International practice in IT-enabled public sector reform.* London: Routledge.

Knee, J. A. (2021). *The platform delusion: Who wins and who loses in the age of tech titans.* London: Penguin.

Kokas, A. (2023). *Trafficking data: How China is winning the battle for digital sovereignty.* Oxford: Oxford University Press.

Lamdan, S. (2023). *Data cartels: The companies that control and monopolize our information.* Stanford: Stanford University Press.

Lehdonvirta, V. (2022). *Cloud empires: How digital platforms are overtaking the state and how we can regain control.* Cambridge, MA: MIT Press.

Ma, W. (2021). *The digital war: How China's tech power shapes the future of AI, blockchain and cyberspace.* Chichester: Wiley.

Mayer-Schönberger, V., & Cukier, K. (2013). *Big data: A revolution that will transform how we live, work and think.* London: John Murray Publishers.

Moazed, A., & Johnson, N. L. (2016). *Modern monopolies: What it takes to dominate the 21st century.* New York: St. Martin's Press.

Montero, J., & Finger, M. (2021). *The rise of the new network industries: Regulating digital platforms.* London: Routledge.

Nielsen, R. K., & Ganter, S. A. (2022). *The power of platforms: Shaping media and society.* Oxford: Oxford University Press.

OECD (2005). *E-government for better government.* Paris: OECD.

O'Mara, M. (2019). *The code: Silicon Valley and the remaking of America.* London: Penguin Books.

O'Neill, C. (2016). *Weapons of math destruction: How big data increases inequality and threatens democracy.* New York: Broadway Books.

Osborne, D., & Gaebler, T. (1993). *Reinventing government: How the entrepreneurial spirit is transforming the public sector.* New York: Plume.

Pahlka, J. (2023). *Recoding America.* New York: Metropolitan Books.

Parker, G. G., van Alstyne, M. W., & Choudary, S. P. (2016). *Platform revolution: How networked markets are transforming the economy – and how to make them work for you.* New York: Norton.

Pollitt, C., & Bouckaert, G. (2000). *Public management reform: A comparative analysis*. Oxford: Oxford University Press.
Shapiro, C., & Varian, H. R. (1999). *Information rules: A strategic guide to the network economy*. Cambridge MA: Harvard Business Review Press.
Thomas, P. N. (2023). *Platform regulation: Exemplars, approaches, and solutions*. Oxford: Oxford University Press.
Turner, F. (2006). *From counterculture to cyberculture: Stewart brand, the whole earth network, and the rise of digital utopianism*. Chicago: University of Chicago Press.
Van Dijk, J. (2019). *The digital divide*. London: Polity Press.
Wheeler, T. (2023). *Techlash: Who makes the rules in the digital gilded age?* Washington: Brookings Institution Press.

2 Infrastructure Development

Hakan Erek

Introduction

The telecommunication industry can be considered as the backbone of the digital economy. OECD also asserts that improving access to connectivity is one of the fundamental dimensions of digital transformation (OECD, 2020). Widespread and high-quality telecommunication services (especially broadband services) contribute to society and the economy through various channels including network effects, accessibility and universal service and innovation (OECD, 2021). In this broader perspective, having a robust telecommunication infrastructure offers benefits like improved collaboration, enhanced productivity, effective decision-making, cost reduction and an improved customer experience.[1]

As mentioned earlier, since the telecommunication industry forms the basis for digitalization, focusing on the development of telecommunication infrastructure is important, in that sense, it is possible to analyze the industry at different layers such as physical infrastructure and technology, finance (revenue and investment) and consumer (price, coverage, data usage and data speed).

In the case of Türkiye, mobile and fixed telecommunication markets exhibit distinct dynamics, therefore it would be beneficial to examine them in two separate parts. Each part has its own regulatory landscape, figures and financial subparts.

First, we will provide introductory information about the legal framework in Türkiye and recent developments. The telecommunication industry is highly regulated, so the structure of the legal framework has a substantial impact on both the costs and revenues of the industry. Second, we will present some figures about both mobile and fixed markets in Türkiye like 4G/fiber penetration and discuss the historical development of the industry. The purpose of this section is to illustrate what Turkey's current landscape reflects about its historical development. Additionally, this section will include some international benchmarks for comparison. In the following section, the financial situation of the industry will be discussed by using historical sectoral revenue and investment trends in Türkiye and other countries. The fifth section

DOI: 10.4324/9781032692937-2

will be a general discussion about digitalization and drawing insights from the preceding sections. Finally, there will be a conclusion section at the end of the study.

Mobile Communication Services

Mobile communication services can be considered as the main driver of digitalization in Türkiye. A substantial part of the application ecosystem works via mobile connectivity. That shows itself in figures about digital banking usage, e-commerce activities and public services like education (EBA) and health (HES). Therefore, understanding the elements affecting mobile connectivity is essential.

Regulatory Landscape

The legal framework and license regime play a crucial role in determining the landscape for network investment, making it essential to understand these aspects. Consequently, the regulatory landscape is a separate topic for both industries. Mobile communication services were initiated in 1994 with an "annual authorization regime".[2] Turkcell İletişim Hizmetleri A.Ş. (Turkcell) and Telsim Mobil Telekomünikasyon Hizmetleri A.Ş. (Vodafone).[3] In 1998, the Ministry made an auction for GSM services (2G) and 900 MHz, and two operators (Turkcell and Vodafone) won the right to provide 2G services by using the spectrum on 900 MHz. Hence, the concession agreement regime started in Türkiye. Moreover, the number blocks were also allocated with the auction. In summary, 2G concession agreements include the right to use 900 MHz, the right to provide 2G services, and the right to use number blocks.

In the beginning, Türkiye's mobile communication market was a duopoly, Aycell Haberleşme ve Pazarlama Hizmetleri A.Ş.[4] and İŞ-TİM Telekomünikasyon Hizmetleri A.Ş. entered the market in 2001 by getting the right to use 1,800 MHz and to provide 2G services. In 2003, the last movers merged,[5] and Türkiye's mobile market transformed into a three-player market.

In 2008, there was another auction for IMT-2000/UMTS (3G) services and the spectrum associated with 3G services. All three operators participated in the auction, and each of them has gained the right to provide 3G services. In addition, the Information and Communication Technologies Authority (hereinafter ICTA) has imposed obligations related to coverage and quality of services. This is a common practice, as many other countries also implement similar obligations on operators to widen mobile connectivity and ensure a basic level of services beyond the competitive output. However, the Turkish market has a distinctive feature, in fact, ICTA has also mandated some Research & Development (R&D) and Small and Medium Enterprises (SME) (as purchasing) obligations. In this context, operators were required to maintain a certain level of coverage and speed (as usual) while they also had a responsibility to purchase certain levels of their needs from SMEs and to invest in R&D topics. That feature differentiates Türkiye from other countries because none of the other countries have such obligations.

In 2015, the Ministry organized an auction for IMT-Advanced (4.5G) services and the spectrum associated with 4.5G services. All operators participated in the auction. At the end of the auction, various bands[6] were allocated. The 4.5G auction was a milestone for the Turkish mobile communication industry since it also brought features as the first of its kind. For instance, as a result of an amendment done in the Electronic Communication Code (Law no:5809), the concession regime was replaced with an authorization regime, and the 4.5G auction was done as an authorization.[7] 4.5G was particularly significant as it brought fast mobile broadband to Türkiye. Moreover, ICTA imposed localization obligation on operators in addition to existing obligations (coming from 2G and 3G) and specific obligations for coverage and quality. Notably, after the 4.5G auction, operators gained the flexibility to use all of their spectrum for any technology, in other words, technology agnostics were introduced. Prior to the 4.5G auction, all of the operators had to use spectrum for the services associated with that spectrum.

We have attempted to summarize the general history and significant developments in the Turkish mobile communication industry. Let's underline the key characteristics of the industry. First of all, both 2G and 3G concessions and 4.5G authorization are Build-Operate-Transfer contracts. In fact, all operators are obliged to transfer all network assets to the public or an entity designated by the public. Thus, unlike operators in other countries, operators in Türkiye do not own the network assets. This distinctive feature is particularly noteworthy for Turkey.

Second, although the concession agreements and authorization document foresee room for renewal, the whole process is unclear.[8] As expected, due to a lack of ownership, it becomes critical for operators to know how many years they can utilize the assets to make accurate investment decisions. The unclear situation poses a threat to the transfer of the assets. Although there are different concession agreements and authorization for each technology, due to the economics of scope and economics of scale, there is one accumulated mobile communication network. Therefore, if an operator decides to cease one of its concessions while retaining the others, the transfer of the common assets becomes problematic.

Third, as is well known, operators have coverage and quality of service obligations in accordance with the spectrum they hold. In Türkiye, it can be stated that operators have too many non-traditional[9] obligations such as purchasing equipment from SMEs, having R&D indicators or localization. These obligations exert significant pressure on operators in terms of both financial and transaction costs. Moreover, the localization obligation stands apart from other localization efforts in Türkiye. For instance, in the renewable energy industry, the regulatory framework foresees additional support for local products, and there is no obligation for electricity generators. In telecommunication case, the operators are practically compelled to produce their own local products.

Finally, as mentioned earlier, Türkiye has established a concession agreement or authorization for each technology. As a result of that approach, coverage and quality obligations are monitored separately; in other words, the operators try to meet different targets for various technologies instead of meeting one indicator for the voice service and one indicator for the data service. Such an approach imposes a huge operational burden on both the operators and ICTA.

In conclusion, Türkiye possesses its own distinctive regulatory framework in the mobile communication industry. Non-traditional obligations, fragmented structure of quality and coverage obligations, non-ownership features and unclear process for extension make Türkiye different from other countries and determine the investment decision of the operators.

Historical Figures and Features of the Mobile Telecommunication Industry

Sharing some historical figures about the Turkish telecommunication market is critical to understand the development of the market and maturity level. Such a sharing also indicates the readiness of the society for more digitalization. It would be better to begin with the penetration rate based on different technologies. Trends in the industry are shown in Figure 2.1.

As seen in Figure 2.1, the mobile penetration rate exceeds 100%, but it must be kept in mind that there are still 2G customers, so the penetration rate is not equal to the rate of connected customers (mobile). In any case, exceeding the 100% threshold indicates that mobile communication services

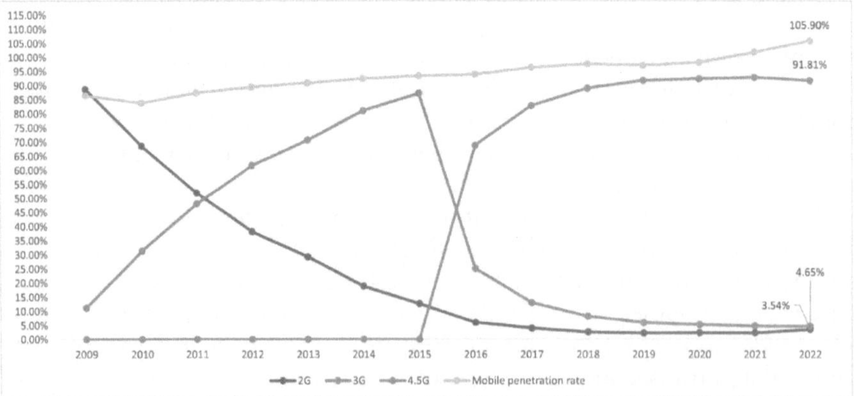

Figure 2.1 Mobile penetration rate and subscription rate in different technologies (2009–2022) (ICTA, 2024).

are extensive. Moreover, approximately 95% of the consumers have access to mobile internet.

When we look at the technology-based distribution, the 4.5G customer rate is much higher than other technologies as expected. Türkiye's mobile industry has exceeded the 90% threshold in 4.5G technology just in three years. In that sense, it can be concluded that both the number and the rate of data customers[10] increased very quickly. One more feature about the increase of 4.5G deserves attention, in fact, the number of 4.5G customers increased by 5% between 2020 and 2021 (75.9 m to 80.2 m). Such a jump seems to be related to the COVID-19 pandemic and indicates that remote activities, such as education or working, directly rely on solid mobile broadband connectivity.

The rate of 2G and 3G customers is continuously diminishing. Especially, there is an obvious offset between the rate of 3G customers and 4.5G customers. It is not surprising because data usage on mobile devices began with 3G, and in that sense, a data customer generally switches to 4.5G to have faster speed and better service. Moreover, new smart devices are compatible with 4.5G, so new customers start their mobile connectivity with 4.5G technology.

In spite of the diminishing rate of customers in legacy technologies like 2G and 3G, due to the regulatory framework, operators are under obligation to provide legacy technologies. In other words, operators keep some portion of their spectrum in old technologies, however, it is possible to have higher capacity with the same spectrum by allocating the spectrum to the latest technologies (BEREC, 2023).[11]

Another technical parameter is the number of fixed wireless access (FWA) customers. As known, FWA[12] is an additional revenue stream for mobile operators, whereas it enables customers, who do not have access to fixed broadband services, to have broadband services with extensive usage.

Let us start with figures about FWA in Türkiye. The trend in the number of FWA customers is shared in Figure 2.2.

Figure 2.2 The number of FWA customers in Türkiye (2015–2022) (ICTA, 2024).

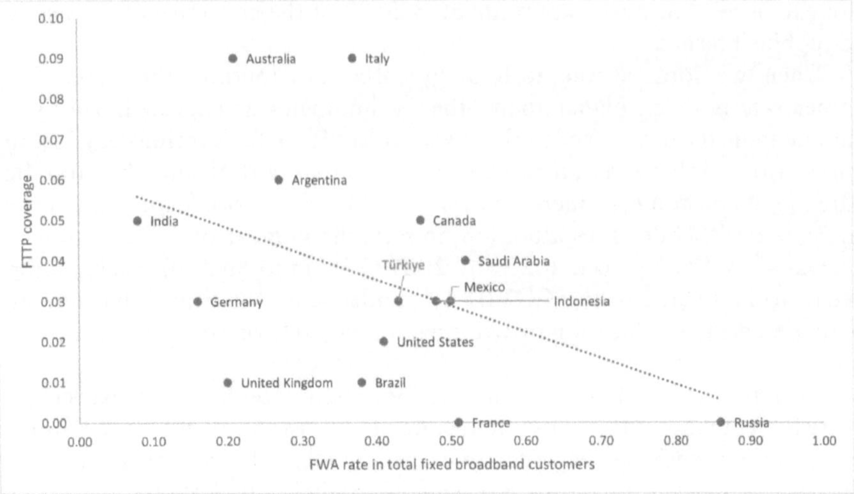

Figure 2.3 Relation between FTTP and FWA rate in total fixed broadband customers (2021), (OMDIA, 2023a, 2023c).

Note: The total number of residential and business premises covered by the optical fiber network. As known, FWA is expected to be more extensive with 5G technology. For making a right comparison, we choose 2021, because 5G was not online in most of countries or existed with very limited extent. China, Japan and Korea are eliminated since they represent extreme values.

In spite of the recent rise in FWA customers, the general trend of FWA is declining in Türkiye. For example, FWA customers decreased by 67% in the period between 2015 and 2020. To draw accurate conclusions, there is a need for comparison, as done previously. The graph in Figure 2.3 indicates the relation between FTTP and FWA rates in total fixed broadband customers.

Figure 2.3 indicates a reverse relation between the fiber coverage and the share of FWA. This is not surprising considering the fundamental feature of FWA, which is to provide broadband services to customers without access to fixed broadband. Even though Türkiye's position appears to be average, Türkiye is under its potential in FWA. Huge traffic increase and restricted allocation of spectrum might be the potential reasons behind the low penetration of FWA in Türkiye.

As the importance of mobile connectivity speed increases, the fiber penetration rate of base stations in mobile communication networks becomes critical on top of the spectrum and newer technologies. In fact, the need for fiber is directly related to increasing demand, and fiber can lift heavy traffic by locating in places that are close to users (OECD, 2019).

It would be beneficial to Türkiye's figures and its place in the world. G-20 countries serve as a good benchmark for Türkiye, considering its competition with countries in terms of economic competitiveness. The figures can be seen in Figure 2.4.

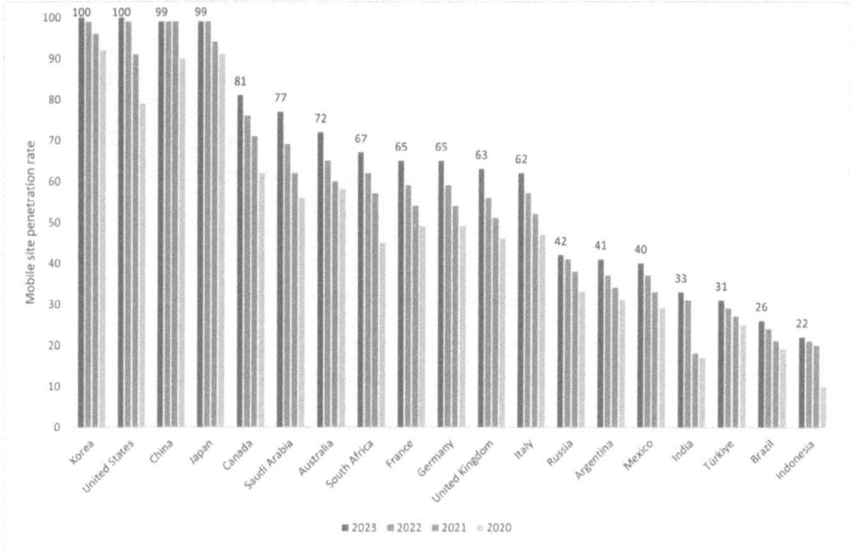

Figure 2.4 Fiber penetration rate of mobile sites in G-20 countries (2020–2023) (OMDIA, 2023c).

Türkiye is ranked as the third-worst country in terms of fiber penetration of mobile sites. Despite increasing penetration rate from 25% to 31%, Türkiye's pace lags behind that of other countries. For example, Türkiye was in a better position than India in 2020 and 2021, India has since surpassed Türkiye.

Under the current regulatory framework, there is no regulated tariff for fiber access to mobile sites. Nevertheless, the Turkish regulatory body initiates its studies about specific tariffs for fiber to mobile sites. Considering the current position of Türkiye, such an initiative appears to be accurate.

If the fiber penetration of mobile sites is not high enough, the allocation of the spectrum or latest technologies such as 5G would not result in improvements in the capacity, speed and quality of mobile connectivity.

In conclusion, the Turkish mobile communication industry has experienced rapid mobile broadband penetration after the introduction of 4.5G technology. Furthermore, the COVID pandemic appears to have accelerated this penetration. However, customers in legacy technologies have continuously diminished since the introduction of the latest technology. In terms of mobile connectivity, Türkiye has mature conditions for further digitalization.

As an important source of revenue for mobile operators, FWA has not expanded as it should. Huge traffic increase and limited spectrum seem the primary reasons. On the other side, FWA serves as a quick solution for areas lacking fiber connection, so the low level of FWA penetration may have a retarding effect on digitalization in non-fiber places.

The last thing that needs to be mentioned is the situation of fiber penetration of mobile sites, as shown earlier. Türkiye lags behind most G-20 countries in terms of fiber penetration of mobile sites. That poses a risk to Turkish mobile networks.

To sum up, at the basic level, mobile infrastructure is widespread in Türkiye, but the penetration of FWA and fiber penetration of mobile sites lag behind the required level for further digitalization.

Financial Situation in the Mobile Telecommunication Industry

Digitalization entails an increase in connected devices, a substantial rise in traffic and a growing demand for improved services. Thus, a significant demand for more investment for the network. Therefore, the capability of making investments, in other words, revenues of the industry, needed to be discussed.

It is good to start by showing the revenues and investment expenditure of the whole industry. Relevant figures are shared in Figure 2.5.

As indicated in Figure 2.5, the Turkish mobile industry's Average Revenue per User (ARPU), the basic indicator of operators' revenue, has been diminishing for eight years. On the other side, operators have allocated a higher portion of their revenues to investments.

When examining the details of the cost side, there is a general increase in terms of equipment, energy and devaluation of the Turkish Lira. In fact, the Wireline Voice and Data Network Equipment Index increased by 14% in

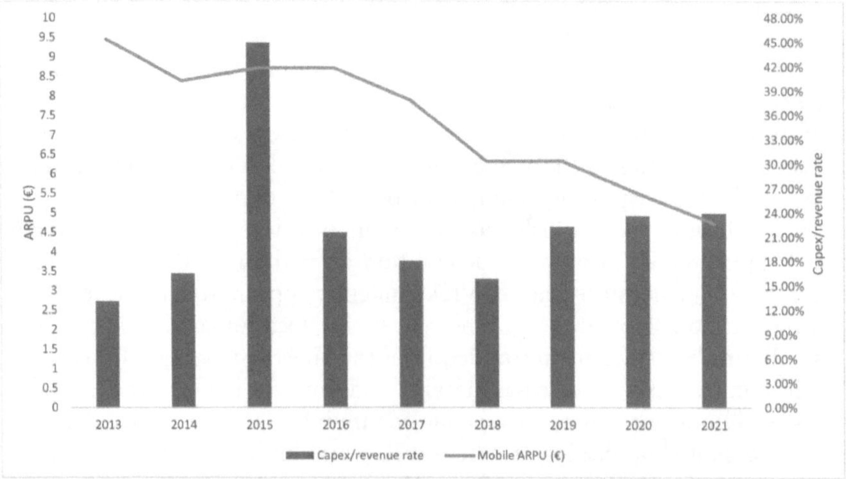

Figure 2.5 Mobile ARPU (€) and Capex/revenue rates of the industry (2013–2021)[13] (OMDIA, 2022).

the Dec. 2021–Dec. 2022 period,[14] similarly, the Communication Equipment Manufacturing Index also increased by 5.14% in the same period.[15] These figures highlight that the global telecommunication industry faces price increases in the equipment used in the network. Although it is not a capital expenditure, the rise in energy costs is another issue, in fact, the index for electricity, gas and steam increased by 284%.[16] In addition to the economic developments, the devaluation of the Turkish Lira (39% value loss in 2022)[17] puts mobile operators in a more difficult position.

The increase and expected increase in the traffic volume, increasing cost of investment (due to the aforementioned reasons) and declining revenue have a negative impact on the financial sustainability of the industry.

It is important to grasp how investments made by operators affect mobile telecommunication networks. Thus, we can see the potential consequences of declining revenues and increasing needs. In this context, it would be helpful to look at the relation between average capital expenditure/revenue rate and average mobile download speed.

For measuring the impact, mobile download speed seems an accurate choice since it is standard for whole countries, and it is affected by the usage and area, in other words, download speed can be linked with the capital expenditure. On the other hand, the 11-year average capital expenditure/revenue rate is used because we see extensive rollout work or spectrum actions at different times, so using the average brings all markets to baseline.

Figure 2.6 shows the relation between mobile download speed (2023) and average capex/revenue (2011–22).

As seen in Figure 2.6, there is a reverse relation between mobile download speed and average capex/revenue rate. Upon closer examination, it becomes evident that developing countries exhibit a high capital expenditure/revenue rate and relatively low download speed. This is expected, considering that some developing countries have low-level mobile penetration rates, and they try to expand the coverage. The reverse situation holds true for developed countries, they have already reached a certain level of mobile penetration and coverage. However, Türkiye's position seems different since Türkiye's mobile penetration rate is above 100%, and the coverage level is about 95%; in other words, Türkiye's mobile telecommunication network is at the level of developed countries. Therefore, filling the penetration or coverage gap is not an element behind the relatively high capital expenditure/revenue rate.

There are three possible explanations for Türkiye's situation. These include (i) investment in legacy technologies, (ii) excessive coverage obligations and (iii) other obligations related to localization, R&D and SMEs.

First, as mentioned in the earlier parts, customers in Türkiye have access to 2G, 3G and 4.5G services, and the customer share of legacy technologies is increasingly diminishing. Despite this, the operators allocate certain parts of their spectrum sources to old technologies instead of increasing spectrum efficiency by using the same sources with the latest technologies. The rationale behind this practice is closely related to the provisions in the concession

Figure 2.6 Relation between mobile download speed (2023)[18] and average Capex/revenue rate (2011–2022) (OMDIA, 2023b).

agreements. In fact, operators are obliged to provide relevant services to customers by the end of the concession agreement or authorization period.

Second, concession agreements and authorizations stipulate a certain coverage level for different technologies; in accordance with these obligations, operators have about 95% coverage, but ICTA pushes operators to increase the coverage (the increase sometimes practically means 100% coverage) by relying on gray areas in concession agreements or authorization. Such an approach may be another reason behind the higher capex/revenue rate in Türkiye. In fact, the operators invest in covering sparsely populated remote regions. While such expenditures have an impact on the total capital expenditure, their impact on the speed is very limited.

Lastly, as mentioned in the first section, operators in Türkiye face some "non-traditional" obligations. Meeting those obligations may be another reason behind the picture shared earlier. For the sake of the obligations, operators use more expensive local equipment rather than imported ones, or operators need to buy more local products to meet the needs because of the capacity gap.

In conclusion, even though operators in Türkiye allocate a higher portion of their revenues to investments compared to other countries, mobile download speed lags behind countries with lower or same level capital expenditure/revenue rate. Some elements of the Turkish regulatory framework such as keeping legacy technologies, forcing more coverage and non-traditional obligations can be the reason for the situation. Easing the regulatory framework would be beneficial for both operators and customers.

The combination of the financial situation of the industry and the situation in Figure 2.6 is a call for action. Diminishing revenues, rising demands due to digitalization, increasing cost of investments (energy, equipment, devaluation of local currency) and legal obstacles on investment optimization make the situation unsustainable for the operators. Such conditions pose a threat to Türkiye's digitalization process and mobile telecommunication network.

Fixed Communication Services

Fixed communication services are behind mobile communication services in terms of the level of development in Türkiye. The fixed infrastructure is very critical for further digitalization, because connected home devices, all kinds of remote activities and handling huge mobile traffic depend on solid fixed infrastructure. Therefore, we need to grasp the factors shaping fixed infrastructure development.

Regulatory Landscape

Before 1995, all postal, telegraph and telecommunication services were provided by a public entity, PTT. In 1995, PTT was divided into two parts. PTT was responsible for postal and telegraph services while the newly established Türk Telekomünikasyon A.Ş. (Türk Telekom) was responsible for general telecommunication services.[19]

Fixed broadband services, such as ADSL, were initiated, in 2003 with a very restricted extent, and ADSL service became widespread in 2005. The year 2005 is also significant because Türk Telekom, a public entity, was privatized in the same year. In other words, the privatization of Türk Telekom can be considered the starting point of competition in Turkish broadband services. The privatization process has also brought some structural changes to the market. In fact, the Turkish Competition Authority (TCA) recommended the structural unbundling of Kablo TV services from Türk Telekom's fixed broadband services to keep an alternative infrastructure from the undertaking of Türk Telekom. Moreover, TCA advocated the legal unbundling of retail services from the wholesale activities of Türk Telekom.[20]

The first recommendation was fulfilled with the law no. 5335, in which Kablo TV activities were transferred to another public entity, Türksat A.Ş. The second recommendation was added to the decision of the Turkish Privatization Authority. According to this, the privatized entity must actualize the legal unbundling of retail activities in the following six months. Under these circumstances, Türk Telekom was privatized, and TTNET A.Ş. was founded as an internet service provider (ISP) in 2006. There are certain rules for alternative ISPs about extending authorization, whereas there is no specific and publicly available procedure for the extension of the concession agreement of Türk Telekom. Moreover, as a part of the concession agreement, Türk Telekom is expected to transfer all relevant assets (like copper and fiber) to ICTA or an entity pointed by ICTA. In that sense, Türk Telekom's concession agreement is parallel to concession agreements in the mobile industry.

Unlike the mobile telecommunication industry, ISPs do not have separate concession agreements or authorization for different fixed broadband technologies. Therefore, Türk Telekom has one concession agreement, and in the scope of that agreement, Türk Telekom provides ADSL and fiber services. Moreover, there is one player, Türk Telekom, with the concession agreement and other ISPs take only relevant authorization from ICTA to provide fixed broadband services. In other words, Türk Telekom is the incumbent player and all other ISPs are the second movers.

ICTA tries to regulate wholesale activities with its secondary legislation such as Market Analysis Regulation and Access and Interconnection Regulation. In Market Analysis Regulation, ICTA evaluates the structural features, the competition and the situation of the players in the market and defines relevant markets. If necessary, ICTA determines one or more players as "having significant market power" and decides to bring the obligations in terms of access, tariff or behavior. Under the current regulatory framework, Türk Telekom is the only player that has significant market power. According to ICTA, Türk Telekom has significant market power in relevant markets of wholesale fixed local access and wholesale fixed central access. As a result of having significant market power, Türk Telekom is subject to certain obligations such as providing full access to its copper network and virtual unbundling of local access to its fiber network,[21] having facility sharing, being subject to tariffs (based on costs and no margin squeezing).[22]

In the scope of Access and Interconnection Regulation, ICTA aims to enhance the utilization of the current infrastructure and promote competition in relevant markets. In this regard, ICTA has a decision about Procedures and Principles on Facility Sharing, in which ICTA aims to increase collaboration among ISPs' infrastructure investment and source efficiency and to prevent duplicate works. In accordance with Procedures and Principles, the Electronic Communication Infrastructure Information System (EHABS) was founded, and all operators have begun to check the availability of other players' infrastructure before they plan to invest in a location.

In conclusion, there are some similarities between regulatory frameworks in mobile and fixed industries such as the concession structure and uncertainty about the extension. Behaviors in the secondary legislation seem to differentiate, in fact, ICTA tries to promote efficient use of resources and prevent duplicate investments; in other words, ICTA tries to be supportive for ISPs, whereas the very same ICTA seems to push the mobile operators in terms of quality, coverage and other non-traditional obligations and does not support the efficient use.

Historical Figures and Features of the Fixed Telecommunication Industry

Like the mobile telecommunication industry, there are different service types in the fixed telecommunication industry. Currently, ISPs provide fiber, xDSL,[23] cable[24] and other types of services.[25]

Examining the historical development of the number of customers in different services is a good starting point for discussion. The relevant figures are shared in Figure 2.7.

In 2007, Türkiye had five million fixed broadband customers while in 2022, the number increased to 19 million, representing a more-than-threefold increase. When we specifically consider the fiber customers, the number of subscribers has increased from 154,000 to 5.7 million. Despite the significant increase in fiber customers, the fiber service is not the dominant type of fixed broadband service. XDSL service has remained the most widespread fixed broadband service in Türkiye.

Technological development and digitalization naturally lead to an increase in the number of fiber customers. Therefore, the international benchmarks are essential to evaluate Türkiye's development. As we did in the mobile

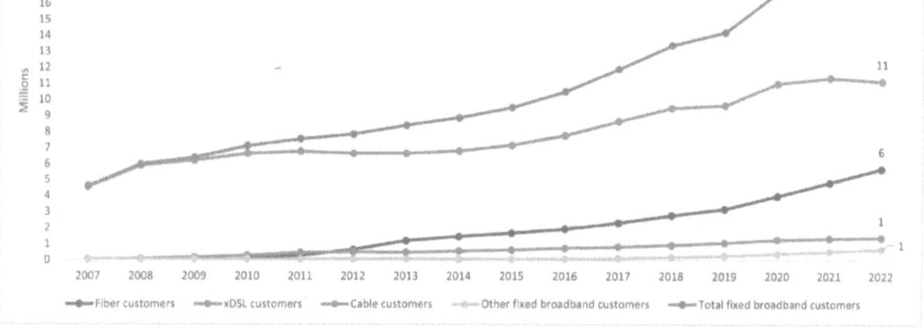

Figure 2.7 The number of customers in different fixed broadband services (ICTA, 2023).

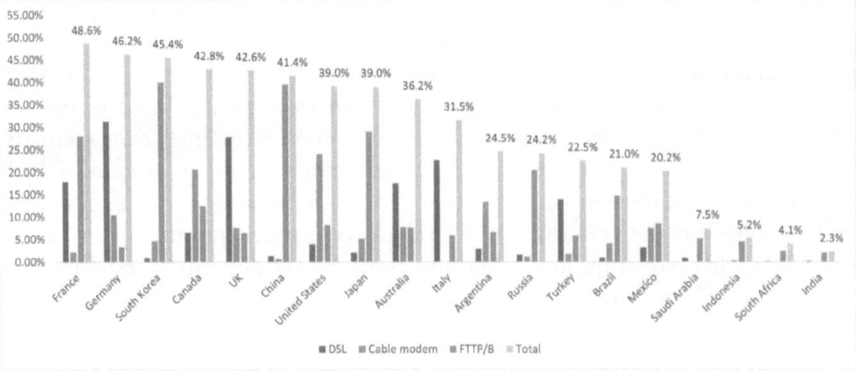

Figure 2.8 The population penetration of fixed broadband (2022) (Analysys Mason, 2023).

telecommunication section, G-20 countries are accurate benchmarks to compare. The benchmark is shared in Figure 2.8.

As seen in the visual, the increase in Türkiye's penetration rate falls behind that of most other G-20 countries. In this sense, it can be stated that Türkiye's growth rate appears strong, but it is not sufficient to be prominent in the global competition. Moreover, the countries behind Türkiye, such as Saudi Arabia, South Africa, India and Indonesia, are in a better position in terms of FWA rate. That situation verifies the conclusion mentioned in the previous section.

The penetration of the latest technology in the fixed industry lags behind the penetration of the latest technology in the mobile industry. This can be considered normal since the mobile network is more extensive than the fixed one; in addition, switching to new technologies in mobile is easier. For example, customers generally use devices that are compatible with multiple technologies, and the equipment of operators is also multi-technology. When we come to the fixed industry, the customers may need to change their modem devices to switch to fiber; furthermore, as the first requirement, the customers need FTTH in their location, which might be required for new investments.

In summary, there is progress in the fixed telecommunication industry, but Türkiye seems to be far from the required level for digitalization.

Financial Situation in the Fixed Telecommunication Industry

As done in the financial conditions topic in the mobile telecommunication section, it would be good to begin with basic financial figures for fixed telecommunication services. Figure 2.9 shows the fixed ARPU ($) and annual capital expenditure/revenue rate of the industry.

The Turkish fixed telecommunication industry seems to have similar dynamics with the mobile telecommunication industry. In that sense, the fixed industry also sees diminishing revenues in terms of the US dollar, and there is

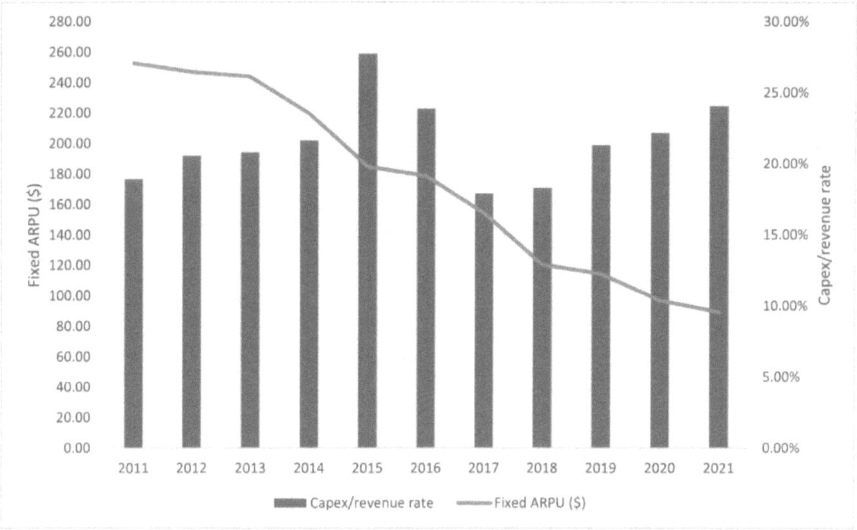

Figure 2.9 Fixed ARPU ($) and Capex/revenue rates of the industry (2013–2021) (Analysys Mason, 2023; OMDIA, 2023c).

an increasing trend in capital expenditure/revenue rate. Most of the reasons behind the cost increase are also applicable for the fixed industry. Beyond the cost, it might not be surprising to see an increase in capital expenditure/revenue. Unlike the mobile industry, the fixed industry in Türkiye is in an expansion period (especially in terms of fiber), so more civil works for more fiber or fixed broadband coverage mean higher capital expenditure, and it is natural.

As done in the previous section, it would be beneficial to show the impact of investments made by ISPs on the fixed telecommunication network. Unlike the previous analysis, we are examining the relation between the 11-year average capital expenditure/revenue and the fiber coverage (instead of fixed mobile speed). This is because the mobile industry has a relatively more established network compared to the fixed one, so the impact of investments in the mobile industry is expected to emerge in the capacity, or in other words, in the mobile download speed. However, when it comes to the fixed industry, we see an expanding network, therefore the impact of the investments can be observed in the coverage.

In light of this discussion, Figure 2.10 shows the relation between the 11-year average capex/revenue rate and the FTTP coverage gap in 2023.

As seen in Figure 2.10, there is a positive relation between the capital expenditure/revenue rate and the FTTP coverage gap. This seems natural, as all countries aim to increase their investment to cover more areas and population. For Türkiye, there is a need for acceleration of the investments, in other words, increasing investment means less gap in the fiber coverage.

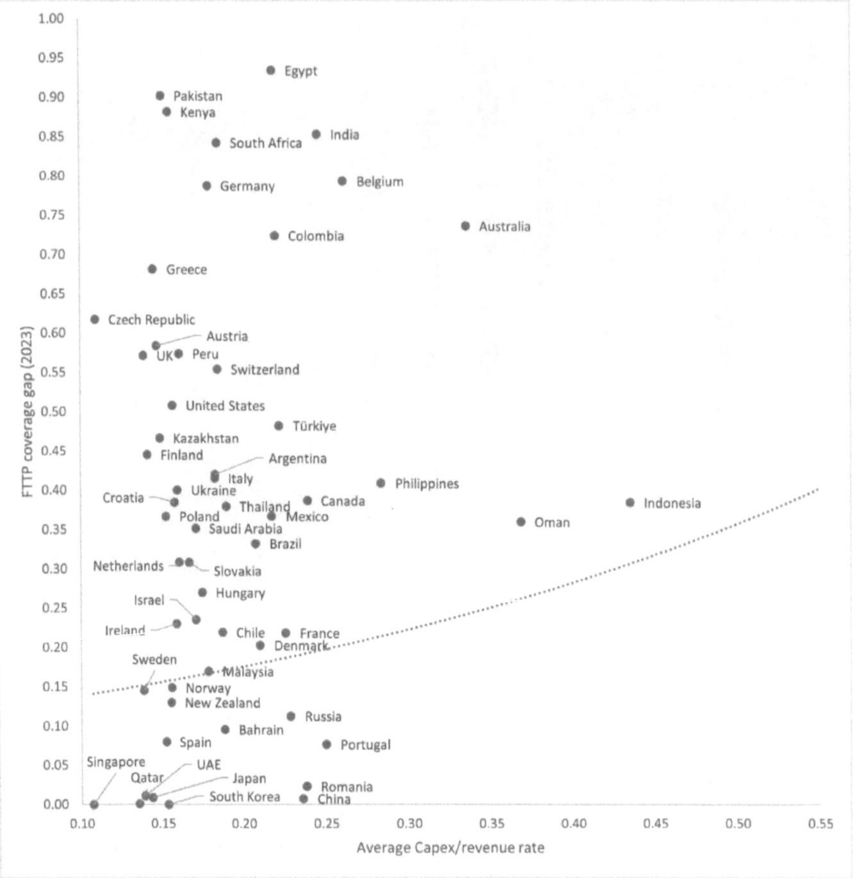

Figure 2.10 Relation between FTTP coverage gap (2023) and average Capex/revenue rate (2011–2022).

Source: OMDIA, 2023b, 2023c.

At this point, it would be helpful to mention some limitations in the regulatory framework. As underlined in the first part of the study, ICTA has brought a regulation about common investments among ISPs.

In the scope of the regulation, if an ISP decides to build a fiber infrastructure, it needs to check that area from ICTA's central system, and if another ISP has available capacity, the relevant ISP applies to the capacity owner to use that capacity instead of having greenfield investment. Even though ICTA's approach focuses on the efficient use of sources, that regulation practically slows down investment efforts. Furthermore, the regulation can be abused to prevent alternative investments by competitors. Reconsidering the implementation of that set of rules may mobilize the sources of alternative ISPs in

Türkiye, and such a move accelerates fiber investments and close the gap in the FTTP coverage.

Another issue that needs to be mentioned is the structure of the fiber wholesale company, Türk Telekom. The company is vertically integrated, and its subsidiary, TTNET, is active as an ISP in providing retail fixed broadband services. The current structure of the company makes conditions more difficult for Türk Telekom to focus on wholesale business (expansion of the network, developing new products etc.).

There are two solutions for the aforementioned restriction. The first one is to establish a joint venture with the participation of ISPs and the joint venture just focuses on the development of wholesale access. The second one is the reorganization of Türk Telekom and ensuring the independence of the wholesale company within the same undertaking. For the second option, it is possible to mention the United Kingdom's example, in which incumbent wholesale was reorganized as a more independent unit in 2017.[26] After that, we saw significant progress in FTTP coverage in the United Kingdom. In fact, the FTTP coverage gap has reduced from 88% to 57% in the 2020–2023 period.

To sum up, there is a need for more investment to increase the FTTP coverage in Türkiye. The current regulatory framework and the structure of the incumbent wholesale company seem to slow down the country's fiber development. Steps accelerating the fiber development such as easing sharing rules, restructuring the incumbent company or establishing a joint wholesale company are beneficial for Türkiye's position in global competition.

Concluding Remarks

Thus far, we have discussed three features of the Turkish telecommunication industry, and each feature has an impact on the other. In fact, the regulatory framework shapes the investment decision, revenue sources and access conditions for connectivity, whereas the density and demands of consumers set the priorities of operators. Ultimately, increasing investments enable customers to access connectivity under better terms. In total, all of these factors and relations affect the digitalization of the country. It would be better to show the contribution of the development of the infrastructure on digitalization. In that point, we can refer to the Türkiye Digital Society Index (TDSI)[27] (Köksal & Bakis, 2023) and the European Commission's Digital Economy and Society Index (DESI) (European Commission, 2022). Both approaches see infrastructure and figures about the customers as critical elements.

In the TDSI, a turning point occurred in 2014, after which the TDSI experienced accelerated growth.[28] This jump overlaps with figures in mobile and fixed services; in fact, in the 2014–2015 period, we observed the peak in 3G customers, the transition to 4.5G services, an increase in xDSL connections and an acceleration in fiber customers. Consequently, the increase in mobile and fixed broadband subscriptions can be regarded as the driver of digitalization in Türkiye.

Despite its different methodology,[29] DESI sees connectivity as a main pillar. DESI focuses on broadband connectivity and coverage on both mobile and fixed sides. In terms of mobile subscription and mobile coverage, Türkiye is on par with EU countries (Vodafone Türkiye & Policy Analysis Lab, 2023) while the country lags behind in terms of some indicators such as fiber penetration, average download speed, transition to 5G and so on. The significance of connectivity (or infrastructure) is understood by the fact that six out of seven top DESI scorer countries also achieved the highest scores in connectivity in 2022.

Improving connectivity leads us to the financial conditions of the industry, since requirements for ranking up in digital indexes need 5G, higher fiber penetration, higher speed for both mobile and fixed internet and lower latency, and all of those factors need further capacity, spectrum and coverage investments. According to the European Commission's Investment and Funding Needs for the Digital Decade Connectivity Target report, the EU needs €148 billion to complete the FTTP coverage and full 5G access (European Commission, 2023). Similarly, the International Monetary Fund estimates that global digital infrastructure needs $418 billion for a universal 4G cellular network with 40–50 GB monthly data use (IMF, 2023). As seen substantial investment is needed for better and more extensive telecommunication infrastructure. In this context, having sustainable revenues is essential for the telecommunication industry to make necessary investments. In light of the figures shared earlier, the Turkish telecommunication industry faces challenges.

As highlighted earlier, in such a regulated industry, the regulatory framework is fundamental for further development and digitalization. This is because the framework determines which technology will be used (using legacy technologies, no 5G for now), it increases the cost of investment by bringing extensive coverage and non-traditional obligations and makes access to connectivity harder by raising the cost for both suppliers and consumers (GSMA, 2017).[30]

To sum up, the development of infrastructure is indispensable for the digitalization of society and the economy. In Türkiye, there is a solid basis for digitalization in spite of some weaknesses in fiber and using the latest technologies. However, financial conditions in the industry and regulatory framework are not supportive of further digitalization.

The telecommunication industry is the backbone of the overall process of digitalization in all countries. Without a robust mobile or fixed network offering high speed and extensive coverage, establishing a digital economy becomes challenging. In this context, Türkiye has indicated critical development. For example, in the mobile industry, Türkiye has exceeded 100% mobile penetration rate and has had about 95% mobile coverage. On the other hand, a substantial portion of the revenue in fixed industry is allocated to capital expenditure.

Despite these advancements, there are notable weaknesses in the industry. Both mobile and fixed telecommunication industries have experienced diminishing revenues, and it may not be financially sustainable to actualize the required investments in the network. For the mobile industry, operators face heavy obligations like keeping legacy services alive, extensive coverage and some non-traditional obligations. These challenges appear to impede operators from making efficient and effective investments.

In light of these weaknesses, there are some areas for development in the Turkish telecommunication industry. For both mobile and fixed industries, there are declining revenues. Various support mechanisms can be considered to mitigate the chance of the failure to actualize necessary investments due to declining revenues. The EU's Digital Europe Programme can be a good benchmark for Turkish policymakers.

Another area of development for the mobile industry is easing the obligations and simplifying the regulatory framework. It would be helpful that ICTA embraces a more balanced approach to coverage and other non-traditional obligations. Moreover, three different concession agreements or authorizations bring complex providing services and reporting issues. Thus, the simplification and the unification of some obligations will be beneficial for the industry. The situation of legacy technologies can be a starting point for ICTA, and BEREC's discussion paper can be a good benchmark for Türkiye (BEREC, 2023).

For the fixed industry, removing all obstacles before the investments is the most crucial area of development. Actions that can ease the fiber investment, such as using the capacity of other networks (like electricity and gas), enabling alternative ISPs to invest, restructuring the incumbent wholesale company, or establishing a new joint venture for wholesale activity, are critical to achieving this goal.

It needs to be emphasized that despite its significance, the solid telecommunication infrastructure is not the only enabler of digitalization, a solid infrastructure just prepares the conditions for digitalization. Beyond that, there is a need for digital adoption in society (like digital literacy, use of digital tools and development of digital skills) (IMF, 2023). For example, in the light of DESI'20 data, the third cluster consisted of Germany, France and Spain, which have higher connectivity scores than the countries in the second cluster (like the United Kingdom, Ireland and Belgium), the countries in the second cluster have a higher DESI score than the countries in the third cluster (Sevgi, 2021).

In conclusion, while Türkiye has made progress, there is a long way to go for both mobile and fixed industries. In international benchmarks, Türkiye appears to lag behind. Accurate and urgent public interventions, as mentioned and discussed earlier, would be beneficial not only for the Turkish telecommunication industry but also for customers and the digital economy built on the telecommunication network.

Notes

1 The Importance of Communication Infrastructure in the Age of Digital Transformation, (2023.10.29) https://utilitiesone.com/the-importance-of-communication-infrastructure-in-the-age-of-digital-transformation (The Last Access Date: 29.01.2024).
2 In that regime, two operators (mentioned in the text) had authorization from the Ministry annually.
3 Vodafone has bought the assets of Telsim in 2006 in an auction. Therefore, in the rest of the chapter, the term "Vodafone" will be used.
4 It was subsidiary of national incumbent company in fixed communication market (Türk Telekom).
5 The following time, the merged entity was named as AVEA. At the end, it was renamed as "Türk Telekom Mobile" and became fully part of Türk Telekom.
6 800 MHz, 900 MHz, 1800 MHz, 2100 MHz and 2600 MHz.
7 That amendment makes Türkiye's regulatory framework closer to that of the EU.
8 ICTA has published a process about renewal of 2G concession agreements (www.kap.org.tr/Bildirim/1134152). However, that was specific to 2G concession agreements, in other words, there is still no general set of rules for renewal of spectrum rights. Such a deficiency has negative impact on investment horizon.
9 The term traditional means obligations that are directly related with telecommunication services like coverage, access or quality.
10 The introduction of 4.5G technology enables customers to access fast mobile broadband services. Mobile application ecosystem has grown in parallel with 4.5G.
11 In BEREC's draft report on practices and challenges of phasing out of 2G and 3G, Berec states that phasing out legacy technologies increases the spectrum efficiency and quality of the services (p. 3). Correspondingly, the 12th Development of the Republic of Türkiye also mentions the similar needs. Therefore, it is expected that upgrading legacy technologies will be discussed in short term.
12 In regulatory framework, FWA service defined as mobile communication services, so FWA can be provided only by mobile operators that have right due to their concession agreements and authorizations.
13 The jump in 2015 is directly related to 4.5G auction. The fee of auction is also included in the capital expenditure.
14 Economic Research Federal Reserve Bank of St. Louis, https://fred.stlouisfed.org (The Last Access Date: 29.01.2024)
15 Economic Research Federal Reserve Bank of St. Louis, https://fred.stlouisfed.org (The Last Access Date: 29.01.2024)
16 Turkish Statistical Institute Domestic Producer Price Index, Dec. 2022.
17 Central Bank of the Republic of Türkiye – www.tcmb.gov.tr/kurlar/kur2022_tr.html (The Last Access Date: 29.01.2024)
18 Speedtest, www.speedtest.net/global-index (The Last Access Date: 29.01.2024)
19 Competition Board's decision dated 21.07.2005 and numbered 05–48/681–175.
20 Competition Board's decision dated 02.09.2004 and numbered 04–57/797.
21 For the sake of the promotion of fiber penetration, ICTA Board decided to exclude fiber access services for years or the time when total fiber customers reach 25% of all fixed broadband customers from the market analysis (Board's decision dated 03.10.2016 and numbered 2011/DK-10/511).
22 ICTA Board's decision dated 31.12.2019 and numbered 2019/DK-SRD/338.
23 Fixed broadband services based on DSL technology.
24 Services provided via Kablo TV's infrastructure.
25 Fixed broadband services based on frame relay, metro Ethernet, ATM and BPL technologies.

26 www.openreach.com/about/our-story
27 Index covers three components. These are (i) connectivity, (ii) use of internet (like social media, e-commerce) and (iii) digital public services.
28 TDSI increases from 23.1 in 2014 to 49.4 in 2021.
29 DESI covers five pillars; these are (i) human capital, (ii) connectivity, (iii) use of internet, (iv) integration of digital technology and (v) digital public services.
30 Türkiye has the highest share of tax and fee payments in total industry revenue.

References

Analysys Mason. (2023). *Fixed broadband and voice quarterly metrics Q1 2023.* https://www.analysysmason.com/research/content/data-set/fixed-broadband-voice-quarterly-metrics-rdmb0/

BEREC. (2023). *Draft report on practices and challenges of phasing out of 2G and 3G.* https://www.berec.europa.eu/en/document-categories/berec/reports/draft-berec-report-on-practices-and-challenges-of-the-phasing-out-of-2g-and-3g

European Commission. (2022). *Digital economy and society index.* https://digital-strategy.ec.europa.eu/en/library/digital-economy-and-society-index-desi-2022

European Commission. (2023). *Investment and funding needs for the digital decade connectivity target.* https://digital-strategy.ec.europa.eu/en/library/investment-and-funding-needs-digital-decade-connectivity-targets

GSMA. (2017). *Delivering mobile connectivity in Mena: A review of mobile sector taxation and license extension.* https://www.gsma.com/solutions-and-impact/connectivity-for-good/public-policy/wp-content/uploads/2017/07/MENA-Snapshot-Study-Executive-Summary_May-2017.pdf

ICTA. (2023). *Annual statistical bulletin at provincial level on the electronic communication sector 2023.* https://www.btk.gov.tr/uploads/pages/yillik-il-istatistikleri/2023.pdf

ICTA. (2024). *Türkiyeelectronic communication sector quarterly market data report 4Q2023.* https://www.btk.gov.tr/uploads/pages/pazar-verileri/2023-4-kurum-disi-7nisan-rev.pdf

International Monetary Fund. (2023). *Estimating digital infrastructure investment needs to achieve universal broadband.* https://www.imf.org/en/Publications/WP/Issues/2023/02/10/Estimating-Digital-Infrastructure-Investment-Needs-to-Achieve-Universal-Broadband-529669

Köksal, E., & Bakis, O. (2023). *Türkiye digital society index.* BETAM Research Note, 23/269. https://dx.doi.org/10.2139/ssrn.4400548

OECD. (2019). *Enhancing access and connectivity to harness digital transformation.* https://www.oecd.org/digital/broadband/enhancing-access-digital-transformation.pdf

OECD. (2020). *Digital economy papers: Going digital integrated policy framework.* OECD Digital Economy Papers, No. 292, https://doi.org/10.1787/dc930adc-en

OECD. (2021). *Broadband policy and technology developments.* OECD Digital Economy Papers, No. 317. https://doi.org/10.1787/e273ff77-en

OMDIA. (2022). *Communication provider revenue and capex tracker – 2Q2022.* https://omdia.tech.informa.com/om026377/communications-provider-revenue-and-capex-tracker--2q22

OMDIA. (2023a). *Fixed wireless access subscription forecast – 1Q23.* https://omdia.tech.informa.com/om033535/fixed-wireless-access-subscription-forecast--1q23

OMDIA. (2023b). *Communication provider revenue and capex tracker – 2Q23.* https://omdia.tech.informa.com/om031662/communications-provider-revenue-and-capex-tracker--2q23

OMDIA. (2023c). *Fiber development index – 2023*. https://omdia.tech.informa.com/om032629/fiber-development-index-2023

Sevgi, H. (2021). Analysis of the digital economy and society index (DESI) through a cluster analysis. *Trakya Üniversitesi Sosyal Bilimler Dergisi*, *23*, 37–52.

Vodafone Türkiye & Policy Analysis Lab. (2023). *Digital Türkiye 2030: Economic impacts and policy framework*. https://www.palglobal.org/en/47103/Digital-Turkey-2030-Economic-Impact-and-Policy-Framework

3 Policies and legislation

A historical overview and current perspectives on digitalization in Türkiye

Fatma Davarcıoğlu Özaktaş and Şahin Ardıyok

Introduction

In the digital age, it is critical for governments to have the capacity ensure that their citizens are able to get the most out of technological developments. This would not only increase the social and economic conditions of individual citizens but also contribute to the overall social welfare of the country as well as its economic growth. The government may achieve these goals by creating the most efficient infrastructure to increase the digital capabilities and opportunities of its citizens and by internalizing digitalization itself and transforming its own services.

An efficient infrastructure requires widespread availability of affordable and high-speed internet. Conventional economic wisdom sets out that the best way to ensure this is by establishing a competitive marketplace for the provision of internet services. Türkiye also adopted this approach in the late 1990s and decided to liberalize the telecommunications sector by following the best practices established by the EU. However, Türkiye made some unsuitable policy choices on the way and ended up with a below-optimal fixed and mobile broadband internet infrastructure. As to the internalization of digitalization, Türkiye did much better and managed to establish a well-functioning e-government infrastructure. The background of these issues, Türkiye's mistakes, achievements, current problems, and potential steps that may be taken in the future are discussed in the following sections.

In this chapter, the first section delves into the liberalization of telecommunications services in Türkiye. This section begins by addressing the factors triggering the liberalization in Türkiye, followed by an examination of the EU accession and progress in adaptation, which emphasizes on the regulation of mobile communications services and the regulation of fixed internet services. In the second section, fixed and mobile internet markets are assessed and problems and future policies regarding the fiber expansion and the 5G rollout are scrutinized. The third section explores the information society and the digitalization process while the fourth section focuses on broadband in digitalization. Finally, in the fifth section, e-government services in Türkiye are examined in light of various indicators.

DOI: 10.4324/9781032692937-3

Liberalization of the telecommunications services in Türkiye

In this section, we provide the historical background of the liberalization of telecommunications services in Türkiye and how it was affected by the EU accession process. We focus on the evolution of the mobile and fixed internet services markets and provide insight into the interplay between the regulatory framework and market structure.

Factors triggering the liberalization in Türkiye

The first primary legislation related to the electronics communication sector of Türkiye was adopted (and is still partially in force) in 1924. Act No. 406 created a legal monopoly by granting the Post and Telegraph Agency (PTT) exclusive authority over all sorts of electronic communications services within Türkiye (Arıöz, 2005, p. 22). PTT remained as a state-owned monopoly of postal services, telegraph services and fixed telephony services until 1993, when fixed telephony services were separated via Statutory Decree no. 509, and Türk Telekom was formed to take over as the provider of fixed telephony and other similar services (Eke, 2010, pp. 85–106).

In 2000, the electronic communications sector in Türkiye was liberalized by the enactment of Act. No. 4502. It removed legal entry barriers in electronic communications markets[1] and established the Information and Communications Technologies Authority (ICTA).[2] It took over the regulatory duties originally overseen by the Ministry of Transport and Infrastructure (MoTI).[3]

Liberalization in the electronic communications sector was encouraged as a result of the Uruguay Rounds that were conducted within the scope of the World Trade Organization (WTO) in 1994. While the initial decisions rendered after the Uruguay Rounds, which came into force on 1 January 1995, did not include any agreement relating to the electronic communications sector, the signing states resolved to reach an agreement concerning this issue by 30 April 1996. As agreed, negotiations were finalized on this date, and a fourth protocol was added to the General Agreement on Trade in Services. As a result, the signatories, including Türkiye, agreed to liberalize the electronic communications sector (Arıöz, 2005, p. 22).

In the course of the Uruguay Round negotiations and the period that followed, Türkiye has made several commitments related to telecommunication services. It was declared that

> in the field of telecommunications, initiation of a dialogue between the European Union (EU) and Türkiye on regulatory matters, with a view to approximating Turkish legislation with that of the EU, would be beneficial. Technical assistance from the EU in this framework would be welcome by Türkiye.
>
> (Republic of Türkiye Ministry of Foreign Affairs, 1998)

Accordingly, Türkiye followed the EU example while designing the ex ante rules with respect to the liberalization of the telecommunications market.

The market structure in the telecommunications markets of EU Member States was similar to Türkiye's before the privatization era, as state monopolies mostly controlled the telecommunication networks. The regulatory framework, considering the telecommunications markets in the EU, was mainly shaped by the 1987 Green Paper of the Commission (European Commission, 1987) that was also agreed upon by the Council by a Resolution of 30 June 1988 (The Council of the European Communities, 1988). According to the Green Paper, Member States were required to liberalize all telecommunications services except for the public switched telephone network (PSTN) infrastructure and fixed-voice telephony services. Furthermore, the Member States were also required to have an Open Network Provision (ONP) to regulate the relationship between monopoly infrastructure providers and competitive service providers (Larouche, 2000, p. 5).

EU accession and progress in the adaptation

The early regulatory framework in Türkiye became outdated in a short time with the EU's enactment of the New Regulatory Framework (NRF) in 2002.[4] Relevant legislation in Türkiye was once again revised in 2008 with the entry into force of Electronic Communications Act No. 5809 and relevant secondary legislation subsequently issued by the ICTA. Act no. 5809 established the regulatory framework, and relevant secondary legislation was modeled after the NRF. In the Türkiye 2009 Progress Report of the EU Commission, it was stated that the adoption of this Act "is a significant step towards aligning Türkiye's regulatory framework with the EU acquis, notably as regards the authorization rules and the tasks of the regulator" (European Commission, 2009, p. 51).

Regulation of Mobile Communications Services and Ongoing Issues

Mobile services were first provided in Türkiye in 1994, under the terms of revenue-sharing agreements signed between the operators (Telsim and Turkcell) and Türk Telekom. In 1998, Telsim and Turkcell signed concession agreements with the MOTI and were granted 25-year licenses for the provision of GSM services. In 2000, İŞ-TIM and Türk Telekom were granted the right to provide GSM services. In 2004, İŞ-TIM and Türk Telekom merged their activities under the name of TT-TIM and continued operating in the GSM market through the Avea brand.[5] Authorizations following the IMT-2000/Universal Mobile Telecommunications System (3G) auction that took place in 2008 were also made via concession agreements between the ICTA and the same operators. Finally, the auction for IMT-Advanced (4.5 G) was held in 2015, and the same operators were given rights of use over the relevant spectrum via agreements signed with the ICTA.

It is critical to note that the concession agreements for fixed telephony services, GSM and 3G, as well as the right-of-use agreements for 4.5G, require operators to transfer to the ICTA free of charge any software and equipment (including towers, masts, pipes, containers, tubes, energy transfer lines, antennas and so on) that may affect the functioning of the system. Moreover, while the terms of both the 3G concession agreement and the 4.5G right-of-use agreement were set to expire in 2029, the term of the initial GSM concession agreement was normally to expire in 2023. To remedy this problem, the terms of the GSM concession agreements were also extended to 2029 (Public Disclosure Platform, 2024).

Regulation of Fixed Internet Services and Ongoing Issues

As to fixed internet services, infrastructure-based competition in Türkiye remained significantly limited when compared to the EU Member States, especially during the x-DSL era. This was due to two main factors, namely underdevelopment of the cable TV (CATV) infrastructure and the lack of infrastructure investments by alternative ISPs.

First, in many EU Member States, the CATV network represents an important technology for the provision of next-generation access (NGA) services; however, this is not the case in Türkiye, despite the efforts of the Turkish Competition Authority (TCA). The TCA required that, before privatization, Türk Telekom's assets related to satellite communications – along with its CATV assets – be transferred to Turksat and suggested that the CATV assets be privatized separately.[6] Ultimately, the CATV assets were never privatized. Furthermore, the state remained an important stakeholder in Türk Telekom. As a result, Turksat had no incentive to develop the CATV infrastructure, which could end up cannibalizing revenues generated via Türk Telekom. Hence, the CATV broadband internet infrastructure remained underdeveloped, and as at the second quarter of 2023, only 1.5% of fixed internet subscribers use the CATV infrastructure (ICTA, 2023b).

Second, unlike the ISPs in EU Member States, alternative ISPs in Türkiye made no significant investments to install their own xDSL infrastructure. This is because almost all ISPs preferred to act as resellers of Türk Telekom's services or to have bitstream access to Türk Telekom's infrastructure with minimal investment. The main reason for this was that the ICTA placed too much emphasis on pricing while neglecting other parameters, such as access conditions, quality of service and dispute resolution mechanisms. Accordingly, despite the presence of ex ante regulations requiring local loop unbundling (LLU), no ISPs preferred to take the risk and invest in the LLU (Dalgıç-Tetikol et al., 2022, pp. 313–314). It could be claimed that this was not in line with the aim of ICTA's aim, which had adopted a ladder of investment[7] approach that aimed to incentivize the alternative ISPs to gradually make more xDSL infrastructure investments.

The ICTA changed its approach concerning fiber networks, and rather than promoting service-based competition as the first base of the ladder of investment, it announced a regulatory holiday for FTTB/H investments,[8] urging all alternative ISPs to invest in their networks directly. In hindsight, it seems that the ICTA's gamble paid off, as many alternative ISPs invested heavily in their own FTTB/H infrastructure and currently have considerable networks of their own. Currently, the main problem facing the operators in investing in their own FTTB/H infrastructure is related to regulations concerning rights of way that operators must obtain to develop their networks.[9]

Market assessment and future policies

There are certain regulatory hurdles to overcome before expanding the existing fiber networks and authorizing operators for the provision of 5G services via a new auction. While these regulatory obstacles constitute only one part of the whole picture, which involves various economic, political and legal parameters, overcoming them is crucial for improving Türkiye's electronic communications infrastructure.

Fiber expansion

To expand their fiber networks, the right of way is *sine qua non* for operators. Right of way is usage rights granted to operators, allowing them to pass above, below or through privately or publicly owned land for installing, removing, maintaining and repairing electronic communications networks. Obtaining rights of way may be difficult for operators due to the need to obtain approvals from relevant public authorities and the need for coordination with other operators. Indeed, the more difficult it is to obtain rights of way, the more difficult it becomes for alternative operators to compete with the incumbent operator (Dursun, 2020, pp. 24–25).

In Türkiye, Act No. 5809 contains certain provisions that require both private and public owners of land to accept, under reasonable circumstances, operators' requests for rights of way. Yet the obligation imposed on public owners is more comprehensive: they are required to finalize such requests in 60 days in a transparent manner and without discriminating between operators with equal standing. Moreover, the Act further stipulates that the right of way will not be granted if an electronic communications network exists on which colocation and facility-sharing obligations have been imposed. In other words, operators must apply for colocation or facility sharing (if possible) before requesting a right of way.[10] Hence, inefficiencies in facility-sharing procedures would also hinder operators' efforts to expand their networks[11] (Dursun, 2020, p. 41).

In Türkiye, the Information System for Electronic Communication Infrastructures (EHABS) entered into service in 2019 to make it easier for operators to obtain information regarding the existing networks and determine whether to request the right of way or apply for facility sharing. However, EHABS did not manage to eliminate the complications regarding these procedures. Furthermore, the relevant legislation in Türkiye requires operators to pay additional fees for rights of way, raising even higher barriers.[12] To boost operators' investments in fiber networks and increase the level of infrastructure-based competition, it is crucial to both revise the regulations that oblige operators to apply for colocation or facility sharing before being able to request rights of way and introduce new legislation prohibiting public authorities from charging fees for right of use.

As a final remark, some TCA decisions indicate that the incumbent operators may be motivated to intentionally slow down the processes and hinder the expansion of competitors' networks (Turkish Competition Authority, 2016). These issues could be resolved by fine-tuning the existing ex ante regulations of the ICTA regarding colocation and facility sharing and supporting these with effective ex post interventions by the TCA when necessary.

Plans for the 5G rollout

Both the ICTA and the government acknowledge the importance of the 5G rollout, but for now, no concrete plans have been made public as to how the operators would be authorized to provide 5G services (ICTA, 2010, pp. 57–60).

One of the reasons why Türkiye is lagging in its rollout of commercial 5G services is the government's ambitious plans to ensure that all elements of the 5G networks are developed within Türkiye. So far, the "End-to-end Domestic and National 5G Communications Network Project" has been initiated and the "Communications Technologies Cluster" has been formed. Moreover, the ICTA, together with contributions from private firms, made a call to support national projects that aim to develop 5G technologies and provide financial support to various firms (ICTA, 2023b). It should also be noted that the President of Türkiye declared that the country would not be introducing 5G technology before a national tech infrastructure was created. Comparing the advantages and disadvantages of this policy choice falls outside the scope of this chapter. However, it should be noted that this is not the only factor that is slowing down the 5G rollout in Türkiye.

As mentioned in Section 1.2., operators who are authorized to provide mobile communications services in Türkiye will be required to transfer to the ICTA free of charge the relevant equipment and software used for the provision of GSM, 3G and 4.5G services by 2029. However, such equipment and software would be critical for providing 5G services if they obtain authorization to do so. If the ICTA and the relevant authorities plan to auction off spectrum for the provision of 5G before 2029, they must first remove this legal uncertainty. One way to do that would be to tie the upcoming 5G auction to the former GSM, 3G and 4.5G authorizations and ensure that the operators that become authorized to provide 5G services would be able to use the existing software and equipment. While this would be a relatively straightforward solution – so long as the relevant spectrum for 5G services is allocated to the existing operators – significant complications may arise if new entrants are introduced.

In any case, the auction design would be of utmost significance, and the ICTA must receive as much input as possible from all stakeholders. This would require a comprehensive public consultation process, which could take a long time. Hence, even if Türkiye decides to wait until the development of an end-to-end domestic and national 5G communications network, the ICTA should start working on designing an auction that could address the existing problems. The first and most crucial step in that respect would be to open transparent communication channels with the stakeholders and engage with as many relevant parties as possible.

Another issue that could create problems for the future development of Turkish mobile markets is that the strategic investment arm and equity solutions provider of the Republic of Türkiye, the Türkiye Wealth Fund (TWF), currently controls both Türk Telekom and Turkcell (Türkiye Wealth Fund, 2023). In other words, two of the three existing mobile operators in Türkiye are controlled by the same entity. While the operators have separate legal entities, strategic decisions, including decisions concerning substantial investments, are inevitably influenced by the TWF. Accordingly, the TWF may prefer to restrict the infrastructure-based competition between Türk Telekom and Turkcell to maximize its profit, which could result in a reduction in the total amount of investments made. The negative effects of such a strategy on infrastructure-based competition may be partially eliminated by way of contractual requirements concerning the imposing on operators' minimum investments as well as minimum geographical coverage obligations via the right-of-use agreements to be signed after the 5G auction. Still, considering regulation is a suboptimal alternative to competition, it might be difficult to completely negate potential harms that may be caused by the joint ownership of the two operators.

Information society and the digitalization process

"Information society" includes the digital transformation in the social and public spheres through the widespread use of information and communication technologies (ICT). The digitalization of public services enables the public sector to provide faster, more transparent and accessible services through the effective use of information and communication technologies in public services. "E-government" refers to an approach that enables citizens to access public services through digital platforms, facilitating the public's interaction with the government and simplifying bureaucratic processes. When the concepts of information society, digitalized public services, broadband access and e-government applications come together and are integrated, the foundations are laid for a sustainable, participatory development model that is open to development.

The success of ICT in disseminating information in the economic and social spheres enables the formation of an information society and the realization of an economic, social and cultural transformation. An information society – where change is continuous and rapid and where information technologies are at the center – is the last stage of the evolution process of society. "Lifelong learning," "digitization" and "dynamic and open society" are the key concepts of the information society (Güner, 2020, p. 128).

Since the late 1990s, the focus has been on the transformation to an information society, with the viewpoint that the information society is the driving force of economic and social transformation. In this context, strategies, action plans and programs have been established in the world and in the EU in particular, to ensure coordination in the main themes of technological development, digitalization, information communication technologies and digital transformation. The common goal of these efforts, each of which has its own objectives and action plans, can be perceived as preparing younger generations for the digital age, ensuring internet and broadband access, network and information security, providing online services for education, health and some other public services and creating an e-business environment (Akçam, 2006, pp. 3–12).

In Türkiye, efforts to transition to an information society started in 1993 with the World Bank's *Informatization and Economic Modernization Report*. This included action-plan proposals for (i) preparing the human factor, (ii) legal infrastructure in the computer, software and communication networks referred to earlier and (iii) an information economy. However, this first initiative could not be realized because the loan agreement with the World Bank was never finalized.

The next concrete step was the Turkish National Information Infrastructure Master Plan (TÜBİTAK, 1999) prepared by the Ministry of Transportation and the Scientific and Technological Research Council of Türkiye (TÜBİTAK). The plan, which aimed to determine Türkiye's information policies in line with general global information technology trends, set out Türkiye's situation, future goals and institutional structure proposals. In 1998, the E-Commerce Coordination Board (1998–2002) was established to develop e-commerce, and policy recommendations were presented. Kamu-NET (1998–2002), which covers the same period, proposed action plans for the coordination, monitoring and financing of public computer networks. However, a lack of coordination between different institutions and organizations in their work on the information society until recently prevented the desired results from being achieved. Therefore, currently, priority has been given to defining the institutional structure for the information society transition. Accordingly, the e-Türkiye Initiative was launched in 2001 with the contribution of 13 working groups from different ministries. Its objective is the e-Europe+ Action Plan prepared for candidate countries of the EU. However, this action plan was never implemented due to political instability. Subsequently, this initiative evolved into the E-Transformation Türkiye

Project (2002 –), which was placed under the responsibility of the Ministry of Development. The Information Society Department (ISD) was established within the same ministry to (i) coordinate the project, (ii) the information and communication technology investments of public institutions and (iii) determine strategies for an information society (ICTA, 2023b).

The objectives of the e-transformation Türkiye project are as follows:

- Regulating information and communication technology policies and legislation in accordance with EU requirements, implementing the action plan specified for candidate countries within eEurope +,
- Ensuring the participation of citizens in decision-making processes with information and communication technologies,
- Making the public services transparent and accountable,
- Implementing good governance principles by utilizing information and communication technologies in the provision of public services,
- Disseminating the use of information and communication technologies,
- Integrating public investment projects in the field of information and communication technology and ensuring coordination between investors organizations (ICTA, 2023b).

In line with these objectives, a number of action plans were prepared and put into practice. The "2003–2004 Short Term Action Plan (KDEP)," "2005 Action Plan" and "2006–2010 Information Society Strategy and Action Plan" were prepared and put into practice in 2005–2006. In connection with all these processes, the "E-Transformation Türkiye Executive Board," "Transformation Leaders Board" and "Advisory Board" were established to effectively transform the country into an information society.

The "2015–2018 Information Society Strategy and Action Plan" was prepared by the Ministry of Development with the participation of all stakeholders – including public agencies, universities, private companies, NGOs and individuals. It set out eight pillars for strategies and targets, with a focus on employment and growth. They are (i) information technologies sector; (ii) broadband infrastructure and sectoral competition; (iii) qualified human resources and employment; (iv) diffusion of ICT into society; (v) information and internet security and protection of personal information; (vi) ICT-supported innovative solutions; (vii) internet entrepreneurship and e-commerce and (viii) user-centric and effective public services (ICTA, 2023b).

All these studies have as their goal to generate advanced science and technology by using information and communication technologies effectively, to make it sustainable by connecting it to education and industry, to create an information society prepared for global competition and thus to achieve a sustainable development process.

The information society measurement criteria and indicators are listed as (i) infrastructure for accessibility to information and communication technologies, (ii) broadband internet access, (iii) usage rates, (iv) skills, (v) technology development capacity, (vi) use of digital public services and (vii) barriers to all these.

Broadband in digitalization

An information society is rooted in fast and continuous access to information. Thus, infrastructure and internet bandwidth are important determinants of digital transformation. Broadband accelerates data uploading, downloading and information transfer by providing a high-speed internet connection. For this reason, the expansion of broadband internet access is accepted as a basic indicator in the transition to an information society. It is used as one of the components in the calculation of the digital transformation index (Güner, 2020, p. 132).

Expanding broadband access also reduces social inequalities by ensuring equal access to information. In countries with high broadband internet access rates, digital public services such as online education and health services, electronic commerce and e-government are more developed (ICTA, 2008). A widespread and advanced broadband network facilitates adaptation to new technologies and supports digital transformation and technological innovation. This leads to a structure that is open to innovation, increases efficiency, reduces transaction costs and provides a competitive advantage at the national and international levels. On the other hand, the fact that a technologically advanced infrastructure is attractive to investors is another factor supporting economic growth (TÜBİSAD, 2022, p. 38).

The importance of broadband internet access can also be listed in terms of its benefits to stakeholders, which can be listed as telecommunications operators, equipment and content providers and the public. Accordingly, with the increasing importance of information-based applications, broadband services have come to occupy an important place in operators' investments. Computer/equipment manufacturers and software developers benefit from the increased demand in their markets resulting from the use of broadband services. In sectors that rapidly access information and innovations through a widespread broadband network, transaction costs are reduced, and efficiency, productivity, quality and competitiveness are increased.

On the other hand, the development of broadband improves social welfare through specific applications such as e-health, e-learning, e-business, e-government, working at home through electronic communications, media and entertainment (ICTA, 2010, pp. 57–58).

In line with the social and economic benefits of broadband services, governments prioritize the strengthening and expansion of broadband infrastructure. Accordingly, national broadband strategies and action plans include the necessary measures to achieve these objectives.

In Türkiye, the main targets of the National Broadband Strategy and Action Plan (NBSAP) for 2023 are stated as (i) providing broadband service at a speed of at least 100 Mbit/s to every household; (ii) developing the infrastructure to carry fixed and mobile broadband internet; (iii) increasing the internet usage rate of the population between the ages of 16 and 74 to over 80%; (iv) making our country a regional hub and transit point in communication and (v) establishing strong internet exchange points (Republic of Türkiye Ministry of Transport, Maritime Affairs and Communications, 2017). With the motto, "broadband for everyone from everywhere," the NBSAP addresses the basic principles for developing broadband and fiber infrastructure across the country, increasing broadband access capacity and speed as well as increasing demand for broadband services.

Currently, there are 74.8 million mobile and 19.5 million fixed broadband subscribers in Türkiye. Approximately 11 million of the fixed broadband subscribers rely on xDSL, whereas there are approximately 6.5 million fiber and 1.5 million cable fixed broadband subscribers. Accordingly, the penetration rate is 22.8% for fixed broadband and 87.8% for mobile broadband. Both of these are considerably below the OECD averages, which are 34.9% and 127.9% respectively. Moreover, nearly 50% of the fixed broadband subscribers have a download speed below 24 Mbps, and only 2.4% have a download speed over 100 Mbps (ICTA, 2023b).

The data, obtained by monitoring the broadband speed measurements from approximately 1.3 billion speed tests in 220 countries around the world over a 12-month period, indicate that globally, the average speed is gradually increasing. Accompanying the increase in average speed, Türkiye ranks 127th among 220 countries with 24.84 Mbps as in 2023. In addition to the world average, the country has a speed below the regional average of 30.41 Mbps. With this rate, Türkiye ranks 10th among 15 countries in its region (see Figure 3.1).

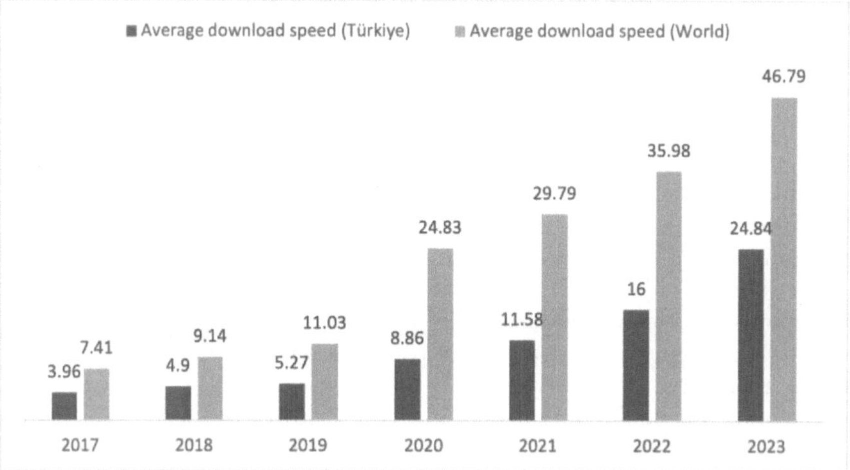

Figure 3.1 Global and Turkish internet download speed average[13](Mbps) (2017–2023) (Cable.co.uk, 2023).

According to Speedtest data, as of August 2023, the mobile download speed in Türkiye is 32.48 Mbps, below the world average of 43.20 Mbps. As for fixed broadband download speed, the world average is 82.77 Mbps, whereas in Türkiye, it is 34.61 Mbps. In terms of download speeds, Türkiye ranks 66th among 145 countries in mobile speeds and 107th among 182 countries in fixed broadband speeds (Speedtest, 2023).

Like internet access speed, the cost of internet access varies from country to country. According to a Cable.co.uk study of broadband pricing in 219 countries, the world faces huge inequalities in terms of getting online. As of 2023, when the average price of 219 countries is $57.07, Türkiye ranks 18th with $13.17 in a ranking from cheap to expensive (see Table 3.1).

These figures indicate that broadband internet in Türkiye is considerably slower and more expensive when compared to developed countries, and this may be a competitive disadvantage for Türkiye.

Digitalization of government services: e-government

Developments in information technologies, which effect the daily life of individuals as well as working conditions – from the production processes of enterprises to decision-making processes – inevitably have effects on the public sector, which is another part of society. Digital transformation of the public sector can be understood as the technological change that this sector undergoes in its business processes to provide more efficient services, by switching from traditional methods to digital technologies as a result of changing social needs with the impact of developing information and communication technology opportunities (Nart, 2019, p. 2837). In other words, the public, as an important factor in creating and increasing economic and social welfare, realizes its digital transformation when it incorporates into its service delivery all kinds of technological developments that serve this purpose.

The social structure renewed by technological change has forced the public sector to change its management approach as well as the way it provides services. New public administration is the replacement of the traditional principles of strict rules, excessive centralization and hierarchical structure with a structure in which the public interacts with citizens, and bureaucracy is no longer a wall between citizens and the public.

The reflection of this new understanding of the production process is that public intervention is minimized, the market is prioritized, and the public assumes a regulatory and supervisory role. Thus, the public sector – whose service areas have also differentiated – is changing the way it provides services by digitalizing them. Information technologies have started to be used, applying a private-sector management style to the public sector. The traditional public sector is now being replaced by e-government. Therefore, one of the factors pushing the public sector toward digitalization is the change in management approach. Another factor is the widespread use of smart devices

Table 3.1 Broadband prices

Rank	*Name*	*Packages measured*	*Average package cost per month TRY*	*Cost per megabit, per month TRY*	*Cheapest broadband package measured TRY*	*Cheapest broadband package measured (USD)*	*The most expensive broadband package measured*	*The most expensive broadband package measured (USD)*	*Conversion rate (USD) (Rates Frozen: 30/03/2022)*	*Average cost of broadband (Per month in USD)*	*Average cost of broadband (Per megabit per month in USD)*
18	Türkiye	41	249.00	4.28	169.00	$8.94	900.00	$47.60	0.05289	$13.17	$0.23

Source: Cable.co.uk (2023).

and mobile applications, which have brought changes in information and communication technologies as well as the increasing demands of citizens to receive some services in this way (Howard, 2001, p. 6).

On the other hand, the public sector's desire to increase interaction with its citizens as well as the savings brought by digital solutions in service delivery are also factors that trigger digital transformation. As a matter of fact, digital transformation efforts are ongoing all over the world due to cost pressures and to provide services more efficiently. Countries can achieve significant benefits through good planning, appropriate investments and implementing a process that is sensitive to the needs of its citizens. Accordingly, digital transformation of the public sector makes public services more citizen-oriented, prevents inefficiency caused by unnecessary bureaucratic procedures and ensures that services are provided at lower costs, are faster and more efficient, uninterrupted, of a high quality and continuously accessible. Accurate, reliable and rapidly accessible information reinforces trust in the state. It also ensures impartiality and equality in public service delivery (Cordelia, 2007, p. 268). Digital transformation improves service delivery, optimizes management processes and uses public resources efficiently as well as increases the transparency of public institutions. All these changes, provided that data security is ensured, will have a positive impact on the public–citizen relationship and serve the public sector's goal of increasing citizen satisfaction.

The concrete form of the digital transformation of the public sector is e-government. E-government is an application that enables public services to be provided at lower costs and more efficiently with the developing information technology, as well as enabling citizens to fulfill their responsibilities to the public more easily and safely (Göçoğlu, 2020, p. 619).

E-government is a platform that contributes to the transparency and accountability of the public sector and aims to identify citizen needs faster. Performance management is an efficiency management system that aims to produce the best service at the lowest cost (Avaner & Fedai, 2019, p. 158; Duman & Aktel, 2021, p. 617).

E-government applications, which provide horizontal coordination instead of a centralized structure, also strengthen the interaction among the public sector, private sector and civil society. As a matter of fact, in the literature, the concept of digitalization in public administration refers to a multidirectional relationship from the state to the state, from the state to companies, from the state to its employees, from the state to citizens, from the state to civil society organizations and from all of them back to the state. In a structure where a multidimensional integrated network is formed, increased interaction between the parties brings transparency, accountability and reduced bribery and corruption. On the other hand, the participation of large masses in governance reinforces the democratization dimension (Turkish Ministry of Development, 2018, pp. 34–38, 72).

E-government in Türkiye

Digitalization and electronic service delivery in public administration first started in the United States in the mid-1980s and then moved to Europe in the early 2000s. In Türkiye, although many projects for digital transformation started in the 1990s, initiatives for the transition to e-government in particular were launched in the 2000s within the scope of EU harmonization. Although different projects were carried out during this period, initiatives in the field of e-government were based on the e-Türkiye+ Project as an extension of the e-Europe+ project. In 2006, within the e-Transformation Türkiye project, the "2006–2010 Information Society Strategy and Action Plan" pointed to the implementation of e-government with a focus on modernization in citizen-oriented public administration.

The goal of the 2016–2019 National E-government Strategy and Action Plan is to accelerate Türkiye's digital transformation and achieve social, economic and environmental development. The vision of the National E-government Strategy and Action Plan has been defined as "improving the quality of life for society with efficient e-government."

The following strategic aims have been determined to achieve the vision of an e-government ecosystem: (i) ensuring efficiency and sustainability of the e-government ecosystem; (ii) implementing common systems for infrastructure and administrative services and (iii) realizing transformation in public services, enhancing usage, participation and transparency (Republic of Türkiye Ministry of Transport, Maritime Affairs and Communications, 2017, p. 15).

The task of institutionalizing the transition to e-government lies with the digital transformation offices. In this respect, the purpose of the establishment of digital transformation offices is stated as "gathering the work on digital transformation, cybersecurity, national technologies, big data and artificial intelligence, which are carried out separately under different institutions, under one roof, in line with developing technologies, social demands and reform trends in the public sector" (Digital Transformation Office, 2023). In other words, the digital transformation offices – which also assume the role of coordination between government agencies by gathering the digital applications that different units provide to public services by using different infrastructures on a single platform – are also responsible for carrying out studies to make the e-government process effective and efficient (OECD, 2004, pp. 2–7).

Coordinated by the Digital Transformation Office, operated by Türksat A.Ş. and updated simultaneously with technological developments, the e-government application gathers an increasing number of services under a single roof.

E-government with indicators

In the e-government application (which has reached a total of 16,841,987,021 logins since its launch in 2008), the number of users registered in the system as of November 2023 is 64,122,503. Of the total number of users,

33,619,017 are male and 30,503,486 are female (see Figure 3.2). The age breakdown of users shows that although users have become more homogeneous over the years, the majority of users are in the 35–44 age group (see Figure 3.3).

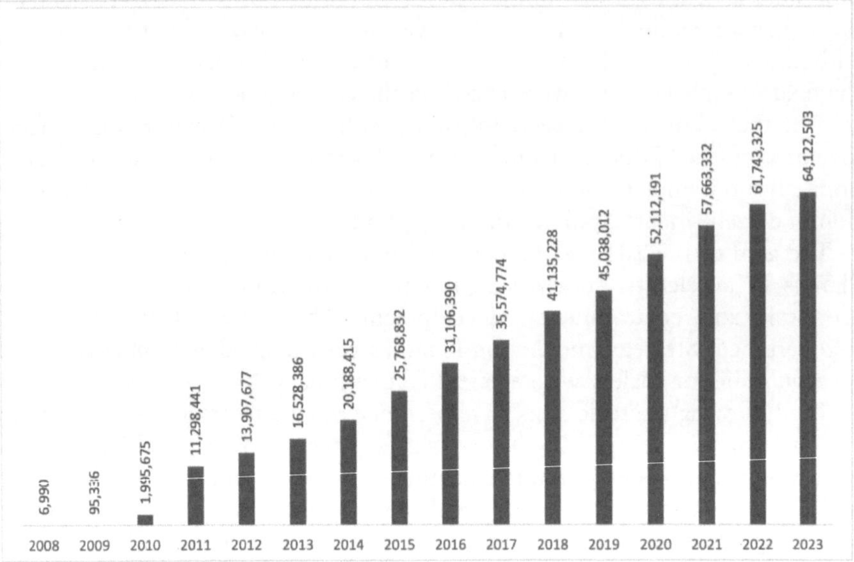

Figure 3.2 Number of E-government gateway users (Digital Transformation Office, 2023).

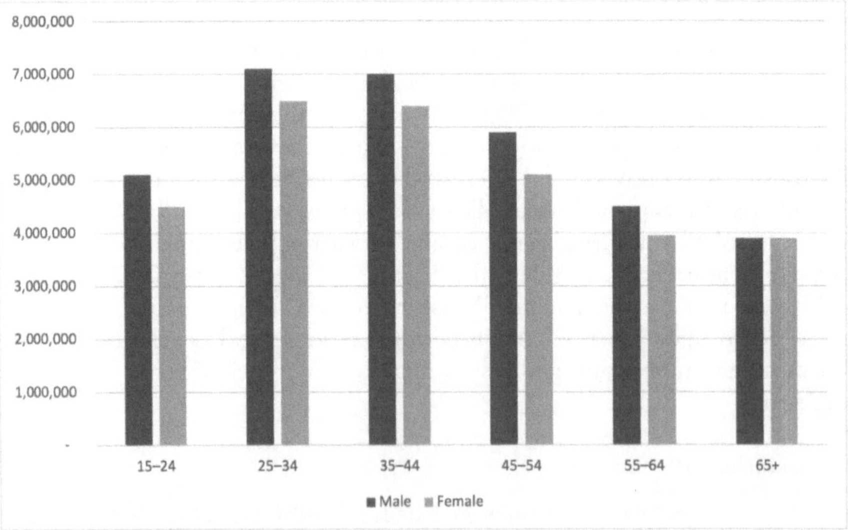

Figure 3.3 E-government gateway user distribution by age (Digital Transformation Office, 2023).

As of 2023, the total number of services reached 7,506 provided on the web and on the mobile application. Looking at the number of services by institution, the number of institutions providing services reached 1,016, up from nine in 2008.

Through the e-government gateway web page and mobile application based on data from 2022, in which the opinions and suggestions of one million users were collected, the E-government Gateway satisfaction rate of users is 95.3% (Digital Transformation Office, 2023).

E-government performances vary according to the country's economic, social, political, cultural and, most importantly, technological developments. An international indicator in this regard is the e-government development index, which has been calculated by the United Nations every two years since 2001. In this index, which is calculated as an equally weighted average of the Online Service Index, Telecommunication Infrastructure Index and Human Resources Index, Türkiye ranks 48th among 193 countries in 2022 and 24th in the Online Service Index (OECD, 2023) (see Table 3.2).

The European Commission E-Government Benchmarking Report dated October 2023 compares a total of 35 countries, including 27 EU countries, European Free Trade Association countries and candidate countries for membership. According to the report, Türkiye ranks 10th among 35 countries in terms of overall average.

The report covers four main topics: user orientation, transparency, key enablers and cross-border services. The e-government portal performs best in user orientation, where it ranks 3rd in the overall ranking. Türkiye ranks 6th in transparency and key enablers and 20th in cross-border services (see Table 3.3).

In line with the current policies in Türkiye, e-government indicators follow a positive trend. To ensure the effectiveness of e-government services and the sustainability of such development, the improvement of technological infrastructure is the primary objective. Due to the lack of technical infrastructure, there are large differences in internet use in terms of region, gender, age and education – in other words, a digital divide will prevent e-government services from achieving their objectives. Therefore, the public sector should also

Table 3.2 UN e-government survey 2022: Türkiye's performance

	Rank	*E-Government Development Index (EGDI) Group*	*EGDI*	*Telecommunication Infrastructure Index (TEA)*	*Online Services Index (OSI)*	*Human Capital Index (HCI)*	*E-Participation Index (EPI)*
Türkiye	48	Very High	0.7983	0.6626	0.86	0.8722	0.7841

Source: UN (2022).

Table 3.3 E-government benchmark: Türkiye's performance

	Score	*Rank*
Türkiye	81	10
User centricity	99	3
Online availability	98	4
Mobile friendliness	98	11
User support	100	1
Transparency	78	6
Service delivery	75	5
Personal data	78	14
Service design	81	7
Key enablers	93	6
eID	90	7
E-documents	86	1
Pre-filled forms	97	
Digital post	100	1
Cross-border services	55	20
Online availability	50	
User support	100	1
eID	4	
E-documents	44	

Source: European Commission (2023).

take measures to eliminate the digital divide. Other measures that can be taken to strengthen the system include protecting personal data by strengthening the legal infrastructure, financing the ever-renewing e-government system and training service providers in service areas.

Conclusion

In line with the social and economic benefits of broadband services, governments prioritize the strengthening and expansion of broadband infrastructure. Accordingly, national broadband strategies and action plans include the necessary measures to achieve these objectives.

The digital revolution transformed conventional societies into information societies where access to information became a fundamental aspect of everyday life. This created brand-new opportunities for personal and societal development and progress. In this new order, access to digital services – and the infrastructure that made the provision of these services – became significant for all citizens, and governments were expected to ensure that their citizens could get the best out of the digital revolution. The actions of the governments to promote, foster and adopt digitalization also impacted the trajectory of their growth and constituted an important factor affecting the current state of affairs.

Türkiye reacted to these developments by following the best practices established mainly by EU and EU Member States and adopting policies both to develop the digital infrastructure and to digitize the services its government provides to its citizens. Indicators show that Türkiye has made significant progress with respect to the digitalization of government services in accordance with its development plans. So far, Türkiye managed to establish a well-functioning institutional framework whereby various bodies cooperate effectively to develop the e-government infrastructure.

However, a significant indicator of the digital development level of countries is broadband internet use and speed. It is seen that Türkiye is far behind development with below-average speed and above-average prices. In this chapter we identified some important causes behind these symptoms. Some of these causes, such as the underdevelopment of infrastructure-based competition in broadband internet, are rooted in mistakes made in the past, and the best that can be done is to learn from these mistakes. Some others stem from inefficiencies associated with the existing regulations such as colocation and facility sharing and may be remedied by changing the regulatory framework. Finally, some of these causes are directly related to the policy choices, such as auction design or state ownership of service providers and may be resolved by adopting policies that prioritize creating a competitive market structure rather than other political objectives.

Notes

1 Türk Telekom's monopoly in fixed telephony services and leased lines were to be preserved until the end of 2003. Satellite service providers and internet service providers (ISPs) that were providing services in accordance with revenue-sharing agreements were authorized to have licenses.
2 The NRA established by Act no. 4502 was named the Telecommunications Authority (TA), whereas the ICTA was established with the coming into force of Act no. 5809. However, to avoid confusion, we do not make a distinction between the TA and the ICTA.
3 The Ministry still retains some of the regulatory duties, such as setting strategies and policies regarding electronic communications services which are based on scarce resources such as numbering, internet domain names, satellite position and frequency allotment. Competences of the Ministry are listed under Article 5 of Act No. 5809.
4 The NRF consists of the Framework Directive, EU Authorization Directive, EU Access and Interconnection Directive, EU Universal Services and User's Right Directive and EU Communications Privacy Directive.
5 In 2015, Türk Telekom acquired sole control of Avea, which was later rebranded as TT Mobil. In 2006, Telsim was acquired by Vodafone. As of 2020, there are three MNOs in the Turkish mobile communications market – Turkcell, Vodafone and TT Mobil.
6 (TTAŞ'nin Özelleştirilmesi Hakkında 1998/4 sayılı Özelleştirme Yoluyla Devralmalarının Hukuki Geçerlilik Kazanabilmeleri için Rekabet Kurumu'na Yapılacak Ön Bildirimlerde ve İzin Başvurularında Takip Edilecek Usul ve Esaslar Hakkında Rekabet Kurulu Tebliği Çerçevesinde Hazırlanan Rekabet Kurumu 2. Daire Görüşü. [the TCA Opinion])
7 According to the ladder of investment approach, the alternative operators are first granted access to the whole of the electronic communications network, and they are incentivized to build their network elements as they enlarge their consumer

base until they build and possess all the network elements other than the ones that are natural monopolies (e.g. a local loop) (Dikici, 2012, p. 78).

8 On 3 October 2011, it was announced that FTTH/B access would not be included in the market analysis over the next five years or until the share of FTTH/B access reaches 25% of the fixed broadband. In that sense, the regulatory holiday seems an indication that the ICTA has the intent to induce infrastructure-based competition (Dalgıç-Tetikol et al., 2022, p. 388).

9 This problem is not specific to Türkiye, as the OECD acknowledged that obtaining rights of way is the most fundamental problem preventing effective expansion of FTTB/H networks (OECD, 2014). That being said, it should be noted that the magnitude of the problem is considerably higher in Türkiye when compared to EU Member States due to certain idiosyncratic regulatory barriers.

10 Similar regulations are also in place in countries such as Italy and Croatia, where fiber network coverage is lower compared to the EU average, whereas no such requirement is imposed on operators in countries such as Sweden, the United Kingdom, the Netherlands and Ireland, where fiber network coverage is very high (Dursun, 2020, p. 43).

11 Facility-sharing and colocation procedures are regulated by the ICTA, whereas regulations regarding rights of way are issued by the Ministry of Transport.

12 The EU Commission stated that fees requested by municipalities in Türkiye for granting right-of-use to operators constitute an entry barrier (European Commission, 2023). Similarly, according to the OECD, financial burdens imposed on operators due to right-of-use fees slow down the deployment of broadband networks and hinder infrastructure-based competition (OECD, 2010).

13 Data received over 12 months, until 30 June 2023.

References

Akçam, S. (2006). Avrupa Birliğinde Bilgi Toplumuna Geçiş Çalışmaları. *TOBB information services department*. www.tobb.org.tr/BilgiHizmetleri/Documents/Raporlar/ab_bilgi_toplumu.pdf

Arıöz, A. (2005). *Telekomünikasyon Sektöründe Serbestleşme Süreci* [Specialization Thesis, Turkish Competition Authority]. www.rekabet.gov.tr/Dosya/uzmanlik-tezleri/69-pdf

Avaner, T., & Fedai, R. (2019). Türk Kamu Yönetiminde Ofis Sistemi: E-Devlet Uygulamalarından Dijital Dönüşüm Ofisine. *Amme İdaresi Dergisi*, *52*(2), 149–172.

Cable.co.uk. (2023). *Worldwide broadband speed league*. www.cable.co.uk/broadband/speed/worldwide-speed-league

Cordelia, A. (2007). E-government: Towards the e-bureaucratic form? *Journal of Information Technology*, 22(3), 265–274. https://doi.org/10.1057/palgrave.jit.2000105

The Council of the European Communities. (1988). *Council resolution of 30 June 1988 on the development of the common market for telecommunications services and equipment up to 1992*. Council Resolution No C 257/1. https://eur-lex.europa.eu/legal-content/EN/TXT/PDF/?uri=CELEX:31988Y1004(01)

Dalgıç-Tetikol, D., Köksal, E., & Güloğlu, B. (2022). *Determinants of internet adoption in Turkey and the need for a more coherent vision on information and communication technologies policy*, 23(4), 311–336. https://doi.org/10.1177/17835917221143060

Digital Transformation Office. (2023). *E-government gateway statistics, 2023*. https://cbddo.gov.tr/en/statistics/e-government-statistics/

Dikici, M. (2012). *Toptan Genişbant Erişim Modellerinde Ücretlendirme Politikası: Yatırım Merdiveni Yaklaşımı Işığında Analitik Bir İnceleme* [Master Thesis, Ankara

University]. https://dspace.ankara.edu.tr/xmlui/bitstream/handle/20.500.12575/31961/tez.pdf?sequence=1&isAllowed=y
Duman, E., & Aktel, M. (2021). Türkiye'nin E- Devlet Kapısı (Dijital Türkiye Portalı). *Süleyman Demirel Üniversitesi Hukuk Fakültesi Dergisi*, *11*(2). https://doi.org/10.52273/sduhfd.957529
Dursun, S. (2020). *Elektronik Haberleşme Sektöründe Altyapıya Dayalı Rekabet Sorunları ve Çözüm Önerileri* [Specialization Thesis]. https://rekabet.gov.tr/Dosya/uzmanlik-tezleri/09-selin-dursun-20200923173352978-pdf
Eke, E. (2010). Türk Telekomünikasyon Sektöründe Serbestleşme. *Süleyman Demirel Üniversitesi Vizyoner Dergisi*, *2*(1), 85–106. https://dergipark.org.tr/tr/download/article-file/214013
European Commission. (1987). *Towards a dynamic European economy – Green Paper on the development of the common market for telecommunications services and equipment* [Green Paper]. COM (87) 290final. https://eur-lex.europa.eu/legal-content/EN/ALL/?uri=CELEX%3A51987DC0290
European Commission. (2009). *Türkiye 2009 progress report*. COM (2009) 533 final. www.ab.gov.tr/files/AB_Iliskileri/Tur_En_Realitons/Progress/Türkiye_progress_report_2009.pdf
European Commission. (2023). *eGovernment benchmark, 2023*. https://digital-strategy.ec.europa.eu/en/library/egovernment-benchmark-2023.
Göçoğlu, V. (2020). Kamu Hizmetlerinin Sunumunda Dijital Dönüşüm: Nesnelerin İnterneti Üzerine Bir İnceleme. *MANAS Sosyal Araştırmalar Dergisi*, *9*(1), 615–628. https://doi.org/10.33206/mjss.538784
Güner, O. (2020). Bilgi Toplumu Göstergeleri Bağlamında Avrupa Birliği Ülkeleri ve Türkiye'ye Dair Bir Değerlendirme. *İşletme Ekonomi ve Yönetim Araştırmaları Dergisi*, *3*(2), 121–143. https://doi.org/10.33416/baybem.673085
Howard, M. (2001). E-government across the globe: How will 'e' change government? *Government Finance Review17*(4), 6–9.
ICTA. (2008). *Teknoloji, Hizmetler, Düzenleme ve Dünyadaki Gelişmelerle Genişbant*. www.btk.gov.tr/uploads/pages/slug/teknoloji-hizmetler-duzenleme-ve-dunyadaki-gelismelerle-genisbant.pdf
ICTA. (2010). *Genişbant ve Fiber: İktisadi Düzenleyici İncelemeler, Deneyimler ve Öneriler*. www.btk.gov.tr/uploads/pages/slug/genisbant-ve-fiber-iktisadi-duzenleyici-incelemeler-deneyimler-ve-oneriler.pdf
ICTA. (2023a). *Annual market data releases*. www.btk.gov.tr/pazar-verileri
ICTA. (2023b). *Türkiye Elektronik Haberleşme Sektörü Üç Aylık Pazar Verileri Raporu*. www.btk.gov.tr/uploads/pages/pazar-verileri/2023-2-kurumdisi.pdf
Larouche, P. (2000). *Competition law and regulation in European telecommunications*. Oxford and Portland Oregon: Hart Publishing.
Nart, S. (2019). Kamu Kurumlarının DNA'sı Dijital Dönüşüme Hazır mı? Meritokrasi Perspektifinden bir değerlendirme. *MANAS Sosyal Araştırmalar Dergisi*, *8*(3), 2834–2851. https://doi.org/10.33206/mjss.531781
OECD. (2004). *E-transformation Türkiye project: Turkish case for e-government, OECD meeting of senior officials from centres of government on using new tools for decision-making: Impacts on information, communication and organization*. www.bilgitoplumu.gov.tr/wp-content/uploads/2014/04/E-Transformation_Türkiye_Project.pdf
OECD. (2010). Land use restrictions as barriers to entry. *OECD Journal: Competition Law and Policy*, *10*(2), 7–73. https://doi.org/10.1787/clp-10-5kmjlgt6ngq4
OECD. (2014). *The development of fixed broadband networks*. Paris: OECD ILibrary. https://doi.org/10.1787/20716826
OECD. (2023). Digital government studies digital government review of Türkiye. *OECD digital government studies*. https://doi.org/10.1787/3958d102-en
Public Disclosure Platform. (2024). *Turkcell İletişim Hizmetleri A.Ş. Special case disclosure*. Retrieved January 25, 2024, from www.kap.org.tr/Bildirim/1134152

Republic of Türkiye Ministry of Foreign Affairs. (1998, July 17). *A strategy for developing relations between Türkiye and the European Union proposals of Türkiye* [Press release]. www.mfa.gov.tr/a-strategy-for-developing-relations-between-Türkiye-and-the-european-union_br_proposals-of-Türkiye_br_july-17_-1998_br_.en.mfa
Republic of Türkiye Ministry of Transport, Maritime Affairs and Communications. (2017). *Ulusal Genişbant Stratejisi ve Eylem Planı (2017–2020)*. www.sp.gov.tr/upload/xSPTemelBelge/files/lxlRY+Ulusal_Genisbant_Stratejisi_ve_Eylem_Plani_2017-2020.pdf
Speedtest. (2023). *Turkey median country speeds August 2024*. https://www.speedtest.net/global-index/turkey
TÜBİTAK. (1999). *Turkish national information infrastructure master plan*. http://www.bilgitoplumu.gov.tr/Documents/1/Yayinlar/991000_TuenaRapor.pdf
TÜBİSAD. (2022). *Türkiye'nin Dijital Dönüşüm Endeksi*. www.tubisad.org.tr/tr/images/pdf/DDE-2022-Raporu-Final.pdf
Turkish Competition Authority. (2016). *Decision numbered 16–20/326–146 and dated 09.06.2016*. www.rekabet.gov.tr/Karar?kararId=b89d44a3-cd12-4cc6-b566-151fb893ab28
Turkish Ministry of Development. (2018). *11. Kalkınma Planı: E-Devlet Hizmetlerinin Geliştirilmesi Çalışma Grubu Raporu*. www.sbb.gov.tr/wp-content/uploads/2022/08/e-Devlet-Hizmetlerinin-Gelistirilmesi-Calisma-Grubu-Raporu.pdf
Türkiye Wealth Fund. (2023). *Technology and telecom*. Retrieved January 25, 2024, from www.tvf.com.tr/en/our-portfolio/technology-and-telecom
UN (2022). *UN e-government survey 2022*. https://publicadministration.un.org/egovkb/en-us/Reports/UN-E-Government-Survey-2022

4 Development of E-Commerce

Zeynep Şengören Özcan and Aslı Ak

Introduction

Rapidly growing in Türkiye as well as worldwide, e-commerce represents one of the main aspects of the digital economy. Its distinct dynamics attract attention from all industries, international organizations and regulatory authorities. Many reports worldwide reflect the digital economy's increasing diffusion, particularly during the COVID-19 pandemic, and its significance in trade and economic growth.

Consequently, e-commerce has triggered many debates in different fields of law, including competition, data protection, tax, customs and consumer protection laws. Recent regulatory attempts toward e-commerce in Türkiye (ECT) heightened the interest and fueled the debates around it. In that regard, this chapter explores the development of ECT, covering its growth, driving factors, key players, consumer behavior and prospects. Comparisons with global trends and approaches will be provided, where appropriate, to further highlight the similarities or uniqueness of ECT.

The chapter starts with identifying the growth and drivers of ECT: advancements in technology, demographics and external factors that have all created an ideal environment for the growth of ECT. The chapter then provides an overview of the e-commerce market structure, including leading players, their market status, the role of e-marketplaces and the competitive dynamics. Consumer behavior in ECT is also examined, focusing on factors influencing purchasing decisions. Trust, competitive pricing and delivery convenience are identified as key drivers, with localized strategies essential for success. Insights into the future of e-commerce in Türkiye are subsequently discussed, anticipating ongoing growth and exploring further opportunities such as social commerce, e-export and emerging technologies, mainly AI.

Growth of E-Commerce in Türkiye

In its simplest terms, for e-commerce to grow and flourish in any place at any given time, three fundamental conditions must be fulfilled. First and foremost, necessary technological advancements, infrastructure and safeguards

DOI: 10.4324/9781032692937-4

must be in place. The existence of an adequate level of technology is the first step that paves the way for consumers' access to e-commerce channels. Second, e-commerce must appeal to an audience. In other terms, there must be enough consumers and business users who are keen and able to conduct transactions through e-commerce channels. For this condition to be fulfilled, the society must be technologically literate. Third, for e-commerce to establish itself as a permanent phenomenon, there must be long-term favorable changes in consumer behavior, either through natural adaptation or by external factors acting as catalyzers, such as the COVID-19 pandemic.

It is safe to say that the growth of ECT has been affected by all these factors, and potentially many more, in recent years. The sector has experienced enormous growth, increasing its nominal sales volume almost sixfold from TRY 136 billion to TRY 800.7 billion between 2019 and 2022 (ETBP, 2022) with further growth anticipated for 2023. Adjusted for inflation, ECT grew by approximately 3.2 times between 2016 and 2022, indicating an annual compound growth rate of 43% (TÜSİAD, 2022, p. 52). Global Data's study covering 48 countries constituting more than 90% of the world GDP indicates that Türkiye became the fastest-growing country in e-commerce in 2019 and 2020 (TÜSİAD, 2021, p. 12). In addition, the studies indicate ongoing growth, anticipating a 23.7% annual compound growth rate for ECT for 2020–2025, whereas the global rate is estimated at 11.7% (PwC, 2023, p. 12).

The proportion of e-commerce in total GDP also implies growth potential. With a proportion of 2.7%, Türkiye ranks 23rd among 94 countries (Deloitte, 2021, p. 53). Additionally, Türkiye's ratio of e-commerce to total commerce was 15.7% in 2020 (ETBP, 2020), which was behind the worldwide average of 17.8% (Statista, n.d.) and countries like the United Kingdom, Korea and China (UNCTAD, 2021b).

While acknowledging the current and future importance of this sector for the country, this section also delves into the recent growth and development of ECT, scrutinizing the intricate interplay of the main factors that underpin its rise. Through a lens focused primarily on the statistics and facts of the sector, this section endeavors to unravel the multifaceted dynamics that have propelled ECT.

From technological advancements and high internet penetration to the surge in smartphone adoption, the emergence of robust online payment systems and the development of a logistics infrastructure, each element plays a pivotal role in the growth story. Understanding the demographic nuances, with a special emphasis on the young, tech-savvy population, allows us to appreciate the intricacies of consumer behavior in this unique market. Finally, we explore the changing consumer preferences and transformative impact of the COVID-19 pandemic that has further underscored the rapid evolution of ECT.

Although it might seem simple to identify and categorize these factors, understanding their true impact on the growth of electronic commerce requires considering them together and within a specific context. It is important to note that Türkiye's e-commerce ecosystem, much like the global case, results from a combination of factors constantly influencing one another. Therefore, any future predictions should be made holistically.

Technological Advancements

Despite the lack of a uniform e-commerce definition, one can find a commonality in all attempts: the emphasis on the use of technology. Whether it be a "sale or purchase of goods or services . . . through electronic transactions conducted via the internet or other computer-mediated . . . networks" (Eurostat, 2023), "sale or delivery of goods and services by electronic means" (World Trade Organization, n.d.) or "all economic and commercial activities being conducted online through electronic medium" (Turkish E-commerce Act, 2014), one thing is for certain: We need the technological infrastructure to realize e-commerce transactions.

Fast-forwarding 30 years from its first-ever connection to the global internet network in 1993 (Parlak, 2005, p. 30), Türkiye reached an internet penetration rate of 83.4% in January 2023 (DataReportal, 2023). The data suggest that Türkiye's internet penetration is at a more advanced level when compared to the 65.7% internet penetration rate worldwide (Statista, 2024). However, Digital's annual reports show that progress has mostly been made over the last ten years, where the rate almost doubled against an increasing population (DataReportal, 2014–2023). That said, it is clear that Türkiye still has a long way to go in internet penetration to catch the penetration rates (see Figure 4.1) observed in Northern America (92%), Northern Europe (97.4%) and Western Europe (93.5%) (DataReportal, 2023).

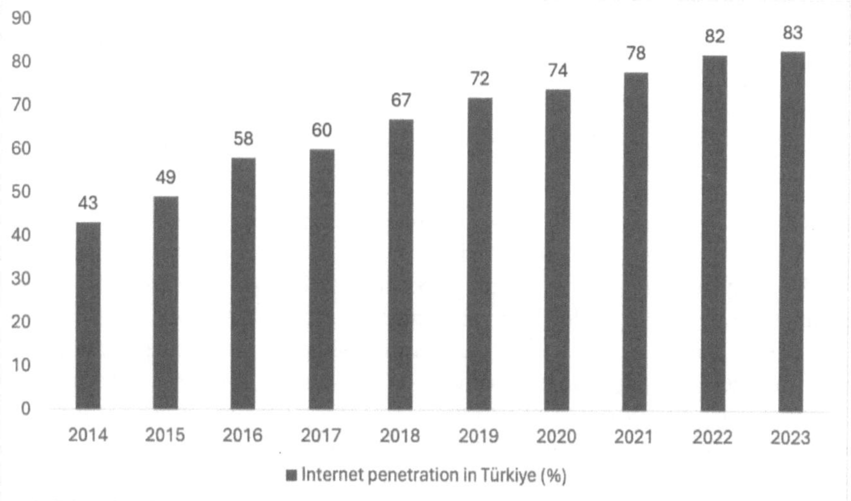

Figure 4.1 Internet penetration in Türkiye between 2014 and 2023 (DataReportal, 2014, 2015, 2016, 2017, 2018, 2019, 2020, 2021, 2022, 2023).

Increasing smartphone adoption in Türkiye also supported growth in e-commerce, fueled by the expansion of internet penetration and global technological advancements. Indeed, one may argue that smartphone adoption and the growth of e-commerce are indissociable (Mangır & Allahverdi, 2022, p. 139). As opposed to standard mobile phones, smartphones serve a critical role in the growth of e-commerce as they allow their users to download and use applications that make e-commerce possible with just a few taps. While only 30% of the total population in Türkiye had smartphones in 2014 (DataReportal, 2014–2023), the same metric proved to be 97.6% in the first days of 2023 for internet users aged between 16 and 64 (DataReportal, 2023).

Luckily, the tech-savvy approach on the demand side was not neglected. Increased access to the internet and the emergence of e-commerce platforms and marketplaces in Türkiye, starting from the early 2000s, were not the only technological advancements leading to today's e-commerce ecosystem. Clearly, the rapid advancement in online banking and payment services were driving factors in establishing the trust relationship between merchants and customers who do not meet physically. Further to the contributions of existing banks and financial institutions, many sector players took the initiative to establish their own e-money and payment service institutions to offer additional benefits to their customers under their own brands. Although many examples such as *Trendyol Cüzdan* and *hepsipay* proved to be successful, regulatory interventions resulted in the suspension of some of these initiatives (Ulukan, 2022).

Developments in the field of logistics are also closely related to the technological infrastructure. Ensuring fast, secure and reliable delivery options to consumers acts as a competitive advantage for enterprises using their own delivery methods or relying on third-party services. In any case, with the growth of e-commerce, merchants started to seek ways to improve customer experience by providing them next-day delivery options, the ability to track their order status and easily initiate returns through websites or applications.

Demographics

The rapid adaptation to the advancements in technology undoubtedly has to do with the demographics of a society. The Turkish Competition Authority (TCA) acknowledges that a young population facilitates society's fast adaptation to technological developments and creates further potential in that area (TCA, 2022, p. 20). Other studies also suggest a negative relationship between age and adaption to e-commerce (Hamad & Schmitz, 2019, p. 22). Although varying for different products, females have presented a more willing approach toward online shopping (Hamad & Schmitz, 2019, p. 22). Some studies also featured a positive relationship between adaption to ecommerce and demographic factors such as education, income and marital status (Hamad & Schmitz, 2019, p. 29). In that sense, it is crucial to understand the overarching demographic group or groups serving the growth of ECT.

DataReportal reported the median age for the Turkish population as 31.6 for January 2023, with only 8.8% of the population being older than 65 (DataReportal, 2023). With an up-and-coming generation of future consumers under the age of 24 constituting 38.1% of the population, it is safe to argue that Türkiye will continue to preserve the enhancing effects of its young generation for a considerable amount of time.

Overall, the distribution of female and male population seems balanced with 49.9% and 50.1% respectively (DataReportal, 2023). Accordingly, it may not be possible to argue that one group has dominance over the other in its impact on the growth of ECT. That said, statistics align with past studies and show that women are more active e-commerce customers in Türkiye, accounting for 58% of the transactions concluded in 2022 (İyzico, n.d., p. 17).

In terms of literacy, Türkiye presents pleasing figures of overall literacy in adults aged 15+ being 96.7% (94.4% in females and 99.1% in males) (DataReportal, 2023). Though there still is room for improvement, analyzing these metrics together with the median age of the population and the continued increase in internet penetration and smartphone use, the literacy level in Türkiye can be another metric supporting the current and future growth of e-commerce.

The Turkish Statistical Institute's (TÜİK) figures reported labor force participation as 51.4% for 2021, 32.8% for women and 70.3% for men (TÜİK, 2023) specifically. It is also noted that among women with a higher education degree, the labor force participation exhibited a rate of 67.6%. What seems to be a positive correlation between employment and the level of education can also be leveraged for the further growth of e-commerce.

All in all, the demographics of Türkiye paint a positive picture for the future of e-commerce with a young and technologically able population with high literacy rates.

COVID-19 Pandemic and Changing Consumer Preferences

December 2019 marked the start of a global downturn like no other, which affected all aspects of life globally – the COVID-19 pandemic (WHO, 2020). The fast, irrepressible and cross-border spread of the disease has led to worldwide lockdowns, shifting the traditional ways of commerce everywhere, with an even worse impact than the 2008–2009 financial crisis (UNCTAD, 2021a, p. 11).

Unlike many sectors and industries, e-commerce showed growth during the COVID-19 pandemic. The use of electronic channels for the sale or purchase of products and services, an already popular and growing phenomenon, gained significant acceleration as both consumers and businesses sought ways to minimize the adverse impacts on commerce. Indeed, some argue that even the most technologically conservative groups have set their doubts aside, and the number of both consumers and businesses that went online has increased (Güven, 2020, p. 252).

Not only did it overturn how business is conducted, but the COVID-19 pandemic also shifted Turkish consumers' preferences significantly. Following the footsteps of the rest of the world, Turkish households channeled their resources heavily toward online grocery shopping, health, personal care and cleaning products, books and stationery and dried nuts (Güven, 2020, p. 258). The increase in online sales of these categories was reported as "186% for groceries, 168% for healthcare products, 108% for cosmetics, 69% for books and stationery and 42% for dried nuts" (Güven, 2020, p. 258). The changes in consumer preferences were a direct result of the increased sensitivity toward keeping healthy and of the increased hours spent at home due to lockdowns and travel regulations. Another explanation here can also be presented as the tendency to keep stock of items that have been increasing in price due to high demand, resulting from the uncertainties brought by the pandemic (Özbay & Özcan, 2021, p. 28). On the contrary, Turkish consumers gave up on their spending on travel and accommodation, luxury consumer goods, clothing and accessories (TCA, 39; Güven, 2020, p. 263).

Changes in demand found a response on the supply side as well. Offering their products on e-marketplaces, enterprises increasingly joined the online world. While there were 68,457 businesses engaged in e-commerce in 2019, this number increased to 256,861 in 2020, demonstrating a 275% increase during the COVID-19 pandemic. This increasing trend also followed through with 484,347 and 548,688 businesses engaged in e-commerce in 2021 and 2022 respectively (ETBP, 2021–2022).

These figures indicate that the ECT is still developing and not yet mature. The share of e-commerce within the total trade and GDP reveals the potential for growth. Considering the young population and room for an increase in internet use, ECT is expected to maintain its development in the following years. Recent market entries, exits and expansion of incumbent firms affirm the immaturity and dynamism of ECT.

Moreover, enterprises rapidly improved their logistics structures and offered "contactless delivery," mobile wallet options and wearable technologies, which allowed their customers to engage in daily transactions with the minimum contact possible (TÜSİAD, 2022, p. 9). As a matter of fact, the number of contactless transactions made via cards has increased by 250% from 2020 to the first half of 2021 (TÜSİAD, 2022, p. 9).

Although it is not possible to state that these consumer preferences have proven to be permanent with respect to product choices, it is evident that COVID-19 acted as a catalyzer for larger circles of consumer groups developing a habit of e-commerce. Even after the lift of restrictions to social life, consumers demonstrate a tendency to continue using e-commerce channels due to time-efficiency benefits and the variety of product and service choices offered online, especially with respect to their food and grocery needs (TÜSİAD, 2022, p. 10). When asked about their reasons for shopping online, 57.3%, 49.4% and 43.5% of Turkish consumers have brought forward the benefits of free delivery, easy returns policy and coupons, and discounts, respectively (DataReportal, 2023). Another prominent reason is the ability to observe other consumers' experiences through their reviews, likes or comments, which under normal circumstances cannot easily be obtained during a traditional physical shopping experience.

Accordingly, one may argue that although the attention that COVID-19 attracted has faded away throughout the years, its impact on the growth of e-commerce, consumer and business user preferences has proven to be a permanent one. While consumers exploit the benefits offered in terms of ease of ordering, payment and logistics, enterprises also make use of the opportunities provided to them by e-marketplaces or their own investments to increase the quality and variety of their offerings to more customers.

Overview of the Competitive Dynamics and Leading Players in Türkiye

Overview of the E-Commerce in Türkiye and the Main Players

The origins of ECT can be traced back to the late 1990s, when Türkiye's Supreme Council of Science and Technology decided to launch the e-commerce web. Some date it back to the use of the internet (Demirdöğmez et al., 2018, p. 2222; Toplu Yılmaz & Bayram, 2020, p. 44) while others to electronic fund transfers in 1992 (Aydemir, 2004). Since then, efforts to promote and regulate the sector have continued with the involvement of government and civil society. E-commerce obtained its first comprehensive legal regulation in 2014 with the Turkish E-Commerce Act. In 2017, the Electronic Commerce Information Centre (ETBİS) was established to keep the data of operational companies and publish regular statistics on its platform, ETBP. Recently, in 2022, the Turkish E-Commerce Act was amended to meet the needs of the dramatically growing sector and tackle the problems arising from the asymmetric power of e-marketplaces (The Preamble of the Act Amending the Turkish E-Commerce Act; Act No: 7416, 2022). Additionally, the TCA has proposed an amendment in the Competition Act targeting competition concerns arising from market power and data use, possibly impacting e-commerce.

Although e-commerce was first developed globally with the help of big retailers such as Amazon (Sarıçiçek, 2020, p. 129), ECT was pioneered by local e-marketplaces or classified advertisement platforms, that is, e-commerce intermediaries. Hepsiburada, still a prominent e-marketplace in Türkiye, entered the market in 1998, followed by Türkiye's leading online advertising platform, Sahibinden, in 2000. Local brands Gittigidiyor (e-marketplace) and Yemeksepeti (food delivery platform) were launched in 2001, operating via B2C and C2C models. ECT diverges from the rest of the world, where e-commerce emerged with electronic data interchange as B2B (Oğuz et al., 2022, p. 154). Accordingly, unlike the United States – where technology and supply side played pivotal roles in the advancement of e-commerce – consumer demand is expected to drive ECT (Kepenek, 1999, p. 24).

ECT produced more local enterprises, such as Çiçeksepeti, Markafoni, Trendyol and N11. The latest local entrant into the market was Getir, with grocery delivery. It later diversified its activities, ranging from taxis to professional services, and received acknowledgment for its growth (Simpson, 2021; Üner et al., 2021; Dillet, 2022).

Still, the contribution of global players' investments is indisputable. German player Limango entered the market, and the shares of Markafoni and Gittigidiyor were acquired, respectively, by Naspers and eBay. The interest of the global players in the Turkish e-commerce market continued after 2015 with the acquisition of Yemeksepeti by DeliveryHero. In 2018, Amazon entered the Turkish market, and Alibaba took control of promising market player Trendyol. Local players in e-commerce accessed global funding as well. Hepsiburada achieved global investment, becoming the first Turkish company listed in NASDAQ (Podder & Hu, 2021), and Getir raised global funding (Levingston & Hammond, 2023) as well as Trendyol (KPMG, 2021, p. 5; Reuters, 2021). Although some players, like eBay, Limango and Naspers, have exited the market over the years, recent funding and the investments of the existing global players are evidence that enthusiasm for ECT endures.

Overview of Competition in the Market

E-Marketplaces

The number of undertakings using the e-marketplaces increased by 331% in 2020 and 90% in 2021 (see Figure 4.2). COVID-19 led to more undertakings using e-marketplaces to reach customers. This trend kept on even after the pandemic, and 97% of undertakings engaged in e-commerce operated through e-marketplaces in 2022. In that regard, Turkish e-commerce businesses prefer outsourcing certain aspects of their operations rather than managing their e-commerce website (PwC, 2023, p. 15).

It is clear e-marketplaces allow small and medium enterprises (SMEs) to increase their brand awareness and exposure to larger target audiences while benefiting from the logistics and payment infrastructure that e-marketplaces provide either directly or through third parties (TÜSİAD, 2022, p. 10). Considering this, it is unsurprising that SMEs prefer e-marketplaces as their e-commerce channels. Indeed, aiming to promote SMEs with comparatively less engagement in e-commerce (OECD, 2019; Falk & Hagsten, 2015, p. 361), the OECD considers e-marketplaces as a market response to overcome growth barriers, such as legislative consistency, taxation, e-payment and the need for complementary skills (2013, p.5). In this respect, e-marketplaces in Türkiye are commonly preferred by SMEs. About half of the sellers in e-marketplaces are single proprietorships and have only one employee (TCA, 2022, pp. 94–95).

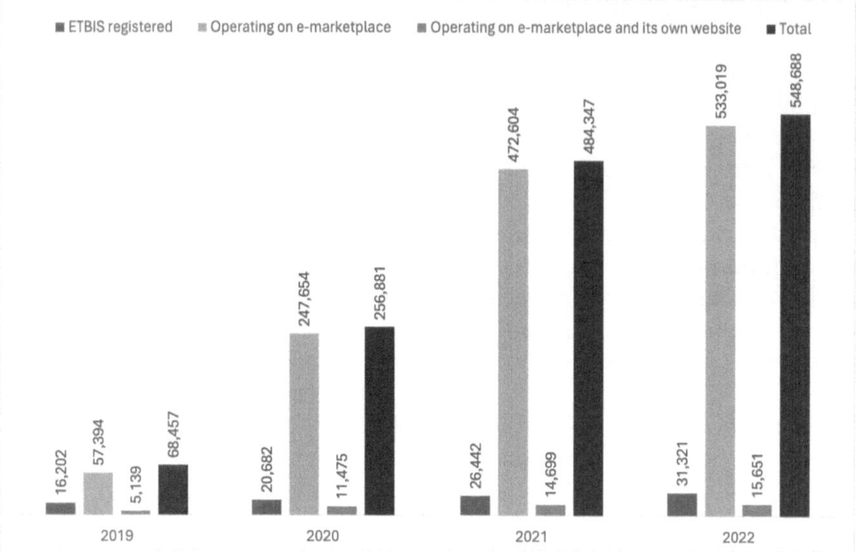

Figure 4.2 Number of undertakings operating in e-commerce (ETBP, 2022).

SMEs, due to their number and share in total employment, play a vital role in the economy – so much so that they accounted for 99.8% of the total number of start-ups in 2020 (KOSGEB, 2020). In that sense, e-marketplaces have not just played a significant role in initiating the development of ECT but have also maintained their growth by allowing SMEs access to e-commerce. Because e-marketplaces serve as a gateway for SMEs in Türkiye, firms' dependence on the marketplaces raises some competition concerns (TCA, 2022). In 2020, 72% of businesses using e-marketplaces engaged with one e-marketplace. This rate increased to 75% in 2021 and 80% in 2022 (ETBP, 2021–2022), indicating that businesses' dependence on e-marketplace has augmented over those three years (TCA, 2022, p. 91).

The common observation for e-marketplaces in several countries is that a single player tends to dominate the market. However, ECT presented a more competitive market structure with several remarkable players until 2019. Although some of the largest global companies operate in Türkiye, they cannot stand out in Türkiye as they did globally. The superiority of local players, highly evident in the initial stages of e-commerce, still prevails to some extent. Currently, the largest e-commerce players in Türkiye are Trendyol (affiliated with Alibaba) and Hepsiburada.

Another observation is the higher significance for Türkiye of e-marketplaces in e-trade. Marketplaces accounted for 47% of all online sales in 2019, whereas the TCA (2022) estimates that sales through e-marketplaces reached 80% of total e-commerce. Hence, the structure of e-marketplaces has become a decisive factor for ECT, in general. The TCA's (2022) market inquiry puts forth that Trendyol is the leading player in e-marketplaces, preferred by 46% of consumers. If the consumer is younger, the likelihood that they use Trendyol online shopping is even higher.

Though e-commerce exhibited a competitive outlook, the TCA (2022, p. 97) pointed out a downturn in 2018. While Trendyol gained significant market share, and Hepsiburada and Amazon preserved their position, Gittigidiyor and N11 lost market share dramatically. Indeed, Gittigidiyor shut its operations in June 2022, and Getir took over N11. Supporting its market concentration findings in the report, the TCA also concluded that Trendyol holds dominance in a recent decision.[1] Hence, the 2022 e-commerce market outlook can be described as relatively concentrated: Trendyol is the dominant player, and Hepsiburada is the main rival. Both players operate a hybrid e-marketplace model, yet the weight of third-party sellers has risen over the years (TCA, 2022, p. 159). In that sense, the e-marketplace sector in Türkiye can be said to follow the global tendency of tipping.

Sectoral Distribution and the Rise of Fast Delivery

Türkiye deviates from the world in the sectoral distribution of e-commerce. The most prominent distinction is that the home appliances category, ranking first in Türkiye (PwC, 2023, p. 14), was not among the top five categories globally. On the other hand, clothing and footwear, food and beverages and electronics are the next most preferred categories for e-commerce – both in Türkiye and globally. The total share of the leading five categories globally is around 45% while it is 33% in Türkiye. This implies that ECT covers a wider range of categories (PwC, 2023, p. 14) and is less concentrated in category distribution.

Analyzing the category distribution in Türkiye in depth, home appliances come first each year, followed by clothing, footwear and accessories. Third on the list belongs to electronics. Due to COVID-19, the airline sector could not show any prominence in 2020, yet it rose to rank fourth for both 2021 and 2022. The groceries segment increased in 2021, thanks to the effect of COVID-19, and sustained its position in 2022.

The groceries segment is a noteworthy example of the industry's prospects for improvement and diversification. The volume of the supermarket segment increased by 283% in 2020 and continued to grow, reaching TRY14 billion in 2022. New entrant Getir and incumbent Yemeksepeti unveiled the potential of fast grocery delivery, and many supermarket chains as well as the e-marketplace sector leader Trendyol expanded their operations accordingly. These players serve the Turkish instances of quick commerce, which allows new entrants and increases competition and service differentiation (TUSİAD, 2022, p. 57). Studies revealed that 60% of consumers plan to shop for groceries online after the pandemic (TÜSİAD, 2021, p. 20), which indicates the continuity of the demand for online grocery and quick commerce in Türkiye.

Geographical Distribution

E-commerce companies are mainly concentrated in big cities. ETBIS data suggests that 37% of e-commerce companies are headquartered in İstanbul. The three big provinces in Türkiye accommodated 53.3% of e-commerce companies in 2022. This concentrated structure has persisted since 2020, though the collective weight of the most significant three and five provinces has slightly diminished over the years. Studies recommend tailored approaches for different geographies, including multi-channel opportunities (TÜSİAD, 2021, p. 3).

Ecosystem, Super-App and Related Sectors

Today, digital platforms are recognized to compete as ecosystems (Jacobides & Lianos, 2021), which enables them to interconnect related or complementary services around a core service by benefiting from economies of scale and scope and network effects (OECD, 2020a). Hence, platforms can integrate various products and services and facilitate data sharing between services (TCA, 2023, p. 155). Ecosystems are also highly intertwined with the concept of super apps, which are commonly defined as a "closed ecosystem of many apps that people would use every day because they offer such a seamless, integrated, contextualized and efficient experience" (Mast, 2020).

The leading e-commerce actors in Türkiye diversified and enlarged their businesses with a vision of becoming super apps: Trendyol has extended its operation into fast grocery delivery, food delivery and secondhand C2C (Dolap). Other examples of super-apps in Türkiye are Yemeksepeti (food, fast grocery and local business delivery services) and Getir (food, fast grocery and local business delivery services, taxi -*BiTaksi*-, short-term car rental and local employment). While competition intensifies, super-apps are expected to grow to maintain consumer loyalty by providing them with an uninterrupted single-sourced experience (TÜSİAD, 2022, p. 15).

Additionally, economies of scale and scope allow marketplaces to widen their operations toward logistics, storage and payment services (TCA, 2022, p. 163). In that sense, Trendyol (Trendyol Express), Hepsiburada (hepsiJet), Amazon and N11 have investments in the logistics sector. Moreover, Trendyol (with Wallet) and Hepsiburada (with HepsiPay) have payment system operations.

Even if e-commerce players are not directly part of the logistics or payment sector, the development of e-commerce goes hand in hand with the development of the logistics sector. Struggling to cope with the surging demand after COVID-19, the logistics sector created alternative methods and introduced new players (TÜSİAD, 2022, p. 75). The amendment to the Road Transport Regulation in 2021 reduced cargo companies' requirements for serving e-commerce and facilitated sector development and delivery performance. With the expansion of e-commerce, new storage and delivery methods are also expected to be adopted in the following years, that is, more dark stores operating 24/7 and closed to consumers as a necessity of quick commerce (TÜSİAD, 2022, p. 57) or the enhancement of delivery points around the country.

In that regard, e-commerce has amplified the growth and investment in complementary sectors (TÜSİAD, 2022, p. 52). It also created new industries and business models, initiating transformations in some conventional industries, for example, e-commerce expenditures provided employment opportunities for 1.9 million people, corresponding to 7.2% of the overall employment in Türkiye in 2020 (Deloitte, 2021, pp. 5–7).

Advertising

Advertising is a valuable component for promotion in each sector. However, it has become vital in ECT, particularly for e-marketplaces. The TCA (2022, pp. 166–167) determined that Trendyol launched an "advertising attack," with its campaign highly exceeding the budgets of its rivals. This helped it gain its current market position. In that regard, advertising in e-marketplaces is acknowledged as a competition driver. As a matter of fact, consumers have stated that online advertising is the top decisive factor in using e-marketplaces for the first time (TCA, 2022, p. 75). Therefore, the discussion regarding antitrust violations by creating barriers via advertisements (Varol, 2020) becomes a more credible risk in e-marketplaces. Traces of these concerns can also be followed in the E-Commerce Act amendments, including restrictions on using brand names in advertisements and advertisement and discount budgets. It is not evident how amendments will affect the market structure; however, e-marketplaces should allocate an advertising budget in Türkiye to gain market power and create brand awareness.

Consumer Behavior and Profile

The rise of B2C and C2C models placed consumers at the heart of e-commerce. Because of consumers having a central role, concerns about consumer protection have escalated (OECD, 2023, 2020b). To "fully exploit the opportunities" of e-commerce, building consumer trust becomes one of the critical elements (Coppel, 2000, p. 3). On the contrary, a lack of trust would discourage the development of e-commerce.

The TCA's consumer survey (2022, pp. 55–80) sets forth insights regarding how the lack of consumer trust risks discouraging e-commerce. Accordingly, privacy and fraud concerns, along with the lack of trust in sellers, are listed as the most prominent factors demotivating consumers from using e-commerce. This is followed by the need for physical experience and difficulties in returning products. Then comes trust and recognition of the e-marketplace, as consumers value recognition and trustworthiness most when choosing the e-marketplace. These insights indicate that there are still areas for improvement in building trust in e-commerce, such as privacy regulation, trusted payment systems and brand awareness.

Among other remedies, consumer reviews help address the trust problem, as they provide authentic perceptions about the product and the transaction or delivery process. Indeed, reviews diversify e-commerce from conventional business. In that sense, 71% of consumers in Türkiye find reviews helpful (Statista, 2023a). The survey also reveals that a multitude of reviews is a decisive factor in choosing the e-marketplace, as 70.5% of consumers have read the reviews before purchasing on e-marketplaces (TCA, 2022, p. 81).

A detailed consumer behavior analysis in e-commerce could be a pathfinder for further growth. Reasonable prices come first among the motivations of consumers to use e-commerce, followed by timesaving and product variety (TCA, 2022, p. 54). Other research suggests that consumers in e-commerce value free delivery, easy returns and coupons/discounts the most (PwC, 2023, p. 40; Statista, 2023a). The quality of the service and the system as well as trust and enjoyment are also significant for shopping behavior in Türkiye (Çelik & Yılmaz, 2011, p. 16). Income is another factor affecting consumer behavior (Alkan et al., 2021, p. 102; Oğuz et al., 2022). Studies also covering Türkiye show that a 1% increase in GDP per capita leads to a 7.29% increase in e-commerce (Oğuz et al., 2022). Research also indicates a positive relationship between education and e-commerce. In line with the global trends, the demographic groups in Türkiye using e-commerce more than others are young, (DataReportal, 2023), educated and have a high income (Alkan et al., 2021). While male users prefer purchasing electronics the most, female users buy mainly clothes (TCA, 2022, p. 71).

Highly related to the increasing use of mobile devices, consumers prefer mobile channels in e-commerce (ETBP, 2022); in previous years 70% of users chose mobile devices in e-commerce. That said, Turkish consumers have not widely adopted mobile and digital wallets or alternative payment systems. Only 6% of payments in 2022 were made via wallets, and the majority of consumers used credit cards for e-commerce payments (DataReportal, 2023). The rates of different payment methods have been stabilized over the three years: credit cards 61%; EFT/transfers 36% and cash 3% (ETBP, 2022).

In light of these data and explanations, it can be inferred that consumers value security, low prices, consumer experience and free delivery in ECT. The majority of e-commerce consumers are young and educated with high incomes, they consult consumer reviews in their purchases and use mobile channels and credit cards.

The Future of ECT

The contribution of e-commerce to consumer experiences, business growth and economic development is evident. Consumers can access a broader range of products and suppliers at high speed and comfort; business can expand their operations without being limited to their physical boundaries, and the cost savings help to increase competition and efficiency (OECD, 2013, 2019; Alkan et al., 2021, p. 95; Falk & Hagsten, 2015). With all these advantages, the sector is expected to grow, yet at a slower pace than in previous years. PwC (2023, p. 11) relates this trend to the increasing maturity and stability of the market. However, the growth rate of Eastern Europe, which includes Türkiye, is anticipated to exceed the rest of the world in the next five years (PwC, 2023, p. 11). Where the Turkish e-commerce market is concerned, the rise in use as a result of COVID-19 is expected to continue, as the pandemic has altered consumer behavior (TCA, 2022, p. 19; TÜSİAD, 2022, p. 10).

Though Türkiye has great potential with its young population, rising internet use and myriad SMEs, the journey toward business and consumer integration to e-commerce at higher levels is not without challenges or limitations. Barriers hindering the growth of e-commerce are summarized as legislative consistency, taxation, e-payment, the need for complementary skills – especially for small business (OECD, 2013, pp. 4–5) – and the costs associated with delivery and returns, which discourage e-commerce engagement (OECD, 2019; Eurostat, 2001).

In that regard, relieving the concerns of consumers and businesses alike is the key to accelerating the advancement of ECT. Regarding logistics, COVID-19 forced current retailers and marketplaces to invest in the sector by encouraging new entrants. The geography and dispersed settlement could be future challenges for the sector, complicating the provision of a standardized service in each region. As to alternative payment methods, they have not been widely adopted in Türkiye. However, the rising FinTech sector in Türkiye (Ernst & Young, 2022) indicates an opportunity for new financial solutions in ECT.

Considering the weight of SMEs in the economy, their integration into e-commerce is vital for e-commerce growth. Indeed, studies present that the effects of e-sales are more substantial for small firms than for medium and large ones (Falk & Hagsten, 2015, p. 366). As marketplaces serve as a gateway and facilitator of integration, recent regulations, mostly on marketplaces, will shape the future of ECT. The new E-commerce Act includes license fees, limitations on advertising and restrictions on expanding operations to delivery and payment systems, which may discourage the growth of marketplaces. The direct and indirect effects of these provisions and the actors' responses will be under close examination of e-commerce studies in subsequent years.

Another opportunity for SMEs to increase online sales is e-export. The studies on e-export put forth the effects of e-commerce on reducing trade barriers and distance-related costs (Terzi, 2011; Martens, 2013; PwC, 2023; Toplu Yılmaz & Bayram, 2020; Chmielarz et al., 2021). However, e-export has remained limited in Türkiye, where 91.3% of e-commerce consists of internal trade (ETBP, 2022). Cross-border disputes, limited language skills, or differences in regulation challenge cross-border e-commerce (OECD, 2019). As e-export provides a remarkable opportunity, barriers hindering the exploitation of this opportunity also reveal the issues that need to be dealt with for further improvement.

Recent trends in e-commerce suggest the use of social media by labeling it "social commerce" (PwC, 2023; TÜSİAD, 2022). With its high adoption rate in Asia Pacific and the United States, social commerce also has high potential for Türkiye. Regarding social media use, Türkiye ranks sixth, exceeding the global average, with users spending approximately three hours a day on social media. Instagram and YouTube are the most preferred platforms in Türkiye (TCA, 2023). Online advertising is also seeing an increase in use by influencers and as such is the subject of a new guideline in Türkiye (TCA, 2023, p. 37). In that regard, social commerce is expected to rise and become a norm soon (TÜSİAD, 2022 p. 96).

Another global trend is that the business connects directly to customers without the use of intermediaries. As e-commerce matures, the likelihood increases that businesses will use their own channels (Deloitte, 2021, p. 7). However, intermediaries in Türkiye play a crucial role in the trust of e-commerce, which is not expected to dramatically change in the next years. In order for global trends to catch on and increase direct sales, more investment is needed in brand awareness and the digital consumer experience.

Lastly, artificial intelligence is expected to transform e-commerce, as it will change all industries. Where AI has already been used – and where potential remains strong – is in the areas of customized experience, such as recommender systems, pricing algorithms, better market and demand analyses and forecasts and the ability to monitor operations from start to delivery (Zhang et al., 2021; TÜSİAD, 2022; Cheng et al., 2023). Introducing and encouraging the use of AI tools helps firms operate more efficiently and take advantage of future trends.

Conclusion

E-commerce, which has shown dramatic growth recently, is regarded as the key to economic growth. With this crucial role and its interconnection with different industries, e-commerce continues to be a mainstay of global discourse. With its above-average growth rate, Türkiye holds significant potential for e-commerce. Recent amendments will shape ECT, which in turn increases the need to understand the dynamics of ECT.

ECT has developed dramatically recently, with an annual compounded growth rate reaching 43%. This growth is far above the world average. The underlying factors of this growth are the rapid advancement of technology leading to increased internet penetration, smartphone adaptation and support by basic financial services, which has been welcomed by the young demographics of Türkiye. Another factor that affected consumer habits and availability of SMEs in e-commerce came from the push created by the restrictions attached to the COVID-19 pandemic, which has proven to be more permanent than the pandemic itself, luckily.

In terms of anticipated growth, increasing the number of transactions and businesses joining ECT, the sector presents an immature, dynamic and more competitive market structure when compared with global trends. The development of fast grocery delivery serves as a compelling example of innovation in ECT. The weight of e-marketplaces and their role in SME integration cannot be overlooked, yet this dependency on e-marketplaces has escalated antitrust concerns. The sector has exhibited a more concentrated structure, so there has been a trend toward tipping after 2019 when Trendyol gained significant market share with the help of a massive advertising campaign. The expansion to related and complementary fields has created new opportunities and new entries. This trend is expected to continue; however, the effects of the E-Commerce Act on this trend may be adverse.

ECT consumers value security, low prices, consumer experience and free delivery. The majority of e-commerce consumers are young, educated, high-income and male. They consult consumer reviews when making purchases and use mobile channels and credit cards.

Examining ECT and global trends, Türkiye has noteworthy potential for further growth, based on market forecasts. Investments in trust and digital infrastructure, for better brand awareness and a better consumer experience, are absolutely needed for further growth. ECT holds substantial potential for further development in social commerce and e-export. Like all sectors, AI solutions provide numerous opportunities to serve efficiently. Enhancing AI capabilities is inevitable if ECT continues to maintain its development.

Note

1 TCA decision dated 26.07.2023 and numbered 23–33/633–213.

References

Alkan, Ö., Küçükoğlu, H., & Tutar, G. (2021). Modeling of the factors affecting e-commerce use in Turkey by categorical data analysis factors affecting e-commerce use. *International Journal of Advanced Computer Science and Applications*, *12*(1), 95–105. https://doi.org/10.14569/IJACSA.2021.0120113

Aydemir, S. (2004). Elektronik Ticaret Alanındaki Rekabet Sorunları. *Uzmanlık Tezi.* Ankara: Rekabet Kurumu.

Çelik, H. E., & Yılmaz, V. (2011). Extending the technology acceptance model for adoption of shopping by consumers in Turkey. *Journal of E Commerce Journal of Electronic Commerce Research*, *12*(2), 152–161.

Cheng, X., Cohen, J., & Mou, J. (2023). AI-enabled technology innovation in e-commerce. *Journal of Electronic Commerce Research*, *21*(1).

Chmielarz, W., Zborowski, M., Fandrejewska, A., & Atasever, M. (2021). The impact of e-commerce on globalization processes: Comparison of Poland and Turkey. *European Research Studies Journal, XXIV*(3), 682–698.

Coppel, J. (2000). E-commerce: Impacts and policy challenge. *OECD Economics Department Working Papers*, (252). https://doi.org/10.1787/18151973

DataReportal. (2014, July 7). *Digital 2014: Middle East, North Africa & Turkey regional overview.* https://datareportal.com/reports/digital-2014-middle-east-north-africa-turkey-regional-overview

DataReportal. (2015, January 22). *Digital 2015: Turkey.* https://datareportal.com/reports/digital-2015-turkey

DataReportal. (2016, January 29). *Digital 2016: Turkey*. https://datareportal.com/reports/digital-2016-turkey

DataReportal. (2017, February 1). *Digital 2017: Turkey*. https://datareportal.com/reports/digital-2017-turkey

DataReportal. (2018, February 1). *Digital 2018: Turkey*. https://datareportal.com/reports/digital-2018-turkey

DataReportal. (2019, January 31). *Digital 2019: Turkey*. https://datareportal.com/reports/digital-2019-turkey

DataReportal. (2020, February 18). *Digital 2020: Turkey*. https://datareportal.com/reports/digital-2020-turkey

DataReportal. (2021, February 11). *Digital 2021: Turkey*. https://datareportal.com/reports/digital-2021-turkey

DataReportal. (2022, February 15). *Digital 2022: Turkey*. https://datareportal.com/reports/digital-2022-turkey

DataReportal. (2023, February 13). *Digital 2023: Turkey*. https://datareportal.com/reports/digital-2023-turkey

Deloitte. (2021). *The transformative power of economy: E-commerce impact analysis: An overview of the e-commerce ecosystem in Turkey*. www.tubisad.org.tr/en/images/pdf/the-transformative-power.pdf

Demirdöğmez, M., Gültekin, N., & Taş, H. Y. (2018). Türkiye'de E-Ticaret Sektörünün Yıllara Göre Gelişimi. *OPUS – Uluslararası Toplum Araştırmaları Dergisi*, *8*(15), 2216–2236. https://doi.org/10.26466/opus.453147

Dillet, R. (2022). *Getir is now worth nearly $12 billion after raising another $768 million*. TechCrunch. https://techcrunch.com/2022/03/17/getir-is-now-worth-nearly-12-billion-after-raising-another-768-million/?guce_referrer=aHR0cHM6Ly93d3cuZ29vZ2xlLmNvbS8&guce_referrer_sig=AQAAAHKE47m6yHN7QfeG0bPf6mOxdBlBrlaPs4VDvAJPg0WxjscTyJv-4Ib_G6grzvivkvAvE4VUXqj7jEY8u4L6BLs5RpXiMVcXEj2bySILYEFA5b7MliJMb_Wjn6u8gH_RdL2QX4LNvILlfE83HpR7IxP-rXmHRjKcwD3HDdc9Q7zc&guccounter=2

Ernst & Young. (2022). *Dünyada ve Türkiye'de FinTech*. www.ey.com/tr_tr/ey-turkiye-yayinlar-raporlar/dunya-ve-turkiye-fin-tech-pazari-yeni-nesil-dijital-bankalarin-gelecegi

ETBP. (2020). *İstatistikler (2020 Yılı İstatistikleri (Ocak – Aralık))*. T.C. Ticaret Bakanlığı, Elektronik Ticaret Dairesi Başkanlığı. www.eticaret.gov.tr/istatistikler

ETBP. (2022). *İstatistikler*. T.C. Ticaret Bakanlığı, Elektronik Ticaret Dairesi Başkanlığı. www.eticaret.gov.tr/istatistikler.

Eurostat. (2001). *E-commerce in Europe – results of the pilot surveys carried out in 2001 (PDF)*. European Commission, Eurostat. https://ec.europa.eu/eurostat/web/products-statistical-books/-/ks-43-02-721

Eurostat. (2023, August 29). *Glossary: E-commerce*. European Commission, Eurostat. https://ec.europa.eu/eurostat/statistics-explained/index.php?title=Glossary:E-commerce#:~:text=E%2Dcommerce%20can%20be%20defined,mediated%20(online%20communication)%20networks

Falk, M., & Hagsten. E. (2015). E-commerce trends and impacts across Europe. *International Journal of Production Economics*, *170*, 357–369. https://doi.org/10.1016/j.ijpe.2015.10.003

Hamad, H., & Schmitz, M. (2019). The impact of demographic variables and consumer shopping orientations on the purchasing preference for different product categories in the context of online grocery shopping. *Journal of Marketing and Consumer Research*, *52*, 21–32. https://doi.org/10.7176/JMCR/52-05

Güven, H. (2020). Covid-19 Pandemik Krizi Sürecinde E-Ticarette Meydana Gelen Değişimler. *Eurasian Journal of Social and Economic Research*, *7*(5): 251–268.

İyzico. (n.d.). *2022 Türkiye e-ticaret ekosistemi* (market research report). https://media.iyzico.com/b/2023/07/2022-e-ticaret-ekosistemi-raporu.pdf

Jacobides, M. G., & Lianos, I. (2021). Ecosystems and competition law in theory and practice. *Industrial and Corporate Change*, *30*(5), 1199–1229. https://doi.org/10.1093/icc/dtab061

Kepenek, Y. (1999). Ekonomik Yönleriyle Elektronik Ticaret, İGEME in Aydemir, S. (2004). Elektronik Ticaret Alanındaki Rekabet Sorunları. In *Uzmanlık Tezi*. Ankara: Rekabet Kurumu.

KOSGEB. (2020). *Küçük ve Orta Büyüklükteki Girişim İstatistikleri, 2020*. T.C. Sanayi ve Teknoloji Bakanlığı, Küçük ve Orta Ölçekli İşletmeleri Geliştirme ve Destekleme İdaresi Başkanlığı. www.kosgeb.gov.tr/site/tr/genel/detay/8044/kucuk-ve-orta-buyuklukteki-girisim-istatistikleri-2020

KPMG. (2021). *Turkish startup investments review Q3 2021*. Turkish-startup-investments-review-2021-q3.pdf (kpmg.com)

Levingston, I., & Hammond, G. (2023). Getir valuation slashed to $2.5bn as delivery startup raises new cash. *Financial Times*. https://www.ft.com/content/6037cacb-4161-4c36-af14-9f9821daa6e5

Mangır, F., & Allahverdi, Z. F. (2022). Dünyada ve Türkiye'de E-Ticaret Sektörü Genel Durum Analizi: Fırsatlar ve Zorluklar. *Cyberpolitik Journal*, 7(14), 128–154.

Martens, B. (2013). What does economic research tell us about cross-border e-commerce in the EU digital single market? *JRC-IPTS working paper on the digital economy*. https://doi.org/10.2791/83255

Mast, S. (2020). Are digital ecosystems the secret to building and growing a strong economy? *Forbes*. www.forbes.com/sites/forbestechcouncil/2020/08/20/are-digital-ecosystems-the-secret-to-building-and-growing-a-strong-economy/

OECD. (2013). Electronic and mobile commerce. *OECD digital economy papers*, No. 228, OECD Publishing, Paris. https://doi.org/10.1787/5k437p2gxw6g-en

OECD. (2019). *Unpacking e-commerce: Business models, trends and policies*. OECD Publishing, Paris. https://doi.org/10.1787/23561431-en

OECD. (2020a). *Executive summary of the hearing on competition economics of digital ecosystems*. https://one.oecd.org/document/DAF/COMP/M(2020)2/ANN6/FINAL/en/pdf

OECD. (2020b). *Protecting online consumers during COVID-19 crisis*. https://read.oecd-ilibrary.org/view/?ref=130_130819-ay45n5rn74&title=Protecting-online-consumers-during-the-COVID-19-crisis

OECD. (2023). Recommendation of the council on consumer protection in e-commerce. OECD/LEGAL/0422. https://legalinstruments.oecd.org/en/instruments/OECD-LEGAL-0422

Oğuz, S., Yaşar Dinçer, F. C., & Yirmibeşoğlu, G. (2022). E-commerce in EU countries and Turkey: An econometric analysis. *Studies in Business and Economics*, *17*(3), 152–161. https://doi.org/10.2478/sbe-2022-0052

Özbay, F., & Özcan, A. (2021). The examined of the influence of Covid-19 on e-commerce and consumer behavior: A study on Turkey. *Aydın Faculty of Economics Journal*, 6(1), 21–33.

Parlak, A. (2005). *İnternet ve Türkiye'de İnternetin Gelişimi* [Thesis, Fırat Üniversitesi]. http://hasanbalik.com/projeler/bitirme/39.pdf

Podder, S., & Hu, K. (2021). *Turkey's Hepsiburada valued at $4.38 bln in strong Nasdaq debut (July 1)*. Reuters. www.reuters.com/world/middle-east/turkeys-hepsiburada-valued-36-bln-strong-nasdaq-debut-2021-07-01/

The Preamble of the Act Amending the Turkish E-Commerce Act; Act No: 7416. (2022). www5.tbmm.gov.tr/sirasayi/donem27/yil01/ss345.pdf

PwC. (2023). *Amazon Turkey SME E commerce outlook*. www.pwc.com.tr/amazon-turkiye-sme-e-commerce-outlook-2023

Reuters. (2021). *Turkey's Trendyol raises $1.5 bln, valuing it at $16.5 billion*. Reuters. www.reuters.com/world/middle-east/turkeys-trendyol-raises-15-bln-valuing-it-165-billion-2021-08-09/

Sarıçiçek, C. (2020). Me, myself and Amazon: The challenges digital marketplaces pose to EU competition law. *Rekabet Dergisi*, *21*(1), 122–199.
Simpson, F. (2021). *Rapid UK expansion for fast-delivery grocery franchise Getir*. Forbes. www.forbes.com/sites/fionasimpson1/2022/10/11/rapid-uk-expansion-for-fast-delivery-grocery-franchise-getir/
Statista. (n.d.). *E-commerce as percentage of total retail sales worldwide from 2015 to 2027*. www.statista.com/statistics/534123/e-commerce-share-of-retail-sales-worldwide/
Statista. (2023a, June 9). *Attitudes towards online shopping in Turkey as of March 2023*. www.statista.com/forecasts/1003017/attitudes-towards-online-shopping-in-turkey
Statista. (2023b, October 25). *Number of internet and social media users worldwide as of October 2023*. www.statista.com/statistics/617136/digital-population-worldwide/
Statista. (2024, May 6). *Worldwide internet user penetration from 2014 to April 2024*. https://www.statista.com/statistics/325706/global-internet-user-penetration/
TCA. (2022). E-Pazaryeri Platformlari Sektör İncelemesi Nihai Raporu. *Rekabet Kurumu*. https://www.rekabet.gov.tr/Dosya/geneldosya/e-pazaryeri-si-raporu-pdf
TCA. (2023). Çevrim içi Reklamcılık Sektör İncelemesi Ön Raporu. *Rekabet Kurumu*. https://www.rekabet.gov.tr/Dosya/cevrimici-reklamcilik-on-raporu-20231009170548088.pdf
Terzi, N. (2011). The impact of e-commerce on international trade and employment. *Procedia-Social and Behavioural Sciences*, *24*, 745–753. https://doi.org/10.1016/j.sbspro.2011.09.010
Toplu Yılmaz, Ö., & Bayram, O. (2020). Covid-19 pandemi döneminde Türkiye'de e-ticaret ve e-ihracat. *Kayseri Üniversitesi Sosyal Bilimler Dergisi*, 2(2): 37–54. https://doi.org/10.51177/kayusosder.777097
TÜİK. (2023). *İstatistiklerle Kadın, 2022*. TÜİK. https://data.tuik.gov.tr/Bulten/Index?p=%C4%B0statistiklerle-Kad%C4%B1n-2022-49668&dil=1#:~:text=az%20oldu%C4%9Fu%20g%C3%B6r%C3%BCld%C3%BC-,Hanehalk%C4%B1%20i%C5%9Fg%C3%BCc%C3%BC%20ara%C5%9Ft%C4%B1rmas%C4%B1%20sonu%C3%A7lar%C4%B1na%20g%C3%B6re%202021%20y%C4%B1l%C4%B1nda%2015%20ve%20daha,ise%20%62%2C8%20oldu
Turkish E-Commerce Act (Elektronik Ticaretin Düzenlenmesi Hakkında Kanun). (2014). www.mevzuat.gov.tr/mevzuatmetin/1.5.6563.pdf
TÜSİAD. (2021). *Çok Kanallı Perakende ve Covid 19 (market research report)*. https://tusiad.org/tr/yayinlar/raporlar/item/10775-tusiad-cok-kanalli-perakende-raporu
TÜSİAD. (2022). *E-ticaretin önce çıkan başarısı, tüketici davranışlarında değişim ve dijitalleşme (market research report)*. www2.deloitte.com/content/dam/Deloitte/tr/Documents/consulting/E-ticaretin-one-cikan-basarisi-2022.pdf
Ulukan, G. (2022). *Trendyol, yeni e-ticaret yasası nedeniyle Trendyol Cüzdan para yükleme dahil birkaç hizmetini durdurdu [Güncellendi]*. Webrazzi. https://webrazzi.com/2022/11/28/trendyol-yeni-e-ticaret-yasasi-nedeniyle-trendyol-cuzdan-hizmetini-durdurdu/
UNCTAD. (2021a). *COVID-19 and e-commerce a global review*. https://unctad.org/system/files/official-document/dtlstict2020d13_en_0.pdf
UNCTAD. (2021b). *Global e-commerce jumps to $26.7 trillion, COVID-19 boosts online sales*. https://unctad.org/conference/ntfc-global-forum-2022/news/global-e-commerce-jumps-267-trillion-covid-19-boosts-online-sales
Üner, M. M., Evirgen, C., & Cavusgil, S. T. (2021). Getir: A remarkable example of a digital disrupter from an emerging market. *California Management Review*. https://cmr.berkeley.edu/2021/09/getir-a-remarkable-example-of-a-digital-disrupter-from-an-emerging-market/
World Health Organization. (2020, June 29). *Listings of WHO's response to COVID-19*. www.who.int/news/item/29-06-2020-covidtimeline
World Trade Organization. (n.d.). *Electronic commerce*. www.wto.org/english/thewto_e/minist_e/mc11_e/briefing_notes_e/bfecom_e.htm#:~:text=Electronic%

20commerce%2C%20or%20e%2Dcommerce,other%20public%20or%20private%20organizations

Varol, N. (2020). Reklam Harcamaları ve Rekabet Hukuku. *Rekabet Dergisi, 73*, 5–62.

Zhang, D., Pee, L. G., & Cui, L. (2021). Artificial intelligence in e-commerce fulfillment: A case study of resource orchestration at Alibaba's smart warehouse. *International Journal of Information Management, 57*. https://doi.org/10.1016/j.ijinfomgt.2020.102304

5 Foreign and Turkish Digital Platforms

Fatih Cemil Özbuğday

Introduction

Türkiye, with its huge consumer market, youthful population, and increasingly tech-savvy workforce, is not only nurturing a thriving ecosystem of local digital enterprises but also attracting an increasing number of foreign investments. According to the Presidency Investment Office, Türkiye's digital economy accounted for 5.2% of its GDP in 2019 and is projected to grow to 8.5% by 2023 (Investment Office, 2023).

The digital ecosystem in Türkiye is currently undergoing a significant transformation, marked by the rapid growth of local online platforms that have garnered both domestic and international interest. Some of these platforms have attracted substantial investments from major global players, some of which have even achieved a decacorn status. This surge in investment activity has also been accompanied by the entry of numerous global platforms into the Turkish market, resulting in intense competition for the attention of Turkish consumers. This mix of local and global forces raises important questions about the competition and interaction between foreign and Turkish digital platforms.

Despite its discernible impact and economic significance, the competitive interaction between local and global digital platforms has not received much attention in academic literature (Eferin et al., 2019). This chapter aims to contribute to the understanding of this phenomenon, with an emphasis on the unique setting of Türkiye. Consequently, the objective of this chapter is threefold. First, we aim to address this gap by developing a simple conceptual framework that is grounded in the principles of within-country and cross-country network externalities. Second, we augment our analysis by providing a comprehensive review of the changes in ownership structures among local digital platforms, coupled with industry-specific cases in Türkiye. The case studies include music streaming, video streaming, meal delivery, and classified advertising markets. Finally, we apply our conceptual framework to these real-world scenarios, thereby offering both theoretical and practical insights into the competitive interaction between local and global digital platforms in Türkiye.

DOI: 10.4324/9781032692937-5

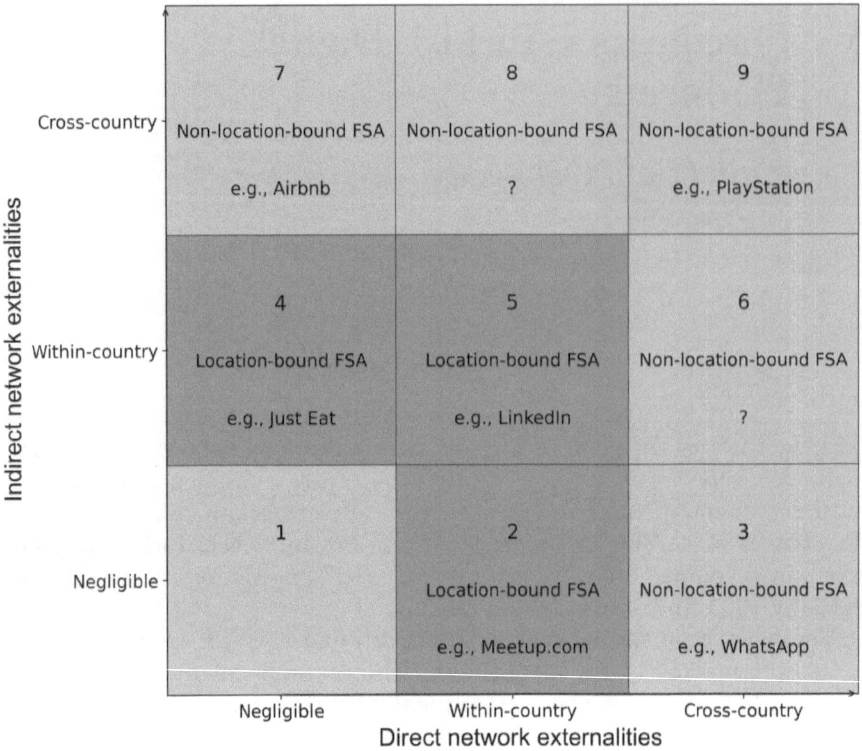

Figure 5.1 The geographic scope of network externalities and firm-specific advantages derived from existing user base. Adapted from Stallkamp and Schotter (2021).

Dynamics of Competition Between Local and Foreign Digital Platforms

The nature of competition in digital markets is fundamentally different from that in traditional markets, largely because of the role of platform-based competition and network externalities (Cennamo, 2021). While traditional markets focus on product-based competition, digital markets are driven by platform-based models in which the value of a platform increases with its user base. Network externalities, both direct and indirect, significantly shape the strategies and outcomes for these digital platforms (Katz & Shapiro, 1985; McIntyre & Srinivasan, 2017).

A key challenge for new platforms is the "chicken-and-egg" problem: attracting users to a platform that becomes valuable only after a robust user base has been established (Caillaud & Jullien, 2003). Overcoming this initial barrier can lead to a competitive advantage as the size of the user network becomes a crucial differentiator. This often leads to a positive feedback loop, potentially resulting in "winner-takes-all" market scenarios (Schilling, 2002).

However, existing literature often overlooks the influence of national borders on these dynamics (Lee et al., 2016). Network externalities can vary significantly in geographic scope (Stallkamp & Schotter, 2021). For instance, platforms such as job search engines are largely constrained by national borders owing to regulatory and language barriers, whereas others, such as mobile operating systems, benefit from global network externalities. Moreover, distance also plays a role in constraining the impact of network externalities, even in the digital age. Location-based services such as Uber and Tinder rely heavily on spatial proximity, whereas platforms such as eBay are less affected by distance but still show some level of influence (Agrawal et al., 2015). This dichotomy introduces the concepts of location-bound and non-location-bound firm-specific advantages (FSAs) (Anand & Delios, 1997).

Therefore, the landscape of digital market competition is intricately shaped by network externalities that can be constrained or amplified by geographical and distance factors. These dynamics can give rise to location-bound or non-location-bound FSAs, shaping not just domestic competition but also international market entry and growth strategies for digital platforms.

Figure 5.1, adapted from Stallkamp and Schotter (2021), presents a conceptual framework for categorizing digital platforms and industries based on the extent and geographical scope of their network externalities. The horizontal axis represents direct network externalities, whereas the vertical axis captures indirect network externalities, both ranging from negligible to cross-country externalities. The matrix is divided into nine cells, each designated with a specific number based on the type of firm-specific advantages they are likely to exhibit: either non-location-bound FSA or location-bound FSA. Examples of companies or platforms are also provided for specific cells to offer practical illustrations.

According to the classification by Stallkamp and Schotter (2021), if a platform has at least one type of cross-country network externality, its large user base can act as a non-location-bound firm-specific advantage to facilitate international expansion (Cells 3, 6, 7, 8, and 9). In contrast, platforms with predominantly within-country network externalities find their firm-specific advantages to be location-bound, making international expansion more challenging (Cells 2, 4, and 5). Thus, understanding the types of network externalities, whether within-country or cross-country and direct or indirect, provides critical insights into the international strategies that platform firms can effectively adopt.

One central issue discussed is the "chicken-and-egg" problem, which represents the difficulty in attracting a critical mass of users to a platform in a new market. In sectors with predominantly within-country network externalities, new entrants may find it difficult to compete with established local platforms because of the early mover advantages and positive feedback loops created by network externalities (Zhu & Iansiti, 2012). One strategy to overcome this hurdle of competing with established local platforms is through acquisitions or alliances, which allow new entrants to leverage the incumbent's existing local user base. By contrast, when cross-country network externalities are significant, the situation becomes quite different. In such scenarios, a foreign entrant can capitalize on its existing global user base, creating a powerful non-location-bound firm-specific advantage. This makes it easier for late entrants with large global networks to challenge local incumbents, thereby making independent entry more feasible compared to markets limited by within-country network externalities (Stallkamp & Schotter, 2021).

Overall, these discussions serve as a conceptual framework for our analysis. Based on these discussions, we propose the following hypotheses on market entry strategies and competitive dynamics and test them through a series of real-world case studies in Türkiye.

Hypothesis 1: In markets characterized by within-country network externalities, late-entrant foreign platforms are likelier to enter through acquisitions or alliances with local platforms to mitigate competitive disadvantages.

Hypothesis 2: In markets characterized by cross-country network externalities, late-entrant foreign platforms are more likely to enter independently, leveraging their global user base to compete with local incumbents.

Hypothesis 3: In sectors with primarily within-country direct or indirect network externalities, local incumbent platforms are expected to dominate, making it difficult for foreign entrants to gain a significant market share.

Hypothesis 4: In platforms with cross-country direct or indirect network externalities, foreign platforms are expected to compete more effectively with local incumbent platforms.

Evolving Ownerships of Local Digital Platforms in Türkiye

Before moving on to the analysis of competition between local and foreign digital platforms across multiple industries and applying the conceptual framework to a series of cases in various markets, we first examine prominent changes in the ownership structures of digital platforms in Türkiye.

As Türkiye's digital economy continues to grow, the Turkish digital platform sector has attracted significant attention from foreign investors, as evidenced by the changes in ownership structures. These ownership changes primarily occur through two forms: acquisitions and investment rounds. In addition, there is one prominent case of an initial public offering. We examine some of the noteworthy case studies in detail here.

Zynga's Acquisition of Peak Games

The acquisition of Peak Games by Zynga in June 2020 represents a significant event in the digital economy, not just for its substantial financial value but also for its impact on Türkiye's position in the global digital market. Founded in 2010, Peak Games established itself as a leading mobile game developer.

The massive scale of the transaction makes the acquisition of Peak Games intriguing. The American video game company Zynga purchased Peak Games for $1.8 billion, with half of the payment in cash and the other half in Zynga stock (Bloomberght, 2022). After the acquisition, Peak Games continued to operate independently.

In November 2021, Zynga was acquired by Take-Two Interactive, the parent company of Rockstar Games and 2K, for $12.7 billion (Wikipedia, 2023). Peak Games remains an operational subsidiary of Take-Two Interactive.

Alibaba's Investment in Trendyol

Alibaba's investment in Trendyol (trendyol.com), now Türkiye's leading e-commerce platform, is another case study of international capital infusion into Türkiye's digital economy. Founded in 2010, Trendyol has since grown to offer an extensive range of products, including fashion and electronics. In 2018, Alibaba acknowledged the company's potential and invested $728 million to acquire a significant shareholding. This stands out as one of the largest foreign direct investments in a Turkish digital entity.

As of August 2021, Trendyol received $1.9 billion in funding across five rounds (Crunchbase, 2023a). Its most recent fundraising event was a $1.5 billion private equity round, which has increased its valuation to an impressive $16.5 billion (Azevedo, 2021).

Delivery Hero's Takeover of Yemeksepeti

The acquisition of Yemeksepeti (yemeksepeti.com) by Delivery Hero in 2015 serves as a noteworthy case study for international acquisitions in Türkiye's emerging digital economy. Founded in 2000, Yemeksepeti was a trailblazer in the online meal delivery market in Türkiye, which solidified its position as the market leader prior to its acquisition. With an estimated value of $589 million, the acquisition was one of the most significant in the Turkish digital ecosystem at the time (Emeafinance, 2015).

Yemeksepeti's post-acquisition operational independence sets it apart. Unlike other acquisitions in which the target company was fully assimilated, Yemeksepeti maintained its operational autonomy under Delivery Hero's umbrella.

The acquisition served as a strategic turning point for both the companies. For Yemeksepeti, the infusion of capital from the acquisition allowed for further expansion, solidifying its market position and resulting in a user base exceeding 30 million and approximately 80,000 partner restaurants (Yeşilyurt, 2022). For Delivery Hero, a German-based company, the acquisition offered rapid entry into the Turkish market.

Investments Getir Received

Getir (getir.com) was established in 2015 and has since transformed the shopping experience for Turkish consumers by utilizing a network of dark stores and couriers to provide rapid delivery of daily necessities straight to customers' doorsteps. The company raised $1.8 billion over seven rounds of funding (Crunchbase, 2023b). The latest funding round, a $768 million Series E round in March 2022, elevated Getir's valuation to $11.8 billion (Ersoy, 2022), making it a leading player in the quick commerce industry.

Aided by substantial financial backing, Getir ventured beyond Türkiye's borders to establish operations in various European countries and Brazil. However, the company encountered a series of challenges that required a reevaluation of its global strategy. Regulatory issues in France forced the firm to exit the French market in 2023 (Dillet, 2023). Similar withdrawals were announced for Italy, Portugal, and Spain as part of a realigned strategy to focus on profitability in its core markets. The situation was further exacerbated by a 14% reduction in its global workforce in 2022, which was attributed to escalating operational costs and intensifying competition. Despite these challenges, Getir remains a dominant player in the quick commerce sector, with a valuation of $12 billion as of May 2022 (Lunden, 2022).

eBay's Acquisition of GittiGidiyor

The acquisition and eventual closure of GittiGidiyor (gittigidiyor.com) by eBay provide another case study. Founded in 2001, GittiGidiyor quickly became one of Türkiye's leading e-commerce platforms with a business model similar to eBay's auction-based format. By 2007, GittiGidiyor had caught eBay's attention, leading the American e-commerce giant to acquire a minority stake initially and then a majority stake of $217.5 million in 2011 (Andaç, 2011).

GittiGidiyor appeared to thrive under eBay's ownership for several years. Its workforce grew by 40%, registered users increased to 33 million, and the platform experienced a growth rate of 50% (Kara-Kaşka, 2022). Despite this promising trajectory, eBay made the strategic decision to close down GittiGidiyor in June 2022, citing market conditions and strategic imperatives as key drivers.

Initial Public Offering by Hepsiburada

Founded in 1998, Hepsiburada (hepsiburada.com) has grown to become the leading e-commerce platform in Türkiye. In July 2021, Hepsiburada became the first Turkish company to list on the NASDAQ stock exchange. The company raised $738 million in its initial public offering of a 20% stake, reaching a value of $3.9 billion (Ersoy, 2021). Since then, the controlling shareholders have not changed.

Industry-Specific Analyses

In this section, we present industry-specific analyses that provide a comprehensive understanding of the interplay between local and global digital platforms. Our examination is centered on four key industries: music streaming, video streaming, meal delivery, and classified advertising markets. Through this in-depth analysis, we aim to illustrate how various forms of network externalities, market characteristics, and strategic decisions affect the competitive landscape, thereby offering valuable insights into the coexistence and rivalry between the local and international players in these sectors.

Music Streaming Markets

The music industry has undergone a radical transformation in the modern landscape of digital economics. The widespread adoption of music streaming services has revolutionized the way music is consumed, distributed, and monetized. With more than 616.2 million global users, the impact of these digital innovations is significant (Statista, 2023a). Streaming has become the foundation of the financial model of the music industry, providing on-demand and universally accessible content for consumers. In 2022, the proportion of "Total Streaming" in total revenues is approximately 67%, signifying that streaming has become a predominant source of revenue. According to the International Federation of the Phonographic Industry (IFPI), this 67% of revenue share emanates from diverse streaming avenues; 18.7% is attributable to ad-supported streams while a substantial 48.3% is derived from subscription-based audio streaming services (IFPI, 2023).

The music streaming industry is dominated by a global oligopoly with a small number of key players, including Spotify, Apple Music, Amazon Music, and Tencent Music, which hold significant market shares. Spotify, in particular, has disrupted the industry by commanding over 30% of global streaming subscribers. By the end of 2022, it had 205 million premium users, leaving competitors behind. However, the market is dynamic, with emerging players such as Deezer, a French Unicorn (Statista, 2023a). In some countries, local music streaming companies have established a strong position, such as Gaana in India or Melon in South Korea.

Network externalities shape user behavior and market dynamics in music streaming. Direct within-country externalities arise when local users create playlists that suit cultural or musical tastes, thereby increasing the platform's value. Direct cross-country externalities occur when a platform creates a global community that enables sharing and discovery beyond geographic boundaries. Inclusivity broadens the platform's music selection by showcasing international influences and drawing a more diverse user base from various countries. Indirect network externalities also benefit the platform: its appeal to artists and labels grows with its user base. A larger user pool encourages more artists to join, thus increasing the platform's music library and the value for current and potential users. Thus, the large user base of global music streaming companies is a firm-specific advantage that helps their international expansion.

Furthermore, Figure 5.2, which details the music engagement mix for 2022, shows a more complex picture. Although music streaming is a dominant force in the music industry, it is important to recognize that other digital platforms also play a significant role in music consumption. Platforms such as YouTube, ad-supported streaming services, and short-form video apps such as TikTok provide alternative ways for people to enjoy music.

However, the success of the music streaming industry is not a uniform experience but is influenced by diverse geographical contexts, each with its unique market conditions and consumer behaviors. Although global giants such as Spotify and Apple Music have achieved success in multiple markets, their dominance is not consistent. For instance, in the South Korean market, the local music streaming service Melon dominates with a 55% market share, almost matching the share of YouTube's free version. Spotify and Apple Music, which are typically dominant in other markets, have a relatively subdued presence with 6% and 5.6% shares, respectively (Statista, 2023b). Thus, local platforms may be able to secure a significant market share despite the presence of established international players.

Music Streaming in Türkiye

Türkiye's music streaming market reflects global trends and offers unique insights. The empirical data reveal trends in this market. The proportion of Turkish individuals purchasing or subscribing to music streaming services or downloads in the last three months has been 30.08% in 2023, increasing from 14.52% in 2020 (TurkStat, 2023). This is in line with the global trend of increasing adoption of digital media and could also reflect changes in consumer behavior or the influence of market entrants. The financial projections for Türkiye's music streaming market also indicate an upward trend and align with the global patterns discussed earlier. In particular, the industry is expected to grow at a strong compound annual growth rate (CAGR) of 7.95% from 2023 to 2027, resulting in a projected market volume of US$75.90 million by the end of this period (Statista, 2023c).

Several key trends are worth noting when examining the Turkish music industry's recent financial landscape. One of the most significant is the meteoric rise in revenues generated from streaming services expressed in US dollars (USD). In 2018, streaming accounted for $7.4 million, which escalated impressively to $53.7 million by 2022. When viewed as a share of the music industry's total revenue, streaming increased from 59.2% in 2018 to 85.5% by 2022. This shift is consistent with global trends where streaming has become the main revenue generator for the music industry. A closer look at the composition of digital sales reveals that subscription streaming services have been particularly successful, growing from $5.1 million in

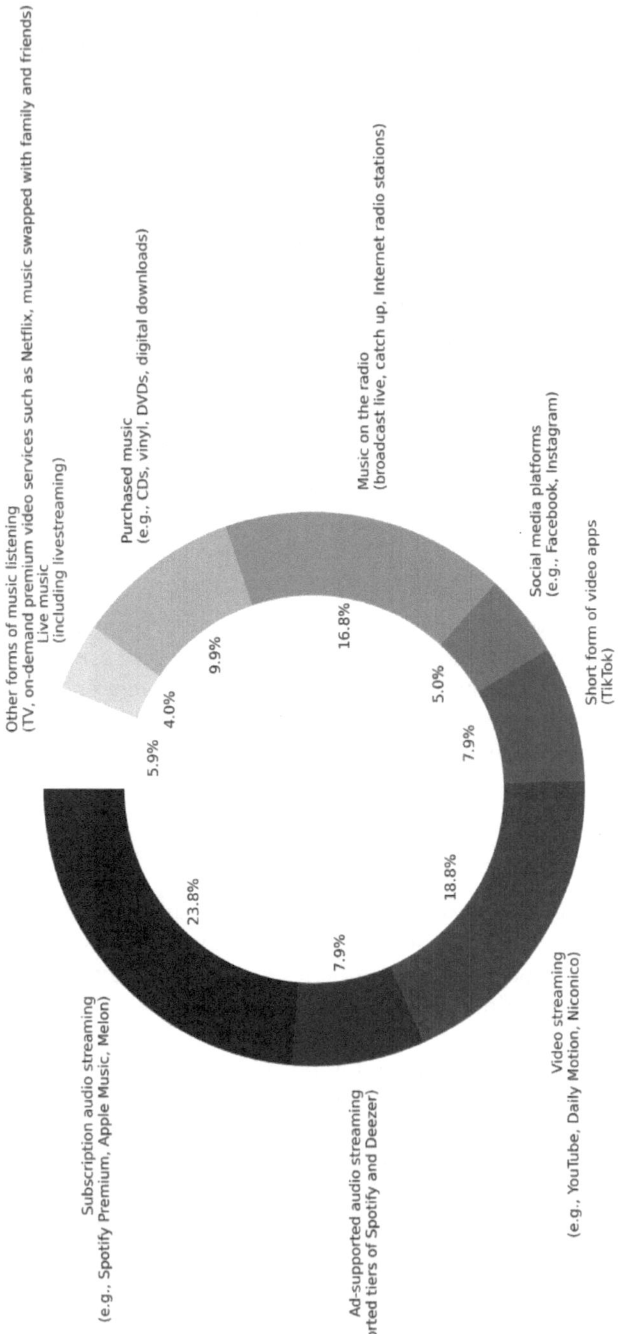

Figure 5.2 The music engagement mix, 2022 (IFPI, 2023).

2018 to $26.3 million in 2022. Ad-supported audio streaming also saw a significant increase, from just $0.4 million in 2018 to $13.4 million in 2022, indicating the popularity of the freemium model in Türkiye. Moreover, ad-supported video streaming revenues have also grown substantially from $1.8 million in 2018 to $14 million in 2022, surpassing audio. This suggests that visual elements are becoming increasingly significant in music consumption (MUYAP, 2023).

Given the positive financial outlook for music streaming in Türkiye, it is essential to analyze the key players in the market, as their strategies and services will shape its future. While concrete data on market share and user numbers may be elusive, some indicators, such as app ranking on Google Play Store and Apple App Store, offer a glimpse of market dynamics. These metrics indicate the predominance of global platforms, such as Apple Music, Spotify, and YouTube Music, in Türkiye's digital music arena. These global platforms have been able to use their size and extensive music libraries to attract a broad audience. Deezer, a global player, has a smaller presence than its competitors. DailyMotion, Facebook, and TikTok, which are not solely music streaming services, also contribute to the digital music ecosystem through their video content.

Transitioning to the local sphere, Fizy and Muud offer a unique value proposition. Unlike stand-alone streaming services, these are extensions of mobile phone operators that use music to increase customer engagement and brand loyalty. Finally, TRT Dinle, a platform from Türkiye's public broadcaster, the Turkish Radio and Television Corporation (TRT), adds a public service element to the digital music landscape.

Video Streaming Markets

Online video streaming or over-the-top (OTT) media services have transformed the global media landscape and greatly impacted consumer behavior. Consumers in developed digital economies are increasingly forgoing traditional pay-TV subscriptions in favor of more affordable, customizable, and diverse video options. Subscription Video-On-Demand (SVOD) platforms, which enable users to access an unlimited library of digital video content for a fixed monthly fee, have gained prominence. By the end of 2021, global SVOD subscriptions surpassed 1.2 billion (Statista, 2023d).

However, SVOD is not the only option in this evolving landscape. Consumers have other video streaming choices that cater to their specific preferences, such as Transactional Video-On-Demand (TVOD), Broadcaster Video-On-Demand (BVOD), and Ad-Supported Video-On-Demand (AVOD). Hybrid models offer a combination of these options. The Free Ad-Supported Streaming TV (FAST) segment has also attracted consumers. Other popular platforms, such as Twitch, TikTok, Facebook, X, Instagram (Reels), and even WhatsApp (Status), are also part of the broader video streaming ecosystem, but they occupy specialized niches that do not fit neatly into traditional categories.

The video streaming industry exhibits a blend of oligopoly and competitive markets, with dominant players, such as Netflix, Amazon Prime, and Disney+, controlling the SVOD sector. YouTube dominates the AVOD sector, whereas the FAST sector experiences intense competition. In this highly fragmented market landscape, users commonly subscribe to multiple platforms (multihoming) to access a diverse range of content.

Both domestic and international network externalities are significant in video streaming, similar to music streaming. Within-country network externalities may originate from localized content such as domestic TV shows, movies, or user-generated videos. If a platform has a large user base in a country, it may motivate more content creators from that country to upload localized content, thus making the platform more attractive to domestic users. Cross-country network externalities arise when a platform is popular globally and users from many countries contribute content. This variety of content appeals to international tastes and can introduce users to new cultures. These externalities can be a non-location-bound advantage for global video streaming companies with large user bases.

Market shares in the video streaming industry vary by geography and service type. For example, YouTube universally dominates the AVOD segment. However, for SVOD services, competition has become far more nuanced (Budzinski et al., 2021). For instance, while Netflix is the most popular streaming service in multiple countries, Amazon Prime Video has emerged as the second most popular platform. The situation was different in the United Kingdom and Finland, where national public broadcasting companies took the lead (Audience Project, 2019).

Video Streaming in Türkiye

Recent statistics provide evidence of Türkiye's growing potential in the video streaming sector, highlighting its upward trajectory in this field. The proportion of digital content and online services purchased or subscribed by individuals over the internet for private use in the last three months has been 30.69% in 2023, increasing from 18.02% in 2020 (TurkStat, 2023). This upward trend suggests a thriving market.

The Turkish video streaming market, which is both dynamic and full of potential, is an intriguing blend of local and global entities that compete for consumer attention. According to a report in the second quarter of 2023, BluTV, a homegrown platform that offers a vast collection of both Turkish and international content, is currently leading the SVOD category with a notable 38% market share. Following closely behind are several international giants, such as Netflix, Amazon Prime Video, and Disney+, which capture 27%, 19%, and 8% of the market, respectively. Another global player, Mubi, holds a smaller share of 4% (Gazete Duvar, 2023). The landscape also encompasses other homegrown platforms such as Puhu TV, Exxen, and Gain, which together account for approximately 4% of the SVOD market.

YouTube dominates the AVOD segment, highlighting the ubiquitous reach of the global platform (Gaming in Turkey, 2020).

In the BVOD space, Türkiye has platforms like TRT's TRT İzle, which streams content from the national broadcaster. TRT İzle is publicly funded, reflecting a commitment to public service rather than purely to commercial goals. Moreover, many traditional broadcasters have also entered the AVOD market and migrated their content online to expand their reach. However, the TVOD segment remains underdeveloped, with limited market presence compared to its SVOD and AVOD counterparts.

Meal Delivery Markets

The home-delivered restaurant meal market is undergoing a significant transformation, owing to the emergence of new online platforms that compete for market share and customer loyalty. Financial projections for the meal delivery market are bullish, with revenue expected to reach US$0.39 trillion by 2023 (Statista, 2023e). This upward trajectory in the meal delivery market has also attracted investors.

Given the current state and upward trajectory in the meal delivery market, it is worth examining the major companies that have successfully navigated it. The global meal delivery market is highly competitive, with a few major players dominating the industry. Key players in this space include Just Eat Takeaway.com, Delivery Hero, GrubHub, Foodpanda, Deliveroo, Ele.me, Meituan Waimai, and UberEats (Research and Markets, 2023). It is also worth noting that alliances and ownership ties exist among these companies, with some functioning as subsidiaries of larger enterprises. For instance, Just Eat Takeaway.com acquired GrubHub, expanding its presence in the American market, whereas Delivery Hero owns Foodpanda, extending its reach across Asia and Eastern Europe. This consolidated landscape highlights the high stakes involved in competition in this sector.

One major reason for the high stakes is the network externalities. Although network externalities are important, as shown in Cell 4 in Figure 5.1, the dynamics are somewhat different for meal delivery services. These services benefit predominantly from within-country indirect network externalities. This is because the service's core offering, local delivery, is inherently location-specific (Belleflamme & Neysen, 2017).

Meal Delivery Market in Türkiye

Türkiye is currently experiencing a significant shift in the meal delivery industry, which reflects global trends. The proportion of individuals in Türkiye who have ordered food online for personal use, including from restaurants, fast-food chains, and catering services, has increased from 22.5% in 2020 to 47.6% in 2023 (TurkStat, 2023). Predictions suggest that, by 2027, the meal delivery segment in Türkiye is expected to have a substantial user base of approximately 37.7 million people (Statista, 2023f). Considering these remarkable growth metrics, it is crucial to focus on the key players influencing the meal delivery market in Türkiye.

Recent decisions made by the Turkish Competition Authority (TCA) have highlighted the competitive landscape of the online meal delivery market in Türkiye (Turkish Competition Authority, 2022a, 2022b, 2022c). These investigations have identified key national players in the industry as well as small local actors.

The main contenders, Yemeksepeti, Getir Yemek, and Trendyol Yemek, serve dual roles in the market. They act both as intermediaries, aggregating a variety of restaurants and cuisines for consumers to choose from, and as delivery platforms equipped with their own logistics fleets.

Yemeksepeti has been the most experienced and largest player in Türkiye's online meal delivery market, having commenced operations in 2000. The company was acquired by Delivery Hero of Germany in 2015, which resulted in full control of Yemeksepeti by the global food delivery network. Its long history and widespread presence have enabled Yemeksepeti to dominate the Turkish meal delivery industry for many years.

In recent years, the market has become more competitive with new players. In February 2019, Getir Yemek, a subsidiary of Getir, launched its meal delivery service in Istanbul and has since expanded to cover all cities in Türkiye. Another notable entrant is Trendyol Yemek, which began operations in 2020 and is owned by Alibaba, the Chinese e-commerce giant. In 2020, Fuudy also entered the market and distinguished itself from its competitors by focusing on the luxury food ordering segment.

Although Yemeksepeti has long dominated Türkiye's online meal delivery market, newer players such as Getir Yemek and Trendyol Yemek have managed to capture significant market shares in a relatively short period of time. Getir Yemek, which entered the market with a strong push in 2019, has experienced stable growth since its launch, even in the face of stiff competition from a well-established player. It was able to leverage its existing Getir user base to gain a foothold in the market rapidly. Trendyol Yemek, which entered the market approximately 1.5 years after Getir Yemek, has also quickly consolidated its position. It used its multi-category e-marketplace to establish itself as a strong competitor against Yemeksepeti's long-standing dominance. Notably, Trendyol Yemek and Getir Yemek have similar numbers of active users, suggesting that the market is becoming increasingly competitive. While these new players have risen, some other competitors have either withdrawn from the market (Glovo and Scotty Yemek) or become inconsequential. However, it is worth noting that Yemeksepeti continues to hold its ground firmly, retaining over 40% of its market share as of the first half of 2022, which still places it above its closest rival, Getir Yemek.

Classified Advertising Markets

Classified advertising represents a unique segment within the broader advertising ecosystem. Unlike display advertisements or sponsored content, which often aim for mass reach and branding impact, classified advertisements are usually more transactional and targeted. Classified advertising platforms allow the posting of specialized advertisements, commonly abbreviated as classified-ads or classifieds. These advertisements serve specific needs, such as job recruitment, property sales, or secondhand goods, and connect individual buyers and sellers.

From an industrial organization perspective, classified-ads platforms function as multi-sided markets that connect sellers and buyers across various sectors. As the network grows on one side, benefits accrue on the other, leading to network externalities. Notably, these network externalities often tend to be within-country. That is, the platform's value increases disproportionately when local sellers list more items, thereby attracting more local buyers seeking items in close geographical proximity. Conversely, an increase in local buyers encourages more local sellers to list items, thereby creating a virtuous circle of localized growth.

The classified advertising landscape is undergoing significant transformation on a global scale. According to recent data, the global digital classified advertising market was valued at approximately $19.10 billion in 2020 (Million Insights, 2023). Furthermore, the online classified-ads platform market is estimated to experience substantial growth, with its size likely to reach $22.98 billion by 2027, with a CAGR of 2.22% projected from 2023 to 2027 (Statista, 2023g).

The major players in the online classified market that contribute to these trends have various brands under their umbrella (Similarweb, 2023). The landscape of classified advertising platforms is both diverse and concentrated and is characterized by a variety of ownership structures that range from global conglomerates to local business groups. Several prominent names recurrently appear as key players in this landscape.

Naspers, a South African media group, and its subsidiary Prosus wield substantial influence in the classified-ads ecosystem. They own various platforms, and their extensive portfolio illustrates their global reach, spanning from Brazil to Indonesia. On the other hand, the platforms owned by the Schibsted Media Group are largely concentrated in the European region, indicating Schibsted's regional focus as opposed to a global outreach strategy. Adevinta, another major player, has a similar European orientation.

In North America, online classified markets are dominated by platforms such as Craigslist, eBay, and Facebook Marketplace (Sawers, 2022). Craigslist is one of the pioneers in the classified advertising space and covers a wide range of categories, including jobs, housing, and services. eBay, traditionally an e-commerce giant, also operates in the classified advertising sphere with eBay Classifieds in addition to its auction-based sales model. Facebook Marketplace leverages its extensive user base to facilitate the person-to-person sales of goods and services within local communities.

Classified-Ads Markets in Türkiye

In Türkiye, classified-ads platforms have a highly localized ownership structure, unlike many other countries. The most prominent platform, Sahibinden (sahibinden.com), is owned by the Türkiye-based Aksoy Group and primarily serves the Turkish market. A recent decision by the TCA further probed into the nature of the classified-ads markets in Türkiye (Turkish Competition Authority, 2021). In this decision, the TCA mainly considered online platform markets for "real estate sales and rental services" and "second-hand vehicle sales activities" as part of classified-ads markets.

According to the findings, Sahibinden has maintained a dominant market position in the real estate sales and rental services sector since 2015, consistently securing a market share of over 40% (based on metrics such as number of corporate members, corporate member income, and page views). The data indicate that Sahibinden's market share remains significantly ahead of competitors such as Hepsi Emlak, Zingat, and Emlakjet. Despite the declining trend, Sahibinden faces minimal competitive pressure and continues to dominate the market. Similarly, Sahibinden enjoys a robust presence in the online platform market for secondhand vehicle sales activities, holding more than 40% of its market share since 2015. The sector includes competitors, such as Arabam (arabam.com). Despite a decrease in market share, Sahibinden still maintains a near-monopoly status in terms of revenue and page views. The data suggest that the company has sustained its market leadership over the years and faced minimal competitive threats in this sector.

In the context of online platforms for real estate and secondhand vehicle sales, Sahibinden appears to face primary competition, if any, from local entities such as Hepsi Emlak, Emlakjet, and Arabam.com. This suggests that the platform operates in an environment where within-country network effects are especially strong. The case of Letgo, which is partially owned by the international OLX Group and Naspers, underscores the significance of local network effects. Despite initial interest and buzz, Letgo could not achieve the same level of market penetration as Sahibinden did.

Finally, Armut (armut.com), a local Turkish online services marketplace offering over 2,000 services, is a popular online marketplace in Türkiye. It has a slightly different model from the traditional classified-ads markets. Instead of serving as a platform where buyers and sellers post listings for goods, services, or information, Armut operates with two main business models: pay-per-lead and book-now models. That said, Armut shares similarities with classified-ads markets in that it serves as an intermediary between service providers and consumers. However, Armut often plays a more active role in the transaction process by offering features such as reviews, verified service providers, and a more structured quoting process. This makes Armut more similar to platforms such as Thumbtack in the United States or MyBuilder in the United Kingdom, which are online marketplaces for services rather than traditional classified-ads sites.

Discussion and Conclusion

The digital landscape of Türkiye serves as a vibrant showcase of how local and global platforms can coexist and compete in various sectors. For instance, contrary to common narratives in other markets, Türkiye's video streaming sector presents a unique case in which a local platform leads the market. BluTV, in particular, has managed not only to hold its own but also to outperform global giants such as Netflix and Amazon Prime Video. Similarly, Sahibinden dominates in the classified advertising space. The platform has kept foreign competitors at bay. However, as a counterexample of the dominance of local platforms, the market structure of the Turkish music streaming industry indicates the dominance of global platforms, such as Spotify.

Yemeksepeti is a prominent player in the meal delivery sector with a substantial local network. Now a part of the global Delivery Hero network, Yemeksepeti exemplifies how a local brand can dominate a digital market, become part of an international conglomerate, and still maintain its local appeal and market share. In the realm of e-commerce, Trendyol is a noteworthy case. Although it began as a local venture, it is now owned by Alibaba, one of the world's largest e-commerce entities. Despite its global backing, Trendyol maintains a strong local identity. It competes effectively with other global platforms, such as Amazon, making the Turkish e-commerce landscape a balanced field of local and global influences.

An examination of these cases and the prominent changes in the ownership structures of digital platforms in Türkiye in relation to the previously outlined hypotheses leads to the following conclusions:

- Alibaba's investment in Trendyol supports Hypothesis 1. The local expertise and customer base of Trendyol would represent within-country network externalities that made it attractive for Alibaba to invest rather than build anew.
- Delivery Hero's acquisition of Yemeksepeti matches with Hypothesis 1. Yemeksepeti had a strong local network and market dominance, suggesting that within-country network externalities played a role.
- eBay's Acquisition of GittiGidiyor: eBay's initial acquisition of GittiGidiyor aligns with Hypothesis 1. However, the eventual closure makes this a complex case. This could suggest the challenges of leveraging within-country network externalities over time.
- The other cases of ownership changes are not relevant to any of the proposed hypotheses.
- The Turkish music and video streaming industries seem to support Hypothesis 2, as global platforms such as Spotify and YouTube have entered independently, leveraging their global user bases.
- The case of Sahibinden supports Hypothesis 3, as it is a local platform that dominates its market characterized by within-country network externalities. Furthermore, until the takeover by Delivery Hero, the case of Yemeksepeti was also a testament to the validity of Hypothesis 3.

- Spotify's dominance in Türkiye's digital music arena aligns with Hypothesis 4.
- Likewise, the strong presence of global platforms, such as Netflix, in the Turkish SVOD sector verifies Hypothesis 4.

Based on a detailed examination of Türkiye's digital platforms and their ownership structures, the evidence collectively offers a validation of the conceptual framework proposed to understand the dynamics of competition and interaction between foreign and Turkish digital platforms. Additionally, the empirical cases from Türkiye not only support the hypotheses but also enrich our understanding by providing insights. For instance, the eBay–GittiGidiyor case serves as a cautionary tale, suggesting that maintaining a competitive advantage grounded in within-country network externalities can be challenging even after a successful acquisition.

A limitation of this chapter is its narrow focus on network externalities as the primary factor influencing the competition between local and international digital platforms. It overlooks other important elements, such as firms' management techniques and technological capabilities, the impact of regulatory frameworks on international business strategies, and the costs of adapting to different linguistic, cultural, and institutional landscapes (Stallkamp & Schotter, 2021). Therefore, this chapter may not capture the full complexity of digital competition.

References

Agrawal, A., Catalini, C., & Goldfarb, A. (2015). Crowdfunding: Geography, social networks, and the timing of investment decisions. *Journal of Economics & Management Strategy*, *24*(2), 253–274. https://doi.org/10.1111/jems.12093

Anand, J., & Delios, A. (1997). Location specificity and the transferability of downstream assets to foreign subsidiaries. *Journal of International Business Studies*, *28*, 579–603. https://doi.org/10.1057/palgrave.jibs.8490112

Andaç, Ş. (2011, September 12). Yeni ekonomi avcısı gittigidiyor'un eBay'e satışından pişman. *Milliyet*. www.milliyet.com.tr/ekonomi/yeni-ekonomi-avcisi-gittigidiyorun-ebaye-satisindan-pisman-1437339

Audience Project. (2019). *Insights 2019: Traditional TV, online video & streaming* (R. Werliin Ed., pp. 1–55). www.audienceproject.com/wp-content/uploads/audienceproject_study_tv_video_streaming.pdf

Azevedo, M. A. (2021, August 9). Turkey's first decacorn: Trendyol raises $1.5B at a $16.5B valuation. *TechCrunch*. https://techcrunch.com/2021/08/09/turkeys-first-decacorn-trendyol-raises-1-5b-at-a-16-5b-valuation/

Belleflamme, P., & Neysen, N. (2017). The rise and fall of take eat easy, or why markets are not easy to take in the sharing economy. *Communications & Strategies*, (108), 59–174.

Bloomberght. (2022, January 10). *Peak games'in sahibi satılıyor*. www.bloomberght.com/peak-games-in-sahibi-satiliyor-2296228

Budzinski, O., Gaenssle, S., & Lindstädt-Dreusicke, N. (2021). The battle of YouTube, TV and Netflix: An empirical analysis of competition in audiovisual media markets. *SN Business & Economics*, *1*(9), 116. https://doi.org/10.1007/s43546-021-00122-0

Caillaud, B., & Jullien, B. (2003). Chicken & egg: Competition among intermediation service providers. *RAND Journal of Economics*, 309–328. https://doi.org/10.2307/1593720

Cennamo, C. (2021). Competing in digital markets: A platform-based perspective. *Academy of Management Perspectives*, *35*(2), 265–291. https://doi.org/10.5465/amp.2016.0048

Crunchbase. (2023a, September 27). *Trendyol group*. www.crunchbase.com/organization/trendyol/company_financials

Crunchbase. (2023b, September 27). *Getir*. www.crunchbase.com/organization/getir/company_financials

Dillet, R. (2023, June 21). *Quick commerce startup Getir plans to exit France amid regulatory issues*. https://techcrunch.com/2023/06/21/quick-commerce-startup-getir-plans-to-exit-france/

Eferin, Y., Hohlov, Y., & Rossotto, C. (2019). Digital platforms in Russia: Competition between national and foreign multi-sided platforms stimulates growth and innovation. *Digital Policy, Regulation and Governance*, *21*(2), 129–145. https://doi.org/10.1108/DPRG-11-2018-0065

Emeafinance. (2015, May 7). *Turkey's Yemeksepeti in landmark acquisition*. www.emeafinance.com/live/deals-top/m-a/2641-turkish-firm-in-landmark-acquisition

Ersoy, E. (2021, July 1). *First Turkish firm to IPO on nasdaq hits $3.9 billion value*. www.bloomberg.com/news/articles/2021-07-01/hepsiburada-valued-at-3-9-billion-in-turkey-s-debut-nasdaq-ipo?leadSource=uverify%20wall

Ersoy, E. (2022, January 11). *Getir to seek $12 billion valuation in new investment round*. www.bloomberg.com/news/articles/2022-01-11/getir-said-to-seek-12-billion-valuation-in-new-investment-round?leadSource=uverify%20wall

Gaming in Turkey. (2020). *Türkiye'nin Oyun Sektörü 2020 Raporu*. www.gaminginturkey.com/files/pdf/turkiye-oyun-sektoru-raporu-2020.pdf

Gazete Duvar. (2023). www.gazeteduvar.com.tr/justwatch-acikladi-turkiyenin-en-populer-dizi-ve-film-platformu-blutv-galeri-1627959?p=5

IFPI. (2023). *Industry data*. www.ifpi.org/our-industry/industry-data/

Investment Office. (2023, September 27). *Foreign Direct Investment (FDI) strategy of Turkey*. www.invest.gov.tr/en/library/publications/Lists/InvestPublications/Turkiye-Foreign-Direct-Investment-Strategy-2021-2023.pdf

Kara-Kaşka, M. (2022, June 20). *GittiGidiyor: eBay neden Türkiye pazarından çekiliyor?* www.bbc.com/turkce/haberler-dunya-61862952

Katz, M. L., & Shapiro, C. (1985). Network externalities, competition, and compatibility. *American Economic Review*, *75*(3), 424–440.

Lee, J., Song, J., & Yang, J. S. (2016). Network structure effects on incumbency advantage. *Strategic Management Journal*, *37*(8), 1632–1648. https://doi.org/10.1002/smj.2405

Lunden, I. (2022, May 25). *Getir, the $12B instant delivery startup, plans to axe 14% of staff globally and cut aggressive expansion plans*. https://techcrunch.com/2022/05/25/getir-the-12b-instant-delivery-startup-plans-to-axe-14-of-staff-globally-and-cut-aggressive-expansion-plans/

McIntyre, D. P., & Srinivasan, A. (2017). Networks, platforms, and strategy: Emerging views and next steps. *Strategic Management Journal*, *38*(1), 141–160. https://doi.org/10.1002/smj.2596

Million Insights. (2023). *Classified digital advertising market size, share & trends analysis report*. www.millioninsights.com/snapshots/classified-digital-advertising-market-report

MUYAP. (2023, September 27). *Türkiye Müzik Endüstrisi 2023*. https://tr.mu-yap.org/wp-content/uploads/2023/09/TURKIYE-MUZIK-ENDUSTRISI-2023.pdf

Research and Markets. (2023). *Online food delivery market: Global industry trends, share, size, growth, opportunity and forecast 2023–2028*. www.researchandmarkets.com/report/online-food-delivery

Sawers, P. (2022). *Meta abused its dominant market position to benefit Facebook marketplace, EU's initial findings show.* https://techcrunch.com/2022/12/19/meta-abused-its-dominant-market-position-to-benefit-facebook-marketplace-eus-initial-findings-show/

Schilling, M. A. (2002). Technology success and failure in winner-take-all markets: The impact of learning orientation, timing, and network externalities. *Academy of Management Journal*, *45*(2), 387–398. https://doi.org/10.5465/3069353

Similarweb. (2023). *Most visited classifieds websites.* www.similarweb.com/top-websites/e-commerce-and-shopping/classifieds/

Stallkamp, M., & Schotter, A. P. (2021). Platforms without borders? The international strategies of digital platform firms. *Global Strategy Journal*, *11*(1), 58–80. https://doi.org/10.1002/gsj.1336

Statista. (2023a). *Music streaming worldwide – Statistics & facts.* www.statista.com/topics/6408/music-streaming/#topicOverview

Statista. (2023b). *Most frequently used music streaming or download services in South Korea as of August 2022.* www.statista.com/statistics/943272/south-korea-most-frequently-used-music-streaming-download-services/

Statista. (2023c). *Music streaming – Turkey.* www.statista.com/outlook/dmo/digital-media/digital-music/music-streaming/turkey

Statista. (2023d). *Video streaming worldwide – Statistics & facts.* www.statista.com/topics/7527/video-streaming-worldwide/#topicOverview

Statista. (2023e). *Online food delivery – Worldwide.* www.statista.com/outlook/dmo/online-food-delivery/worldwide#revenue

Statista. (2023f). *Online food delivery – Turkey.* www.statista.com/outlook/dmo/online-food-delivery/turkey

Statista. (2023g). *Classifieds – Worldwide.* www.statista.com/outlook/dmo/digital-advertising/classifieds/worldwide

Turkish Competition Authority. (2021, July 8). *Decision No: 21-34/475-237.* https://www.rekabet.gov.tr/Karar?kararId=caea11c5-f59c-418c-a148-cd8cb12c44f3

Turkish Competition Authority. (2022a, September 15). *Decision No: 22-42/606-254.* https://www.rekabet.gov.tr/Karar?kararId=f6693d81-5d00-4e88-a2dc-cbbdb-fe0a275

Turkish Competition Authority. (2022b, May 18). *Decision No: 22-23/366-155.* https://www.rekabet.gov.tr/Karar?kararId=e7152b1a-f634-4293-9f0d-6ddf0013edb9

Turkish Competition Authority. (2022c, May 18). *Decision No: 22-23/364-154.* https://www.rekabet.gov.tr/Karar?kararId=b6684eb6-1ca3-4551-945e-7487d0930393

TurkStat. (2023, September 27). *Survey on Information and Communication Technology (ICT) usage in households and by individuals.* https://data.tuik.gov.tr/Bulten/Index?p=Hanehalki-Bilisim-Teknolojileri-(BT)-Kullanim-Arastirmasi-2023-49407

Wikipedia. (2023, September 27). *Peak games.* https://en.wikipedia.org/wiki/Peak_Games

Yeşilyurt, E. F. (2022, December 30). *Yemeksepeti 2022'nin sipariş verilerini açıkladı.* www.aa.com.tr/tr/sirkethaberleri/e-ticaret/yemeksepeti-2022nin-siparis-verilerini-acikladi/677842

Zhu, F., & Iansiti, M. (2012). Entry into platform-based markets. *Strategic Management Journal*, *33*(1), 88–106. https://doi.org/10.1002/smj.941

6 ICT Adoption in Türkiye by Industry and Size

A Comparative Assessment With the EU

Hüseyin Taştan

Introduction

Information and communication technologies (ICT) encompass a broad spectrum of technologies and applications that can best be described as "general purpose technologies" (GPTs). As outlined by Bresnahan and Trajtenberg (1995), GPTs exhibit broad applicability across various domains, possess the potential for ongoing improvement resulting in reduced costs, and foster innovation in the development of new products and services. ICTs have the potential to enhance firm performance across all sectors by facilitating the innovation of new production processes, products, and services (Brynjolfsson & Hitt, 2000; Jovanovic & Rousseau, 2005).

Since Brynjolfsson (1993) and Brynjolfsson and Hitt (1996) claimed that the famous Solow "productivity paradox" is resolved,[1] numerous firm-level and macroeconomic studies have shown that ICT has a positive and significant impact on productivity.[2] In developing countries, there is a growing recognition of the crucial role of ICT and workplace digitization in boosting total factor productivity. Several studies at both the firm and industry levels from developing countries have concluded that ICT increases productivity.[3] These studies emphasize not just the direct effects of ICT but also the significance of complementary organizational changes as outlined theoretically by Milgrom and Roberts (1990). Their model suggests that when a firm invests in various ICTs, the resulting benefits on performance metrics like productivity and profitability might hinge on complementary organizational changes. Bresnahan et al. (2002) incorporate complementarities among ICT investments, workplace organization, and product innovation to explain skill-biased technical change characterized by a shift in demand toward highly skilled labor. In their model, a decline in the cost of ICT prompts firms to boost their ICT investments. This, in turn, results in organizational shifts and drives innovations in both products and services. The dynamics of these complementarities further amplify the adoption of ICTs and result in an increase in the demand for highly skilled labor. In this context, organizational change may encompass a shift toward decentralized decision-making processes within a firm, the adoption of collaborative work practices, and

DOI: 10.4324/9781032692937-6

the flattening of hierarchies. Such changes can enhance the efficiency of ICT investments through their intensified utilization.

While the literature has firmly established the positive impact of ICT on productivity, the timing and intensity of ICT adoption can vary significantly among firms, industries, and regions. To understand these variations, several technology adoption theories have been proposed. Among these, the "epidemic model" and the "rank model" emerge as notably influential (Karshenas & Stoneman, 1995; Geroski, 2000). The rank model posits that firm heterogeneity is the driving force behind technology adoption while the epidemic model emphasizes the transmission of new technology within an industry or a region. In particular, the epidemic model highlights the role of learning effects and reductions in adoption costs as primary drivers of new technology diffusion. Evidence from empirical research indicates that the key factors influencing adoption of new technology include the user cost of capital, size, employees' educational level, export status, intensity of R&D activities, and the use of complementary technologies (Battisti & Stoneman, 2005; Stoneman & Battisti, 2010). The literature also emphasizes the significance of complementary organizational and managerial shifts in decisions regarding ICT adoption (Hollenstein, 2004; Battisti et al., 2007; Gallego et al., 2014) and country-specific factors (Haller & Siedschlag, 2011). Andrews et al. (2018) use a cross-country dataset to explore the drivers of ICT adoption for a set of EU countries and Türkiye over the period 2010–2016. They argue that firms' incentive to adopt may depend on the availability of a skilled labor force and competitive pressures, which may be directly affected by policies. Their findings suggest that three primary factors are crucial for digital adoption in firms. First, enhancing the deployment of high-quality broadband infrastructure complements the adoption of advanced digital technologies. Second, the successful adoption of new technologies increasingly relies on more advanced intangible investments. Third, in line with this, the research reveals that greater digital integration is observed in environments characterized by superior management practices, broader access to ICT skills, especially through training for lower-skilled employees, and a more effective alignment of skills with job requirements.

The body of research examining ICT adoption and digitization at the firm level in Türkiye is relatively limited. Findik and Tansel (2015) conduct an investigation into the factors influencing ICT adoption, encompassing various ICT forms, including LAN and WLAN, ERP and CRM systems, as well as narrowband and broadband connectivity. Their findings emphasize the significance of firm-specific resources in shaping the adoption of new technologies. Using Turkish firm-level panel data, Atasoy et al. (2016) provide evidence on the positive impact of ICT applications on employment. Their results suggest that the full effect of some of the ICT applications, such as enterprise systems, may exhibit a time lag, particularly within medium and large firms. Kılıçaslan et al. (2017) find that ICT input increases labor productivity in Turkish manufacturing firms. Taştan and Gönel (2020) recognize the difficulties in separating ICT and non-ICT capital and use a decomposition of labor into ICT and non-ICT using Turkish firm-level data. Using a production function specification in which value-added is the dependent variable, they provide evidence on the positive contribution of both ICT labor and traditional labor. Their results also highlight the importance of complementarity between ICT applications such as enterprise systems and ICT-skilled labor. Taştan (2021) also provides evidence on the positive association between ICT adoption and labor productivity in both manufacturing and service industries in Türkiye.

This chapter examines the adoption of ICTs by Turkish firms across manufacturing and service industries. While aggregated measures of ICT, such as total technology investments, are useful in understanding trends in ICT usage, they may potentially mask developments in the adoption of different types of ICTs. Examining specific forms of ICTs adopted by industries may help us better understand the sector-specific challenges and needs. In addition to analyzing ICT adoption across different industries, this study also segments indicators by firm size. This segmentation is crucial as the challenges and opportunities faced by small and medium enterprises (SMEs) differ markedly from those confronted by large firms. While larger firms might have the capital to invest in advanced technologies, they might encounter difficulties in realizing complementary organizational changes. On the other hand, smaller firms, despite their agility and innovative spirit, might be constrained by resources. By understanding the differences in adoption dynamics across size groups, policymakers can craft strategies tailored to the unique needs and strengths of each firm size category.

We categorize key ICT indicators into four main areas: internet connectivity, e-commerce, enterprise software systems, and advanced digital technologies including artificial intelligence, cloud computing, the internet of things, and robotic systems. This chapter also compares and contrasts the Turkish data to the EU countries. A primary motivation for this comparison is the harmonized methodology and identical questions used in the ICT surveys across both regions, ensuring data consistency and comparability. This juxtaposition helps us understand how Turkish firms are technologically positioned relative to their EU counterparts. This comparative analysis is particularly relevant for Türkiye, considering its European integration ambitions, established trade relationships with the EU, and its ongoing efforts to align more closely with EU standards and regulations.

This chapter is organized as follows. The second section introduces the data. The following sections delve into the adoption of specific technologies and metrics. The third section assesses the measures of internet connectivity. The fourth through sixth sections examine the adoption of e-commerce, enterprise software systems, and advanced ICT applications, respectively. This is followed by a discussion of the findings and, finally, a conclusion with policy implications.

Data

The main sources of data for ICT adoption by firms stem from surveys conducted by the Turkish Statistical Institute (Turkstat, 2023) in collaboration with the statistical office of the EU (Eurostat). As outlined by Eurostat's official metadata (2023), these annual surveys aim to "collect and disseminate harmonized and comparable information on the use of Information and Communication Technologies and e-commerce in enterprises at the European level." ICT survey statistics reported in the Eurostat database cover all 27 EU members as well as candidate countries. The ICT survey covers the following main sectors according to the NACE Rev.2 classification system: Manufacturing (C), Electricity, Gas, and Water Supply (D-E), Construction (F), Wholesale and Retail Trade (G), Transport and Storage (H), Accommodation and Food Services (I), Information and Communication (J), Real Estate (L), Professional Activities (M), Administrative and Support Services (N), Repair of Computers and Communication Equipment (S95.1).[4] The Turkish version of the survey collects data from enterprises with ten or more employees. The breakdowns are presented with respect to firm employment size, categorized as small (10–49 employees), medium (50–249 employees), and large (250+ employees).

Existing research on ICT adoption employs a range of indicators, broadly categorized into inter-firm and intra-firm diffusion (Battisti & Stoneman, 2003; Battisti et al., 2007). Inter-firm diffusion pertains to the adoption of ICTs by individual enterprises within a specific industry or group and is typically quantified by the percentage of firms that have integrated ICT. Such diffusion often reflects industry trends, competitive pressures, and the overarching regulatory environment. On the other hand, intra-firm diffusion focuses on the extent and depth of ICT utilization within a firm, exploring how various departments or functions employ the technology. Empirical evidence suggests that, initially, industries witness a surge in inter-firm diffusion, but as the technology matures, intra-firm diffusion becomes more pronounced (Battisti & Stoneman, 2003).

In line with the literature, in this chapter, we use both types of technology adoption indicators. In accordance with the dynamic nature of ICT trends, the coverage and survey questions have evolved over time and regions. The most recent iteration offers insights into the usage of ICT systems, e-commerce and e-business, internet connectivity, artificial intelligence, cloud computing, and robotic systems, among others. In the following sections, we present several metrics to shed light on the extent of ICT adoption by Turkish enterprises and compare and contrast them with their European counterparts. The metrics are grouped into four categories: internet connectivity, e-commerce, enterprise software systems, and advanced ICTs encompassing artificial intelligence, cloud computing, the internet of things, and robotic systems.

Internet Connectivity

Internet connectivity is foundational for numerous ICTs. A fast and reliable broadband internet connection serves as the backbone that supports various digital technologies and applications. According to Turkstat's (2023) survey (see Table 6.1), 95.4% of small firms, 98.7% of medium-sized firms, and 99.7% of large firms have internet access through either fixed or mobile broadband. Internet adoption rates exceed 92% in all major sectors, with the construction (F) industry exhibiting the lowest adoption rate.

Table 6.1 Internet connectivity metrics

			Internet speed, %			
Size group	*Internet adoption,%*	*Internet-using employees, %*	*<30 Mb/s*	*30–100 Mb/s*	*>100 Mb/s*	*>1 Gb/s*
10–49	95.4	51.1	22.2	35.3	34.0	7.3
50–249	98.7	52.3	14.2	38.4	44.1	10.0
250+	99.7	64.7	4.8	29.5	65.2	16.5
All(10+)	96	57.2	20.7	35.6	36.2	7.9
Industry						
C	96.7	46.1	22.2	37.1	34.7	7.4
D-E	99.5	72.5	20.8	33.6	43.2	9.2
F	92.2	54.2	21.5	30.7	30.6	5.7
G	97.7	64.6	20.2	37.4	38.5	8.7
H	93.9	66.0	21.8	31.6	34.0	6.2
I	94.3	50.7	21.0	37.9	34.7	8.0
J	98.8	92.1	5.0	27.6	66.1	18.9
L-M	99	81.2	18.5	39.7	40.0	10.5
N	94.7	67.4	18.5	31.9	38.9	7.7
S95.1	98.8	83.2	10.6	40.0	45.8	17.6

Notes: "Internet adoption" refers to the proportion of enterprises which have internet access as of 2023 (*Source*: Turkstat, 2023). The column "internet-using employees" shows the proportion of employees using the internet in their daily activities within firms in 2023. "Internet speed" shows the percentage of firms in each speed categories defined as "the maximum contracted download speed of the fastest fixed line internet" in 2023 (*Source*: Eurostat). NACE Rev.2 main sectors are Manufacturing (C), Electricity, Gas, and Water Supply (D-E), Construction (F), Wholesale and Retail Trade (G), Transport and Storage (H), Accommodation and Food Services (I), Information and Communication (J), Real Estate and Professional Activities (L-M), Administrative and Support Services (N), Repair of Computers and Communication Equipment (S95.1).

Despite high adoption levels, firms continue to differ in their choice of internet speed and the extent of internet use within their organizations. To gain a more nuanced understanding of internet connectivity dynamics, we examine two key metrics: the broadband internet speed and the percentage of employees using the internet in their daily tasks.

Broadband Internet Speed

Internet connectivity is not just about ensuring access but also about the quality and speed of that access. A stable and high-speed internet connection is indispensable for advanced ICT applications such as cloud computing and data-intensive processes. Empirical evidence suggests that working in a more digitalized environment with high-speed internet increases labor productivity and firm performance (Akerman et al., 2015; Gal et al., 2019; Hjort & Poulsen, 2019). In Table 6.1, we present the proportion of enterprises in four speed categories according to their maximum contracted download speed of the fastest fixed line internet in 2022. The slowest internet connection (less than 30 Mb/s) is preferred mainly by small firms (22.2%). Approximately, 52% of small- and medium-sized enterprises have speeds under 100 Mb/s. In contrast, 65% of large enterprises contract for speeds equaling or exceeding 100 Mb/s. The highest internet speeds (>1 Gb/s), often termed as ultrafast or "gigabit" internet, are typically found in large firms followed by small- and medium-sized enterprises.

Figure 6.1 offers a comparative analysis of the adoption of internet speeds of at least 100 Mb/s among firms of various sizes in both European countries and Türkiye from 2020 to 2023. The data reveals a positive trend across all firm sizes, reflecting the growing necessity for faster internet in business operations. Small enterprises demonstrate a diverse range of adoption rates across countries. While nations like Denmark, Romania, Portugal, and Spain show higher adoption rates among small businesses (above 70%), Turkish small firms remain behind at about 34%, which is significantly lower than the EU average of 57.5%. On average, medium-sized firms have a higher adoption rate (44.1% in Türkiye, 71.1% in the EU) than small firms in all countries. Denmark, Sweden, and Spain are in the lead, whereas Türkiye aligns at the bottom, far below the EU average. Large firms demonstrate higher adoption levels across all nations and the pace of convergence is faster, but Türkiye (65.2%) still lags behind the EU average of 83.9% in 2023.

To assess Turkish firms' preparedness for the next wave of digital transformation and identify potential areas of investment and policy intervention, we further examine the adoption rates of ultrafast internet, typically characterized by the speeds of 1 Gb/s or more. European firms, particularly medium-size and large firms, display a growing inclination toward the use of ultra-high-speed internet, as depicted in Figure 6.2. By 2023, the adoption rate of ultra-high-speed internet among small Turkish firms stood at 7.3%, slightly down from 2020. Meanwhile, their European counterparts have an adoption rate of 11.3%, reflecting a modest rise from 2020. Medium-sized Turkish firms had a 10% adoption in 2023 and lagged behind the EU average of 17.8%. Large Turkish enterprises increased their adoption to 16.5% in 2023 from their 2020 rate, yet remained below the EU's average of 31.2%.

Figure 6.3 compares the proportion of moderately high-speed internet subscribers (>100 Mb/s) across NACE Rev.2 main industrial sectors and countries. About 34.7% of enterprises in the manufacturing industry (C) have a connection at least 100 Mb/s in Türkiye, compared to the average of about 56.2% in the EU. Denmark, Sweden, Portugal, Finland, Spain, and Romania lead the countries with more than 75% of the firms having a moderately high-speed internet connections in the manufacturing sector. Similarly, Turkish firms tend to have lower rates of adoption, ranging from 30% to 40%, in all main manufacturing and services sectors. This contrasts with the EU, where the average adoption rate lies between 50% and 85% in these sectors. Even in the ICT sector (J) in Türkiye, known for its technological prowess, only 66% of firms adopted high-speed internet compared to the average of about 82.5% in the European firms.

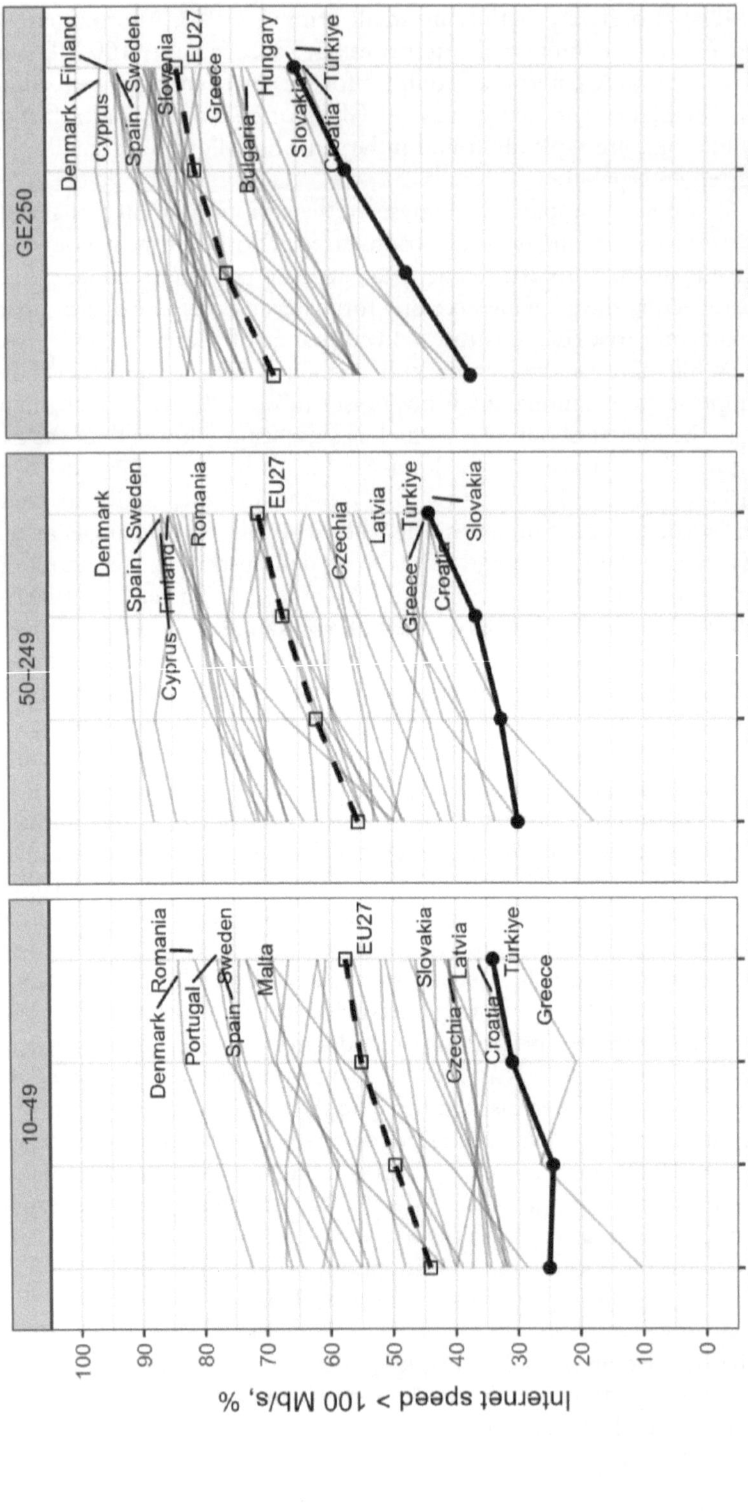

Figure 6.1 Proportion of firms with broadband internet speed of at least 100 Mb/s across firm size groups.

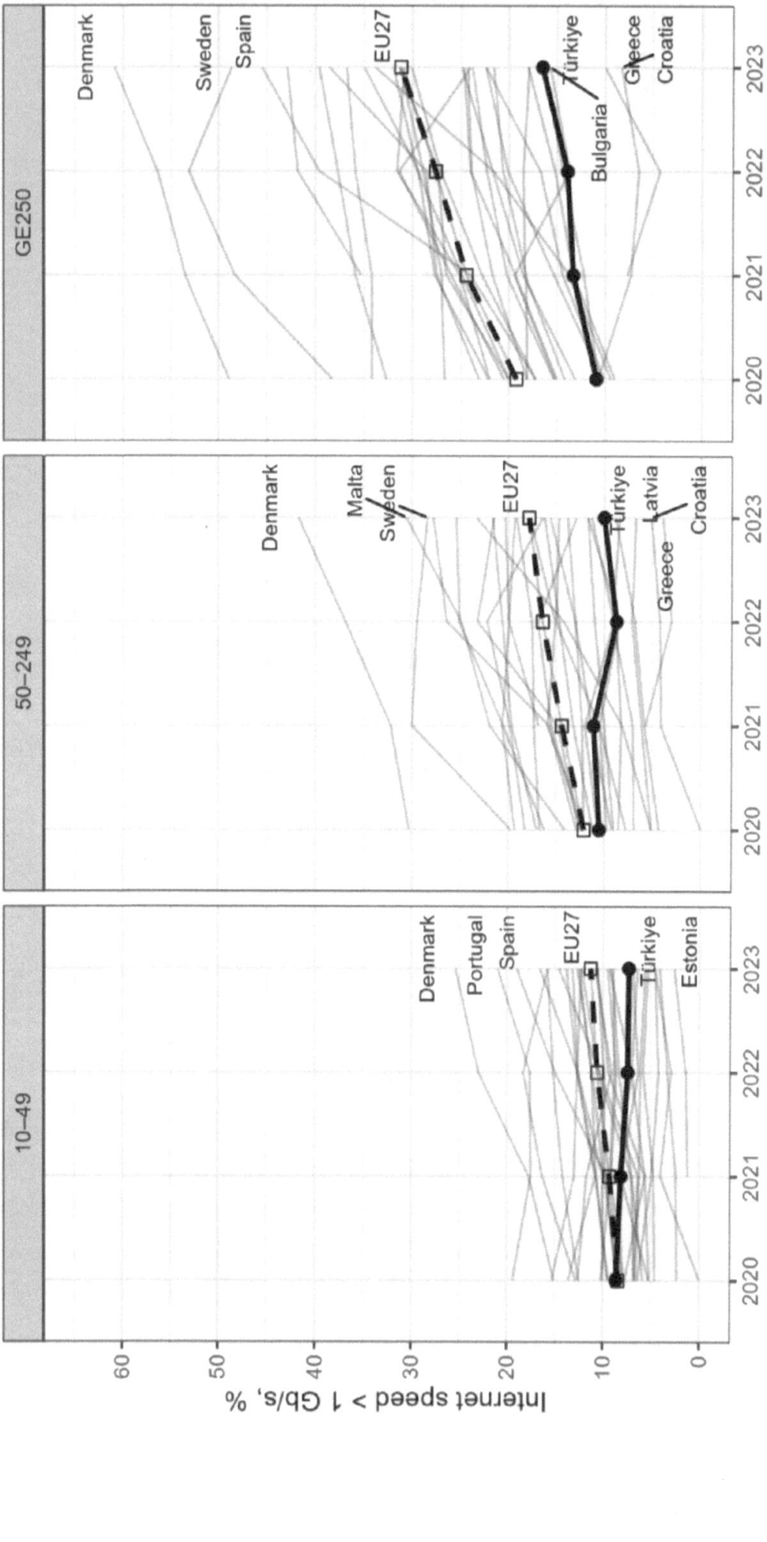

Figure 6.2 Proportion of firms with ultrafast broadband internet speed (at least 1 Gb/s) across firm size groups.

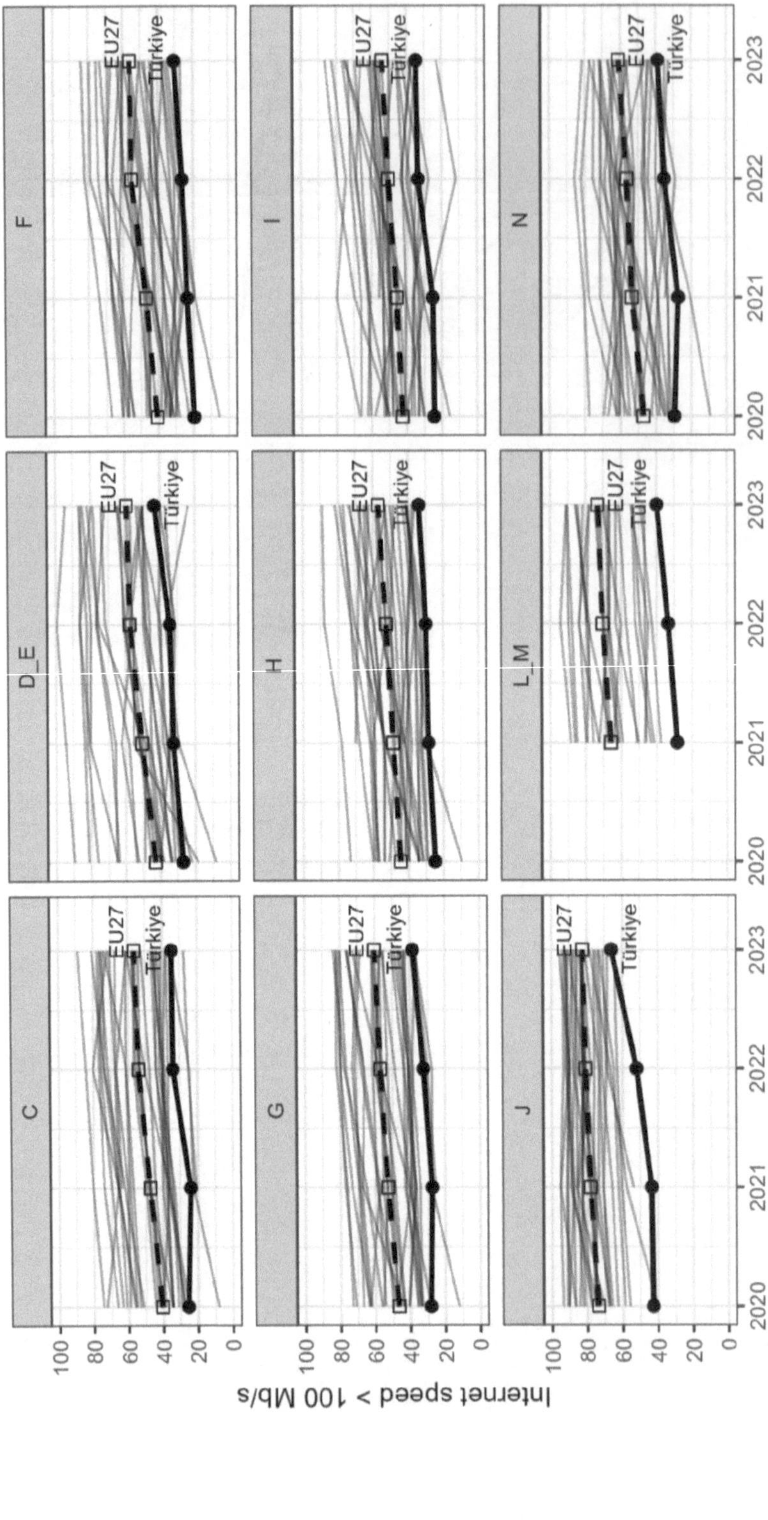

Figure 6.3 Proportion of firms with broadband internet speed of at least 100 Mb/s across NACE Rev.2 1 digit industries.

Proportion of Employees Using the Internet

Firms also differ with respect to the intensity of internet connectivity within their operations. A valuable metric for this intra-firm digital adoption is the proportion of employees actively using the internet in their daily tasks. This measure provides information on the depth of ICT integration within firms. As shown in Table 6.1, for all firms with ten or more employees, the proportion of internet users in their daily tasks is about 57.2% in 2023, more than double from 25.1% in 2010. The notable surge observed in 2021 can, in part, be attributed to the changes brought on by the COVID-19 pandemic. As firms had to adjust rapidly to remote work models and increasing digitalization, there was an inevitable rise in the number of employees relying on the internet for their daily tasks (see Figure 6.4).

Both small- and medium-sized enterprises report about half of their employees being regular internet users in 2023 while larger firms demonstrate a slightly higher adoption rate at around 64.7%. As depicted in Figure 6.4, up until 2021, Turkish firms were trailing their EU counterparts in integrating internet-based ICT into their operational workflows across all size categories. However, by 2023, a significant shift is observable. While small- and medium-sized firms in Türkiye continue to have a slightly lower percentage of internet-using employees compared to the EU average, the gap has noticeably narrowed. Remarkably, larger firms in Türkiye have rapidly adopted internet-based ICT practices, converging with the EU average at 64.4%.

Across main sectors, the Information and Communication sector (J) leads with 92.1% of its workforce using the internet daily, followed by the Repair of Computers and Communication Equipment sector (S95.1) at 83%, emphasizing tech-centric nature and the reliance on digital diagnostics and remote support in these sectors. On the other end, the Manufacturing sector (C) reports the lowest usage, with 46.1% of its employees using the internet daily, reflecting the hands-on nature of many tasks within this sector. About 54.2% of employees in the Construction sector (F) and 72.5% in the utilities sector use internet routinely in their daily tasks. In the services sectors, the Real Estate and Professional Services sector (L-M) demonstrate a significant reliance on internet-based tasks with 81.2% of employees using the internet. Other services sectors, including Wholesale and Retail Trade (G), Transportation and Storage (H), and Administrative and Support Services (N) hover around the 60–70% range, a significant increase from 2015.

Figure 6.5 displays the proportion of employees using the internet within firms across the NACE Rev.2 main sectors in comparison with other countries over the 2015–2023 period. While intra-firm adoption of internet-based ICT has increased almost in all countries and in every sector, the speed of adoption was significantly faster in Turkish manufacturing and service industries during this period. Starting below the EU average in nearly all sectors, Turkish firms not only kept pace with the prevailing growth trends but also outperformed the EU average in the majority of the services sectors.

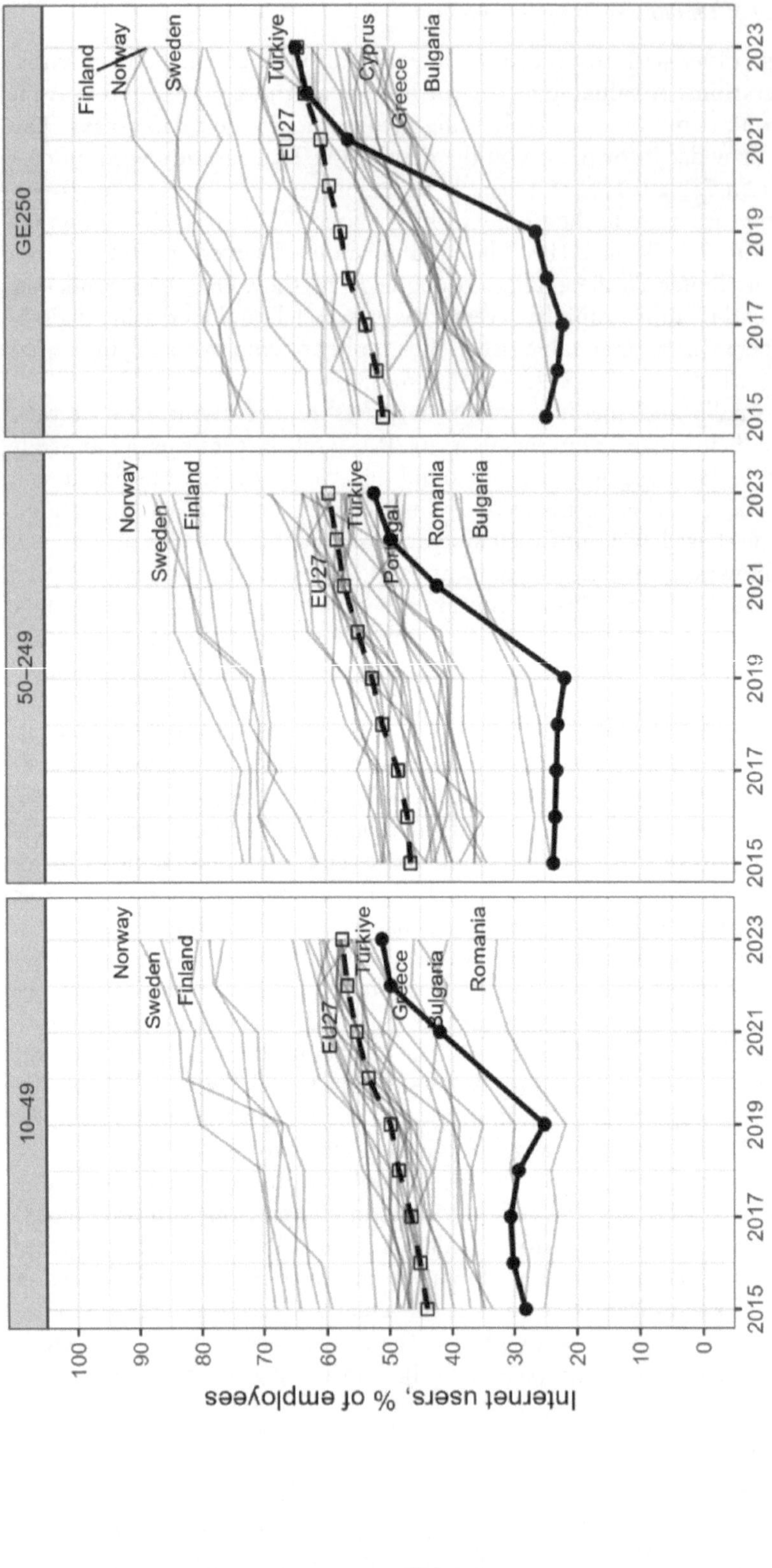

Figure 6.4 Proportion of internet-using employees across firm sizes (2015–2023).

Note: 2020 is not available in Türkiye.

E-Commerce

As more consumers engage in online purchasing, adopting e-commerce technologies has become a necessity for many businesses to remain competitive. E-commerce stands as one of the most transformative ICT technologies for firms, offering opportunities for growth, efficiency, and customer reach. Regardless of size or sector, venturing into e-commerce can redefine market boundaries for enterprises, enabling them to access a global customer base. Additional advantages of e-commerce include reduced overhead costs, efficient inventory management, and a wealth of data that can be utilized to gain deeper insights into consumer behavior, preferences, and buying patterns.

Proportion of Firms With Electronic Sales

E-commerce capabilities among firms are often gauged by the percentage engaged in web- or platform-based electronic sales. Table 6.2 shows the proportion of firms with e-commerce sales across size and industry groups in Türkiye in 2023. On average, across all sizes, 18.2% of firms are engaged in e-commerce activities. As firms grow larger, their engagement in e-commerce also increases, in both Türkiye and other European countries as depicted in Figure 6.6. This could be indicative of the larger firms having more resources to invest in e-commerce platforms or potentially having a broader market reach that necessitates online sales channels.

Figure 6.6 reveals that from 2015 to 2023, e-commerce adoption consistently increased across various European countries, including Türkiye.

Table 6.2 E-commerce and enterprise software adoption

Size group	*E-commerce, %*	*ERP, %*	*CRM, %*	*BI, %*
10–49	17.3	25.3	10.1	4.9
50–249	20.8	47.2	19.5	11.3
250+	31.8	77.5	40.0	30.7
All (10+)	18.2	29.7	12.1	6.4
Industry				
C	17.3	34.8	11.6	6.5
D-E	7.2	41.8	15.3	13.4
F	7.4	17.7	5.7	4.8
G	23.5	36.3	14.5	6.1
H	9.9	22.2	11.5	5.5
I	39.5	21.9	11.1	6.4
J	28.7	41.7	38.8	21.9
L	16.4	37.3	19.7	7.4
M	8.5	26.5	14.0	6.3
N	14.4	23.3	11.7	5.7
S95.1	29.4	45.8	31.7	7.0

Notes: "E-commerce" shows the proportion of enterprises with electronic sales via websites or mobile applications. ERP is the proportion of enterprises using an Enterprise Resource Planning software in their business operations, and CRM is the proportion of enterprises using a Customer Relationship Management software. BI shows the proportion of enterprises using Business Intelligence software (Turkstat, 2023).

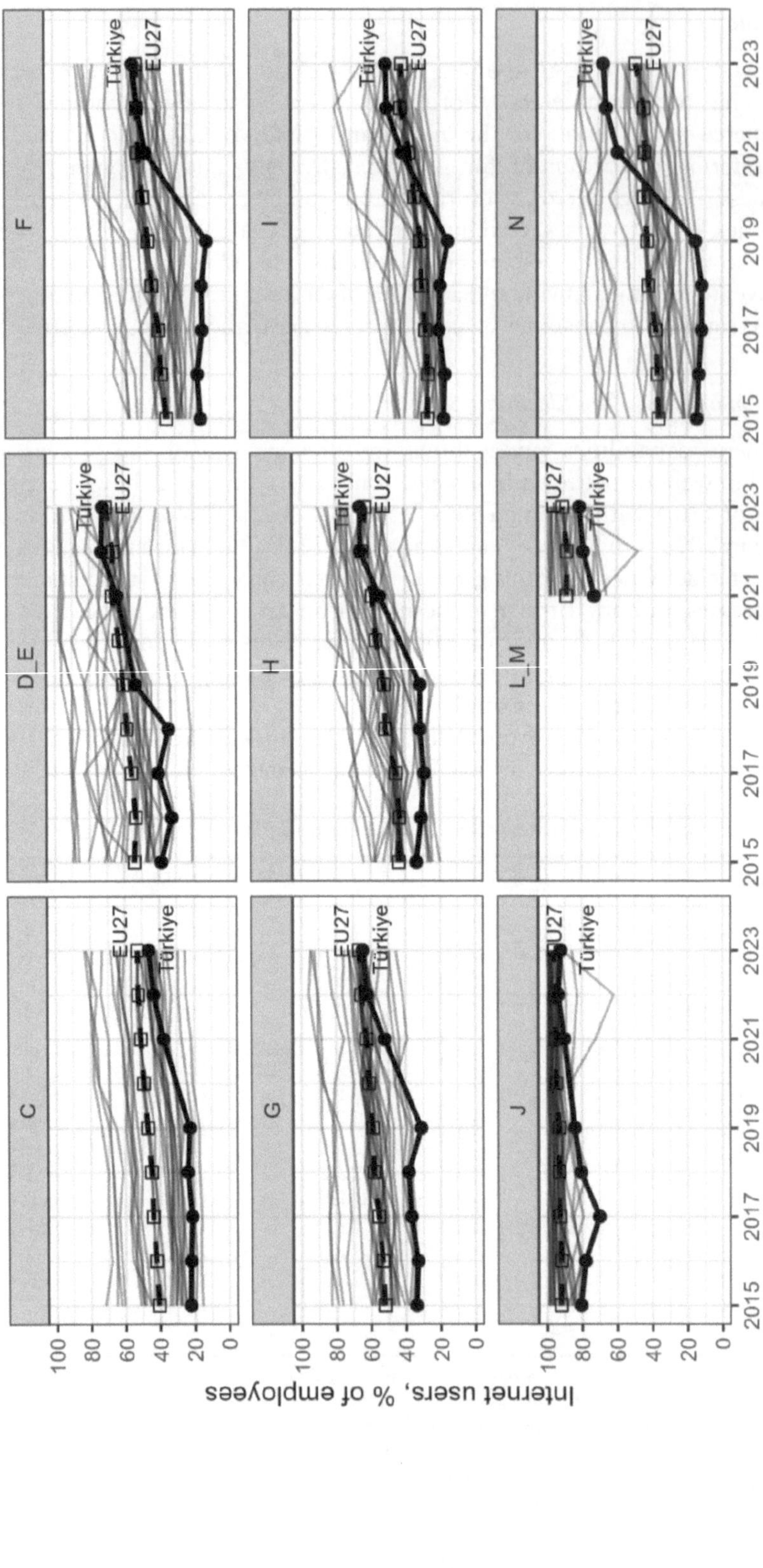

Figure 6.5 Proportion of internet-using employees across NACE Rev.2 main sectors.

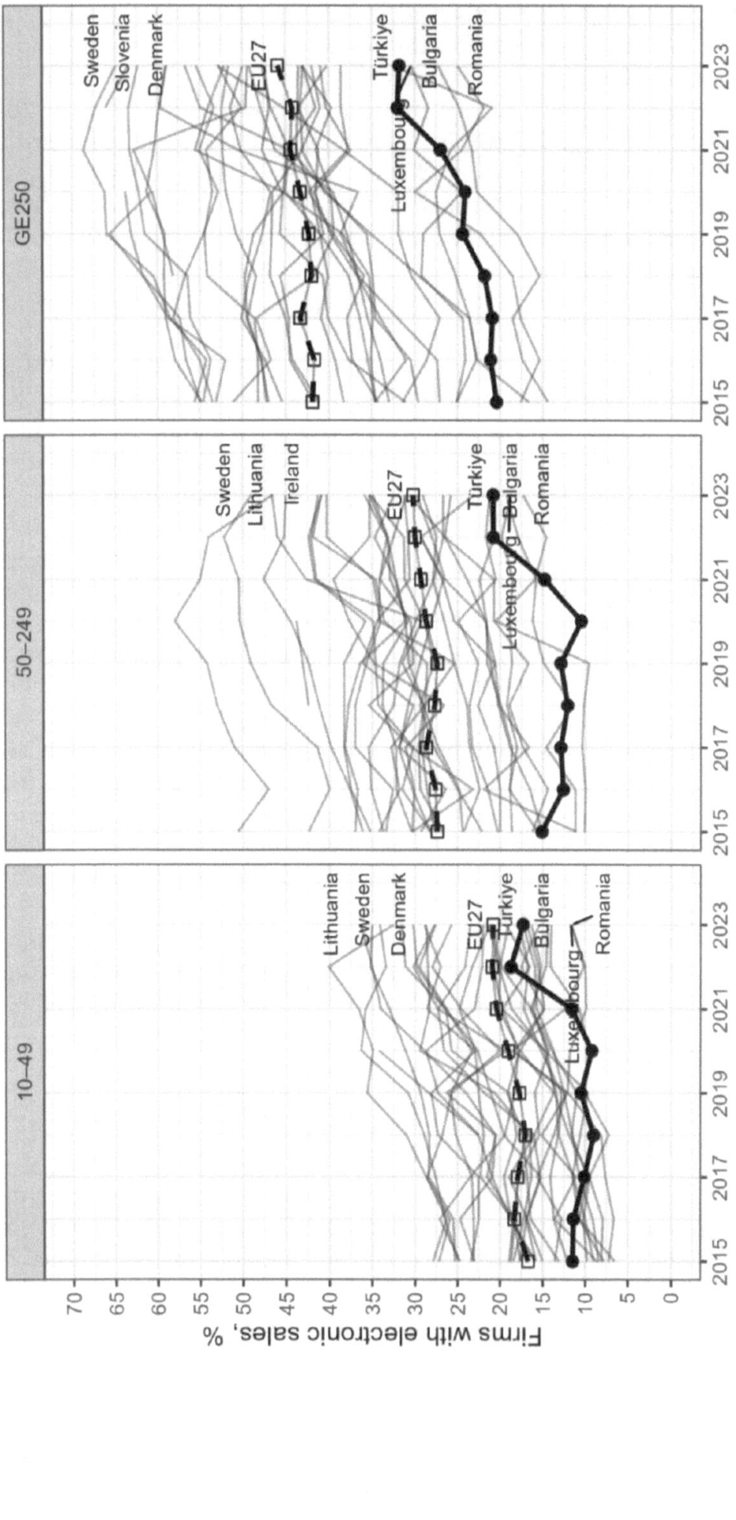

Figure 6.6 Proportion of firms with electronic sales across size groups.

Although Turkish firms generally trailed the EU average during this period, their adoption notably surged after the global pandemic, closing the gap significantly, particularly for smaller firms. By 2023, about 17% of small Turkish firms adopted e-commerce, an increase from just above 10% in 2015, aligning closely with the EU average. However, for medium- and larger-sized firms, a wider disparity remains. While the EU boasts adoption rates of approximately 30% for medium firms and 45% for large firms, Turkish e-commerce adoption rates fall behind, indicating areas for potential growth and alignment in the future.

The rate of e-commerce adoption varies significantly across industries (see Table 6.2 and Figure 6.7). The adoption rate is the highest at about 39.5% in the Accommodation and Food Services sector (I) followed by the ICT sector (J) and the Repair of computers (S95.1). Conversely, sectors D-E (Electricity and water utilities) and F (Construction) display the lowest rates of adoption, both falling below 8%. This might hint at either the traditional nature of these industries or potential barriers preventing firms from moving their operations online. The Wholesale and Retail Trade sector (G) also shows a notable adoption rate, with 23.5% of firms in the sector participating in e-commerce, reflecting the increasing consumer preference for online shopping.

Figure 6.7 displays e-commerce adoption rates across main sectors for European countries over the same period. Until 2020, Türkiye's e-commerce adoption rates consistently fell below the EU averages in nearly all sectors. However, there is a noticeable jump in e-commerce adoption from 2020 onwards. In the manufacturing sector, Ireland and Sweden emerge as frontrunners, with over 40% of their firms engaging in e-commerce in 2023. In comparison, the EU average stands at approximately 21%, whereas Türkiye is slightly behind at around 17%. The wholesale and retail sector shows a slow positive trend over the period in both Europe and Türkiye with the EU average nearing 39% in 2023. Evidently, in sectors like ICT (J), Accommodation and Food (I), Administrative Services (N), Real Estate and Professional Activities (L-M), and Repair of Computers and Communication Equipment (S95.1), Turkish firms not only catch up to but, in some instances, exceed the EU average.

Enterprise Software Systems

The integration of enterprise software solutions, including Enterprise Resource Planning (ERP), Customer Relationship Management (CRM), and Business Intelligence (BI), plays a crucial role in enhancing operational efficiency, fostering customer engagement, and extracting insights from large datasets. Empirical evidence in the literature indicates that enterprise software systems improve various measures of firm performance such as labor productivity and innovation (Hitt et al., 2002; Aral et al., 2006; Engelstätter & Sarbu, 2013; Relich, 2017). Moreover, firms adopting data-driven

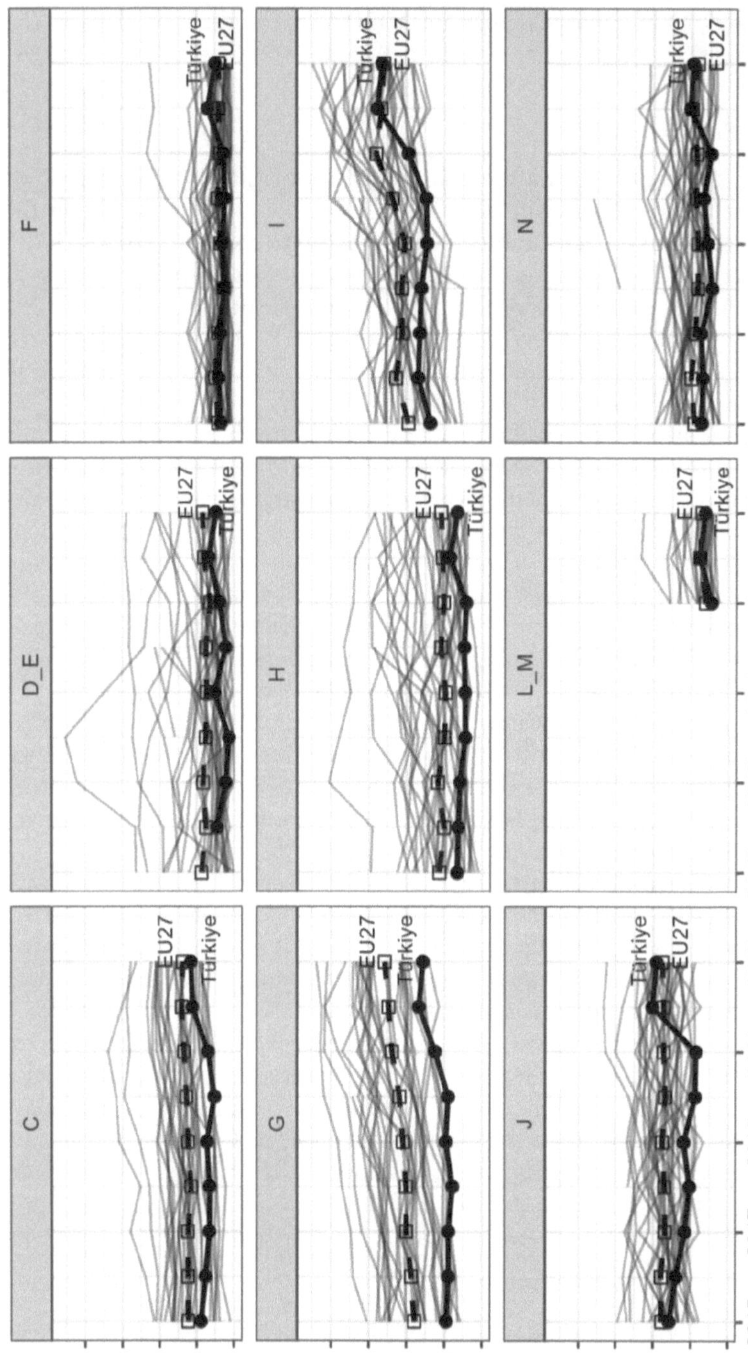

Figure 6.7 Proportion of firms with electronic sales across NACE Rev.2 main sector.

decision-making and business analytics tend to have higher productivity than non-adopters (Brynjolfsson et al., 2011; Brynjolfsson & McElheran, 2016).

Enterprise Resource Planning

Table 6.2 (column 3) shows the adoption rates of ERP systems across size groups and main industries in 2023. Larger firms tend to have a higher ERP adoption rate as expected. Among firms with 250 or more employees, 77.5% have integrated ERP systems into their operations. This percentage is significantly higher than the adoption rates in small- and medium-sized firms, which stand at 25.3% and 47.2%, respectively. This disparity suggests that as firms grow in size, the complexities of their operations may require the comprehensive solutions that ERP systems provide.

Figure 6.8 displays the evolution of ERP adoption rates across size groups over the period 2015–2023. ERP adoption in Türkiye has steadily increased across all firm sizes, whereas the EU average has largely remained stable over the period. While still below the EU average, Türkiye exhibits a distinct convergence trend, particularly after 2017. This trend may reflect the growing acknowledgment of the importance of integrated business management tools.

Industry-wise, ERP adoption exhibits a more diverse pattern (see Table 6.2 and Figure 6.9). The ICT sector (J) has the highest adoption at 41.7%. Close behind is the Repair of Computers sector (S95.1) with an adoption rate of 45.8%. Interestingly, the Water Utilities sector (D-E), despite its more traditional nature, shows a 41.8% adoption rate. This could indicate the need for streamlining utilities' vast operations through ERP systems. On the lower end, the Construction sector (F) and the Accommodation and Food Services sector (I) have adoption rates of 17.7% and 21.9%, respectively.

A gradual upward trend in ERP adoption over the period 2015–2023 is visible in all countries across various sectors as depicted in Figure 6.9. Focusing on Türkiye, the Manufacturing sector (C) has seen a steady growth in ERP adoption, from 24% in 2015 to 34.8% in 2023. The EU average reached 53.6%, a significant rise from 30.2% in 2010 and roughly 40% in 2015, highlighting the region's concerted move toward digitization. Across most sectors, particularly in services, Turkish firms consistently remain below the EU average. For example, the Wholesale and Trade sector's ERP adoption rate has not yet reached the EU average in this sector. However, it is also worth noting that Türkiye has seen considerable growth over these years, given the jump from 18.8% in 2017 to 36.3% in 2023.

Customer Relationship Management

Customer Relationship Management (CRM) systems are software tools that help businesses manage and analyze customer interactions aiming to enhance relationships, streamline processes, and increase profitability. As can be seen in Table 6.2, the adoption of CRM systems appears to grow proportionally

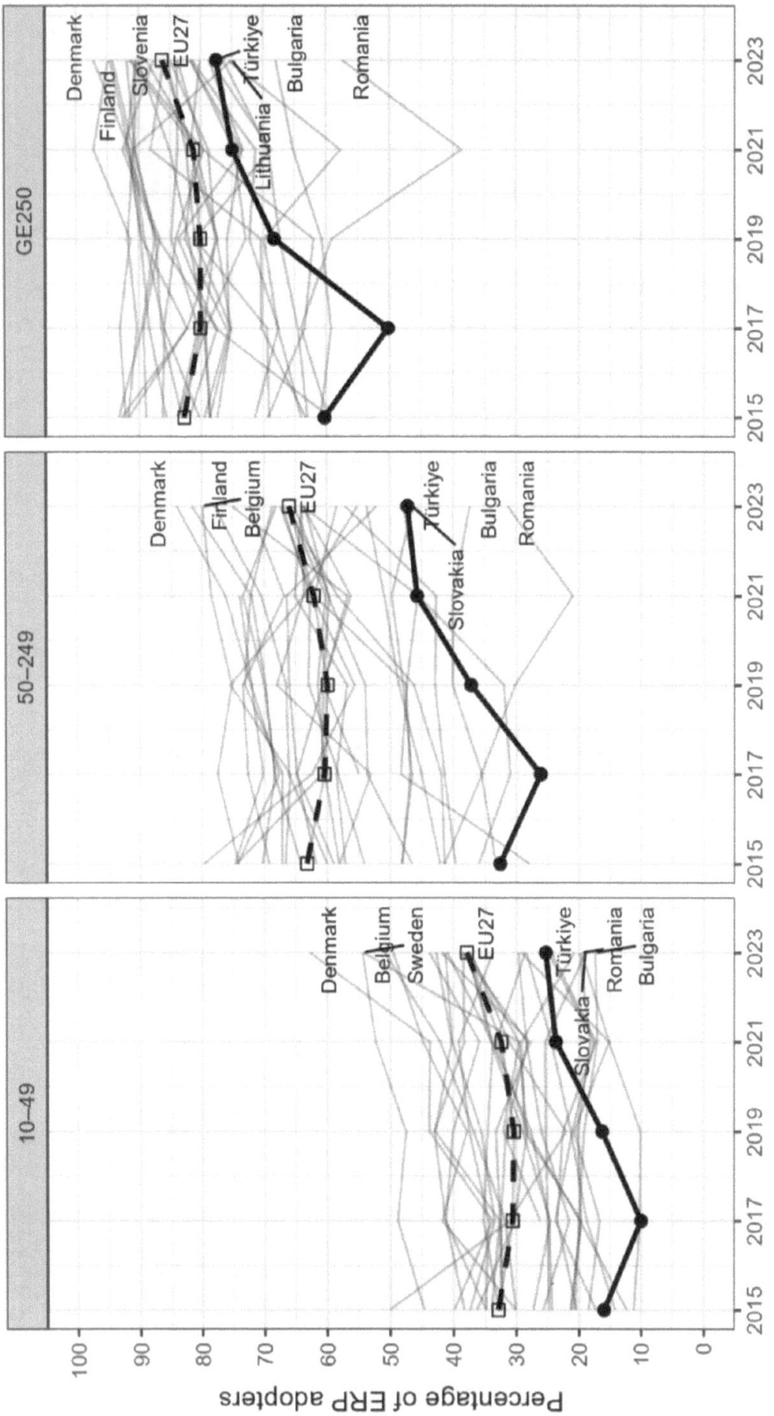

Figure 6.8 Proportion of ERP adopters across size groups.

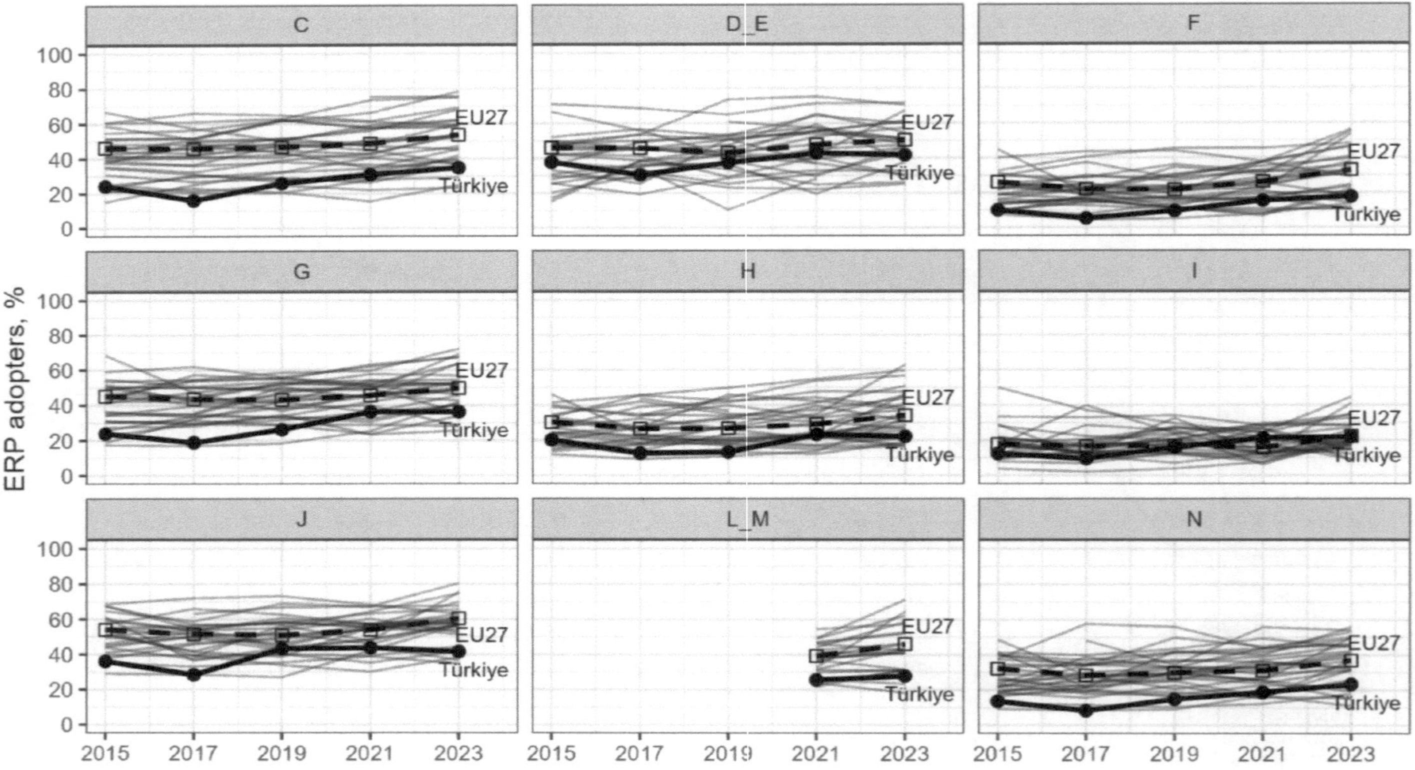

Figure 6.9 Proportion of firms using ERP across NACE Rev.2 main sectors.

with firm size. Large enterprises have a CRM adoption rate of 40.0% which is considerably higher than the rates observed in smaller firms at 10.1%. Medium-sized firms fall in the middle, with an adoption rate of 19.5%.

When we look at the industry breakdown, the ICT sector (J) stands out with a substantial CRM adoption rate of 38.8%. Following closely is the Repair of Computers sector (S95.1) at 31.7%, further emphasizing the ICT industry's inclination toward CRM systems. The Wholesale and Retail Trade sector (G) registers a moderate 14.5% adoption rate, likely due to the sector's direct customer interactions and the importance of customer loyalty in retail. In contrast, the Construction sector (F) has a lower CRM adoption at 5.7%, reflecting the industry's project-centric nature and possibly lesser emphasis on long-term customer relationships.

Business Intelligence

The integration of Business Intelligence (BI) tools is crucial for firms to make informed decisions by leveraging data-driven insights. The last column in Table 6.2 shows the adoption rates of BI systems across different firm sizes and industries in Türkiye for 2022. Only about 4.9% of these firms have adopted BI solutions. This lower adoption rate might suggest that smaller entities could be facing challenges in resource allocation for advanced analytics or perceive BI solutions as more beneficial for larger operations. The adoption rate more than doubles to 11.3%, indicating that as firms grow, they tend to acknowledge the value of data-driven decision-making tools. Large firms have the highest BI adoption at 30.7%.

Industry-level adoption rates suggest that the ICT sector (J) boasts the highest BI adoption rate of 21.9%. The electricity and water utilities sector (D-E) has a relatively high BI adoption rate of 13.4%. While this sector might not be as active in online sales as indicated by relatively low e-commerce adoption, they are keen on using data analytics for decision-making. Manufacturing and services sectors have BI adoption rates less than 7%, slightly higher than the Construction (F) and most of the services sectors.

Advanced Digital Technologies

As the era of Industry 4.0 unfolds, certain technologies emerge as transformative forces reshaping industries and nations. These "Advanced Digital Technologies," encompassing artificial intelligence (AI), cloud computing (CC), the internet of things (IoT), and robotic systems, are not just the next step in ICT but a leap toward a more connected, automated, and data-driven future. For Türkiye, a nation with aspirations of becoming a prominent player in the global digital economy, understanding and adopting these technologies is not just an option but a necessity.[5] This section examines their adoption rates and provides a clear perspective on Türkiye's position in comparison with European nations.

Artificial Intelligence

The integration of artificial intelligence (AI) into business operations has become a topic of growing interest. At its core, AI encompasses a suite of technologies that enable machines to mimic human intelligence, learning from data and making decisions. Sometimes heralded as the most transformative General Purpose Technology (GPT), the potential of AI to revolutionize every industry is immense. Owing to its GPT nature, AI demands significant complementary investments, which can cause initial productivity statistics to appear underestimated, presenting a J-curve behavior. However, when accounting for these investments, especially in intangibles, AI's profound impact on overall productivity becomes evident (Brynjolfsson et al., 2021).

As defined in the ICT surveys conducted by Eurostat and Turkstat in 2021 and 2023, AI adoption refers to the use of at least one of the following technologies:

- Text Mining: Extracting meaningful data from vast quantities of unstructured text.
- Speech Recognition: Transcribing and understanding human speech, making way for applications such as virtual assistants and voice-activated systems.
- Natural Language Generation: Computers generating coherent sentences, often used in chatbots or automated report generation.
- Image Recognition: Identifying and classifying objects or features in an image.
- Machine Learning/Deep Learning: Algorithms that learn and predict from data without being explicitly programmed, a backbone technology for many AI applications.
- Robotic Process Automation: Automating repetitive tasks that were traditionally done by humans, often employed in administrative tasks or data extraction.
- Autonomous Machines: Devices designed to perform tasks without human intervention, from self-driving cars to drones.

Table 6.3 provides the percentage of AI adopters utilizing at least one of the technologies listed earlier across size groups and main sectors. Figure 6.10 complements this by showing the EU-wide adoption, broken down by firm size groups. For small, medium, and large firms in Türkiye, the AI adoption rates in 2023 are 4.9%, 6.5%, and 18.5%, respectively, indicating a significant upward trend in each size category. The EU averages are higher, at 6.4% for small firms, 13% for medium-sized firms, and 30.4% for large firms.

Industry-wise, the adoption of any AI technology surged in 2023 in Türkiye. Figure 6.11 offers a comparative view of AI adoption rates across major industries in both Türkiye and the EU. In Türkiye, the ICT sector (J) leads with an adoption rate of 28.1%, close to the EU average of 29.4%. The Manufacturing (C) and Electricity and Water Utilities sectors (D-E) have AI adoption

Table 6.3 Adoption of advanced digital technologies and e-business

	AI, %		*CC, %*		*IoT, %*	*Robotics, %*
Size group	*2021*	*2023*	*2021*	*2023*	*2021*	*2022*
10–49	2.3	4.9	8.5	13.7	19.6	4.1
50–249	3.6	6.5	19.5	26.6	27.2	8.6
GE250	9.6	18.5	41.0	48.2	35.9	24.1
All	2.7	5.5	10.8	16.4	21.1	5.2
Industry						
C	3.1	6.0	10.4	15.8	21.9	9.3
D-E	4.5	7.2	16.6	23.3	37.0	5.4
F	1.7	4.9	4.4	10.3	13.4	2.2
G	2.3	4.4	13.3	20.5	25.4	4.3
H	1.8	3.5	9.5	10.4	23.8	3.9
I	1.4	3.2	5.6	11.0	21.8	3.8
J	17.6	28.1	41.9	49.6	23.5	4.5
L	2.1	8.2	18.1	21.9	23.6	2.5
M	3.5	6.6	18.1	23.7	15.9	2.2
N	1.7	5.2	10.3	12.0	11.9	2.8
S95.1	–	7.1	23.9	31.7	16.9	3.6

Notes: "AI" refers to the proportion of firms using at least one of the following Artificial Intelligence technologies: text mining, speech recognition, natural language generation, image recognition, machine learning, robotic process automation, and autonomous machines. "CC" represents the proportion of enterprises that purchased cloud computing services over the internet. "IoT" indicates the proportion of enterprises using interconnected devices or systems that can be monitored or remotely controlled via the internet (internet of things). "Robotics" shows the proportion of enterprises that employed industrial or service robots.

rates around 6–7%, indicating they are at the initial phases of embracing AI technologies. These can be compared to the EU averages of 6.8% and 8.8% in the sectors C and D-E, respectively. The Construction industry (F), along with several service industries such as Wholesale and Retail, Accommodation and Food, Real Estate, and Administrative Support Services are at their infancy in Türkiye with AI adoption rates of 3–4%, which are slightly below the EU averages.

Cloud Computing

Cloud Computing (CC) offers businesses a model to access, process, and store data over the internet rather than on in-house systems. Whether utilized as infrastructure, platform, or software, CC offers numerous advantages, including scalability, cost-efficiency, flexibility, and improved collaboration. In this analysis, CC adoption is defined by the percentage of enterprises that procured cloud services over the internet.

As can be seen in Table 6.3, in 2023, CC adoption rates are 13.7% for small firms, 26.6% for medium-sized firms, and 48.2% for large firms in Türkiye. A comparison with EU benchmarks (see Figure 6.10), shows the

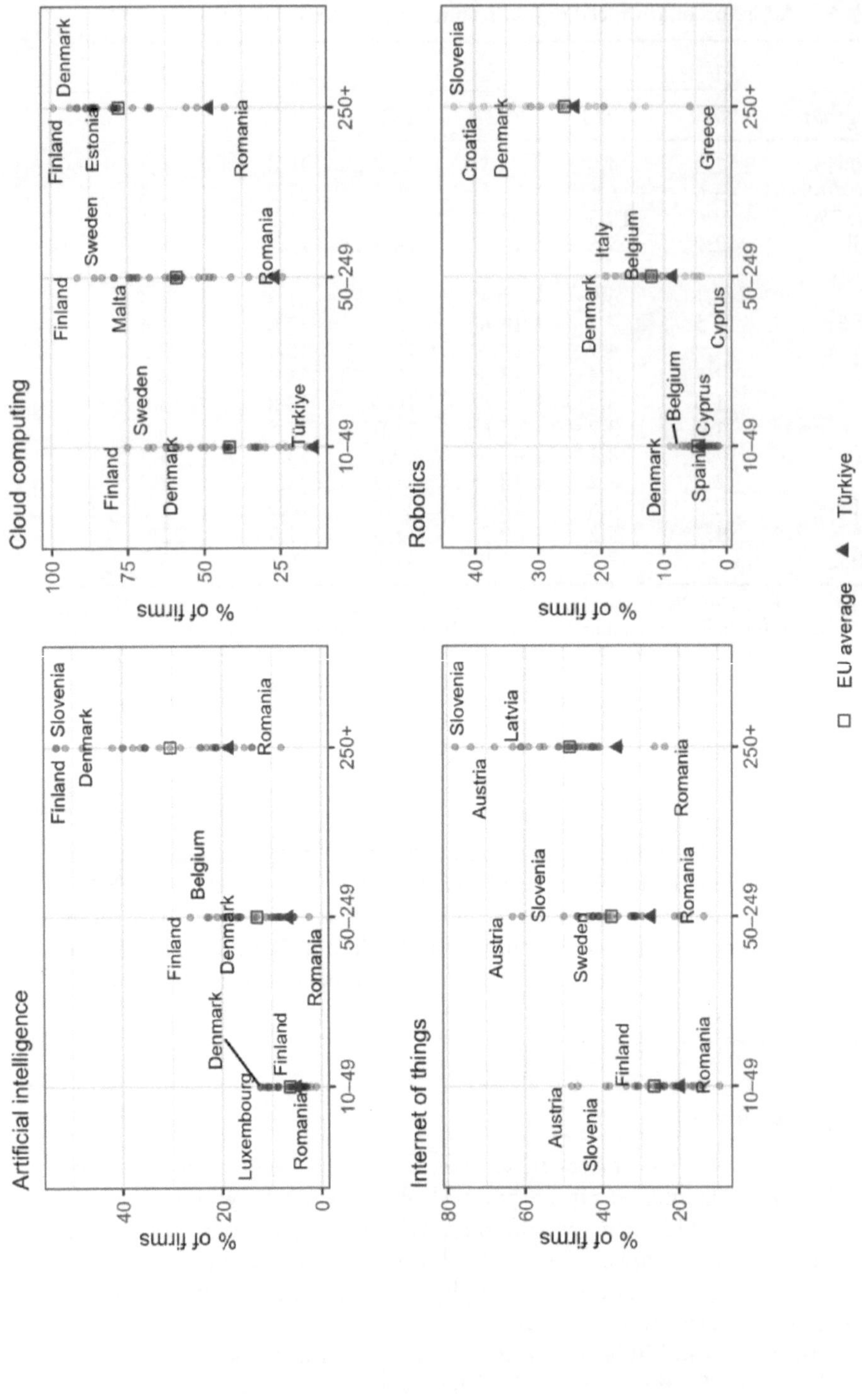

Figure 6.10 Adoption of artificial intelligence (AI), cloud computing (CC), internet of things (IoT), and robotics across size groups.

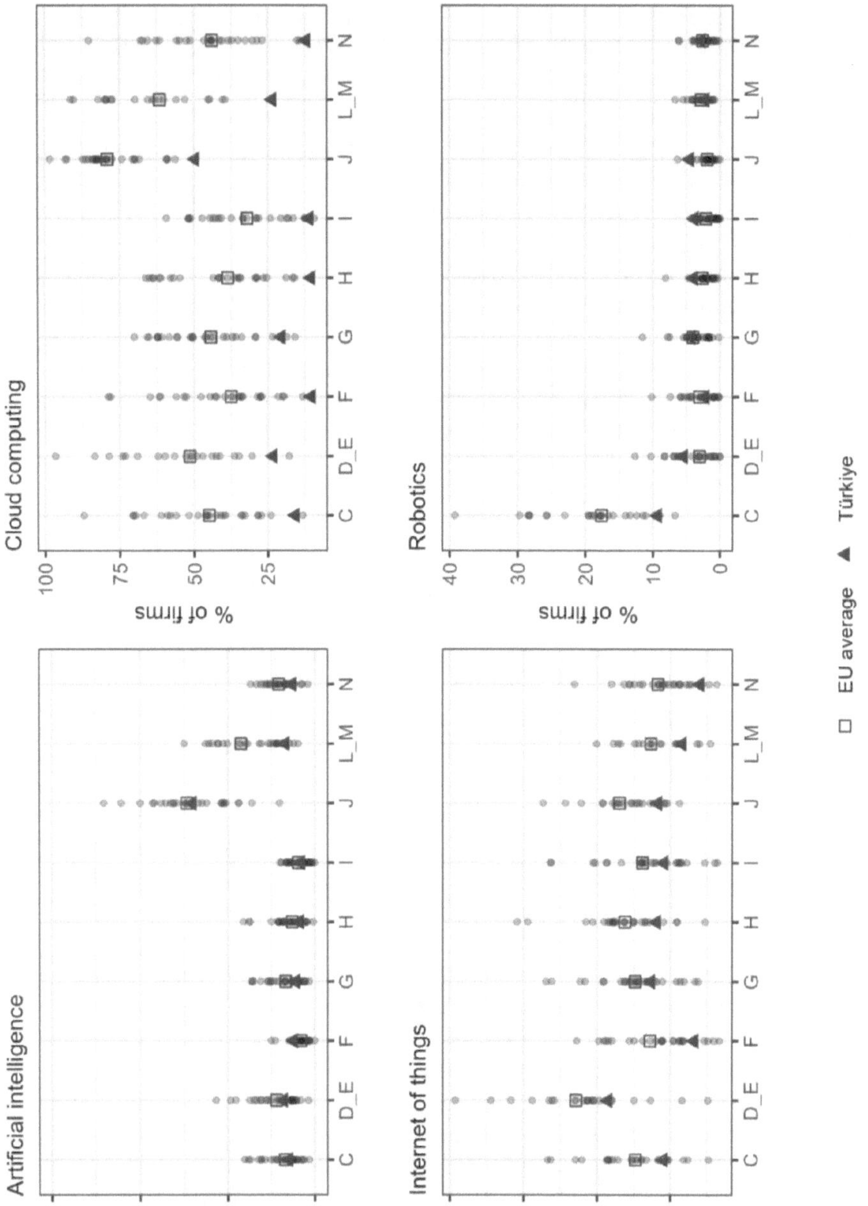

Figure 6.11 Adoption of advanced ICT across industries in EU and Türkiye.

Notes: NACE Rev.2 main sectors are on the horizontal axis; each dot represents a country.

adoption averages at 41.7%, 59%, and 77.6% for small, medium, and large firms, respectively. Sweden, Finland, and the Netherlands lead in small firms while Türkiye has one of the lowest CC adoption rates. In the medium-size category, Türkiye aligns with Bulgaria and Estonia and only surpasses Romania while countries such as Finland and Sweden are at the top. Similarly, large firms still lag significantly behind the EU average.

Industry-wise analysis indicates that the ICT sector (J) stands out with a 49.6% adoption rate in Türkiye but still far below the EU average of 79%. Real Estate (L) and Professional Activities (M) sectors also show a strong inclination toward CC with adoption rates of about 21.9%. The Electricity and Water Utilities (D-E) and the Wholesale and Retail sectors (G) also display adoption rates of about 23.3% and 20.5%, respectively. The remaining sectors, including the Manufacturing (C), Construction (F), Accommodation and Food (H), and Administrative Support Services (N), show varying degrees of adoption, ranging from 10% to 16%.

Internet of Things

The Internet of Things (IoT) connects physical devices, vehicles, appliances, and other items with embedded electronics, software, sensors, and connectivity, enabling these objects to interact, collect, and exchange data. IoT adoption is measured by the proportion of enterprises employing interconnected devices or systems that can be monitored or remotely controlled via the internet.[6] As can be seen in Table 6.3, large firms are at the forefront of IoT adoption with a 35.9% reported usage in 2021. Medium-sized and small firms have 27.2% and 19.6% adoption rates, respectively. The EU averages for comparison are approximately 26.5%, 37.5%, and 48.4% for small, medium, and large firms, respectively. Turkish firms align with France, Portugal, and Hungary in IoT adoption and surpass the Netherlands, Denmark, Bulgaria, and Poland.

When focusing on the IoT adoption across the main sectors, Türkiye offers a mixed picture of technological integration. In the Manufacturing sector (C), IoT usage in Türkiye hovers around the 22% mark, placing it above countries like the Netherlands, Bulgaria, and France but still below the EU average of about 30%. The Electricity and Water Utilities sector (D-E) emerges as a standout, registering a substantial 37.0% adoption rate but below the EU27 average of 45.7%. The Wholesale and Retail sector (G) follows closely with a 25.4% adoption rate, comparable to several EU nations such as France, Belgium, and Hungary, though it trails behind the EU average of about 30%. Interestingly, while being an early adopter in various technologies, the ICT sector (J) has a 23.5% IoT adoption rate, which is below the EU average of 34%. Services sectors including the Accommodation and Food (H), the Real Estate (L), and the Administrative Support Services (N) demonstrate varied adoption rates, hovering between 11% and 24%.

Robotic Systems

Robotic systems, traditionally associated with manufacturing and heavy industries, have started to permeate various sectors as technological advancements render robots more versatile, intelligent, and affordable. From robotic arms in assembly lines to service robots in hospitality, this technology promises improved efficiency, quality, and sometimes even entirely new ways of conducting business.

In this analysis, we focus on the proportion of enterprises employing industrial or service robots as of 2022.[7] As summarized in Table 6.3, for Türkiye, robotic system utilization registers at 4.1% for small firms, 8.6% for medium-sized firms, and 24.1% for large firms. These can be compared to EU averages 4.6%, 12.0%, and 25.8% for respective size groups. Still lagging slightly behind, Türkiye is close the EU averages especially for large and small firms.

Industry-level adoption rates indicate that the Manufacturing sector (C) has a 9.3% adoption rate, trailing the EU average at 18%. Surprisingly, the ICT sector (J), traditionally not a heavy user of robotics, reports an adoption rate of 4.5%, notably higher than the EU's 2% average. The Electricity and Water Utilities (D-E), while not typically associated with robotics, records a 5.4% adoption rate, surpassing the EU average of 3.0%. Other sectors, such as Wholesale and Retail (G), Real Estate (L), and Professional Activities (M), display adoption rates ranging from 2.2% to 4.3%. These figures are either close to or larger than the EU benchmark, which may be an indication of the expanding boundaries of robotic applications beyond traditional domains.

Summary and Discussion

The analysis of internet connectivity metrics across three crucial dimensions – adoption rate, speed categories, and depth of usage – reveals diverse levels of internet engagement among firms in Türkiye. Internet access, whether via broadband or mobile, is widespread among firms across all sectors and sizes with near-universal adoption. Despite this, significant variations exist in terms of speed and depth of internet usage within firms.

While there has been an increasing trend in the proportion of firms that have shifted to high-speed broadband, some disparities still persist compared to the EU countries across all firm sizes and industries. Smaller firms predominantly opt for slower connections, while larger enterprises are more inclined toward high-speed and ultrafast options. The data suggests the presence of potential barriers or challenges, particularly for SMEs. The adoption of ultra-fast internet is on the rise across all firm sizes in the EU, with larger firms experiencing faster growth. However, Turkish SMEs do not show a similar pattern; instead, their adoption of ultra-fast internet appears to remain stagnant. Also, we observe that adoption rates for small firms align closely with the EU27 average, but the disparity becomes more pronounced for medium- and large-sized firms. This suggests that larger Turkish enterprises encounter more substantial challenges or find fewer incentives to adopt ultrafast broadband compared to their European counterparts.

The intensity of internet usage within firms also displays a notable spectrum, with a trend toward increased internet utilization among employees across all sectors. Following the global pandemic, there has been a clear surge in the intensity of internet connectivity within firms, as measured by the percentage of internet-using employees, converging toward the EU average. This suggests a growing reliance on digital connectivity for business operations and a potential shift toward more internet-intensive business models.

Findings suggest that Türkiye's e-commerce landscape has experienced consistent growth. While small enterprises have shown rapid adaptability, aligning closely with the EU average by 2023, disparities continue among medium and large firms. Leading sectors in e-commerce adoption include accommodation and food services, ICT, and wholesale and retail trade sectors. Notably, post-2020, there was a significant rise in e-commerce adoption in all sectors, including the manufacturing industry. This positive trend not only matched the EU average but even surpassed it in certain service sectors.

Enterprise software solutions, especially ERP, have been increasingly adopted by firms in Türkiye. While SMEs have embraced these technologies, their adoption rates still lag behind the EU average. This difference is evident across all sectors, but it is especially pronounced in the manufacturing sector, where the productivity benefits of ERP are highly anticipated. The data also suggests that as companies scale, the adoption of CRM and BI tools increases, possibly driven by a larger customer base, vast datasets to manage, and the complexities associated with it. Overall, the BI adoption rates across various industries and firm sizes indicate a growing awareness and need for data-driven decision-making.

Türkiye's engagement with advanced ICT technologies shows a varied picture in comparison to the EU. AI adoption, while increasing across all sizes and sectors, remains slightly below the EU average, indicating a potential area for growth and deeper integration. Small firms in Türkiye, though in the early stages, are relatively more agile in embracing AI. As expected, larger firms tend to be at the forefront of AI adoption in all countries. The multitude of resources available to them, in terms of both finance and expertise, likely aids in exploring and implementing various AI technologies. While Turkish firms lag behind the EU average, the gap becomes more pronounced in larger firms compared to smaller ones. According to the 2023 survey, among Turkish enterprises that did not use any of the AI technologies, 60.7% complain about high costs, 53.8% about the lack of expertise, 50% about incompatibility with existing equipment and software systems, and 40% about difficulties with the availability and quality of data (Turkstat, 2023).

Cloud computing adoption displays a noticeable disparity among all sizes and sectors compared to their EU counterparts. The widespread use of CC in the EU, across many sectors from manufacturing to services, indicates its established benefits and reliability. Findings indicate that larger firms tend to be more willing to incorporate CC solutions while small firms are more reluctant to adopt it. The reasons behind Türkiye's lower adoption rates warrant further exploration. These factors may include infrastructural constraints, regulatory complexities, or cultural considerations unique to the Turkish business environment.

Türkiye's engagement indicates that while there is a general acknowledgment of IoT's potential, its incorporation largely depends on sector-specific needs, challenges, and perceived immediate benefits. Overall, Türkiye's IoT adoption displays potential and competitiveness in certain sectors, yet there is room for further growth and alignment with the EU. Türkiye's adoption rates in robotic system integration are close to the EU averages across all firm sizes. Industry-wise, while the manufacturing sector is behind the EU average, service sectors such as ICT surpass it, signaling Türkiye's proficiency in adopting robotic technologies in specific industries.

Conclusion

This chapter examines the dynamics of ICT adoption across different industries and firm sizes, with a spotlight on Türkiye's stance vis-à-vis the EU. Despite Türkiye's overall progress in ICT adoption, this chapter uncovers distinct challenges in specific areas, emphasizing the critical need for targeted policy interventions. In particular, the significant gap in high-speed and ultrafast internet adoption between firms in Türkiye and the EU indicates the necessity for substantial improvements in internet infrastructure.

To enhance e-commerce in Türkiye, policies should primarily concentrate on improving digital infrastructure, particularly for medium and large enterprises that are lagging in e-commerce adoption. Initiating training and support programs can also help develop digital and e-commerce skills among these firms. Furthermore, introducing incentives for e-commerce adoption, especially for traditional businesses, could accelerate their digital transition.

Regarding enterprise software adoption, findings suggest that although SMEs are increasingly integrating these technologies, there is still a significant adoption gap compared to the EU, especially in the manufacturing sector. While it is relatively challenging to bolster the adoption of these technologies, policy recommendations could include the development of training and capacity-building programs, focusing on digital literacy and the strategic use of enterprise software, as well as financial incentives or subsidies for SMEs to adopt these systems.

Türkiye's progress in IoT and robotics adoption is noteworthy and promising. However, the disparities in AI and Cloud Computing adoption suggest a need for a multifaceted approach involving policy initiatives, industry collaboration, and educational efforts. Policymakers may consider implementing financial support mechanisms, such as tax breaks, grants, or subsidies, aimed at alleviating the initial costs associated with adopting advanced technologies.

Additionally, fostering partnerships between academia, industry, and government in research and development efforts can drive technological innovation and competitiveness. Overcoming regulatory hurdles and ensuring equitable access to resources will be essential in this endeavor. Moreover, establishing programs to enhance AI-related skills across the workforce is crucial. Collaborations between educational institutions, businesses, and government agencies can facilitate the provision of training, workshops, and certifications in AI and other advanced technologies. Given their economic impact, SMEs should be prioritized for tailored assistance, including grants, training, and policy incentives. Such measures could help SMEs leverage these technologies for innovation and competitiveness, bringing Türkiye's technological capabilities more closely in line with EU standards and enhancing its position in the global technological landscape.

Notes

1 Until the early/mid-1990s, it was far from evident just how much computers, or ICTs in general, had contributed to overall productivity. This phenomenon, commonly referred to as the "Solow paradox" or the "productivity paradox," presented a perplexing situation where one could observe "computers everywhere but not in the productivity statistics" (Solow, 1987). The inability to discern the impact of ICT on productivity is commonly ascribed to measurement challenges. Productivity growth in the United States, particularly since the second half of the 1990s, has been attributed largely to increased levels of ICT investment, their efficient use, and different ICT-related management practices of firms compared to their European counterparts (Jorgenson et al., 2008; Bloom et al., 2008).

2 For comprehensive reviews of this extant literature, we refer to Stiroh (2005), Polak (2017), and Cardona et al. (2013), and Stanley et al. (2018) and Vu et al. (2020) for a macroeconomic perspective.

3 Among others, these studies include Commander et al. (2011) for India and Brazil, Gutierrez (2011) for Colombia, Charlo (2011) for Uruguay, Calza and Rovira (2011) and Brambilla and Tortarolo (2018) for Argentina, Iacovone et al. (2016) for Mexico, and Viollaz (2019) for Peru. More recently, by exploiting the gradual arrival of fast internet in a sample of African countries, Hjort and Poulsen (2019) show that easier and cheaper access to ICT significantly increases both employment and firm productivity.

4 ICT surveys exclude agriculture, financial and insurance services (K), public administration and defense (O), education (P), health and social work (Q), and arts and entertainment (R).

5 Within the context of the broader "Digital Türkiye" vision, the National Artificial Intelligence Strategy was formulated with the goal of fostering an agile and sustainable AI ecosystem. The strategy explicitly aspires to "create value on a global scale for a prosperous Türkiye," emphasizing the nation's commitment to leveraging AI for both national development and global contributions (NAIS, 2021).

6 According to the model survey of Eurostat, examples of IoT include smart-meters, thermostats, lamps, alarm systems, smoke detectors, door locks, cameras, sensors, RFID tags that can be managed via the internet. It excludes plain detection and sensors that cannot be remotely controlled and monitored over the internet.

7 The Eurostat ICT survey defines an industrial robot as "an automatically controlled, reprogrammable, multipurpose manipulator programmable in three or more axes, which may be either fixed in place or mobile for use." This definition

excludes CNC-machines, 3D printers, and devices that are controlled by an operator. Examples of industrial robots include robotic welding, laser cutting, and spray painting. A service robot has a degree of autonomy and can operate in complex and dynamic environments that may require interaction with persons, objects, or other devices. Examples are autonomous guided vehicles, inspection and maintenance robots, and cleaning robots (Eurostat, 2022).

References

Akerman, A., Gaarder, I., & Mogstad, M. (2015). The skill complementarity of broadband internet. *Quarterly Journal of Economics*, *130*(4), 1781–1824. https://doi.org/10.1093/qje/qjv028

Andrews, D., Nicoletti, G., & Timiliotis, C. (2018). Digital technology diffusion: A matter of capabilities, incentives or both? *OECD Economics Department Working Papers*, No. 1476, OECD Publishing, Paris. https://doi.org/10.1787/7c542c16-en

Aral, S., Brynjolfsson, E., & Wu, D. J. (2006). *Which came first, IT or productivity? The virtuous cycle of investment and use in enterprise systems*. In Proceedings of the 27th Annual International Conference on Information Systems, Milwaukee, Wisconsin.

Atasoy, N., Banker, R. D., & Pavlou, P. A. (2016). On the longitudinal effects of IT use on firm-level employment. *Information System Research*, *27*(1), 6–26.

Battisti, G., Hollenstein, H., Stoneman, P., & Woerter, M. (2007). Inter- and intra-firm diffusion of ICT in the United Kingdom (UK) and Switzerland (CH): An internationally comparative study based on firm-level data. *Economics of Innovation and New Technology*, *16*, 669–687.

Battisti, G., & Stoneman, P. (2003). Inter-firm and intra-firm effects in the diffusion of new process technologies. *Research Policy*, *32*, 1641–1655.

Battisti, G., & Stoneman, P. (2005) The intra-firm diffusion of new process technology. *International Journal of Industrial Organization*, *23*, 1–22.

Bloom, N., Sadun, R., & Reenen, J. V. (2012). Americans do IT better: US multinationals and the productivity miracle. *American Economic Review*, *102*(1), 167–201. https://doi.org/10.1257/aer.102.1.167

Brambilla, I., & Tortarolo, D. (2018). Investment in ICT, productivity and labor demand: The case of Argentina. *World Bank Policy Research Working*, Paper No. 8325.

Bresnahan, T. F., Brynjolfsson, E., & Hitt, L. M. (2002). Information technology, workplace organization, and the demand for skilled labor: Firm-level evidence. *Quarterly Journal of Economics*, *117*(1), 339–376. www.jstor.org/stable/2696490

Bresnahan, T. F., & Trajtenberg, M. (1995). General purpose technologies "Engines of growth"? *Journal of Econometrics*, *65*(1), 83–108. https://doi.org/10.1016/0304-4076(94)01598-t

Brynjolfsson, E. (1993). The productivity paradox of information technology: Review and assessment. *Communications of the ACM*, *36*(12), 67–77.

Brynjolfsson, E, & Hitt, L. M. (1996). Paradox lost? Firm-level evidence on the returns to information systems spending. *Management Science*, *42*(4), 541–558.

Brynjolfsson, E., & Hitt, L. M. (2000). Beyond computation: Information technology, organizational transformation and business performance. *Journal of Economic Perspectives*, *14*(4), 23–48. www.jstor.org/stable/2647074

Brynjolfsson, E., Hitt, L. M., & Kim, H., H. (2011). Strength in numbers: How does data-driven decisionmaking affect firm performance? *SSRN Working Paper*. http://doi.org/10.2139/ssrn.1819486

Brynjolfsson, E., & McElheran, K. (2016). Data in action: Data-driven decision making in U.S. manufacturing. *Center for Economic Studies Working Paper*, No. 16–06.

Brynjolfsson, E., Rock, D., & Syverson, C. (2021). The productivity J-curve: How intangibles complement general purpose technologies. *American Economic Journal: Macroeconomics*, *13*(1), 333–372.

Calza, E., & Rovira, S. (2011). ICT, organizational change and firm performance: Evidence from Argentina. In M. Balboni, S. Rovira, & S. Vergara (Eds.), *ICT in Latin America: A microdata analysis*. Santiago, Chile: ECLAC (Economic Commission for Latin America and the Caribbean).

Cardona, M., Kretschmer, T., & Strobel, T. (2013). ICT and productivity: Conclusions from the empirical literature. *Information Economics & Policy*, *25*(3), 109–125.

Charlo, G. (2011). Impact of ICT and innovation on industrial productivity in Uruguay. In M. Balboni, S. Rovira, & S. Vergara (Eds.), *ICT in Latin America: A microdata analysis*. Santiago, Chile: ECLAC (Economic Commission for Latin America and the Caribbean).

Commander, S., Harrison, R., & Menezes-Filho, N. (2011). ICT and productivity in developing countries: New firm-level evidence from Brazil and India. *Review of Economics and Statistics*, *93*(2), 528–541.

Engelstätter, B., & Sarbu, M. (2013). Does enterprise software matter for service innovation? Standardization versus customization. *Economics of Innovation and New Technology*, *22*(4), 412–429.

Eurostat. (2022). *Eurostat model questionnaire for the community survey on ICT usage and e-commerce in enterprises*. Retrieved October 1, 2023, from https://ec.europa.eu/eurostat/cache/metadata/en/isoc_e_esms.htm

Eurostat. (2023). *Reference metadata for ICT usage in enterprises*. Retrieved October 1, 2023, from https://ec.europa.eu/eurostat/cache/metadata/en/isoc_e_esms.htm

Findik, D., & Tansel, A. (2015). Resources on the stage: A firm level analysis of the ICT adoption in Turkey. *TEK Working Paper*, No 2015/12. Retrieved August 24, 2023, from www.tek.org.tr/pdf/286_9122022_181109.pdf

Gal, P., Nicoletti, G., Renault, T., Sorbe, S., & Timiliotis, C. (2019). Digitalisation and productivity: In search of the holy grail – Firm-level empirical evidence from EU countries. *OECD Economics Department Working Papers*, No. 1533, OECD Publishing, Paris. http://doi.org/10.1787/5080f4b6-en

Gallego, J. M., Gutierrez, L. H., & Lee, S. E. (2014). A firm-level analysis of ICT adoption in an emerging economy: Evidence from the Colombian manufacturing industries. *Industrial and Corporate Change*, *24*(1), 191–221.

Geroski, P. A. (2000). Models of technology diffusion. *Research Policy*, *29*, 603–625.

Gutierrez, L. H. (2011). ICT and labor productivity in Colombian manufacturing industry. In M. Balboni, S. Rovira, & S. Vergara (Eds.), *ICT in Latin America: A microdata analysis*. Santiago, Chile: ECLAC (Economic Commission for Latin America and the Caribbean).

Haller, A. S., & Siedschlag, I. (2011). Determinants of ICT adoption: Evidence from firm-level data. *Applied Economics*, *43*(26), 3775–3788.

Hitt, L. M., Wu, D. J., & Zhou, X. (2002). Investment in enterprise resource planning: Business impact and productivity measures. *Journal of Management Information Systems*, *19*(1), 71–98. http://doi.org/10.1080/07421222.2002.11045716

Hjort, J., & Poulsen, J. (2019). The arrival of fast internet and employment in Africa. *American Economic Review*, *109*(3), 1032–1079.

Hollenstein, H. (2004). Determinants of the adoption of Information and Communication Technologies (ICT): An empirical analysis based on firm-level data for the Swiss business sector. *Structural Change and Economic Dynamics*, *15*, 315–342.

Iacovone, L., Perreira-Lopez, M., & Schiffbauer, M. (2016). Competition makes IT better: Evidence on when firms use IT more effectively. *World Bank Policy Research Working Paper*, No. 7638.

Jorgenson, D. W., Ho, M. S., & Stiroh, K. J. (2008). A retrospective look at the U.S. productivity growth resurgence. *Journal of Economic Perspectives*, *22*(1), 3–24. www.jstor.org/stable/27648221
Jovanovic, B., & Rousseau, P. L. (2005). General purpose technologies. In P. Aghion & S. N. Durlauf (Eds.) (pp. 1181–1224). Elsevier. https://doi.org/10.1016/s1574-0684(05)01018-x
Karshenas, M., & Stoneman, P. (1995). Technological diffusion. In P. Stoneman (Ed.), *Handbook of the economics of innovation and technological change* (pp. 265–297). Oxford: Blackwell.
Kılıçaslan, Y., Sickles, R. C., Atay Kayış, A., & Üçdoğruk Gürel, Y. (2017). Impact of ICT on the productivity of the firm: Evidence from Turkish manufacturing. *Journal of Productivity Analysis*, *47*, 277–289. https://doi.org/10.1007/s11123-017-0497-3
Milgrom, P., & Roberts, J. (1990). The economics of modern manufacturing technology, strategy and organization. *American Economic Review*, *80*(3), 511–528.
NAIS. (2021). *National artificial intelligence strategy 2021–2025, republic of Türkiye, ministry of industry and technology, digital transformation office*. Retrieved October 1, 2023, from https://cbddo.gov.tr/en/nais
Polak, P. (2017). The productivity-paradox: A meta-analysis. *Information Economics & Policy*, *38*, 38–54.
Relich, M. (2017). The impact of ICT on labor productivity in the EU. *Information Technology for Development*, *23*(4), 706–722.
Solow, R. M. (1987, July 12). We'd better watch out. *New York times book review*. (p. 36).
Stanley, T. D., Doucouliagos, H., & Steel, P. (2018). Does ICT generate economic growth? A meta-regression analysis. *Journal of Economic Surveys*, *32*, 705–726. https://doi.org/10.1111/joes.12211
Stiroh, K. J. (2005). Reassessing the impact of IT in the production function: A meta-analysis and sensitivity tests. *Annales d'Économie et de Statistique*, *79/80*, 529–561. https://doi.org/10.2307/20777587
Stoneman, P., & Battisti, G. (2010). The diffusion of new technology. In B. H. Hall & N. Rosenberg (Eds.), *Handbook of the Economics of Innovation* (Vol. 2, pp. 733–760). North-Holland: Elsevier. https://doi.org/10.1016/s0169-7218(10)02001-0
Taştan, H. (2021). Firmaların Bilişim Teknolojisi Kullanımı ve Verimlilik İlişkisi. In O. Kent et al. (Eds.), *Türkiye Ekonomisinde Büyüme Kalkınma ve Eşitsizlik – A.* Suut Doğruel'e Armağan: Efil Yayınları.
Taştan, H., & Gönel, F. (2020). ICT labor, software usage, and productivity: Firm-level evidence from Turkey. *Journal of Productivity Analysis*, *53*(2), 265–285.
Turkstat. (2023). *Survey on Information and Communication Technology (ICT) usage in enterprises micro data set (Girişimlerde Bilişim Teknolojileri Kullanım Araştırması)*. Turkish Statistical Institute. https://data.tuik.gov.tr/Bulten/Index?p=Girisimlerde-Bilisim-Teknolojileri-Kullanim-Arastirmasi-2023-49393
Viollaz, M. (2019). Information and communication technology adoption in micro and small firms: Can internet access improve labour productivity? *Development Policy Review*, *37*, 692–715. https://doi.org/10.1111/dpr.12373
Vu, K., Hanafizadeh, P., & Bohlin, E. (2020). ICT as a driver of economic growth: A survey of the literature and directions for future research. *Telecommunications Policy*, *44*(2), 101922. https://doi.org/10.1016/j.telpol.2020.101922

7 Digitalization of society – Türkiye Digital Society Index

Emin Köksal and Ozan Bakış

Introduction

Türkiye took a major step toward digitalization via the deployment of fixed broadband internet by the early 2000s. With the introduction of third-generation (3G) mobile technologies in 2009, the digitalization opportunities for society went one step further. In the following years, with the deployment of fiber access in fixed broadband and fourth-generation (4G) technologies in mobile, Turkish society began to carry out various activities over the internet. With the COVID-19 pandemic, developments in digitalization accelerated, and many services – from shopping to entertainment, from education to health – have been provided digitally.

In this chapter, we try to find answers to the following questions: how can we measure the progress of Turkish society, which has been familiar with information communication technologies (ICT) for more than 20 years? How has society performed in terms of access to the internet, activities carried out on the internet, and digital public services? Is there any difference in digitalization performance by geographical regions? Is there any difference in terms of gender and age groups regarding digitalization? Do individuals at different education levels follow different paths in digitalization? How much has digitalization progressed during the COVID-19 pandemic?

To seek answers to such questions, we proposed the Türkiye Digital Society Index (TDSI).[1] We design the TDSI as a composite index that aims to measure and monitor the digitalization of households. To the best of our knowledge, it is the most comprehensive index designed for Türkiye so far. The TDSI has a structure that allows us to assess Türkiye's progress, at various demographic and regional breakdowns, toward a digital society, in three basic categories (connectivity, use of the internet, and digital public services).

The plan of the chapter is as follows. The second section reviews sources related to measuring the digitalization of society. The third section introduces the structure and data source of the TDSI. The fourth section evaluates the index results. The fifth section analyses the disparities in the digitalization performance in gender, age, and education level. The final section concludes the discussion.

DOI: 10.4324/9781032692937-7

Measuring digitalization of society

Before designing the TDSI, we reviewed the sources published in this field and searched for datasets that could measure digitalization in Türkiye. Several institutions and organizations have developed proposals for digitalization measurement based on many indicators (see ITU, 2003, 2016; UNCTAD, 2006). We found the Digital Economy and Society Index (DESI), which measures EU countries' progress toward a digital economy and society, to be an inspiring work for the design and structure of the TDSI.

The DESI was introduced in 2014, and its framework has been updated regularly (European Commission, 2023). It combines a relevant number of indicators (37 in total) classified into five categories and 12 sub-categories for the EU countries. The five categories that put the characteristics of the DESI are as follows: (1) Connectivity considers the evolution of ICT, by including indicators related to mobile and fixed broadband coverage, take-up, and price indexes. (2) Human Capital essentially focuses on users' skills, distinguishing between basic and advanced competencies. (3) The Use of Internet Services, traditionally referred to the internet usage in practice, included types of activities and transactions. (4) Integration of Digital Technology accounts for the digital transformation of businesses. Finally, (5) Digital Public Services evaluates digital penetration in public administrations such as the number of actual digital services users and the availability of digital services for business.

The TDSI has similarities and differences from DESI in terms of its scope and design. First of all, the DESI evaluates and compares digitalization in EU member countries, but the TDSI is constructed only for Türkiye. Therefore, the TDSI scores cannot be directly compared with other countries. At first sight, it looks like a disadvantage. However, a Türkiye-specific index allows us to design a more comprehensive measurement with more detail. Using the data source at its maximum, we can calculate the index scores at demographic and geographical breakdowns, which do not exist in the DESI. In addition, focusing on Türkiye allows us to widen the coverage. While the DESI started from the year 2014, the TDSI's coverage started in 2004. Another remarkable difference from the DESI is in the coverage of categories. The TDSI does not include any indicator related to the digitalization level of businesses. It aims to measure and monitor the level of digitalization of households or society. It is also worth noting that the TDSI does not directly consider the human capital category that reflects the skills of ICT users.

Another related study we came across is *Türkiye's Digital Transformation Index*, conducted by TÜBİSAD Informatics Industry Association with a series of reports (TÜBİSAD, 2020, 2021b, 2022). These reports provide index scores based on the indicators related to legislation, infrastructure, usage, skills, and economic and social impact dimensions of digital transformation. The index study is based on surveys with professionals in the IT sector, national and international statistics, and administrative data. Unlike the

TDSI, the TÜBİSAD's index has a macro perspective and uses indicators such as the share of research and development expenditure in national income, nature of legal processes, and ease of doing business in the ICT sector in Türkiye. In fact, TÜBİSAD's index is an informative study in its field. However, the digitalization of society is included in a limited way and over macro-level data. In this regard, the potential for comparison with the TDSI is limited.

The data and the structure of the TDSI

Before evaluating the TDSI scores, in this section, we present the data that we use and then introduce the structure and the methodology of the TDSI.

The data source of the TDSI

The TDSI's main data source is TURKSTAT's Household Information Technologies Usage Survey (HITUS).[2] The survey has been conducted each year since 2004 (except 2006) and aims to obtain data about the ICT that households and individuals have and use.

Data included in the HITUS is in the following areas:

- Available ICT in households
- Access and use of ICT by individuals and/or households
- Use of the internet and other electronic networks for different purposes by individuals and/or households
- Obstacles to the use of ICT and the internet
- Use of e-commerce
- Use of e-government applications
- Awareness of ICT security

The survey has been carried out in April each year over a representative sample determined by TURKSTAT. Although demographic information (age, gender) is included for all members of households, questions regarding education level, labor force status, and use of ICT are asked only of individuals between the ages of 16 and 74.

As of 2011, the survey sample has also become representative at the regional level with the Nomenclature of Territorial Units for Statistics – Level 1 (NUTS 1). Although it varies from year to year, the survey has been conducted with an average of more than 10,000 households and nearly 30,000 individuals. In this respect, it has the most representative sample for Türkiye and has the largest coverage of time. It is worth noting that although we have access to the survey in 2022, we do not use it. The survey questions – especially in the connectivity category – are revised by TURKSTAT. And, this revision creates inconsistency in TDSI scores. Therefore, we calculate the TDSI scores till 2021. Sample information of the HITUS that we use for the TDSI is given in Table 7.1.

Table 7.1 Sample information of the HITUS used for the TDSI

Year	*Number of households*	*Number of individuals (aged 16–74)*	*Regional breakdown*
2004	9,571	24,462	rural/urban
2005	10,151	27,013	rural/urban
2007	4,533	12,289	rural/urban
2008	5,161	13,314	rural/urban
2009	4,773	12,524	rural/urban
2010	5,094	13,236	rural/urban
2011	10,235	26,355	NUTS 1–12 Region
2012	10,605	27,394	NUTS 1–12 Region
2013	11,620	29,577	NUTS 1–12 Region
2014	9,825	25,024	NUTS 1–12 Region
2015	9,847	24,798	NUTS 1–12 Region
2016	11,276	27,934	NUTS 1–12 Region
2017	12,781	31,961	NUTS 1–12 Region
2018	12,822	28,888	NUTS 1–12 Region
2019	12,956	31,666	NUTS 1–12 Region
2020	14,498	36,011	NUTS 1–12 Region
2021	13,660	30,530	NUTS 1–12 Region

Table 7.2 Structure of the TDSI

Main category	*Sub-category*
Connectivity	Internet connection technologies of households
	fixed internet
	mobile internet
Internet use	Digital activities on the internet
	communication
	social media
	knowledge
	entertainment
	e-banking
	e-commerce
Digital public services	Use of digital services (e-government)
	passive use (obtaining information, downloading form)
	active use (filling form, application)

The structure of the TDSI

Considering the scope of the HITUS and its evolution over time, the TDSI is designed to present the progress of Turkish society's digitalization performance at best possible. It is structured as a composite index, with 17 indicators in three main categories and ten sub-categories. A summary of its structure can be seen in Table 7.2. We also provide the list of indicators and the calculation methodology in the Appendix Table 7.A.

TDSI scores consist of the contribution of the values calculated for the main and sub-categories with certain weights (see Appendix). Therefore, the TDSI scores for each category (main or sub) are not only comparable over time, but also we can monitor the digitalization performance at the category level.

Moreover, thanks to the representation of the HITUS at the NUTS 1 level, we are able to calculate the index scores for 12 different regions since 2011. Thus, we calculate digitalization performance at the regional level and assess inter-regional differences.

In addition, since HITUS is a micro dataset – that contains information at the individual level – it allows us to calculate index scores by gender, age group, and education level. Thus, we monitor the digitalization process of Turkish society with demographic variables.

Türkiye Digital Society Index (2004–2021)

With the TDSI two main types of analysis are possible: (1) a general performance assessment and (2) zooming in to developments in each category over time. In this section, we will explore these analyses.

The TDSI scores and the digitalization performance of Türkiye

The TDSI scores and contributions of the three main categories are shown in Table 7.3. As seen, households in Türkiye have made significant progress between 2004 and 2021. The TDSI score, which was 2.19 in 2004, has

Table 7.3 TDSI and development in main categories (2004–2021)

Year	*Connectivity*	*Use of internet*	*Digital public services*	*TDSI*
2004	0.41	1.26	0.51	**2.19**
2005	0.70	1.34	0.39	**2.43**
2007	2.81	3.76	0.64	**7.21**
2008	3.82	3.83	0.77	**8.42**
2009	4.46	5.03	0.71	**10.20**
2010	6.23	5.69	1.32	**13.23**
2011	6.86	5.60	1.55	**14.01**
2012	8.10	6.18	2.04	**16.32**
2013	8.84	7.36	1.88	**18.09**
2014	12.12	8.24	2.76	**23.12**
2015	15.30	9.11	3.09	**27.50**
2016	16.82	10.35	4.47	**31.64**
2017	17.84	12.35	5.83	**36.02**
2018	19.93	14.54	6.42	**40.89**
2019	21.64	15.53	6.93	**44.11**
2020	21.72	16.32	6.20	**44.24**
2021	23.54	18.48	7.43	**49.45**

increased to 49.45 in 2021. And in all three categories, the scores have continuously increased over time.

It is possible to take a closer look at the progress of the TDSI scores in Figure 7.1. In this figure, we explore three phases of development for Turkish society's digitalization. A ten-year take-off period between 2004 and 2013; a further rise in digitalization level from 2014 to 2019; and after a pause in 2020, an increase in digitalization during the COVID-19 pandemic.[3]

Also, we picture the contribution of each sub-category (connectivity, use of internet, and e-government) between 2004 and 2021 in Figure 7.2.

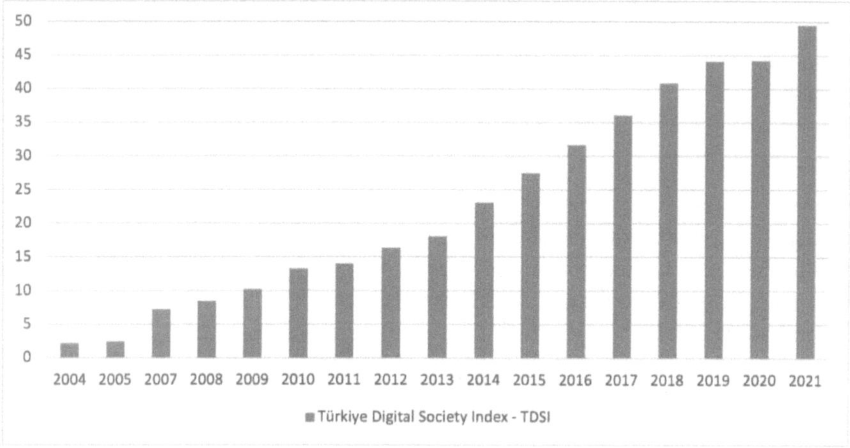

Figure 7.1 TDSI scores (2004–2022).

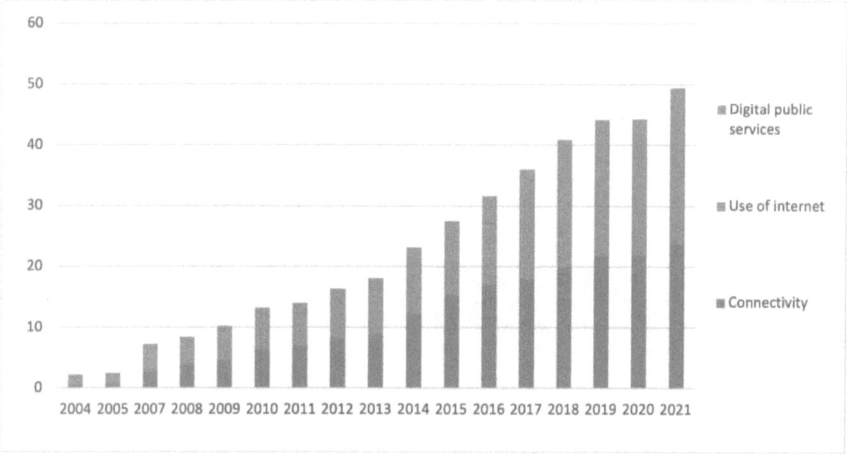

Figure 7.2 Contribution of main categories.

It is noteworthy that the contribution of each sub-category to the index has increased over the years, except for the use of digital public services in 2020.

When we evaluate Table 7.3 and Figure 7.1 together, we see that all three categories have contributed to the increase in the TDSI scores in the first period (between 2004 and 2013). In the period following 2014, an initial increase in connectivity, then a rise in the use of the internet, and especially an increase in the use of digital public services contributed to the TDSI scores. During the pandemic, all categories significantly contributed to the TDSI scores. In the following subsection, we zoom in on the development in each category.

Development in three main categories

Connectivity

Connectivity reflects the availability of households' fixed and/or mobile internet connections. The connectivity category in the TDSI considers both broadband and narrowband connections. However, considering the contribution to digitalization, we weighted more the broadband internet than the narrowband (see Appendix). Figure 7.3 shows the contribution of the connectivity category to the TDSI scores by connection technologies.

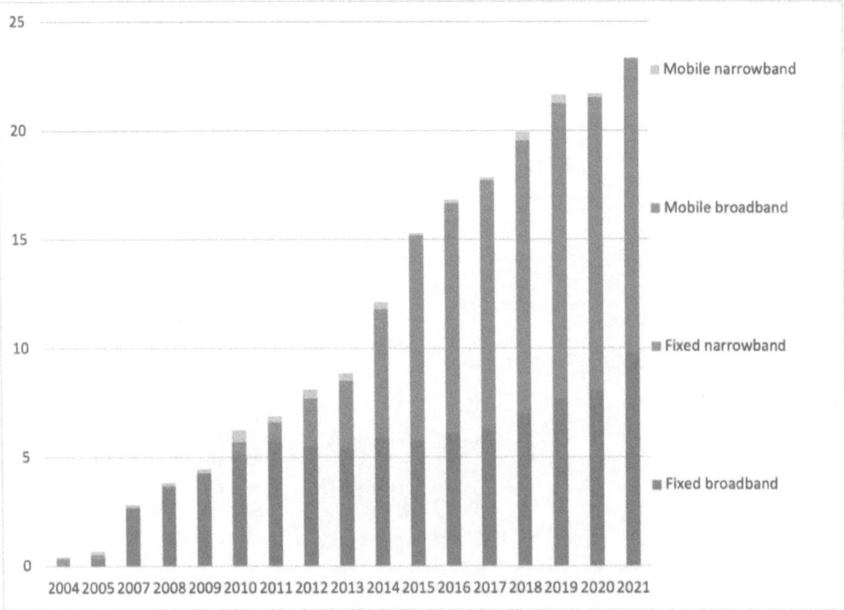

Figure 7.3 Development of connectivity dimension.

As seen in Figure 7.3, the increase in fixed broadband internet continued until 2011. After 2011, it decelerated till the 2021 COVID-19 pandemic. After 2011 a much larger contribution to the index scores has come from mobile broadband technology. It is worth noting that, third-generation (3G) mobile broadband technology was launched in 2009, and fourth-generation (4G) became available in 2016. The saturation of the increase in penetration of mobile broadband technologies started in 2019. During the COVID-19 pandemic, while the contribution of mobile broadband remains almost the same as the previous years, fixed broadband has increased. As expected, we can say that factors such as remote working and online education increase the demand for internet connection at home.

Use of internet

The use of the internet category consists of sub-categories that cover various activities carried out on the internet. The contribution of this category is shown in Figure 7.4 in detail. At first sight, households' activities have increased over time, but certain sub-categories have contributed more than others, such as e-commerce, e-banking, and social media.

E-commerce activity has followed a consistent increase over time. One can ask while the retail e-commerce volume has grown by double digits (see TÜBİSAD, 2021a), why e-commerce activities of households have increased relatively moderately. We would like to remind our readers that the e-commerce activity considered in the HITUS indicates whether individuals have purchased any products or services through the internet in the last three months, regardless of their e-shopping frequency of volume. This situation can be interpreted as a moderate increase in the number of individuals engaged in e-commerce, even though the volume of e-commerce has increased

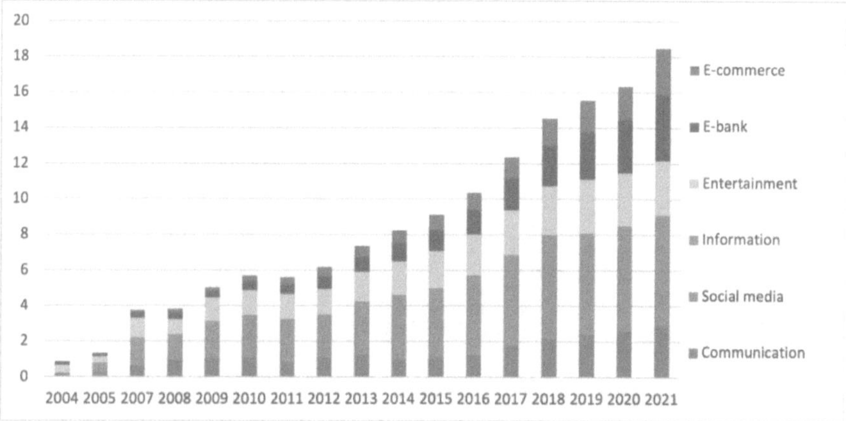

Figure 7.4 Development of the use of the internet.

rapidly. Nevertheless, in 2021, during the COVID-19 pandemic, the increase in e-commerce activity is greater than in the previous years.

E-banking, like e-commerce, also contributes to the index scores by a steady increase. Both the increase in accessibility in mobile applications of banks and developments in payment methods contribute to this field (see TÜBİSAD, 2021a). E-banking is an important part of digitalization as it is also an indicator of financial literacy (see Andreou & Anyfantaki, 2021). Again, during the COVID-19 epidemic, there was an extraordinary increase in e-banking, as in e-commerce.

In the TDSI, the information acquisition sub-category is designed as a combination of three activities: (1) searching for information about goods and services, (2) reading online news sources, and (3) searching for health-related information. Although information in many different fields can be accessed via the internet, the opportunity and ability of users to access this information is an important element in terms of digitalization (see van Deursen et al., 2016). As seen in Figure 7.4, the contribution of this sub-category has increased steadily over the years.

Social media use is another area that has increasingly contributed to the TDSI scores. We should note that while we created this sub-category for the years before 2012 – when today's social media platforms did not yet exist or were not widespread – we consider the use of chat rooms, MSN, and other messengers. As seen in Figure 7.4, the contribution of this sub-category has gradually increased by 2014, which coincides with the widespread usage of mobile broadband.

The communication sub-category consists of email and voice/video call activities over the internet. As seen in Figure 7.5, while the contribution

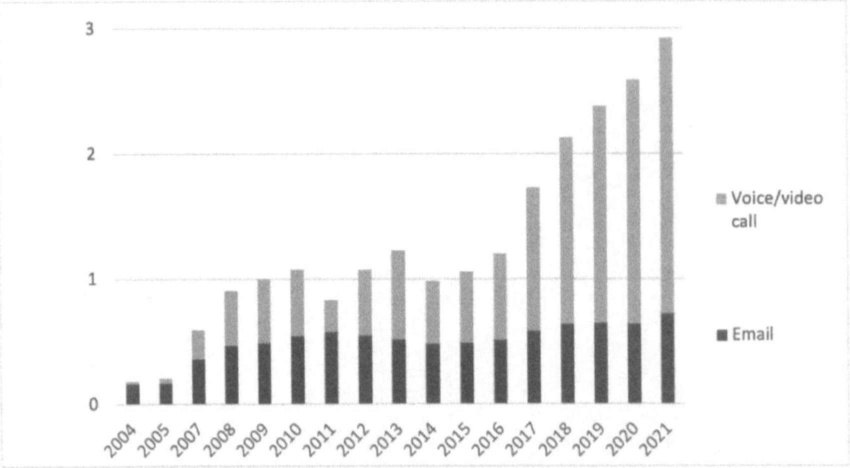

Figure 7.5 Development of the communications sub-category.

of email – as a basic internet activity – to the index scores generally remains constant, it is noteworthy that voice/video calls have begun to increase dramatically by 2017. We think that two factors explain this dramatic increase: the introduction of 4G in 2016 and the launch of the video call feature of the widely used communication application WhatsApp in 2016. As expected, this increase has accelerated during the COVID-19 epidemic.

Use of digital public services

The development in the use of digital public services (e-government) and its contribution to the TDSI scores is shown in Figure 7.6.

There are two sub-categories for the use of digital public services: (1) passive use and (2) active use. Passive use covers activities such as obtaining information and downloading forms from the websites or applications of public institutions. Active use includes filling out forms, applications, appointments, and so on. As seen in Figure 7.7, both active and passive use contributed to the index scores in a steady upward trend until 2020. In 2020, the contribution of active use to the index decreased compared to 2019. However, during the COVID-19 epidemic, both active and passive use increased. We argue that it is mostly due to getting an appointment for vaccination and displaying other COVID-19-related information, such as test results, digital vaccine cart, and so on via using the e-Pulse application.

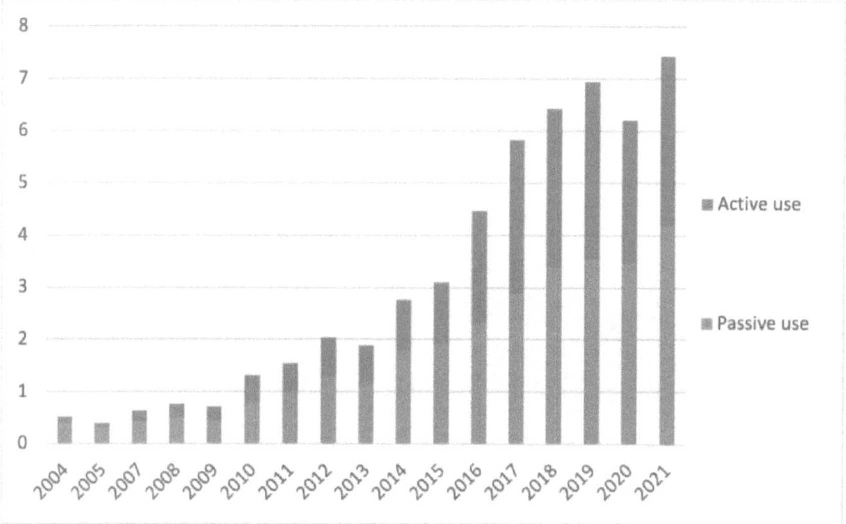

Figure 7.6 Evolution of the use of digital public services.

Regional and demographic disparities (inequalities)

One of the fundamental features of the TDSI is its ability to provide index scores in regional and demographic breakdowns. Although the demographic breakdown can be provided since 2004, the regional index scores can be calculated since 2011 due to the coverage of the dataset. Before going forward in this section, we would like to remind you that our motivation for calculating regional and demographic indexes is to investigate whether there are digital inequalities (see OECD, 2001; see Hargittai & Hsieh, 2013) that suggest significant differences in digitalization level and digitalization performance over time between regions, gender, education level, and age groups.

We provide the regional index scores in Table 7.4 for 12 regions at the NUTS-1 level. We show the changes in index scores between 2011 and 2021 to see the digitalization performance of each region. As seen in Table 7.4, western and coastal regions, especially the TR1 (Istanbul) region, stand out as the regions with the fastest increase in the index between 2011 and 2021. These regions also have higher digitalization performance than Türkiye, as shown by TDSI scores. On the other hand, the central and eastern regions started digitalization relatively at lower levels and have made less progress.

To make it more visual, we also picture the regional scores on a map in Figure 7.7. It shows the index scores in 2021 for each region by different tones in black and white. The picture indicates a west–east disparity that signifies a decrease in digitalization level from the west to the east. Although beyond the scope of our analysis, one can argue that these results imply that the digital inequality is likely to be associated with differences in regional development.

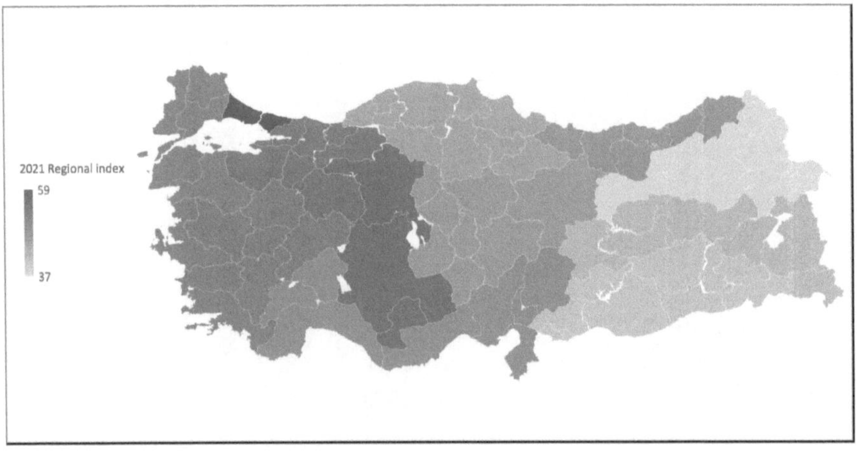

Figure 7.7 Map of index scores by regions in 2021.

Table 7.4 Regional index scores in 2011 and 2021

Region	*2011*	*2021*	*Change*
TR1 Istanbul	19.18	58.94	39.76
TR3 Aegean	13.91	50.30	36.39
TR5 Western Anatolia	16.89	52.91	36.02
TR6 Mediterranean	11.53	47.24	35.71
TR2 West Marmara	14.45	49.92	35.47
TDSI	**14.01**	**49.45**	**35.44**
TR4 Eastern Marmara	17.10	51.98	34.87
TR9 Eastern Black Sea	11.88	46.58	34.69
TR8 Western Black Sea	10.10	43.42	33.32
TRB Middle East Anatolia	7.65	40.56	32.9
TRC Southeastern Anatolia	7.01	39.27	32.26
TR7 Central Anatolia	13.31	44.88	31.57
TRA Northeastern Anatolia	6.96	36.59	29.64

Gender gap in digital inequality has been discussed in the literature since the early years of the internet (see van Dijk & Hacker, 2003a; Hargittai & Shafer, 2006). As in many other areas compared to men, women are more disadvantaged in terms of access and use due to their social roles, interests, and behaviors (van Dijk & Hacker, 2003b). This difference may emerge more sharply, especially in developing countries (Hilbert, 2011). As a developing country, Türkiye is not an exception. Figure 7.8 shows the performance of men and women in digitalization between 2004 and 2021.

In Figure 7.8 (left panel), we see that men start with a higher level of digitalization than women, and the difference has increased over time. The right panel of Figure 7.8, assuming the initial digitalization level is 0 for both men and women, shows that women have lagged behind men between 2004 and 2021. This indicates important evidence that the gap between men and women in terms of digitalization continues permanently.

Level of education is another area that can create inequalities in digitalization among individuals. The relevant literature suggests that individuals with higher education levels may have more advanced skills for both connecting to the internet and using it (see Cruz-Jesus et al., 2016). In addition, there are differences in terms of the purposes for using the internet. For instance, the reasons of those with lower education levels may differ from those with higher education levels; while those with higher education levels use the internet with the motivation to obtain more information and do business, those with lower education levels use the internet to spend their free time (see van Dijk & van Deursen, 2014).

The level and change in digitalization according to education level (primary school or below, secondary school, high school, and higher education) can be seen in Figure 7.9.

Figure 7.9 (left panel) shows that individuals with high education levels started with high digitalization levels, and this difference has gradually

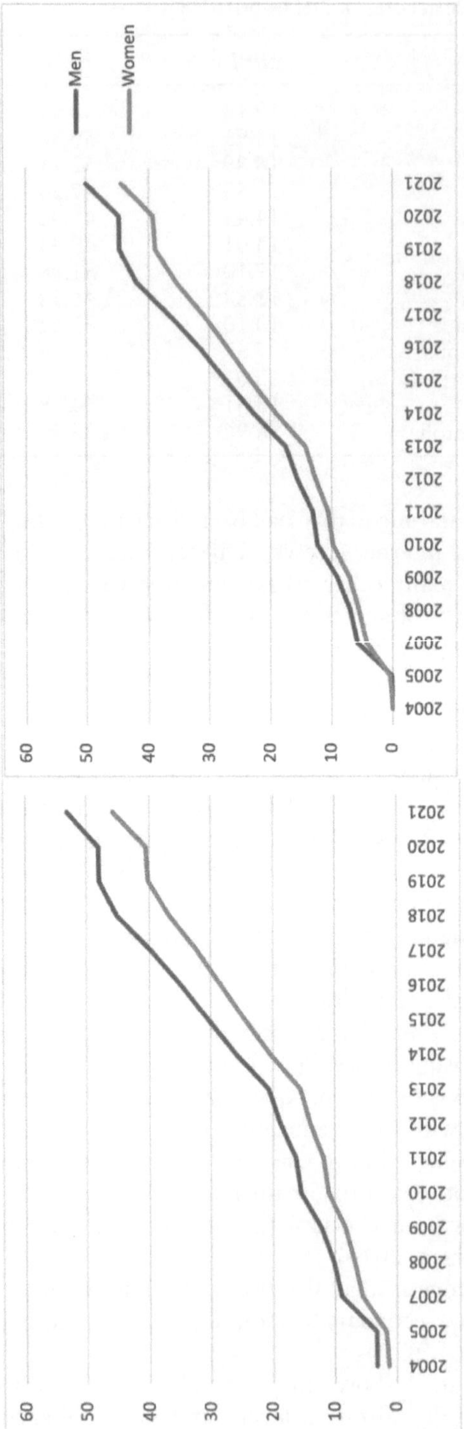

Figure 7.8 Index scores and change in index scores by gender.

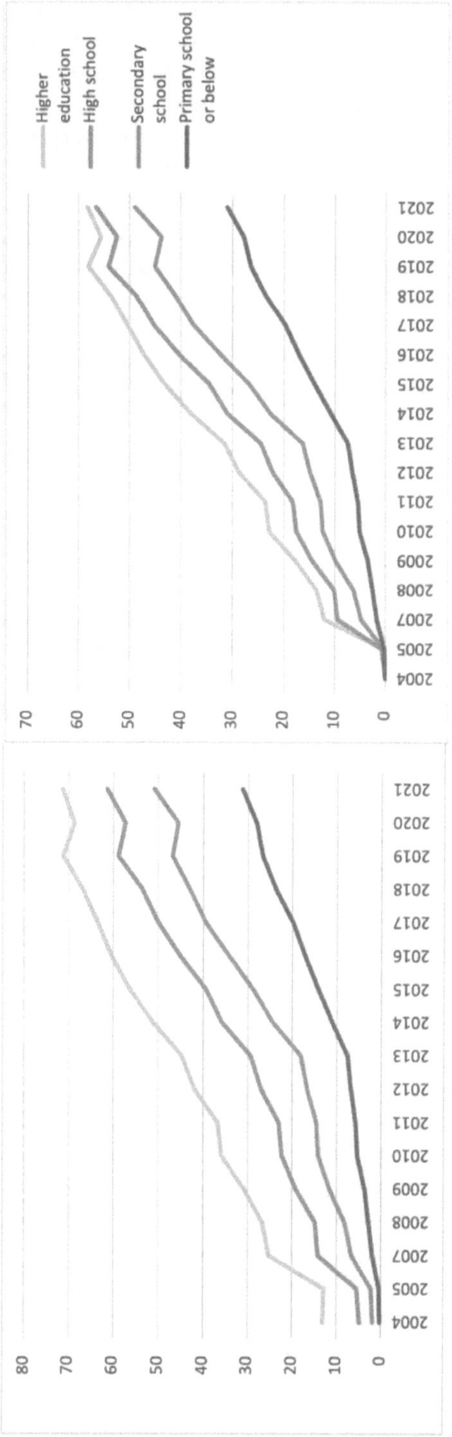

Figure 7.9 Index scores and change in index scores by educational level.

widened between 2004 and 2021. The right panel of Figure 7.9, assuming the initial digitalization level is 0 for all education levels, shows that individuals with high school and higher education have performed better compared to individuals with other educational achievements. Individuals with secondary school education levels have also converged to this performance. However, individuals with primary school education or below have performed very weakly compared to other education levels. This situation is in parallel with the findings in the literature (see Cruz-Jesus et al., 2016) that suggest the difference is not only between those with the highest education level and the lowest education level but also between those with the middle education level and the lowest education level.

Age emerges as another important factor regarding digital inequality. Empirical studies suggest that younger individuals are more likely to access the internet, acquire usage skills, and adapt to it than older individuals (see Niehaves & Plattfaut, 2014; Perrin & Duggan, 2015; Yu et al., 2016). The behavioral pattern revealed by these studies in general indicates that older age groups use the internet less frequently than other younger age groups. Thus, the digitalization of older individuals is an important challenge, especially for societies with aging populations.

Figure 7.10 shows the performance age groups (between 16 and 29, between 30 and 49, and between 50 and 74) in digitalization between 2004 and 2021. We see that the two groups (16–29 and 30–49) have followed a similar path over time, although they started at different levels of digitalization. Figure 7.10 (right panel), assuming the initial digitalization level is 0 for all age groups, confirms the pattern followed by these two age groups. However, the older age group (50–74) has performed weakly compared to the other age groups. These findings are consistent with empirical results in the literature. Moreover, they also point to a digital divide, especially between individuals over the age of 50 and other age groups.

Concluding remarks

In this chapter, we measure Turkish society's digitalization performance by the TDSI. The TDSI allows us to measure the digitalization level of households at various demographic and regional breakdowns (gender, age, education, and region) between 2004 and 2021 in three main categories (connectivity, use of internet, and digital public services). The TDSI shows that Turkish households have made significant progress in digitalization between 2004 and 2021. After a ten-year take-off period between 2004 and 2013, the digitalization level of Turkish society continuously increased until 2019. After a pause in 2020, it has resurged during the COVID-19 pandemic.

However, the TDSI also exhibits digital inequalities that suggest significant differences in digitalization level and digitalization performance over time between regions, genders, education levels, and age groups. When we look at digitalization performance at the regional level, the western and coastal

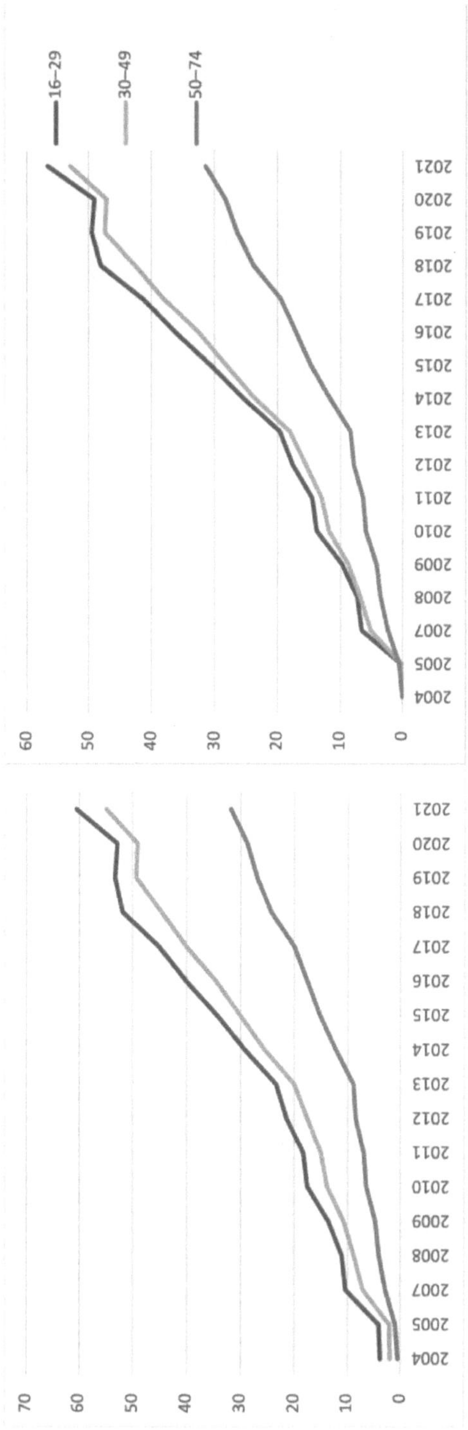

Figure 7.10 Index scores and change in index scores by age groups.

regions stand out as the regions with the fastest rise in the index. On the other hand, the central and eastern regions started at relatively low levels of digitalization and have made less progress. From a demographic point of view, men began with a higher level of digitalization than women. Youths (compared to the older) and those with higher education (compared to lower education) showed higher performance over time.

Besides these findings, one of the insights that this chapter suggests is that we need more studies on Türkiye for digitalization and digital inequalities. Particularly, we need studies that explore the main determinants of digitalization and digital inequalities. How do the income of households, price of ICT services, and availability of infrastructure affect the digitalization level remain significant questions need to be answered. Insights of these studies can guide policies to increase the digitalization level and curb inequalities.

Notes

1 An earlier version of the TDSI can be found in BETAM Research Report titled "Türkiye'de Bilgi İletişim Harcamaları ve Dijitalleşme", available at https://betam.bahcesehir.edu.tr/2022/07/turkiyede-bilgi-iletisim-harcamalari-ve-dijitallesme/.
2 TURKSTAT Household Information Technology Usage Statistics Metadata, available at https://data.tuik.gov.tr/Kategori/GetKategori?p=Bilim,-Teknoloji-ve-Bilgi-Toplumu-102.
3 We remind that the HITUS is conducted in April every year. In Turkey, first COVID-19 restriction came into effect on 10 April 2020. Therefore, the real impact of the pandemic on digitalization can be seen by looking at the values in 2021.

References

Andreou, P. C., & Anyfantaki, S. (2021). Financial literacy and its influence on internet banking behavior. *European Management Journal*, *39*(5), 658–674. https://doi.org/10.1016/j.emj.2020.12.001

Cruz-Jesus, F., Vicente, M. R., Bacao, F., & Oliveira, T. (2016). The education-related digital divide: An analysis for the EU-28. *Computers in Human Behavior*, *56*, 72–82. https://doi.org/10.1016/j.chb.2015.11.027

European Commission. (2023). *Digital Economy and Society Index (DESI) 2022 – Methodological note*. https://ec.europa.eu/newsroom/dae/redirection/document/88557

Hargittai, E., & Hsieh, Y. P. (2013). Digital inequality. In W. H. Dutton (Ed.), *The Oxford handbook of internet studies* (pp. 129–150). Oxford University Press. https://doi.org/10.1093/oxfordhb/9780199589074.013.0007

Hargittai, E., & Shafer, S. (2006). Differences in actual and perceived online skills: The role of gender. *Social Science Quarterly*, *87*(2), 432–448. https://doi.org/10.1111/j.1540-6237.2006.00389.x

Hilbert, M. (2011). Digital gender divide or technologically empowered women in developing countries? A typical case of lies, damned lies, and statistics. *Women's Studies International Forum*, *34*(6), 479–489. https://doi.org/10.1016/j.wsif.2011.07.001

ITU. (2003). *World telecommunication development report: Access indicators for the information society*. www.itu.int/net/wsis/tunis/newsroom/stats/WorldTelecomDevelopmentReport-2003_E.pdf

ITU. (2016). *Measuring the information society report 2016*. www.itu.int/en/ITU-D/Statistics/Documents/publications/misr2016/MISR2016-w4.pdf

Niehaves, B., & Plattfaut, R. (2014). Internet adoption by the elderly: Employing IS technology acceptance theories for understanding the age-related digital divide. *European Journal of Information Systems*, *23*(6), 708–726. https://doi.org/10.1057/ejis.2013.19

OECD. (2001). Understanding the digital divide. *OECD Digital Economy Papers*. https://doi.org/10.1787/20716826

Perrin, A., & Duggan, M. (2015). Americans' internet access: 2000–2015. *Pew Research Center* (Issue June). www.pewinternet.org/2015/06/26/americans-internet-access-2000-2015/; Archived at: www.webcitation.org/6qDiVhx1k

TÜBİSAD. (2020). *Türkiye'nin Dijital Dönüşüm Endeksi 2020*. www.tubisad.org.tr/tr/images/pdf/tubisad-dde-2020.pdf

TÜBİSAD. (2021a). *Ekonominin dönüştürücü gücü: E-ticaret etki analizi*. www.tubisad.org.tr/tr/images/pdf/tubisad-e-commerce_impact_assessment-launchpresentation.pdf

TÜBİSAD. (2021b). *Türkiye'nin Dijital Dönüşüm Endeksi 2021*. www.tubisad.org.tr/tr/images/pdf/tubisad-2021-dde-raporu.pdf

TÜBİSAD. (2022). *Türkiye'nin Dijital Dönüşüm Endeksi 2022*. www.tubisad.org.tr/tr/images/pdf/dde-2022-raporu-final.pdf

UNCTAD. (2006). *The digital divide report: ICT diffusion index*. https://unctad.org/system/files/official-document/iteipc20065_en.pdf

van Deursen, A. J. A. M., Helsper, E. J., & Eynon, R. (2016). Development and validation of the Internet Skills Scale (ISS). *Information, Communication & Society*, *19*(6), 804–823. https://doi.org/10.1080/1369118X.2015.1078834

van Dijk, J., & Hacker, K. (2003a). The digital divide. *The Information Society*, *19*(September 2000), 315–326. https://doi.org/10.1080/01972240390227895

van Dijk, J., & Hacker, K. (2003b). The digital divide as a complex and dynamic phenomenon. *The Information Society*, *19*(4), 315–326. https://doi.org/10.1080/01972240309487

van Dijk, J. A. G. M., & van Deursen, A. J. A. M. (2014). *Digital skills*. Palgrave Macmillan US. https://doi.org/10.1057/9781137437037

Yu, R. P., Ellison, N. B., McCammon, R. J., & Langa, K. M. (2016). Mapping the two levels of digital divide: Internet access and social network site adoption among older adults in the USA. *Information, Communication & Society*, *19*(10), 1445–1464. https://doi.org/10.1080/1369118X.2015.1109695

Appendix

The list of variables used and their weights can be seen in Table 7.A.

Table 7.A List of variables and their weights

Category	*Sub-category*	*Variable*	*Weight*	*Unit*
Connectivity (40%)	Fixed internet	Fixed_broad	0.15	% of households
		Fixed_narrow	0.05	% of households
	Mobile internet	Mobile_broad	0.15	% of households
		Mobile_narrow	0.05	% of households
Internet use (40%)	Communication	Email	0.02	% of individuals
		tel_video	0.03	% of individuals
	Social media	Social media	0.05	% of individuals
	Getting information	Information	0.02	% of individuals
		News	0.02	% of individuals
		Health	0.02	% of individuals
	Entertainment	Music	0.04	% of individuals
		Games	0.04	% of individuals
	E-bank	E-bank	0.08	% of individuals
	E-commerce	E-commerce	0.08	% of individuals
Digital public services (20%)	Passive use of e-government	Public_information	0.05	% of individuals
		Public_form	0.05	% of individuals
	Active use of e-government	Public_active	0.10	% of individuals

Missing observations were completed with the estimates based on trends that completed the time series.

The calculation of TDSI scores can be expressed by the following formula:

$$\text{TDSI}_{(\text{year,k})} = \text{Connectivity}_{(\text{year,k})} \times 0.40 + \text{internet use}_{(\text{year,k})} \times 0.40 + \text{digital public services}_{(\text{year,k})} \times 0.20$$

where *k:* gender, age group, education level, region.

8 The Constitutional Ecosystem of Digital Rights in Türkiye

Harun Muratoğulları

Introduction

The constitutional framework of private economic activity holds particular relevance in the advancement of the digital economy due to its overarching nature and foundational principles that balance innovation with public interests. In general, law is expected to adapt to an ever-changing life as social and commercial relationships evolve through time. This is nothing new, but it is especially pertinent when it comes to the application of the Turkish constitutional framework to the issues involving the internet. The process of interpreting and applying the law in this area is complex due to the involvement of the novel concerns brought forward by digital technologies impacting the established constitutional views around democratic processes and fundamental rights protections. Consequently, a new normative battleground emerges, necessitating those views to be materialized and applied to specific circumstances in the online domain. Against this backdrop, Turkey's aspirations to integrate into advanced economies and actively participate in the global internet ecosystem necessitate a proactive stance from its legal and constitutional framework. This proactive approach is imperative for effectively navigating the rapidly expanding challenges and opportunities presented by the digital economy.

This chapter will introduce Turkey's constitutional approach in dealing with the intricate challenges engendered by the internet, with a meticulous analysis of the jurisprudence of the country's constitutional court in the disputes falling somewhere within the use of the internet. The chapter is divided into four sections. The first section concisely examines the constitutional standing of the international treaties concerning digital human rights under Article 90, positing these instruments as quasi-constitutional "bills of rights" for Turkey. The article significantly ensures that the nation's legal framework will continue to align with the evolving digital rights paradigm in the global context. Then, it proceeds with a relatively abbreviated overview of the fundamental rights system of the country. The last two sections are dedicated to explore the reasoning of the Turkish Constitutional Court with specific regard to the internet phenomenon under two major themes, namely privacy

DOI: 10.4324/9781032692937-8

on the internet and freedom of expression online. By thoroughly analyzing relevant case law and legal principles, this analysis seeks to illuminate Turkey's legal approach to the challenges of the digital era.

A Constitutional Ecosystem Under the Shadow of International Standards

All stakeholders engaged in digital activities within Turkey are afforded protection commensurate with its international constitutional obligations. Article 90 of the Turkish Constitution incorporates international digital rights norms into the country's legal system, ensuring that domestic legislation aligns with international duties in the online domain (see Eren, 2023, pp. 800–807; Atar, 2023, pp. 264–266). Therefore, it is worth noting that Turkey, as a member of major international communities like the Council of Europe and the United Nations, cannot act completely on its own in its regulations of digital space. The human rights norms enshrined in the international treaties to which Turkey is a signatory, alongside the jurisprudence of the judicial bodies overseeing these treaties, function as pivotal guiding principles for the nation in shaping its legislative and policy endeavours pertaining to the online domain. This is why the ECHR's role in the country's online constitutional ecosystem has grown substantially. In that respect, it would not be an overestimation to say that the Convention functions as a de jure "second bill of rights" within the Turkish constitutional framework.

Among these established standards, the freedom of expression is one of the most crucial rights inherent to the right to access the internet, enshrined by Article 10 ECHR, Article 19 ICCPR, and Article 19 UDHR. To this end, any limitations on individual freedoms to express themselves freely online in Turkey must adhere to the stipulations, most relatedly, those outlined in Article 10 of the ECHR. The European Court of Human Rights (ECtHR), of which rulings have been binding to Turkey since 1990,[1] has a substantial body of case law relevant to the internet. This encompasses various aspects, including limitations on freedom of expression online as protected by Article 10 of the ECHR, matters related to data protection and retention within the internet as outlined in Article 8 of ECHR, and the responsibility of states to address violence and other criminal or unlawful activities in the online sphere.

The Turkish Constitutional Framework for the Online Freedoms

The regulation of the online sphere is far from being characterized by *laissez-faire* governance contrary to widespread perception. Indeed, the legal concepts underpinning both criminal and civil law are often also relevant to online activity in a manner that aligns with their application in offline circumstances. This nexus between legal frameworks extends notably to constitutional precepts, wherein Turkey's constitutional architecture grapples with the complexities of the digital domain. Notably, the constitutional judiciary's response thus far has mostly consisted of codifying certain new protections and expanding on existing normative paradigms. This developmental trajectory highlights the continuous effort of the constitutional system to adjust to the demands of the digital age while staying within the boundaries of existing legal frameworks to some degree.

Primarily, Turkey's Constitution is silent with regard to online activity, but the Constitutional Court (hereinafter, "TCC") has consistently advanced the premise that the right to the internet constitutes an inherent right intricately intertwined with the broader spectrum of freedoms, most importantly encompassed by the freedom of expression. This expansive interpretation posited by the TCC underscores the internet's pivotal role as a conduit for the exercise of fundamental liberties, including the rights to seek, receive, and disseminate information, thereby catalyzing novel avenues for the exercise of traditional rights and liberties within the digital milieu. (*Youtube LLC Corporation Service Company and Others*, App no 2014/4705, 29 May 2014). Consonant with the jurisprudential precedents established by the European Court of Human Rights (ECtHR), notably articulated in the landmark case of Ahmet Yıldırım v Turkey (Application no. 3111/10, 18 December 2012), the Turkish Constitutional Court (TCC), in a seminal ruling dated 2 April 2014, adjudicated that the decision rendered by the Presidency of Telecommunication to impose restrictions on access to the entirety of the website *twitter.com* amounted to the violation of freedom of expression. This jurisprudential milestone, epitomized by the case of Yaman Akdeniz ve Diğerleri (Application no. 2014/3986), underscores the TCC's unwavering commitment to upholding fundamental rights within the digital domain, thereby delineating the contours of permissible limitations on online expression in accordance with constitutional imperatives and international human rights standards.

Moreover, the Court has aptly identified the internet's crucial function as a necessary medium that allows for unlimited access to diverse perspectives and the spread of knowledge beyond traditional limits. The case law underscores that the accessibility of the internet and adjudications concerning digital affairs inherently intersect with the expansive purview of the constitutionally safeguarded freedom of expression enshrined within Article 26 of the Turkish Constitution, as evidenced in the seminal case of *Ali Kıdık* (Application no. 2014/5552, 26 October 2017). Viewed through this lens, the discursive landscape of Turkey's constitutional discourse vis-à-vis internet censorship or the regulation of private online data invariably gravitates toward the dialectic tension between the expressive prerogatives of content creators and the competing imperatives, be it the individual rights of purportedly affected parties or the broader societal interests, such as the preservation of public order or the suppression of criminal conduct.

Regarding the first pillar of that debate, from a more global perspective, free speech in the United States is considered "the preeminent right within the American constellation of fundamental rights" (Bollinger, 1988, p. 7) while

European law, notably considering the case-law of the CJEU and ECtHR, views it differently. As Pollicino points out, the metaphor of the marketplace of ideas (Blasi, 2004) is not well-suited to the EU framework of rights protection (Pollicino, 2021, p. 41). Compared to the First Amendment, in which the state's role is interpreted as minimal, Article 10 of the ECHR makes it quite clear that freedom of expression is not an absolute one (see *Handyside v United Kingdom*, App no 5493/72, 7 December 1976). The State parties may lawfully restrict freedom of expression so long as the standards outlined in Article 10.2 are adhered to. This Euro-centric approach is equally effective in the Turkish constitutional setting, and online activity, as one form of freedom of expression, is subject to certain limitations outlined in its relevant article (Article 26 of the Constitution).

Against the backdrop of new chances for free speech provided by new technologies, however, there has equally grown a significant demand for more robust protection for persons against the manifold intrusions facilitated by technological innovations and the ascendance of formidable private digital entities (Pollicino & De Gregorio, 2021). As a response to this, the Turkish legal framework has undergone a conspicuous evolution in its recognition and fortification of the right to privacy and data protection, albeit with a perceptible lag vis-à-vis the advancements witnessed in European jurisdictions. The constitutional basis for the right to data protection in Turkey was originally the rule of law (Article 2), the individual's right to freely develop his/her material and spiritual existence (Article 17), the right to privacy (Article 20), inviolability of the domicile (Article 21), and the right to confidentiality of communication (Article 22). That regime can primarily be characterized by the state obligations of escaping and respect, focusing on the negative aspect of the right. The codification of a new right in 2010 initiated the Turkish shift from a moderately negative and static view of the right to its positive and "aggressive" understanding, if one may say so. Until then, the country had shown a notable lack of progress in aligning with European advancements in the field of personal data legislation, despite being one of the earliest countries to sign the Council of Europe Convention on 28 January 1981 (CETS No.108).

It was only with the Constitutional Amendment of 2010 (Law no. 5982, Article 2) that the right to data protection was, for the first time, recognized as a separate right at the constitutional level with a new paragraph to the provision of the right to privacy, namely Article 20. Accordingly, individuals are entitled to the right to request the state to take the necessary measures to prevent the acquisition of personal data by unrelated third parties. Signifying the horizontal aspect, the amendment also entitles data subjects to be informed about private data concerning themselves, to access such data, to request their correction or deletion, and to learn whether they are used for their intended purposes. Therefore, individuals are granted the right to learn which personal data are used for which purpose, as well as the right to request the correction of this situation or the deletion of their data in case of any inaccuracies in the personal data in question. Following this amendment, the "Law on the Protection of Personal Data" was adopted by the Turkish parliament in 2016 (Law no. 6698, 24 March 2016). The Law is mostly derived from the European Union Data Protection Directive (95/46/EC, 24 October 1995).

Turning now to the restriction regime of constitutional rights in Turkey, the Turkish Constitution, similar to the bills of rights of other liberal democracies, sets forth an extensive catalogue of liberties and rights (Articles 12–74; Eren, 2023, pp. 566–631). Adhering to the conventional approach of categorizing rights as negative, active, or positive, these are organized into three chapters: individual rights, social and economic rights, and political rights (Eren, 2023, pp. 473–476). Article 13 lays forth the ground rules for limiting basic liberties and rights in relation to the constitutional rights limitation system. Accordingly, any limit of constitutional rights should be imposed by law and for specific reasons designated for every fundamental right and freedom in the corresponding article of the constitution. It is also stipulated that the restriction ought to conform with the spirit and wording of the constitution and shall not impede the essence of rights inspired by the 1949 Constitution of Germany (Öden & Esen, 2016). Any restriction also must not contradict the principle of democratic social order, which is akin to the ECHR criterion of "necessary in a democratic society". Finally, a restriction must adhere to the principle of proportionality (see Özbudun, 2011; Tumay, 2009).

Examining the TCC's jurisprudence reveals that its adjudicative attitude on the harmonization of fundamental rights bears striking similarities to the precedents established by the European Court of Human Rights (ECtHR). The TCC's adjudicative framework is built around its firm adherence to a proportionality-based approach, which has been emphasized since it assumed the mandate to adjudicate individual petitions. This modus operandi underscores a pivotal facet of constitutional adjudication in Turkey, in which the proportionality test emerges as a crucial mechanism for reconciling competing interests that may cause conflict. According to the TCC's rulings, instances may emerge where fundamental rights intersect and potentially conflict with one another, necessitating a careful balancing act by the judiciary. In navigating such junctures, the judiciary assumes a critical role in striking a judicious balance that respects the essence of the rights at stake while also ensuring that any restrictions imposed are consistent with the imperative of justification and proportionality in relation to the intended objectives. In this regard, the TCC examines any allegation about the violation of digital rights with its triple test, namely *legality* – whether the restriction is provided for by law, *legitimacy* – whether it depends on a legitimate aim specified in the Constitution, and finally, *necessity in a democratic society* – whether it achieves a fair balance among competing rights, preventing a disproportionate restriction in light of the circumstances while addressing the concerns about harm or violation of personal rights and the other relevant interests that may result from the content.

Key Constitutional Issues Around Private Data

The preceding two sections provided some insight on Turkey's overall constitutional structure that the digital domain is built on. The use of digital technology significantly modifies the manner in which personal data is utilized and raises concerns about fundamental issues of protecting privacy and personal data on the internet, including the issues of consent, limitations on purpose, and even the precise definition of personal data (OECD, 2021). This section will briefly evaluate some critical constitutional aspects of Turkey on the issue of online private data. On 7 April 2016, Turkey enacted its first and primary data protection law, Law No. 6698, on the Protection of Personal Data (LPPD). Many years had passed with no meaningful outcome from legislative attempts to address this issue, primarily as a result of political and administrative obstacles. In the end, the law was largely enacted in accordance with Directive 95/46/EC (1995) as part of the process of harmonization with the EU. That said, it faced a number of unconstitutionality challenges before the TCC due to numerous claims that specific provisions were unconstitutional. The TCC has considered the right to privacy in various occasions, considering different regulatory fields where violations may occur.

The Definition of Private Data

The TCC used the concept of "personal data" for the first time in a 2008 ruling (2006/167, 20 March 2008). The legal reasoning of the Court does not go further, but the reader can infer from the court's words that "all kinds of information related to individuals" fall under the remit of personal data. The TCC maintained, in the following cases, that personal data "refers to all information relating to a person, provided that it is specific or identifiable". In its decisions, the Court states that personal data includes not only names, surnames, dates of birth, and places of birth that reveal a person's identity but also all data such as telephone–passport–social security numbers, motor vehicle registration plates, CVs, email addresses, hobbies, group memberships, family information, and health information that make the person indirectly or directly identifiable (2014/74, 25 December 2014). With these rulings, the TCC has guided the parliament on the definition of personal data based on international documents, before both the Constitutional Amendment of 2010 and the LPPD of 2016. It is also important to mention that the TCC, in its 2014 norm review decision, extended data protection to legal entities (2013/84, 4 December 2014). In the examination of the case, the TCC referred to Article 20 of the 1982 Constitution, emphasizing that this right applies to everyone, regardless of whether they are natural or legal persons. As this ruling shows, Turkey's right to request personal data protection is not confined to natural persons but may also be extended to legal organizations in certain circumstances.

Data Retention: The Principle of Purpose-Bound Processing

A crucial aspect scrutinized during the constitutionality review of Law No. 6698 was the assertion of ambiguity concerning the maximum duration permitted for data retention (2016/125, 23 January 2018). The Law outlined the basic principles for processing personal data in Article 4/2. Among the principles that must be adhered to in data processing is the rule that allows data retention "for the period stipulated in the relevant legislation or required for the purpose for which they are processed". In accordance with prevailing legal frameworks, the storage of personal data is contingent upon either a legislatively prescribed period or, in the absence of such stipulation, a duration deemed necessary for its processing. The contested provision ostensibly underscores the principle of "data minimization", a tenet enshrined in both the Council of Europe Convention of 28 January 1981 for the Protection of Individuals with regard to Automatic Processing of Personal Data (referred to as "CETS No.108") and Article 5(1)(c) of the General Data Protection Regulation (GDPR), which mandates that the lawful retention period not exceed the exigencies of the original purpose for which the data was collected. Conversely, the crux of contention before the TCC pivoted on the perceived vagueness and ambiguity inherent in the formulation of the time frame in question, thus impugning the principle of "certainty", a cornerstone of the rule of law. The TCC's rebuttal to the plaintive arguments invoked nuanced legal reasoning, wherein it espoused the view that the disputed clause, in isolation, does not contravene the principle of legal certainty, citing precedents from the ECHR and the aforementioned CETS 108. The Court's pronouncement mandates that the data controller may only process and retain the impugned data in strict conformity with any time frame stipulated by pertinent legislation. That said, the Court argued that it is imperative to acknowledge the inherent complexity of the personal data landscape, wherein multifarious considerations may preclude the establishment of a uniform time frame for data retention across disparate scenarios. The Court's pronouncement resonates with the nuanced approach adopted by the GDPR, which eschews prescriptive mandates in favour of context-specific determinations regarding data retention periods.

Data Processing Without Explicit Consent

Another issue the TCC was called upon to address in the same case was the exception clause where the consent of the data subject will not be sought, as outlined in Article 5 of Law No. 6698. Given the said article, processing data without explicit consent will be lawful in cases where it is necessary

> for the implementation of a contract, for compliance with a legal obligation, for the establishment, exercise or protection of any right, for the legitimate interests pursued by the data controller provided that this processing shall not violate the fundamental rights and freedoms of the data subject.

The argument put out for annulment was that the exceptions should have been articulated in a more precisely delineated manner. Under this law, so the argument goes, the circumstances falling within the scope of exceptions will likely become more prevalent in practice than the instances necessitating explicit consent. It was maintained that these provisions lack clarity and comprehensibility, specifically regarding the definition of "legitimate interest" of the data controller. Consequently, the essence of the right to data protection would be compromised by the asserted ambiguity (para 20).

Notwithstanding these arguments, it is worth noting that the exceptions asserted as unconstitutional in the present case, similar to the previous challenge, bear a striking resemblance to the exceptions delineated in Article 7 of the EU's Directive 95/46/EC. The TCC acknowledged, with reference to the Directive (para. 33), that despite the evident constraint on the fundamental rights of data subjects, such limitations are confined to the conditions delineated in the Article, ensuring that they do not impede or render the exercise of these rights unattainable. In the opinion of the Court, these exceptions were rather established to safeguard a balance of interests between the data controller and the data subject and to adhere to international law that establishes comparable criteria for the lawfulness of data processing in the absence of explicit consent (para 44–45). The Court further elaborated on the idea of legitimate interest, explaining that it is best viewed as a balance that must be evaluated within the context of protecting both the data controller's and the data subject's rights and freedoms (para 41). If these exceptions are applied in a manner that disproportionately restricts the data subject's rights, the Court has also acknowledged that the data subject may pursue a suitable remedy through an individual complaint or appeal (para 43).

On Article 6 (3), which governs health and sexual data processing, another annulment request was made for instances without permission. The article states that persons or authorized institutions and organizations may only process health and sexual life data under confidentiality for "public health, preventive medicine, medical diagnosis, treatment and care services, planning and management of health services and financing" without the data subject's consent. The request argued that this section lacks definition, provides insufficient protection, and gives data processors considerable discretion. The CC denied the request because the provision falls under the State's positive responsibilities. The Court said the limitation on the right to data protection was meant to safeguard the necessities of a democratic society, where the government sets stricter data processing boundaries.

Conditions for Processing of Special Categories of Personal Data

Additionally, Article 6 (1), which establishes distinct categories of data and more rigorous processing requirements compared to other personal data, was contested on the grounds of being against equality before the law. The article designates the data relating to "race, ethnic origin, political opinion, philosophical belief, religion, sect or other beliefs, appearance and dress, membership of associations, foundations or trade unions, health, sexual life, criminal convictions and security measures, and biometric and genetic data" as "special categories of personal data". The terms "sect" and "dress and attire" were said to be discriminatory and damaging to the rights to freedom of religion, conscience, and thought, as well as in conflict with the OECD Guidelines, the Directive, and relevant international treaties (para 50). The request was once more dismissed by the TCC on the grounds that the Law stipulates the need for tighter standards in processing special categories, including those in dispute. It did not view the contested phrases as a means to expedite the processing of this data. Instead, the purpose is to provide additional safeguards for the protection of these sensitive data (para 57). According to the Court, it is within the discretionary power of the legislator to identify the gaps and deficiencies in the fight against discrimination and to try to eliminate them through positive measures (para 59). In light of the fact that Article 9 of the GDPR prohibits the processing of a comparable set of categories of personal data unless certain conditions are met, it can be inferred that the data privacy approach of Turkish law in respect to special categories appears to be consistent with European norms.

The Right to Be Forgotten

Another aspect of the right to data protection worth mentioning is the balance between freedom of expression and the right to privacy in the context of the right to be forgotten, which is not explicitly stated in either the Constitution or any other law in Turkey. The case law of the TCC appears to have closely mirrored that of the Court of Justice of the EU (*Google Spain SL, Google Inc. v. Spanish Data Protection Agency, Mario Costeja Gonzales*, C-131/12, 13 May 2014) and ECtHR (*Węgrzynowski and Smolczewski v Poland*, App no 33846/07, 16 October 2013) in their rulings on the right to be forgotten. The judgement of the TCC's General Chamber on the application of *N.B.B.*, dating back to 2016, is the most notable on the issue (*N.B.B.*, App no 2013/5653, 3 March 2016). Even though the Court of Appeals has already rendered rulings on the matter (General Assembly of Civil Chambers of the Court of Cassation, no. 2015/1679, 17 June 2015), the TCC's conception of the right to be forgotten was ground-breaking primarily for two reasons: first, it acknowledged the right to be forgotten for the first time, based on the idea that the State has a positive obligation to give people a chance to "turn a new page" by safeguarding their past experiences from public knowledge by citing Articles 5 (Fundamental aims and duties of the State), 17 (Personal inviolability, corporeal and spiritual existence of the individual), and 20 (Privacy of private life) of the Constitution (para 47). Second, even more remarkable, the TCC did not shy away from imposing obligations on non-governmental actors, recognizing the horizontal application of the right to protection of personal data, the German doctrine of "*d*rittwirkung"

(Engle, 2009). The Court noted that the right has force beyond public authorities and extends to private actors as well (para 42). It is important to note that the TCC made such an assessment prior to the enactment of the Law no 6698, on protection of personal data, which does not either explicitly incorporate the right to be forgotten, but places considerable obligations on data controllers, including an obligation to delete personal data when there is no valid justification for its continued retention (Article 7).

The case in point arose out of three news articles, as initially lawful media coverage, about the criminal records of the applicant for alleged drug use, dated back to 1998–1999 within the online archive of a newspaper. The TCC examined the issue from a conflict-based approach to the rights of the two sides between the right to protect one's honour and reputation (as guaranteed by Article 17 of the Constitution) and the freedoms of the press and expression (as guaranteed by Articles 28 and 26, respectively). The Court acknowledged the challenges posed by internet journalism, where it is increasingly difficult for individuals to be forgotten, and accordingly, the need to consider the altered circumstances of communication on the internet (para 37–39). By citing key international laws and court rulings, particularly the CJEU's judgement on *Google Spain*, the TCC emphasized that the right to be forgotten arises from the state's positive obligation to create an environment conducive to the growth of individuals' spiritual well-being (para 46).

The right to be forgotten is not an unconditional right, however. This right, for the Court, cannot be extended to every kind of information found in online newspaper archives; instead, a balance needs to be struck, as per its established criteria, between the rights of both parties (para 66). The Court provided clarification on the criteria for assessing the right to be forgotten, emphasizing that these criteria should be considered on a case-by-case basis. For internet news to be removed from the internet under the right to be forgotten, certain criteria must be met. These include the publication's content, how long it has been online, whether it is considered outdated or accepted as historical information, the news's value to society, whether the subject is a politician or a well-known individual, factors like the article's subject matter, whether the news presents facts or value judgements, and what is of interest to the public in the relevant data (para 50). Applying these standards to the current matter, the TCC agreed with the applicant's assertions and concluded that the result of a criminal proceeding that took place 17 years ago is no longer relevant. Keeping a criminal record concerning drug use serves neither statistical nor scientific reasons on its own. In addition, as the individual in point is neither renowned nor a political figure, his right to be forgotten should be protected in this particular instance. Following the ruling in the *N.B.B.* case, the TCC has further developed its jurisprudence on "the right to digital privacy" in the specifics of the right to be forgotten through a series of subsequent applications (see also *Asli Alp and Şükrü Alp*, App no 2014/18260, 4 October 2017; *Asım Bayar and Veysel Bayar*, App no 2014/4141, 04 October 2017; *C.K.*, App no 2014/19685, 15 March 2018).

Key Constitutional Issues Around Internet Freedom

Unfortunately, Turkey does not have a good record of freedom of expression and internet bans, particularly with regard to the bans on social media platforms such as Wikipedia, YouTube, and Twitter. While there was no constitutional guarantee for internet freedom as an independent right in the Constitution, the first regulation providing the legal framework for state authorities to block internet content was set out in 2007 by the Law on the Regulation of Broadcasts via Internet and Prevention of Crimes Committed through Such Broadcasts (Law no 5651, 4 May 2007). The Law, often known as the Internet Law, deals with various aspects of online content, such as the supervision and control of internet broadcasting, publications, and content considered unlawful (Kaya, 2021). Although access-blocking decisions are frequently made by courts within the scope of Articles 8, 8/A, 9, and 9/A of the Internet Law, the Director of the Information and Communication Technologies Authority (ICTA), a regulatory body tasked with overseeing and regulating the communication and information technologies, may also decide to block access directly within the scope of the legislation. Based on the research of Akdeniz and Güven (2021, p. 10), the ICTA was responsible for blocking 89% of more than 467,011 websites that were prohibited by the end of 2020.

According to Article 8, the judge or prosecutor in the case, or the ICTA, may order the removal of content or the blocking of access during the investigation or prosecution of specific offences, such as child sexual abuse, obscenity, gambling, or inciting suicide. Article 8/A authorizes the President or ministries to request the director of the ICTA to restrict the content based on reasons such as the protection of national security or public order. Last, but not least, if someone claims their personal rights have been violated, the criminal justice of peace can order the removal or prohibition of the offending content within 24 hours without giving the opposing side a chance to be heard or present a defence. Since Law No. 5651 entered into force, the authorized bodies have reportedly blocked access to thousands of URLs, domain names, and websites. Akdeniz and Güven (2023 p. 39) also found that between 2014 and 2022, the courts of first instance issued 6,509 decisions based on Article 9 of the Law, resulting in the blocking of access to 35,023 news items (URL addresses), of which 29,253 were completely removed from the relevant websites in compliance with these decisions. These occurrences of access restriction brought about several individual complaints before the TCC, which has developed an extensive body of case law on the issue.

The Role of the Regulatory Authority in the Digital Environment

The role of public authorities in Turkey's digital constitutionalism has been a subject of intense debate. Connected to this, one of the primary objections raised against the Internet Law concerned Article 8(4), which conferred onto the ICTA the authority to directly order access-blocking in cases where the content or host provider is located outside of Turkey and the content involves sexual abuse of children, obscenity, or prostitution. The TCC found in its judgement of 8 December 2015 that the challenged provision contravened the principle of freedom of information mainly for two reasons (no 2015/76): first, the contested provision confers an ambiguous authority insofar as it can be exercised to impede access to an entire website. According to the Court, the provision authorizes the administration to block access in a manner that lacks clarity regarding its scope and limitations. This was found contrary to the sub-principle of "certainty" under the substantive interpretation of the "restricted by law" requirement in Article 13 of the Constitution. Second, it was argued to have violated Article 22 since it permits the content removal without ensuring judicial scrutiny (para 27). When addressing concerns pertaining to Internet law, the TCC places significant emphasis on the utmost significance of freedom of expression within the context of online interaction. It evaluates the potential consequences of imposing limitations on the dissemination of information and public discussions, particularly when considering actions to ban access that may impede the free exchange of ideas.

Another provision subject to annulment in that respect pertained to Articles 4(3), 5(5), and 6(1) d of the Law, which required the access, hosting, and content providers to submit any requested information to the ICTA (no 2014/87, 8 December 2015). While Article 4(3) limits the scope to the performance of functions passed on to the Presidency, it was evident that this obligation entailed the potential requirement for providers to disclose various personal data of internet users without the knowledge of the individuals or organizations involved. The Presidency was, therefore, granted the authority to obtain any information without a court order or any legal justification.

The requirements placed on access, content, and hosting providers as such would significantly infringe upon the right to privacy of internet users, as protected by Article 8 of the ECHR. With similar concerns, the TCC decided that the aforementioned provisions ought to be annulled due to their contravention of the rule of law (Art 2), restriction clause (Art 13), and Privacy of private life (Art 20) of the Constitution. The Court rightly underlined the importance of "clarity" this time under the principle of the rule of law mentioned in Article 2 of the Constitution (para 163). The rule of law necessitates the establishment of explicit, unequivocal, and easily understandable legal frameworks that eliminate any uncertainty for both persons and the government. The Court further determined that any limitation on confidentiality and safeguarding of personal privacy must satisfy the proportionality test outlined in Article 13 of the Constitution (para 160–162). However, the disputed provisions permitted a practically unconditional transfer of personal data to the Presidency without sufficient limitations, leaving individuals vulnerable and without protection against the administration. The Court determined that Article 20 of the Constitution would be violated so long as there is no restriction on the content, purpose, or scope of such transferred personal data, and the regulation is neither certain nor predictable; consequently, the individuals involved would be unprotected against public authority (para 170).

The Basic Constitutional Principles to Follow in Access-Blocking Cases

As mentioned earlier, pursuant to Article 9 of Law No 5651, individuals in Turkey may apply to the Criminal Judge of Peace on the grounds that their personal rights have been violated and seek a ruling to have the contested information removed from public view and its access restricted. The problem with the Article 9 regime, however, is that it lacks a full-fledged judicial mechanism. Upon the request, the judge may indeed issue a decision to block access within 24 hours through a non-adversarial process that does not involve a hearing and consideration of the defence of the affected parties. In 2015, the TCC addressed the interference with freedom of expression in cases of access blocking based on Article 9 of Law No. 5651 for the first time in the application of *Medya Gündem Dijital Yayıncılık Ticaret* and ruled that the interference was not in accordance with the requirements of the democratic social order since the decisions of the courts of first instance blocking access to internet content did not contain relevant and sufficient grounds to justify the interference (App no 2013/2623, 11/11/2015). The Court has subsequently developed an extensive body of case law concerning the procedure for the removal of the content or blocking access to the publication based on Law No. 5651. Within the purpose of this study, an analysis of the 49 decisions rendered by the TCC on the restriction of content has been carried out. The TCC has formulated the following fundamental principles in cases involving access blocking:

- The method of blocking access according to Article 9 of Law No. 5651, which is established as a "temporary" measure, is an exceptional procedure to be applied only if there is a prima facie case of violation. The following section will provide an overview of this principle.
- The decision made based on the said article of the Law is not the one that resolves the dispute on the merits.
- The decision to block access should be considered as a last resort.
- The blocking access measure should be invoked by the courts in accordance with its purpose. Decisions to block access to websites for the purpose of protecting the reputation and personal rights of individuals should not harm the essence of the rights of the press to criticize and report news.
- The admissibility of news by individuals cannot be justified solely on the basis of court decisions finalizing the allegations against them. A court judgement cannot serve as the only permissible source for news.

- The more important the news or article is in informing the public, the more tolerant the person being written about is expected to be. When online news and ideas impart information regarding matters of public interest, freedoms of expression and press must be afforded increased protection.
- The use of offensive language is protected by freedoms of expression and press.

The Prima Facie Doctrine

The case of *Ali Kıdık* is a crucial ruling by the TCC, establishing constitutional standards for internet blocking in Turkey (App no 2014/5552, 26 October 2017). It raises concerns about how judges can evaluate individual rights violations within a limited time frame without a full trial. What makes this case important in the sense of blocking access to the internet is the prima facie doctrine developed by the TCC in its ruling for Article 9 of the Law. The Court argued that the measure of blocking access to internet publications, as outlined in Article 9 of Law No. 5651, should be implemented as limited to the instances where there is a prima facie indication of the unlawful infringement upon personal rights (para 62–63). Article 9 regime must be construed as a temporary measure against the types of online content with a noticeable risk to further damage personal rights by the lower courts. Its primary objective is to promptly address and rectify any interference with an individual's reputation without further delay. By promptly preventing access to content that palpably harms individuals, disseminates false information, and infringes upon their dignity and reputation, it is aimed at curtailing an ongoing and "prima facie" interference with personal rights (para 83). According to the Court, the purpose of the legislator in Article 9 should be construed as stopping the publication of obvious violations of personal rights, such as "the publication of nude pictures or video footage of a person", until a full-scale lawsuit is completed and without further damage to personal rights (Gözler, 2019). This procedure therefore needs to be utilized as a last resort in a relatively limited area as compared to other legal remedies. The Court established three cumulative aspects that must be taken into account when deciding whether or not a prima facie infringement has occurred (para 83):

1) The illegality of the content must be evident.
2) The incorrectness of the content must be apparent.
3) The damage should be promptly addressed.

The TCC found in the specific case that there is insufficient evidence to substantiate the claim that the aforementioned news has resulted in a conspicuous infringement of the individual's reputation, so leading to a resolution of the matter without resorting to a contentious trial. This landmark decision underscored the need for rigorous regulations and cautioned against unjustifiable, indefinite restrictions, advocating for a measured, prudent approach to online restriction to protect freedom of expression and the press. The TCC has so far applied the doctrine of prima facie breach in many of its judgements (see also *Kemal Gözler*, App no 2014/5232, 19 April 2018; *Özgen Acar*, App no 2015/15241, 31 October 2018; *Barış Yarkadaş*, App no 2015/4821, 17 April 2019; *Kerem Altıparmak*, App no 2015/8193, 27 November 2019).

A Pilot Judgement on Online News Blocking

The Article 9 procedure has faced significant criticism from the Venice Commission of the Council of Europe (no 805/2015, 15 June 2016). This criticism stems primarily from two points: (1) it fails to engage in civil or criminal litigation regarding the defamation claim that underpins the blocking request, which would provide a more accurate assessment of the measure's appropriateness, and (2) it restricts the ability of the judge of the peace to pursue a proportionately less restrictive measure, such as enforcing the publisher to publish the complainant's response. Acknowledging these points, in its decision of *Keskin Kalem Yayıncılık ve Ticaret AŞ and Others* (App no 2018/14884, 27 October 2021), the TCC this time decided to apply the pilot judgement process to address systemic issues affecting nine cases that contained 129 news articles blocked by first instance courts based on Article 9 of Law No. 5651 (Işık, 2022). Referring also to the call of the Organisation for Security and Co-operation in Europe (OSCE) for a fundamental reform of Law No. 5651, which mainly stated that blocking access to websites in Turkey went beyond what was necessary in a democratic society, the TCC accordingly decided to examine whether the problem arises from the law itself. In this regard, the Court concluded that Article 9 of the Law should be reconsidered by the Parliament and drew attention to the following points (para 137):

- The scope of the access blocking procedure upon the request of persons claiming that their rights to honour and reputation have been violated should be clearly and unambiguously reorganized.
- Some criteria should be developed regarding the severity of the unlawfulness of the relevant conduct to be blocked.
- Adversarial proceedings should be allowed.
- There must be an effective appeal process against the decisions of blocking access.
- A set of standards should be provided by law to guide judges in cases where internet content needs to be restricted.

The pilot judgement issued by the TCC was transmitted to the Parliament, and the assessment of the applications within the scope of the judgement was postponed for a period of one year. The Court later on also announced that 334 pending applications were eligible for consideration under the pilot decision.[2] The Parliament has not yet taken any action to amend the relevant legislation as of the time of writing this chapter.

Conclusion

The purpose of this chapter was to provide an overview of the constitutional normative framework pertaining to the digital environment in Turkey while also identifying the challenges that exist within it. Despite the TCC's accomplishment in restoring individual constitutional protections to accommodate the demands of the internet, its endeavours in this respect seem to have been weakened by Turkey's first internet-specific legislation, Law No. 5651. This law sets for unclear boundaries about illegal content and grants excessive powers to the regulatory body, namely the ICTA. The prevailing legal landscape surrounding private data and internet governance in Turkey seems to pivot toward a paradigm of heightened public oversight, ostensibly aimed at circumscribing and regulating private power. Notwithstanding these developments, a nuanced analysis of the TCC's jurisprudential trajectory reveals a discernible assimilation of European constitutional paradigms, indicative of a substantive transfusion of legal concepts from Europe to Turkey. It should be noted that the rulings of the TCC have so far proven that the Turkish Constitution has the capacity to adapt and develop into a living instrument that confronts the complexities of the digital age.

Notes

1 Turkey accepted the right to apply to the ECtHR individually in 1987 (Article 25 of the ECHR) and recognized the ECtHR's mandatory jurisdiction in 1990 (Article 46 of the ECHR).

2 www.anayasa.gov.tr/tr/bireysel-basvuru/pilot-karar-uyarinca-gorusulmesi-ertelenen-basvurular/

References

Akdeniz, Y., & Güven, O. (2021). Engelliweb 2020: Fahrenheit 5651 Sansürün Yakıcı Etkisi. *Free Expression Association.* https://ifade.org.tr/reports/EngelliWeb_2020.pdf.

Akdeniz, Y., & Güven, O. (2023). Engelliweb 2020: Sulh Ceza Hakimliklerinin Gölgesinde Anayasa Mahkemesi. *Free Expression Association.* https://ifade.org.tr/reports/EngelliWeb_2022.pdf.

Atar, Y. (2023) *Türk Anayasa Hukuku* (16th ed.). Ankara: Seçkin Yayınevi.

Blasi, V. (2004). Holmes and the marketplace of ideas. *The Supreme Court Review, 2004*, 1–46. www.jstor.org/stable/3536967

Bollinger, L. C. (1988). *The tolerant society: Freedom of speech and extremist speech in America*. New York: Oxford University Press.

Engle, E. (2009). Third party effect of fundamental rights (Drittwirkung). *Hanse Law Review*, *5*(2), 165–173. https://ssrn.com/abstract=1481552

Eren, A. (2023). *Anayasa Hukuku Dersleri* (5th ed.). Ankara: Seçkin Yayınevi.

Gözler, K. (2019). *Anayasa Mahkemesinin Usulsüz Alıntısı: Ali Kıdık Kararındaki Prima Facie İhlâl Doktrininin Sahibi Kim?* www.anayasa.gen.tr/aym-usulsuz-alinti.htm
Işık, A. (2022). Anayasa Mahkemesi'nin 5651 Sayılı Kanun'un 9. Maddesi Bağlamında İnternete Erişimin Engellemesine Dair Değişen Yaklaşımın Değerlendirilmesi. *Selçuk Üniversitesi Hukuk Fakültesi Dergisi, 30*(3), 967–998. https://doi.org/10.15337/suhfd.1065290
Kaya, M. B. (2021). *İnternet Hukuku* (2nd ed.). İstanbul: On İki Levha Yayıncılık.
Öden, M., & Esen, S. (2016). Fundamental rights and freedoms in Turkey and the Turkish constitutional court. In R. Arnold (Eds.), *The convergence of the fundamental rights protection in Europe* (pp. 127–162). *Ius Gentium: Comparative Perspectives on Law and Justice, 52*. Dordrecht: Springer. https://doi.org/10.1007/978-94-017-7465-9_8
OECD. (2021). *Report on the implementation of the recommendation of the council concerning guidelines governing the protection of privacy and transborder flows of personal data*. https://one.oecd.org/document/C(2021)42/en/pdf
Özbudun, E. (2011). Constitutional law. In T. Ansay & D. Wallace (Eds.), *Introduction to Turkish law* (pp. 19–50). The Hague: Kluwer Law International.
Pollicino, O. (2021). *Judicial protection of fundamental rights on the internet: A road towards digital constitutionalism?* Great Britain: Hart Publishing.
Pollicino, O., & Gregorio, G. (2021). Constitutional law in the algorithmic society. In H. Micklitz, O. Pollicino, A. Reichman, A. Simoncini, G. Sartor, & G. De Gregorio (Eds.), *Constitutional challenges in the algorithmic society* (pp. 3–24). Cambridge: Cambridge University Press. https://doi.org/10.1017/9781108914857.002
Tumay, M. (2009). Restrictions on the fundamental rights in the Strasbourg and Turkish legal orders. *Selçuk Üniversitesi Hukuk Fakültesi Dergisi, 17*(2), 85–128. https://doi.org/10.15337/SUHFD.2017.114
Venice Commission. (2016, June 15). *Opinion No. 805/2015, opinion on law no. 5651 on regulation of publications on the internet and combating crimes committed by means of such publication ("the internet law")*. www.venice.coe.int/webforms/documents/default.aspx?pdffile=CDL-AD(2016)011-e

Court Rulings

CJEU. *Google Spain SL, Google Inc. v. Spanish data protection agency, Mario Costeja Gonzales*, C-131/12, 13 May 2014.
EctHR. *Węgrzynowski and Smolczewski v Poland*, App no 33846/07, 16 October 2013.
General Assembly of Civil Chambers of the Court of Cassation (of Turkey), Decision no. 2015/1679, 17 June 2015.
TCC. *Asım Bayar and Veysel Bayar*, App no 2014/4141, 4 October 2017.
TCC. *Asli Alp and Şükrü Alp*, App no 2014/18260, 4 October 2017.
TCC. *Barış Yarkadaş*, App no 2015/4821, 17 April 2019.
TCC. *C.K.*, App no 2014/19685, 15 March 2018.
TCC. *Kemal Gözler*, App no 2014/5232, 19 April 2018.
TCC. *Kerem Altıparmak*, App no 2015/8193, 27 November 2019.
TCC. *Keskin Kalem Yayıncılık ve Ticaret AŞ and Others*, App no 2018/14884, 27 October 2021.
TCC. *Medya Gündem Dijital Yayıncılık Ticaret*, App no 2013/2623, 11 November 2015.
TCC. *N.B.B.*, App no 2013/5653, 3 March 2016.
TCC. *Özgen Acar*, App no 2015/15241, 31 October 2018.
TCC, no 2006/167, 20 March 2008.
TCC, no. 2013/84, 4 December 2014.

TCC, no 2014/74, 25 December 2014.
TCC, no 2014/87, 8 December 2015.
TCC, no 2016/125, 28 September 2017.
TCC, no 2015/76, 15 December 2017.

9 Regulation of E-Government Services

Beril Taşkin Kapusuzoğlu

Introduction

This chapter delves into the expansion of e-government within Türkiye, tracing its origins back to the early 1990s when the nation began to embrace the digital revolution support of international bodies in a manner consistent with the worldwide movement. The domination of computers and the internet as fundamental drivers of this transition was demonstrated by the widespread adoption of computer technology across Turkish public and private sectors in the 1980s and the establishment of Türkiye's inaugural internet connection in 1993.

The chapter then examines the incorporation of ICT in Turkish government operations, casting light on the strategic regulatory functions assumed by various administrative bodies. An exhaustive and nuanced dissection of the regulatory landscape governing Türkiye's e-government services is divided into three detailed sections: (1) The Era of the Science and Technology High Council, (2) The European Union Harmonization Process, and (3) The Era of the Digital Transformation Office (DTO).

The segment dedicated to The Era of the Science and Technology High Council will examine the early phases of e-government regulations in Türkiye. The focus is on the substantial contributions of the Science and Technology High Council, which established the fundamental parameters that have informed the path of regulatory frameworks in the e-government sphere in Türkiye.

The European Union Harmonization Process segment analyses a critical phase, where Türkiye aligned its e-government policies with the standards set by the EU. The analysis provides insights into the transformative impact of this alignment on Türkiye's digital governance landscape and the supervisory role of the EU over the Turkish e-government services.

The concluding segment of the chapter titled The Era of the Digital Transformation Office casts light on the developments post-2018, when the oversight and regulation of e-government services transitioned to the Digital Transformation Office. This is emphasised as a strategic response to the dynamic alterations within Türkiye's government machinery.

DOI: 10.4324/9781032692937-9

Background of e-government services

In the era of remarkable technological progress, e-government services have become indispensable to public sector management. Termed succinctly as "e-government", this concept embodies the integration of digital technology into the public service sector to augment the efficacy and reach of governmental operations and their interface with the citizenry and the business community. The initial part of this chapter traces the historical path and proliferation of e-government services, emphasising key events and the dynamics instrumental to its growth.

The inception of information and communication technology (ICT) integration in government processes dates back to the utilisation of Herman Hollerith's punched card system in the United States Census of 1890, marking an early instance of such application (Veit & Huntgeburth, 2014). However, in the 1960s, computers played a pivotal role in the execution of administrative functions (Bennett, 1992). From the late 1980s to the early 1990s, there was a rapid increase in the initiation of e-government services on a global scale, with the United States being seen as the pioneer in this arena (Coursey & Norris, 2008). The United States' forefront position in e-government policy implementation was deeply intertwined with the innovation and extensive adoption of computers and the internet within the country. Predating the digital offering of public services as a facet of e-government policy, some public functions began to appear online in the United States in 1985. The advent of the internet's growing development has seen a rise in the number of public services migrating to electronic platforms. A notable early instance was the internet-based payment and electronic submission of tax documents. The initial foray into the electronic tax return system was a collaborative venture between the Federal Internal Revenue Service (IRS) and H&R Block, a frontrunner in the tax preparation sector (Fletcher, 2003).

As with other countries, the driving power for the e-government initiative in the United States has been substantially shaped by the executive arm, particularly the President's Office. The execution of influence predominantly flowed through the conduits of the Office of Management and Budget along with the General Services Administration. The 1993 National Performance Review and a series of ancillary publications highlighted the developing emphasis on information and communication technologies (Dugan, 1999). *The Access America* programme, executed nationwide, was pivotal in transitioning public services to a digital framework (Gore, 1997). Under the guidance of this scheme, the "First Gov" internet portal emerged in 2001 as an e-government gateway, aiming to unite all public services into a singular electronic juncture. Presently, *usa.gov* serves as the portal for the United States' e-government services, providing services via this consolidated electronic channel.

Main reasons behind the expansion of e-government

Several factors have been instrumental in the international expansion of e-government services. The swift progression of technological capabilities, particularly the ubiquity of the internet and the widespread adoption of mobile technology, has significantly smoothed the path of communication and made public services more accessible. Administrations across the globe have used these technological strides to create and refine accessible web-based portals and mobile applications, thereby enhancing civic engagement in public service utilisation. The objectives of cost reduction and the efficient utilisation of resources have also fuelled the drive towards e-government. These initiatives have surpassed traditional service delivery in terms of economic efficiency. The digitisation of service delivery mechanisms, culminating in reduced physical documentation and process automation, enables governmental bodies to reallocate saved resources to more pressing governance priorities (Osborne & Gaebler, 1993).

Another critical factor in the expansion of e-government services is cost-efficiency. In contrast to conventional methods of service provision, e-government approaches are markedly more economical. Automating administrative processes and reducing reliance on paper-based practices allow for a strategic allocation of governmental resources to areas of greater administrative significance. The National Performance Review report of 1993 set explicit targets, aspiring:

> to make the entire Federal Government both less expensive and more efficient, and to change the culture of our national bureaucracy away from complacency and entitlement toward initiative and empowerment. We intend to redesign, reinvent, and reinvigorate the entire National Government.
>
> (National Performance Review, 1993a)

The worldwide growth of e-government services is due to various critical influences, particularly the accelerated expansion of technology and the rapid development of the internet and mobile devices. This has drastically simplified communication channels and facilitated the ease of accessing services (OECD, 2008). Advantageous results were realised following the initiation by US public entities to present electronically select public services. The widespread portrayal of these results significantly boosted the adoption of e-government within public policy by various global institutions, including the EU, which advocated for its uptake amongst member states. The adoption of this new way of delivering public services rapidly extended its global reach. The swift worldwide uptake of e-government policies is also linked to the endorsements and assistance dispensed by esteemed international bodies, including the United Nations, the World Bank, the OECD, and the EU. These entities routinely undertake research, compile analytical reports, and actively promote the commencement of such policies among nations.

The evolution and growth of e-government in Türkiye

Similar to the United States' utilisation of ICT via Herman Hollerith's punched cards in 1890, Türkiye's initial foray into ICT adoption within government operations can be traced back to 1934. This was when the Ziraat Bank first integrated information processing machines into its bureaucratic functions, employing a punched card system to manage office requisitions. The inception of the internet and the e-government initiative in Türkiye did not gain momentum until the 1990s. The encouragement and backing of international institutions such as the United Nations, the World Bank, the OECD, and especially the EU significantly accelerated this progression (Marquardt et al., 2008). This study examines the EU as one of the three key institutions playing a leading role in regulating e-government services in Türkiye.

During the 1980s, the integration of computers became standard practice across the public and private spheres. The inaugural internet connection in Türkiye was activated on April 12, 1993, utilising the network routers within the system room of the Middle East Technical University (METU) Information Processing Department (Dal, 2010). To adapt to the technological evolution, governments across the globe have developed intuitive web portals and mobile applications, thereby simplifying the process for citizens (OECD, 2008). With the worldwide movement towards digital governance, Türkiye commenced its foray into e-government services towards the end of the 1990s and the dawn of the new millennium.

Administrative law considerations in e-government implementation

As shown, the evolution and growth of e-government was inevitable. The advent of the digital era has forced governments worldwide, including Türkiye, to use information and communication technologies (ICTs) while providing government services and processes. Türkiye started constructing the path of its e-government agenda by forming the Supreme Council of Science and Technology (SCST). This included various ministers and bureaucrats and was presided over by the prime minister as chair. It was instituted under Law No. 77, published in the Official Gazette on October 4, 1983. The Council's principal function was to support the government in developing long-term policies for science and technology. Significantly, SCST was the first to broach the topic of offering public services in an electronic format, as outlined in the document Turkey Science and Technology Policy 1993–2003. While the implementation of e-government services has brought about a range of benefits, such as increased efficiency, accessibility, and transparency, it has also given rise to several legal and ethical issues. One such issue concerns clarity around the legal and ethical frameworks governing e-government services to ensure that they are provided relatively, transparently, and accountably. This brings administrative law-related questions to light, particularly regarding the government's accountability in cases of inadequate provision or mismanagement of e-government services. Drawing from Turkish administrative law theory, the responsibility of the state encompasses the reimbursement of damages arising from both intentional and unintentional actions and transactions of the state.[1] The Turkish Constitution, Article 125/7, explicitly states, "The administration shall be liable to compensate for damages resulting from its actions and acts". Consequently, in the context of e-government services, the state's responsibility translates to compensating for damages incurred (Gözler II, 2019b; Ulusoy, 2023).

Nevertheless, the state's legal responsibility to offer e-government services is a complex and multifaceted issue that necessitates a comprehensive analysis. This includes examining legal, economic, and philosophical considerations, as well as administrative law theory, which defines the legal boundaries and obligations of the state. The question of whether the state is legally obliged to provide e-government services is closely linked with the definition of public service and the extent to which it encompasses e-government services (Gözler II, 2019b; Ulusoy, 2023). While various articles of the 1982 Constitution refer to the term public service, there is no explicit constitutional or legal definition. Varied interpretations exist in both scholarly discussions and judicial decisions. Notably, within administrative law doctrine, Truchet highlighted the absence of a clear definition of public service. He emphasised that no one had managed to provide an unequivocal definition; legislators did not prioritise its formulation, judges refrained from defining it to maintain their discretionary powers, and the doctrine fell short in achieving a precise definition (Tan & Bayazıt, 2023). Considering the diverse influences from fields such as law, politics, economics, and philosophy in shaping this concept, it becomes clear why academia and the judiciary have failed to establish a unanimous definition. The ideological approaches of political powers significantly determine the scope of the concept of public service in a country. For instance, socialist authorities tend to broaden the definition of public services, whereas political authorities advocating liberal policies tend to interpret the concept more narrowly. Nevertheless, while the accountability of the state in providing e-government services can be seen as an extension of administrative liability according to Article 125/7 of the constitution, the legal obligation of the state to provide e-government services is not straightforward. It is tied to the broader discussion around the state's role in modern society, particularly the concept of the welfare state (Ulusoy, 2023).

The era of the Supreme Council of Science and Technology

Attempts were made to formulate a science and technology policy in the 1960s and 1970s, but the strategic planning and explicit development of science and technology policies in Türkiye began with the period covered by the

Turkish Science Policy 1983–2003 report. Before the release of this report, TÜBİTAK (The Scientific and Technological Research Council of Türkiye) had undertaken initiatives to collaborate with the OECD to prepare a science policy framework. However, the exploratory studies conducted in 1966 and 1971 did not yield the desired results. Several meetings ensued, but these preliminary actions failed to advance, culminating in the cessation of the initiative without success (Özdaş, 2005).

The Turkish Science Policy 1983–2003 prioritised scientific research in fields critical to technological advancement, explicitly naming electronic engineering, computer sciences, and telecommunications as primary support recipients. It emphasised the importance of investing in micro-hardware and software research and developing digital communication, remote sensing, and satellite communication systems. The Turkish Science Policy 1983–2003 is regarded as a critical document instrumental in formulating Türkiye's e-government policy. Its significance is primarily drawn from its proposition to create the Supreme Council of Science and Technology (SCST). The SCST has been fundamental to the regulation of e-government policies within Türkiye. The Council's role has been critical in not only the preliminary stages of e-government policy formulation but also throughout the development and enactment stages, guided by its decisive resolutions. The primary aim for instituting the SCST was "to ascertain, guide, and harmonise research and development strategies within the realms of science and technology, to be in concert with the goals of economic growth, societal advancement, and national security" (TÜBİTAK, 1993).

The Supreme Council of Science and Technology (SCST)

Although the Supreme Council of Science and Technology (SCST) was formed in 1983, it was not until 1989 that it assembled for its inaugural meeting. The second SCST meeting occurred on February 3, 1993. It marked a pivotal moment by approving the Türkiye Science and Technology Policy 1993–*2003* document, drafted by TÜBİTAK. After providing a brief overview of information technology procurement, utilisation, and associated concerns in public institutions, the Türkiye Science and Technology Policy 1993–2003 outlines the necessary actions in specific sections. It suggests establishing an independent administrative agency involving representatives from other administrative agencies such as The Scientific and Technological Research Council of Türkiye, the Turkish Standards Institution, the Council of Higher Education, the State Statistical Institute, and the Post and Telegraph Organization. This newly proposed entity would oversee the digitalisation and mechanisation of public sector operations, safeguarded from partisan influences (TÜBİTAK, 1993). The Türkiye Science and Technology Policy 1993–2003 document also proposes the establishment of an extensive computer network infrastructure, which would integrate Turkish universities, research establishments, private sector IT firms, and a diverse array of organisations, including banks, financial institutions, and hospitals. This proposition sets an example for the framework of Türkiye's e-government system (BTYK, 1993). Consequently, several recommendations offered by the Türkiye Science and Technology Policy 1993–2003 can be considered preliminary strides in the direction of an e-government policy.[2]

In the same year as the Türkiye Science and Technology Policy 1993–2003, the Informatics and Economic Modernization Report[3] was developed. This report was formulated by the World Bank in collaboration with the Turkish government to address various aspects of the information society in Türkiye. The report included findings related to computer usage, communication networks, human resources for the information economy, the software market, and the legal framework. It concluded,

> Türkiye harbours the capacity to emerge as a dynamic contributor to the informatics revolution and to establish itself as a central information nexus within the global economy. The fruition of this capacity will hinge upon a sustained alliance between progressive governmental policies and entrepreneurial vigour in the private sector.
>
> (The World Bank, 1993)

Although the report proposed an action plan based on these findings, the recommendations were not implemented due to the failure to reach a credit agreement with the World Bank.

Turkish Science and Technology Policy 1993–2003

The Turkish Science and Technology Policy 1993–2003, approved by SCST, holds significance as it is one of the first to address the electronic delivery of public services and remote access to public services. The first annexure of the document was denoted as Issues, Objectives, and Solutions for Türkiye's Information Policies; the importance of the information technology sector was initially emphasised, followed by discussions on the sector's problems, objectives, and proposed solutions (TÜBİTAK, 1993). The document proposed the establishment of an office with minimal bureaucratic influence to oversee computerisation in public institutions and make preparations for the transition to an automation system. Additionally, it suggested that a computer network be established, encompassing universities, research institutions, private-sector computer firms, and other institutions such as banks, financial organisations, and hospitals. Finally, it recommended that all public institutions gradually connect to this network over time (TÜBİTAK, 1993).

Moreover, the Turkish Science and Technology Policy 1993–2003 outlined the characteristics this envisioned computer network should possess. It detailed various characteristics of the network, including the ability to connect to a remote system, enabling public institutions to meet their information communication needs and ensuring confidential and secure information flow when transitioning to an automation system in public institutions. It becomes evident that the groundwork for an e-government framework was being established (TÜBİTAK, 1993).

The Science and Technology Leap Project

The Science and Technology Leap Project focused on empowering Türkiye in science and technology and leveraging these domains for economic and social enrichment. Concluding on February 24, 1995, this project was under the leadership of the President of TÜBİTAK, with a task force constituted by delegates from both the public and private sectors. Within the framework of the project, seven strategic areas were identified for progression. Creating a National Information Infrastructure was emphasised as a critical objective (TÜBİTAK, 1995). The accompanying report with the Science and Technology Leap Project outlined the need for specific electronically administered public services (TÜBİTAK, 1995).

National Information Infrastructure Master Plan

The Türkiye National Information Infrastructure Master Plan (TUENA) is acknowledged as the foundation for the e-government policy. The TUENA's outcome report was submitted to the Ministry of Transport in 1998, and this marks the official start of the e-government policy.

The concept of formulating TUENA was introduced in the Science and Technology Leap Project. Following a series of discussions and debates, it was resolved that the master plan would be developed under the leadership of the Ministry of Transport, with TÜBİTAK providing secretarial support plus a working group composed of selected public and private sector representatives appointed by the Ministry. The report was delivered to the Ministry of Transport in 1998 and updated in the first half of 1999. It was officially announced by the Ministry in the same year. The report outlined the goal of the TUENA project being to

> optimise the overarching socio-economic advantage for enduring development, amplify the domestic input of the information technology sector across hardware, communicative services, software, and content production industries, and to position Türkiye as a frontrunner within its region for capturing a segment of the global information technology marketplace, while also devising policies and frameworks to realise these ambitions.
>
> (TUENA, 1999)

In the formulation of the TUENA project, scenarios and forecasts for the future, participatory methods were naturally employed in the study. Over 200 sector stakeholders participated in direct consultations to contribute their predictions and estimations regarding the infrastructure used in Türkiye in the future. TUENA presented future predictions concerning technological advancements, costs, population, and education (TÜBİTAK, 2002).

The TUENA project, resulting from numerous institutions' and experts' input and reports, is highly comprehensive. This chapter can only emphasise its significance in terms of digitisation, as a detailed examination of the plan would go beyond the scope of this study.[4]

The Electronic Commerce Network

In the context of laying the groundwork for e-government infrastructure, the conception of an Electronic Commerce Network stands out as a notable initiative. The Electronic Commerce Coordination Board was instituted under the authority of the Undersecretariat of Foreign Trade in 1998 to promote electronic commerce within Türkiye. The Electronic Commerce Coordination Board (ECCB) held its first meeting on February 16, 1998. The board decreed that legal, technical, and financial working groups would be established within the ECCB. The "General Coordination of Electronic Commerce" was established within the Undersecretariat of Foreign Trade to establish the legal infrastructure for electronic commerce and identify issues in practice. An "E-commerce Commission" was also established, consisting of representatives from various directorates-general.

During the meeting of the SCST on August 25, 1997, the formation of an Electronic Commerce Network was prioritised. The Council created a task force to develop the necessary legal and infrastructural parameters. Made up of various administrative units, its aim was to adapt to changes in the market quickly, introducing technological innovations, planning production processes, implementing new production, service, and management models comprehensively, and repositioning economic activities on a global scale.

At the SCST meeting of June 2, 1998, reports from established working groups laid the groundwork for four critical long-term e-commerce objectives: (1) building essential technical and administrative infrastructure, (2) creating a legal framework, (3) promoting e-commerce, and (4) aligning national policies with global standards. Following this report, preparing a draft implementation plan before the action plan was considered to realise the legal framework of e-commerce and identify issues in practice. Under the coordination of the Undersecretariat for Foreign Trade, the Electronic Commerce Coordination Council met on April 26, 2000, resolving that established working groups should compile final reports. It was decided that the previously formed working groups should prepare final reports on the ongoing work and future recommendations. An *Electronic Commerce General Coordination* unit was created within the Undersecretariat for Foreign Trade to regulate the process of creating the *Electronic Commerce Network*. An e-commerce commission composed of representatives from various general directorates was also formed. With the Prime Ministry Directive No.

2002/20, titled *e-Türkiye,* on June 19, 2002, activities related to the Electronic Commerce Network were incorporated into programs such as the E-Türkiye Initiative and the E-Transformation Türkiye Project.

Kamu-Net

At the third assembly of the SCST, the idea of establishing a public computer network, known as Kamu-Net (Public-Net), was proposed. It was suggested that Kamu-Net should be prepared to be compatible with TUENA, as the foundations were laid for creating a shared public computer network. Once the conceptual groundwork was established, on February 23–25, 1998, the *Kamu-Net'98 Public Computer Networks Conference* was held. This conference featured presentations from public entities that had already embraced internet applications. It was attended by approximately 460 information technology specialists and senior executives. Following the conference's conclusion, to implement the recommendations arising and to ensure that the related efforts were carried out systematically, the establishment of the *Kamu-Net High Council* and the *Kamu-Net Technical Council* was authorised under Prime Ministry Directive No. 1998/13. Sub-working groups supported both councils, and their responsibilities continued until the publication of the Prime Ministry Directive No. 2002/20, titled *e-Türkiye,* on June 19, 2002. This directive placed all activities in the e-government field under the jurisdiction of the State Ministry and the Deputy Prime Ministry.

The objective of *Kamu-Net* was to create a communal network interlinking the Prime Ministry with central organisational structures, enabling access and shared use of data repositories among public entities. The intent was to increase the operational efficiency of the Prime Ministry and refine the delivery of public services. These two councils faced difficulties in conducting productive work due to individual and institutional disputes and various challenges, such as the 1999 earthquake and the elections that year. The dissolution of these councils' activities coincided with the enactment of Prime Ministry Directive No. 2002/20 titled *e-Türkiye.* Going forward, the *Kamu-Net Technical Council* operated within a reformed framework; the State Ministry and the Deputy Prime Ministry would handle the coordination, implementation, and establishment of institutional infrastructure concerning e-Türkiye. This resulted in an increased representation and political autonomy for the top management in the formation of e-government policies.

Following this reorganisation in 2002, the *Kamu-Net Technical Council* initiated its activities to develop an *e-Government Transition Action Plan.* This plan classified actions into short-, medium-, and long-term objectives, ensuring a systematic approach. Various tasks were identified, including the creation of a *Kamu-Net* website to facilitate public engagement and guide public organisations. This also involved establishing the *e-Government Gateway*, which allows access to electronic services from a single point.

To accelerate e-government adoption, e-institution *Guidelines and Criteria* were introduced to help organisations maximise IT capabilities. Training programmes were initiated to ensure public employees could smoothly transition to the new system. These activities included identifying public services to be moved into the electronic domain, coordinating knowledge transfer between organisations, and ensuring the security of information accessed electronically. Efforts were made to create a coordination framework for the transfer of information between institutions and to ensure the security of electronically accessible information. The council also pioneered the *turkiye.gov.tr* website, regarded as the forerunner to the contemporary *Digital Türkiye/e-Government Gateway* (DPT, 2004).

European Union harmonization process

Comprising only six countries in the early 1950s, the EU has evolved to include 27 nations. The Treaty of the EU prescribes the expansionary path of the EU. Nations aspiring to join the EU are required to comply with the Copenhagen Criteria, which stipulate the necessary political, economic, and jurisprudential conditions for membership (Costa & Peers, 2023). Türkiye lodged its formal request to join the EU in 1987, and the EU acknowledged Türkiye as a prospective member state in 1999. The accession discussions were initiated in 2005.

A fundamental aspect of the EU accession process is the adoption and implementation of the EU acquis. This refers to the shared rights and obligations binding all EU member states. The EU closely monitors and evaluates the progress of all candidate countries throughout the accession process, offering financial and technical assistance to aid reform and harmonisation efforts. While the entire accession process is primarily the responsibility of the candidate country's national government, it is imperative that a comprehensive understanding of the process exists at all levels of government and within civil society (Neumann, 1998). One of the areas of reform and harmonisation of the EU accession process is the e-government. This section will explore the impact that EU harmonisation has had on the regulation of e-government in Türkiye.

E-Europe

The e-Europe initiative, prepared by the EU and part of the EU acquis, holds significant importance in Türkiye's e-government policy. This programme, known as e-Europe, encompasses all EU member states as well as candidate countries like Türkiye. The e-Europe initiative has contributed to shaping and aligning Türkiye's e-government policy. In December 1999, the European Commission launched the e-Europe programme to help improve Europe's digital presence. Following a positive reaction to the e-Europe initiative from Member States, the European Parliament, and principal stakeholders, the Commission submitted a Progress Report to the Lisbon Summit in March 2000. At this Summit, state and government leaders agreed to take action within the defined timelines to advance the e-Europe initiative (COM, 2000).

The e-Europe initiative made tailored recommendations to member and candidate countries to accelerate the renewal and modernisation of their economies, enhance their institutional capabilities, and improve their overall competitiveness. Subsequently, regular monitoring ensured adherence to the targets set, leading to the development of new action plans. These plans include numerous suggestions regarding the integration of e-government: the suggestions and regular monitoring affected not only EU countries but also candidate countries and potential candidate countries. Türkiye signed onto the e-Europe project as a candidate country during the EU leaders' summit on June 15–16, 2001. Hence, e-Europe had significantly influenced Türkiye's e-government policy (Başbakanlık, 2002).

E- Türkiye and E-Transformation Türkiye

The e-Europe initiative, a construct of the EU and an integral part of the EU acquis, wields considerable influence over the formulation of Türkiye's e-government policy. The programme extends its reach to include both EU member states and candidate countries such as Türkiye. It has been pivotal in creating and calibrating Türkiye's e-government policy to meet current standards.

The E-Türkiye initiative started as part of the e-Europe Action Plan on October 9, 2002, through the Prime Ministry's Circular No. 2002/352. Thirteen working groups were established in specific areas under the coordination of the Prime Ministry to draft an action plan. The "e-Türkiye" initiative resulted in a plan covering the years 2001–2002, and the coordination of activities within this framework was entrusted to TÜBİTAK (The Scientific and Technological Research Council of Türkiye). Following the "e-Türkiye" initiative for the years 2001–2002, a new plan was introduced for the 2003–2004 period, named the "e-Transformation Türkiye Project," under the Prime Ministry's Circular No. 2003/12, published on February 27, 2003. This time, the project's coordination, monitoring, evaluation, and direction were assigned to the Undersecretariat of the State Planning Organization (SPO) instead of TÜBİTAK. Under the management of the SPO, the first step was the preparation of a Short-Term Action Plan covering the 2003–2004 period on April 28, 2003. Following the conclusion of this plan in 2004, the 2005 Action Plan came into effect with both encompassing regulations in various fields. The areas and responsible institutions are as follows: (1) legal infrastructure: Ministry of Justice, (2) technical infrastructure and information security: Ministry of Transport, (3) education and human resources: Ministry of National Education, (4) service delivery in the electronic environment: State Planning Organization, (5) common standards to facilitate integrated service delivery between institutions: Turkish Standards Institution, (6) e-health: Ministry of Health (7) e-commerce: Undersecretariat of Foreign Trade, and (8) monitoring activities: Türkiye Informatics Association (DPT, 2003, 2005).

The objectives of the *e-Türkiye* initiative and the subsequent *e-Transformation Türkiye* project are to align with the *e-Europe+ Action Plan* directives. The EU, alongside the SCST, has helped supervise the e-government services in Türkiye. But the e-government project should not be regarded as merely a prerequisite for Türkiye on its path to EU accession. The *E-Transformation Türkiye* has the potential to bring transparency in public administration, efficient and effective processes, citizen participation at all levels of governance, prevention of redundant work and data through interagency information exchange, the provision of high-quality and rapid services to citizens, and the enhancement and acceleration of decision-making processes for public administrators (OECD 2003a, 2003b, 2021, 2023).

The Era of the Digital Transformation Office

Following a referendum in 2017, Türkiye experienced a fundamental political shift from a parliamentary to a presidential governance system. This came into force after the Presidential election held on June 24, 2018.[5]

Emerging Actors in the regulation of e-government services within the presidential government system

The establishment of policy boards, their areas of focus, duties, and authorities are specified in Presidential Decree No. 1. Based on Presidential Decree No. 1, the policy boards function within the framework of the new presidential government system. The President, elected by the citizens, holds individual executive authority and plays a pivotal role in shaping and executing public policies. This represents a departure from the previous parliamentary model. This new era in Turkish governance is characterised by establishing Presidential Policy Boards and Presidential Offices, embodying new dynamics in public policy formulation within the Turkish public administration (Gözler, 2019a; Ulusoy, 2023).

Within the new emerging administrative actors post-2018, the *Science, Technology, and Innovation Policies Board (STIPB)* bears particular relevance to this chapter. Its significance stems from its inception within the Presidential Complex as the successor to the Supreme Council of Science and Technology (SCST), which was dissolved in 2018. The STIPB has assumed a critical function in the evolution of Türkiye's e-government policy, tasked with identifying, steering, and synchronising research and development policies that align with the nation's economic, social, and security ambitions. The role and responsibilities defined for STIPB in Presidential Decree No. 1 are similar to those of SCST. STIPB's duties include identifying policy priorities aligned with Türkiye's national goals, considering the social benefits and socio-economic impacts of information technology, information society, and technological transformation, and providing policy recommendations and advice. Due to separate structures being established within the Presidential system for e-government policies, it is anticipated that STIPB may not have the same direct influence in this area as its predecessor, SCST.

The revision of the Turkish administrative framework to include Presidential Offices is a direct consequence of the enhanced powers conferred upon the President in the post-reform era. This transition was codified with Presidential Decree No. 1, which resulted in the establishment of the Finance Office, Human Resources Office, Investment Office, and Digital Transformation Office. Article 525 of Presidential Decree No. 1 comprehensively defines the offices as bodies "attached to the Presidency" featuring "independent budgets", legal personality, and "autonomous administrative and financial competencies", thus specifying their fundamental characteristics. Occupying a strategic position in the governmental structure, these offices consist of principal and supportive service units, holding a direct presidential link and distinct legal, budgetary, and administrative independence. This restructured organisational model significantly shifts from the conventional Turkish administrative paradigm.[6] By the stipulations defined within the Presidential Decree concerning Presidential Organisation, these offices are instrumental in aiding the President in policy creation and administrative governance tasks. Their roles are similar to those of the Presidential Policy Boards, providing advisory and consultative services. Their responsibilities extend to a broad spectrum of activities, including analysis, reporting, the development and implementation of projects, coordination, partnership, investigation, and surveillance (Gözler, 2019a; Ulusoy, 2023).

The Digital Transformation Office

The Presidential Decree's Article 528 and the subsequent articles contain standard regulations concerning the Presidential Offices. The DTO operates under the direct authority of the President of Türkiye. While the principal office is in Ankara, branches can be established within Türkiye and internationally if required. In line with Presidential Decree No. 48, as promulgated in the Official Gazette on October 24, 2019, the head of the DTO is designated as the *Public Digital Transformation Leader*, a function-specific role that transcends traditional administrative structure. In this capacity, the Public Digital Transformation Leader bears the charge of crafting strategies for digital transformation across the public sector, overseeing the enactment of these strategies, formulating digital transformation roadmaps, and spearheading the digital transformation of public services (OECD, 2021, 2023). Like the SCST, the structure of DTO is distinct from traditional regulatory bodies; however, it plays a crucial role in overseeing e-government services within Türkiye.

An analysis of the organisational architecture of the DTO reveals that the Office President occupies the apex executive role with several critical units reporting directly: The Legal Advisory Office, the Private Secretary Directorate, the Information Technologies Department Presidency, and the Administrative Services Department Presidency. In contrast, a set of specialised departments function under the authority of the Vice President, including the Digital Transformation Coordination Department Presidency, Digital Expertise Monitoring and Evaluation Department Presidency, Cybersecurity Department Presidency, Big Data Artificial Intelligence Applications Department Presidency, International Relations Department Presidency, and the Digital Technologies Procurement and Resource Management Department Presidency. Examining the duties of the DTO, in Article 527 of Presidential Decree No. 1, they are shown as being multifaceted, encompassing advisory services, project development, strategic planning, promotional activities, facilitation, fostering partnerships, and rendering expert opinions. The DTO is entrusted with steering the digital evolution and reform of governmental operations, reflecting its escalating significance in the contemporary policy-making landscape. The office's mission is to articulate policies and strategies conducive to the digital transformation of public services alongside project formulation, facilitation, and consultancy, all while maintaining interdepartmental coordination (OECD, 2021, 2023).

The SCST, established in 1983 and officially convened in 1989, played a crucial role in overseeing e-government services in Türkiye until its dissolution on July 2, 2018. The transition from 2004 to 2016 marked a period of increased regular sessions for the SCST, deviating from its earlier limited sittings. Alongside the SCST, the EU also supervised e-government services. The e-Europe initiative, developed by the EU and a fundamental aspect of the EU acquis, significantly shaped Türkiye's e-government policy, formulating and aligning it to meet with current standards. The political shift from a parliamentary to a presidential governance system introduced new actors to the Turkish administrative structure, influencing the regulation of e-government services. While the Supreme Council of Science and Technology has been disbanded, the Science, Technology, and Innovation Policies Board (STIPB) emerged as its successor on July 10, 2018 with the role of supervising e-government services transitioned to the newly established Digital Transformation Office (DTO). The OECD describes DTO as "the organisation in charge" regarding e-government in Türkiye (OECD, 2021, 2023). Presently, DTO serves as the administrative authority that leads, coordinates, and oversees the e-government services in Türkiye.

Conclusion

In conclusion, the concept of e-government has emerged from integrating digital innovations to enhance the efficiency and accessibility of public services, fostering a more interactive relationship among government bodies, citizens, and the business sector. Türkiye has been working to promote collaboration and cooperation between various public institutions, the private sector, civil society, and international organisations to ensure that e-government initiatives are aligned, integrated, and interoperable. But there are still many persistent and emerging challenges that need to be addressed, such as ensuring digital inclusion, enhancing cybersecurity, fostering innovation, and adapting to changing user needs and expectations. One such challenge is to ensure that all segments of society participate in e-government initiatives. This means addressing the digital divide and digital literacy gaps among different groups of citizens, especially older adults, people with disabilities, low-income individuals, and those living in rural areas who must receive equal access and opportunities. Citizens and businesses need to be made more aware of e-government services and encouraged to provide feedback that can help improve policymaking and evaluation. Another significant challenge facing Türkiye in the future is the need to improve the cybersecurity and resilience of e-government systems and services. With cyber threats and risks constantly evolving and increasing, the government must take proactive and preventative measures to protect e-government infrastructure, data, and users. To do this, Türkiye needs to develop and implement a comprehensive cybersecurity strategy and action plan. This plan should define various stakeholders' roles, responsibilities, and capabilities and establish effective mechanisms and procedures for cybersecurity governance, coordination, and response. Finally, it is essential for Türkiye to keep up with the rapid and ever-evolving changes in the ICT sector. This will require anticipating and responding to emerging trends and opportunities that affect e-government. Additionally, the country should improve the flexibility and agility of e-government systems and services, enabling continuous improvement and optimisation based on user feedback and data analytics.

Notes

1 For further information, please see: Gözler, K. (2019). *İdare Hukuku Cilt II*. Bursa: Ekin Basın Yayın Dağıtım; Ulusoy, A. D. (2023). *Yeni Türk İdare Hukuku*. Ankara: Yetkin Yayınları.

2 For further information and the full report, please see: www.tubitak.gov.tr/tubitak_content_files/BTYPD/btyk/2/2btyk_karar.pdf

3 For further information and the full report, please see: www.bilgitoplumu.gov.tr/Documents/1/Yayinlar/930000_BilisimVeEkonomikModernizasyonRaporu.pdf

4 For further information, please see: TUENA Proje Ofisi (1999). *Türkiye Ulusal Enformasyon Alt Yapısı Ana Planı (TUENA) Sonuç Raporu*. T.C. Ankara: Ulaştırma Bakanlığı.

5 For further information, please see: Gözler, K. (2019). İdare Hukuku Cilt I. Bursa: Ekin Basın Yayın Dağıtım; Ulusoy, A. D. (2023). *Yeni Türk İdare Hukuku*. Ankara: Yetkin Yayınları.

6 For further information and discussions in Turkish administrative law regarding the legal personality of DTO, please see: Üstün, G. (2019). *Cumhurbaşkanlığı Ofislerinin İdari Teşkilattaki Yeri. In Cumhurbaşkanlığı Sisteminde Yürütme Sempozyum Bildiri Kitabı*. İstanbul: Marmara Üniversitesi Yayınevi.

References

Başbakanlık. (2002). *e-Türkiye Girişimi Eylem Planı (Taslak) Ankara, Başbakanlık.*

Bennett, C. (1992). *Regulating privacy: Data protection and public policy in Europe and the United States*. Ithaca: Cornell University Press.

BTYK. (1993). *Bilim ve Teknoloji Yüksek Kurulu, Türkiye Bilim ve Teknoloji Politikası 1993–2003*. Ankara: TÜBİTAK.

COM. (2000). Commission of the European communities. In *eEurope 2002 an information society for all*. Brussels: Commission of the European communities.

Costa, M., & Peers, S. (2023). *Steiner & woods EU law* (15th ed., M. Costa & S. Peers Eds.). Oxford: Oxford University Press.

Coursey, D., & Norris, D. F. (2008). Models of E-government: Are they correct? An empirical assessment. *Public Administration Review*, *68*(3), 523–536.

Dal, S. (2010). Türk Hukukunda İnternet Alan Adları (Domain Names) ve bu Alandaki Son Gelişmeler. *Marmara Üniversitesi İktisadi ve İdari Bilimler Dergisi*, *28*(1).

DPT. (2003). *E-Dönüşüm Türkiye Projesi Kısa Dönem Eylem Planı 2003–2004*. Ankara: DPT.

DPT. (2004). *e-Devlet Proje ve Uygulamaları*. Ankara: DPT.

DPT. (2005). *e-Dönüşüm Türkiye Projesi 2003–2004 KDEP Uygulama Sonuçları ve 2005 Eylem Planı*. Ankara: DPT/Bilgi Toplumu Dairesi.

Dugan, R. E. (1999). Access America, reengineering through information technology. *The Journal of Academic Librarianship*, *25*(1), 46–49.

Fletcher, P. D. (2003). New models of collaboration: A guide for managers. In *IRS E-file: Electronic tax administration in the United States*. Albany: Center for Technology in Government.

Gore, A. (1997). Access America: Reengineering through information technology. In *US national performance review*. Washington, DC: USGPO.

Gözler, K. (2019a). *İdare Hukuku Cilt I*. Bursa: Ekin Basın Yayın Dağıtım.

Gözler, K. (2019b). *İdare Hukuku Cilt II*. Bursa: Ekin Basın Yayın Dağıtım.

Marquardt, K., & Gökçe, O., & Eroğlu, H. T. (2008). E-Avrupa Girişimi ve Türkiye"de EDevlet. In K. Marquardt & O. Gökçe (Eds.), *E-Devlet: Gerçek ya da Hayal*. Konya: Çizgi Kitabevi.

National Performance Review. (1993a). *From red tape to results: Creating a government that works better and costs less: Report of the national performance review*. Washington, DC: USGPO.

Neumann, I. B. (1998). European identity, EU expansion, and the Integration/Exclusion nexus. *Alternatives: Global, Local, Political*, *23*(3), 397–416.

OECD. (2003a, March). The e-government imperative: Main findings. *Policy Brief*. OECD Observer.

OECD. (2003b). *Engaging citizens online for better policy-making*, Paris: Policy Brief.

OECD. (2008). *OECD background paper: Implementing e-government in OECD countries: Experiences and challenges*. Paris: OECD Publishing.

OECD. (2021). *The e-leaders handbook on the governance of digital government*. Paris: OECD Publishing.

OECD. (2023). *Digital government review of Türkiye: Towards a digitally-enabled government*. Paris: OECD Publishing.

Osborne, D., & Gaebler, T. (1993). *Reinventing government: How the entrepreneurial spirit is transforming the public sector*. Reading, MA: Addison-Wesley.

Özdaş, N. (2005). *Konuşmalar. Geçmişten geleceğe Türk bilim ve teknoloji politikaları*. Ankara: Türkiye Bilimler Akademisi.

Tan, T., & Bayazıt, B. (2023). *İdare Hukuku*. Ankara: Turhan Kitabevi.

TÜBİTAK. (1993). *Türk Bilim ve Teknoloji Politikası 1993–2003*. Ankara: TÜBİTAK.

TÜBİTAK. (1995). *Bilim ve Teknolojide Atılım Projesi: Çalışma Komitesi Raporu (95/02)*. Ankara: TÜBİTAK.

TÜBİTAK. (2002) *Bilgi Toplumu Politikaları Üzerine Bir Değerlendirme (Dünya ve Türkiye)*. Ankara: TÜBİTAK.

TUENA Proje Ofisi. (1999). *Türkiye Ulusal Enformasyon Alt Yapısı Ana Planı (TUENA) Sonuç Raporu*. Ankara: T.C. Ulaştırma Bakanlığı.

Ulusoy, A. D. (2023). *Yeni Türk İdare Hukuku*. Ankara: Yetkin Yayınları.

Üstün, G. (2019). Cumhurbaşkanlığı Ofislerinin İdari Teşkilattaki Yeri. In *Cumhurbaşkanlığı Sisteminde Yürütme Sempozyum Bildiri Kitabı*. İstanbul: Marmara Üniversitesi Yayınevi.

Veit, D., & Huntgeburth, J. (2014). *Foundations of digital government leading and managing in the digital era*. Berlin: Springer.

The World Bank. (1993). *Informatics and economic modernization report*. Washington, DC: World Bank.

10 Privacy and Data Protection Regulation

Çiçek Ersoy

Introduction and Legislative Framework for Privacy

In Turkish law, privacy is protected by various legislative sources, including the Turkish Constitution, the Turkish Criminal Code No. 5237, and the Turkish Data Protection Act No. 6698 ("DPA"), which is based on EU Directive 95/46/EC on data protection. The Turkish Criminal Code defines numerous crimes related to the protection of privacy such as "Recording Personal Data" (Art. 135), "Unlawfully Disseminating or Capturing Data" (Art. 136), "Failure to Destroy Data" (Art. 138), and "Preventing and Impairing the System, Altering or Destroying Data" (Art. 244). Besides the criminal sanctions regulated by the Turkish Criminal Code and imposed by the criminal courts, the right to privacy is protected by the Turkish Data Protection Act No. 6698 (**DPA**),[1] which entered into force in April 2016. The Turkish Parliament has recently enacted on March 12, 2024, significant amendments to the Turkish Personal Data Protection Act, which will enter into force on June 1, 2024.[2] The amendments, which aim to harmonize DPA with GDPR, include provisions on the processing of special categories of personal data, cross-border transfer of personal data, administrative fines, and the appeal authority. A further comprehensive revision of DPA is planned by the end of 2024.

The DPA is enforced by the Turkish Personal Data Protection Authority (the Authority), which is a financially and administratively autonomous public legal entity endowed with regulatory and supervisory powers. The Authority comprises the Board of Personal Data Protection (the Board) and the Presidency. The Authority's decision-making body is the Board (Art. 19/IV DPA). The purpose of the DPA is to protect fundamental rights and freedoms, particularly the right to privacy, in the processing of personal data, and to set forth obligations, principles, and procedures which are binding on natural and legal persons who process personal data.

Since 2016, a settled case law has been developed as a result of Board decisions. In the past seven years, the Board has announced various pieces of secondary legislation to ensure clarity and consistency in the implementation of the DPA. These are as follows: the By-Law on Data Controllers' Registry,[3] the By-Law on Erasure, Destruction, and Anonymisation of Personal Data,[4] the

DOI: 10.4324/9781032692937-10

Communiqué on Principles and Procedures to be Followed in Fulfilment of the Obligation to Inform,[5] and the *Communiqué* on the Principles and Procedures for Requests to the Data Controller.[6] Besides this secondary legislation, the Board has announced guidelines that provide a framework for the implementation of the DPA and the secondary legislation. The most important guidelines and draft guidelines are as follows: the Best Practice Guidelines on Personal Data Protection in the Banking Sector,[7] the Guidelines on the Processing of Biometric Data,[8] the Guidelines on the Use of Cookies,[9] the Guidelines on the Right to be Forgotten – Evaluation of the Right to be Forgotten Specific to Search Engines,[10] the Recommendations on the Protection of Personal Data in the Field of Artificial Intelligence,[11] the Guidelines on Personal Data Security (Technical and Administrative Measures),[12] Guidelines on the Protection of Personal Data in Political Elections,[13] Guidelines on the Processing of the Republic of Turkey Identification Numbers,[14] Guidelines on the Protecting Privacy in Mobile Applications,[15] the Guidelines on the Processing of Genetic Data,[16] Guidelines on Deepfake,[17] and the Draft Guidelines on the Investigation of Loyalty Programmes under the Personal Data Protection Legislation.

In implementing the DPA, the General Data Protection Regulation (GDPR) principles are followed and constantly and regularly considered by the Authority. The Board keeps a close eye on GDPR practices and recent global developments, and this approach is successfully reflected in its decisions. The Board often points out the necessity of complete harmonization of Turkish law with the GDPR in different environments and is leading a comprehensive revision of Turkish data protection law to adopt global trends and developments in privacy law.

Scope

Article 2 of the DPA states the material scope of the law. Accordingly, the DPA shall apply to natural persons whose personal data are processed and to natural or legal persons processing such data wholly or partially by automated means or by non-automated means provided that form part of a data filing system.

The protection afforded by DPA applies only to the data of natural persons. DPA does not ensure any protection for the data belonging to legal persons. Regarding the applicability of law, there is no distinction between private corporations and public authorities. Therefore, rules and procedures determined by the DPA apply to all institutions and organizations. Though, about sanctions imposed by the Board, a significant difference exists between private and public authorities. Shall the infringements be committed by the public institutions and organizations, only administrative disciplinary procedures may be applied to the civil servants and other public officers employed in the relevant public institutions but not administrative fines. The public institutions are obliged to inform the Board regarding the disciplinary measures (Art. 18/III DPA).

The DPA includes exceptions under Art. 28/I, which provides that the DPA is not applicable in the following circumstances:

a) Personal data are processed by natural persons within the scope of purely personal activities of the data subject or family members living together with him/her in the same dwelling provided that it is not to be disclosed to third parties and the obligations about data security is to be complied with.
b) Personal data are processed for official statistics and provided that they are being anonymized for purposes such as research, planning, and statistics.
(c) Personal data are processed with artistic, historical, literary, or scientific purposes, or within the scope of freedom of expression provided that national defense, national security, public security, public order, economic security, right to privacy, or personal rights are not violated or the process doesn't constitute a crime.
(ç) Personal data are processed within the scope of preventive, protective, and intelligence activities carried out by public institutions and organizations duly authorized and assigned by law to maintain national defense, national security, public security, public order, or economic security.
(d) Personal data are processed by judicial authorities or execution authorities about investigation, prosecution, judicial, or execution proceedings.

Besides the exceptions of Art. 28/I DPA, the law foresees partial exemptions in specific circumstances. Accordingly, Article 10 regarding the data controller's obligation to inform, Article 11 regarding the rights of the data subject, excluding the right to claim compensation, and Article 16 regarding the obligation to register with the Data Controllers Registry are not applicable in the following cases where personal data processing:

a) is necessary for the prevention of committing a crime or for crime investigation.
b) is carried out on the data which are made public by the data subject himself/herself.
c) is necessary for the performance of supervision or regulatory duties and disciplinary investigation and prosecution to be carried out by the assigned and authorized public institutions and organizations and by public professional organizations, by the power conferred on them by the law,
ç) is necessary for protection of economic and financial interests of State related to budget, tax, and financial matters.

Even though no provisions regarding the territorial scope exist in DPA, in many cases it is determined by the Authority that the DPA shall be applied to the processing of personal data in the context of the activities both in Turkey and also outside the territory of Turkey. If the data processing relates to the data of Turkish citizens or real persons residing in Turkey, but the processing is carried out outside Turkey, DPA may still be applicable. In the case of *Cathay Pacific Airways Limited*, the Board imposed fines for the data breach, by which the residents in Turkey (customers of the company) are affected by the infringement, although the company is not located in Turkey.[18] Likewise, in the case of *WhatsApp*, the Board imposed fines for illegal data processing activities, as the users of *WhatsApp* are residents of Turkey. To sum up, data processing activities carried out for goods and services accessible from Turkey by non-residents and also processing activities related to the monitoring of the behavior of Turkish residents fall within the scope of DPA.[19]

General Concepts

Data Controller, Joint Controller, and Data Processor

A data controller is defined as the natural or legal person who determines the purposes and means of processing personal data and is responsible for the establishment and management of the data filing system (Art. 3/I-g DPA).

Regarding the concept of the joint data controller, there have been several key decisions in which the Board has explicitly stated that the DPA shall be interpreted and implemented in compliance with the GDPR.[20] In the recent *Car Rental* Case,[21] which was about processing personal data through exclusively automated profiling, evaluating the software used by rental companies, and providing these companies with a blacklist, the Board imposed fines on the ground of unlawful data processing. In this case, the Board focused on joint data controllership by car rental firms and software companies, although joint controllership is not regulated by the DPA.

A data processor is defined as the natural or legal person who processes personal data on behalf of the data controller upon its authorization (Art. 3/I-g DPA).

Personal Data

Personal data is defined as any information relating to an identified or identifiable real person (Art. 3/I-d DPA). Data can be defined as "personal data" if these three requirements shall be cumulatively fulfilled: being related to a real person, being identified or identifiable, and being every kind of information.

DPA does not apply to anonymized data. Anonymization means rendering personal data impossible to link with an identified or identifiable natural person, even through matching them with other data (Art. 3/I-b DPA). Pseudonymization is not defined in Turkish law but in By-Law on Erasure, Destruction, and Anonymisation of Personal Data,[22] described as the processing of personal data in such a manner that the personal data can still be attributable to a specific data subject. Therefore, for processing of pseudonym data, DPA is applicable.

Special Category Data

Special categories of personal data means information that reveals racial or ethnic origin, political opinions, religious or philosophical beliefs, clothing and outfit, memberships of unions, associations, or foundations, as well as information about health, sexual life, criminal records, or punitive measures, as well as biometric and genetic data (Art. 6/I DPA). Here clothing and outfit refer to religious clothing like Islamic hijab.

Following GDPR, stricter rules are designed for the processing of special categories of personal data. Besides, regarding the technical and administrative measures, the Board has announced rules for the processing of special categories of data.[23] Accordingly, data controllers shall announce a policy and procedure about special categories of personal data. The Board also pointed out the implementation of the measures that have been determined in the Personal Data Security Guide (Art. 6/IV DPA).

Data Subject

A data subject is an individual who is the subject of personal data and is defined as the natural person whose personal data was processed (Art. 3/I-d DPA). Unlike GDPR, regarding the personal data of children, no special rules are defined in DPA. However, there are cases where the Board emphasizes the specific need for protection regarding the children's data.[24] DPA does not include any specific rules for the processing of personal data of employees.

Data Controller's Registry (VERBIS)

Unlike GDPR and other local laws around the world, Turkey established a registry system for the tracking and documentation of data controllers and related data processing activities. According to Art. 16/II DPA, natural or legal persons who process personal data shall register with the Data Controllers' Registry before the start of data processing. VERBIS is an information system that is accessible on the internet (https://verbis.kvkk.gov.tr/) and established and managed by the presidency under the supervision of the Board and that data controllers will use for the registration with the registry and the other operations related to the registry. Through the system, the data controllers are made public and the right of personal data protection is more effectively exercised.[25] The procedures and principles related to the Data Controllers' Registry are determined through By-Law on Data Controllers' Registry. The exemptions from the registration obligation and data to be submitted within the scope of the registration obligation are explained in the By-Law. In case of any revisions in the Registry records (like amendments in the data processing activities), data controllers shall notify the authority through VERBİS within seven days of the date of revision.

General Principles of Lawful Data Processing

General principles regarding data processing are laid down in Art. 4 DPA. These principles shall be applied for every kind of data processing primarily, and the controller or the processor bears the responsibility of regarding the compliance with these principles.[26] Accordingly, personal data shall be (i) processed lawfully and fairly (principle of lawfulness and fairness); (ii) accurate and, where necessary, kept up to date (principle of accuracy); (iii) collected for specified, explicit, and legitimate purposes and not further processed in a manner that is incompatible with those purposes (principle of purpose limitation); (iv) relevant, limited and proportionate to the purposes for which they are processed (principle of data minimization); and (v) retained for no longer than is necessary for the processing (principle of storage limitation).

Neither the principle of integrity and confidentiality nor the principle of accountability is explicitly regulated by DPA. Though, in many cases of the Board, special reference is made to the principle of accountability. Contrary to GDPR, DPA does not establish any mandatory DPO concept for any company.

Conditions for Lawful Data Processing

The requirements for lawful data processing are laid down in Articles 5 and 6 DPA. Conditions regarding the processing of personal data are limited under the law and cannot be extended. According to Art. 5/I, personal data cannot be processed without explicit consent of the data subject. In the second paragraph of the related article, the DPA defined exceptions to the consent rule and stated that personal data may be processed without the consent of the data subject, only in cases where one of the following conditions is met:

a) if the processing is provided by law;
b) if the processing is mandatory for the protection of the life or physical integrity of the person or of any other person who is bodily incapable of giving his consent or whose consent is not deemed legally valid;
c) if the processing of personal data belonging to the parties of a contract is necessary, provided that it is directly related to the conclusion or fulfillment of that contract;
d) if the processing of personal data is mandatory for the controller to be able to perform his legal obligations;
e) if the processing of personal data concerned is made available to the public by the data subject himself;
f) if the processing of personal data is mandatory for the establishment, exercise, or protection of any right;
g) if the processing of personal data is mandatory for the legitimate interests of the controller, provided that this processing shall not violate the fundamental rights and freedoms of the data subject.

Consent

Under the definition of explicit consent set out in Article 3 of the DPA, three requirements shall be cumulatively fulfilled: First, the expression shall be related to a specified issue; second, the consent expression shall be based on information, declared freely and given voluntarily. Unlike GDPR, DPA does not explicitly request any demonstration that the data subject has consented to the processing of his or her data.

The Board clarified in its *Whatsapp* decision of 12.01.2021 No. 2021/28 the requirements of consent, especially the concept of coupling ban.[27] In this case, the Board imposed fines on *Whatsapp LLC* after concluding an ex-officio investigation concerning the controller's data processing and cross-border data transfer operations. Whatsapp presented consent as a precondition for receiving a service. In the decision, it is stated that the performance of a contract, including the provision of a service, may not be conditional to consent to the processing of personal data that is not necessary for the performance of that contract. The coupling ban is an essential element for the condition of free declaration and voluntary expression of consent. To obtain freely given consent, the data controller shall grant the data subject a real alternative. The consent shall be presented using a clear and plain language and be easily accessible and understandable for the data subjects.[28]

Processing of Special Category Data

The recent amendments to the DPA introduce new and alternative legal grounds for the processing of special category data under the DPA. Subsequently, special category data may be processed only if one of the following legal grounds exist: a) Processing is based on the explicit consent of the data subject; b) Processing is expressly stipulated by law *(e.g. processing of data on criminal convictions under Law No. 5352 on Judicial Records; collection of people's fingerprints under Art. 5 of Law No. 2559 on Police Duties and Powers);* c) Processing is crucial to protect the life or physical integrity of the data subject or of another person where the data subject cannot disclose their consent due to actual impossibility or whose consent is not legally valid *(e.g. processing of data such of previous illnesses to protect the life or bodily integrity of a person who is unable to disclose their consent due to loss of consciousness in an accident)*; ç) Processing is made public by the data subject by the intention of the data subject *(e.g. processing of personal data such as blood type that a person has shared in a publicly accessible environment for use in emergencies, under the condition that the processing complies with such purpose)*; d) Processing is mandatory for the establishment, exercise, or defense of a *right (e.g. Processing of the health data of former employees to exercise the defence rights in front of the labour courts after the termination of the employment contract*; e) Processing for the protection of public health, preventive medicine, medical diagnosis, treatment, and care services, and the planning, management, and financing of health services, under the condition that processing is carried out by persons or authorized institutions and organizations under the obligation of confidentiality *(e.g. processing of a disabled student's disability report by the university in order for a disabled person to benefit from specific accommodation and examination rights)*; f) Processing is mandatory to fulfill legal obligations regarding employment, occupational health and safety, social security, social services, or social aid *(e.g. processing of individuals' health data or criminal conviction data by employers to fulfill the obligation to employ disabled or convicted persons according to the Labour Law No. 4857)*; g) Processing is related to personal data of current or former members of foundations, associations, or other non-profit organizations established for political, philosophical, religious, or trade union purposes, or persons who are in regular contact with these organizations and formations under certain conditions (e.g. *processing of data of donators of the associations)*.

Data Transfers

In principle, personal data can be transferred to third parties in Turkey, if the conditions set out in Art. 5 DPA are fulfilled.

Cross-Border Transfer of Personal Data

Data controllers are required to review their data processing and transfer processes in line with the amendments by September 1, 2024. Besides the consent of the data subject, with the amendments, two alternative mechanisms for the cross-border transfer of personal data are introduced. The prerequisite for all these alternative ways is the presence of legal grounds set out in Articles 5 and 6 of the DPA for lawful data processing. For these mechanisms to be implemented, the Board is expected to publish guidance for the standard contractual clauses and clarify how these mechanisms will work together with the existing transfer mechanisms.

Within the scope of the amendments, a tiered system is presented for cross-border personal data transfers: first, if an adequacy decision of the Board exists, the data may be transferred to a third country or an international organization. In the absence of an adequacy decision of the Board, two requirements shall be cumulatively fulfilled for a legal data transfer: the data subjects shall have the opportunity to exercise their rights and the data controller shall apply for effective remedies in the recipient country, and the following safeguards specified in the DPA shall be fullfilled:

1) Existence of an agreement (which is not an international contract) between public institutions and organizations abroad or international organizations, and public institutions and organizations or professional association with public entity status in Turkey and the Board's approval;

2) Existence of binding corporate rules for companies within a group of undertakings engaged in joint economic activity and the Board's approval;
3) Existence of standard contractual clauses published by the Board and the notification to the Authority within five business days;
4) Existence of a written undertaking containing provisions to ensure adequate protection and the Board's approval.

In the absence of an adequacy decision and appropriate safeguards, it is stipulated that personal data may be transferred abroad in the following cases, provided that it is occasional:

- The data subject's explicit consent to the transfer, provided that they have been informed about the potential risks;
- The transfer is necessary for the performance of a contract between the data subject and the controller or for the implementation of pre-contractual measures taken at the request of the data subject;
- The transfer is necessary for the establishment or performance of a contract between the data controller and another natural or legal person for the benefit of the data subject;
- The transfer is necessary for an overriding public interest;
- The transfer is necessary for the establishment, exercise, or protection of a right;
- The transfer is necessary to protect the life or physical integrity of the data subject or of another natural person where the data subject cannot disclose their consent due to actual impossibility or whose consent is not legally valid;
- The transfer is made from a register that is open to the public or persons with a legitimate interest, to the extent that the conditions laid down by applicable law for accessing the registry and transfer is requested by those having legitimate interest are met.

A further mechanism for cross-border data transfers is the SCC (standard contractual clauses). Under the amendments introduced to Art. 9 DPA, data controllers and data processors shall notify the Authority that they have signed standard contractual clauses within five days of signing. Failure to notify may result in administrative fines of up to one million Turkish Liras.

Rights of Data Subject

The data subject has always the following rights about himself/herself by applying for the controller (DPA Art. 11):

a) To learn whether personal data is processed or not;
b) To request information about personal data if they have been processed;

c) To learn the purpose of processing personal data and whether they are used appropriately for their purpose;
d) To know the third parties to which personal data are transferred in the country or abroad;
e) If personal data are missing or incorrectly processed, request them to be corrected;
d) To request erasure or destruction of personal data;
e) To request that third parties to whom personal data are transferred shall be notified of the procedures for the correction, erasure, or destruction of personal data;
f) To object to the occurrence of a result against the person himself by analyzing the processed data exclusively through automated systems;
g) To demand that the damage is eliminated in the event of corruption due to the processing of personal data unlawfully.

The right to be forgotten is also not explicitly recognized in the DPA, but it is mentioned in decisions of the Constitutional Court (Decision of 3 March 2016, application no. 2013/5653), the Supreme Court General Assembly Civil Chamber (Decisions of 17 June 2015, application nos. 2014/4–56 and 2015/1679), and in recent decisions of the Board (Decision of 23 June 2020, application no. 2020/48).[29] Practice in Turkey regarding the right to be forgotten is based on the well-known *González* decision of the Court of Justice of the European Union (CJEU),[30] and it is clear that the Board adopts a very similar approach to European Law.

Sanctions and Appeal of Board Decisions

The most effective type of sanction, which is applied very frequently, is the administrative fine. The DPA defines five types of violations of law, which will be fined between 47.303 TL and 9.463.213 TL.[31] There exists no turnover-based administrative fine system in Turkish Law. According to Art. 18/II DPA,

- failure to fulfill the obligation to inform provided for in Art. 10
- failure to fulfill the obligations related to data security about Art. 12
- failure to fulfill the decisions issued by the Board according to Art. 15
- failure to fulfill the obligations regarding the registration and notification to VERBIS (Data Controller's Registry)
- failure to fulfill the reporting obligations for data transfers abroad through the standard contract within the specified timeframe (this amendment will come into force by September 1, 2024)

Art. 18/II states that the administrative fines provided for in this article shall be applied to the natural persons and the private law legal persons who are the data controllers. By the amendments of DPA, which will come into force by June 1, 2024, both data controllers and processors bear responsibility for compliance.

Art. 18/II sets out the principles related to the sanctions imposed on the public bodies that infringe the DPA. Shall the infringements be committed by the public institutions and organizations; only administrative disciplinary procedures shall be applied to the civil servants and other public officers employed in the relevant public institutions but not administrative fines. The public institutions are obliged to inform the Board regarding the disciplinary measures.

Challenges against administrative fines imposed by the Board are adjudicated in criminal courts of first instance. But under the amendments, which enter into force on June 1, 2024, the authority of appeal is defined as administrative courts.

There are no provisions in the DPA for the calculation of fines. Therefore, principles set out by Act No: 5326 on misdemeanors, which is a general legislation for minor crimes are applicable. According to Art. 17/II of the Misdemeanours Act, determining the amount of the administrative fine, the following shall be taken into consideration: the seriousness of the crime committed and the negligence and economic situation of the perpetrator.

The Board refers in almost all cases to the nature, gravity, and duration of the infringement, taking into account the nature, scope, or purpose of the processing concerned, as well as the number of data subjects affected and the level of damage suffered by them.

Data Security Requirements for Processing Personal Data

Art. 12 DPA lays down the framework for the data security obligations of the data controller and processor. Accordingly, the data controller is obliged to take all necessary technical and organizational measures to provide a sufficient level of security to:

a) prevent unlawful processing of personal data;
b) prevent unlawful access to personal data;
c) ensure retention of personal data.

Furthermore, the law foresees in Art. 12/II DPA[32] joint liability between the controller and the processor about the data security obligations. The concept and scope of joint liability in practice need to be clarified. Especially, in data breach cases, the bearer of the legal responsibility is mostly the controller, who must notify the incident.

Art. 12/III focuses on the obligations and duties of the controller for ensuring the adequate level of technical and administrative protection of personal data. Accordingly, the data controller is obliged to carry out the necessary audits or have them conducted in its institution or organization.

"Guideline on Personal Data Security"[33] has been announced by the Board to explain the technical and organizational measures in practice to be taken by the controller and to demonstrate the best-practice examples for the processing of personal data. The guidance has been prepared based on the ISO 27001 Information Security Standards and contains an annex list of technical measures. The guidance developed a risk-oriented approach, which enables the companies to design their security measures by analyzing their concrete risks taking into account the cost of implementation, scope of processing, and their risk appetite and tolerance. The guideline describes a minimum standard of measures, and if deemed necessary for ensuring an appropriate level of protection, additional measures may be implemented according to the nature of the sector-specific processed data.

For the security of special category data, specific rules are foreseen. According to the "Notice of the Board on Administrative and Technical Measures for processing special categories of personal data",[34] the data controller is obliged to:

- Prepare a separate policy and procedure for processing special categories of personal data.
- Take certain measures for employees involved in processing such data, such as:
  - Organize the required pieces of training;
  - Sign confidentiality agreements;
  - Determine access rights and regularly make authority checks;
  - Immediately remove authority from employees who change duties or leave the company;
  - Retrieve any data inventory assigned to the employee.
- Take certain measures when processing such data in a digital environment, such as:
  - Keep the data by using cryptographic methods and keep cryptographic authentication keys in secure and different environments;
  - Securely keep data processing logs;
  - Constantly undertake security updates for the data processing environments;
  - If data is accessed through software, take certain specified measures regarding use of the software;
  - Use at least a two-step verification for remote access to data.
- Take certain measures while processing such data in a physical environment, such as:
  - Take adequate security measures depending on the nature of the physical environment (electrical leakage, fire, flood, burglary, etc.);
  - Secure the physical environment and prevent any unauthorized entry.
- Take certain measures for transferring of such data, such as:
  - Use corporate email and registered email systems as well as encryption for transfers via email;

- Use cryptographic encryption and keep the cryptographic keys in different environments for transfers via USBs, CD, or DVDs;
- Use VPN or sFTP methods for transfers between different servers in different physical environments;
- Take necessary measures to prevent risks, such as loss or burglary, and identify the document as "confidential", if data is transferred on paper.

Data Breaches

Article 12/V defines and sets out the procedure in cases of data breaches. Accordingly, data breaches are defined as the unlawful acquisition of personal data by third parties. Notice No. 2019/10 of 24.01.2019 about Procedures and Principles of Personal Data Breach Notification clarifies the details of the obligations and liability of data controllers in case of a data breach.[35] The data controller shall communicate the breach to the data subject (natural person concerned) and notify the Board within the shortest time (72 hours of becoming aware of the breach) by using the notification form.[36] Where necessary, the Board may announce such breach at its official website or in any other way it deems appropriate. In cases where the notification cannot be submitted within 72 hours, the causes for the delay must be presented as well.

Conclusion

Considering the experiences in Turkey in the field of data protection law in the past eight years, a further comprehensive revision of the data protection law and practice in Turkey seems inevitable. To achieve this aim, first the provisions in the DPA (Art. 12/V DPA) regarding data breaches should be revised, and legal practice should be harmonized with the GDPR. Under the current legislation, the Board is to be notified of all incidents without any exceptions, which increases the workload of the Authority. Moreover, to ensure legal security and predictability, transparency of the Board's decisions is of great importance. Publication of the decisions should be made mandatory. Finally, the "Privacy by Design" and "Privacy by Default" principles, which are not explicitly regulated in the DPA, should be adopted in Turkish law.

Notes

1 www.kvkk.gov.tr/Icerik/6649/Personal-Data-Protection-Law
2 The amendments are published in the Official Gazette numbered 32487 and dated March 12, 2024.
3 www.kvkk.gov.tr/Icerik/5442/VERI-SORUMLULARI-SICILI-HAKKINDA-YONETMELIK
4 https://mevzuat.gov.tr/mevzuat?MevzuatNo=24038&MevzuatTur=7&MevzuatTertip=5

5 https://kvkk.gov.tr/Icerik/5443/AYDINLATMA-YUKUMLULUGUNUN-YERINE-GETIRILMESINDE-UYULACAK-USUL-VE-ESASLAR-HAKKINDA-TEBLIG
6 www.resmigazete.gov.tr/eskiler/2018/03/20180310–6.htm
7 www.kvkk.gov.tr/SharedFolderServer/CMSFiles/12236bad-8de1–4c94-aad6-bb93f53271fb.pdf
8 www.kvkk.gov.tr/SharedFolderServer/CMSFiles/bd06f5f4-e8cc-487e-abe1-d32dc18e2d7e.pdf
9 www.kvkk.gov.tr/SharedFolderServer/CMSFiles/fb193dbb-b159–4221–8a7b-3addc083d33f.pdf
10 www.kvkk.gov.tr/SharedFolderServer/CMSFiles/11b6fd99-d42a-45b1-a009–21f2d36ded21.pdf
11 www.kvkk.gov.tr/SharedFolderServer/CMSFiles/25a1162f-0e61–4a43–98d0–3e7d057ac31a.pdf
12 www.kvkk.gov.tr/SharedFolderServer/CMSFiles/7512d0d4-f345–41cb-bc5b-8d5cf125e3a1.pdf
13 https://kvkk.gov.tr/SharedFolderServer/CMSFiles/a4622d77-624b-4105-8064-14933319abc1.pdf
14 https://kvkk.gov.tr/SharedFolderServer/CMSFiles/a828de56-b2b2–43bf-b77d-cc05de5b2c84.pdf
15 https://kvkk.gov.tr/SharedFolderServer/CMSFiles/8ba209bb-fa93–4479–84f0-dd55aac97a0f.pdf
16 https://kvkk.gov.tr/SharedFolderServer/CMSFiles/703442e0–690c-4618–91c3–83e7583170ca.pdf
17 https://kvkk.gov.tr/SharedFolderServer/CMSFiles/015794c4–061b-4560-a0b2-e372ee536642.pdf
18 www.kvkk.gov.tr/Icerik/5487/Cathay-Pasific-Airway-Limited-Hakkinda-Kisisel-Verileri-Koruma-Kurulunun-16-05-2019-Tarih-ve-2019-144-Sayili-Karar-Ozeti.
19 Ekmekçi, Yücedağ, & Akkanat-Öztürk, Aşıkoğlu, Ş.İ. (2024, p. 49).
20 Ersoy (2022, p. 120).
21 www.kvkk.gov.tr/Icerik/7288/2021–1303
22 https://mevzuat.gov.tr/mevzuat?MevzuatNo=24038&MevzuatTur=7&MevzuatTertip=5
23 www.kvkk.gov.tr/Icerik/4110/2018–10
24 www.kvkk.gov.tr/Icerik/6894/2020–255
25 www.kvkk.gov.tr/Icerik/6650/VERBIS
26 Yücedağ (2022, p. 135).
27 www.kvkk.gov.tr/Icerik/7045/WHATSAPP-UYGULAMASI-HAKKINDA-YURUTULEN-RESEN-INCELEMEYE-ILISKIN-KAMUOYU-DUYURUSU
28 Akkurt (2022, p. 171).
29 https://kvkk.gov.tr/Icerik/6871/2020–927, www.kvkk.gov.tr/SharedFolderServer/CMSFiles/95d8ad1b-e849–48c6-ba93–02ecedeffde5.pdf
30 https://eur-lex.europa.eu/legal-content/en/ALL/?uri=CELEX:62012CJ0131
31 These amounts are applied for 2024. Taken the inflation rates into consideration, the amount of fines are renewed yearly.
32 In case of processing of personal data by another natural or legal person on behalf of the data controller, the data controller shall jointly be responsible with these persons for taking the measures laid down in the first paragraph.
33 www.kvkk.gov.tr/yayinlar/veri_guvenligi_rehberi.pdf
34 www.kvkk.gov.tr/Icerik/4110/2018–10
35 www.kvkk.gov.tr/Icerik/5362/Veri-Ihlali-Bildirimi
36 https://ihlalbildirim.kvkk.gov.tr/Home/IhlalBildirim

References

Akkurt, S. S. (2022). Açık Rıza. *Kişisel Verilerin Korunmasına Akademik Bakış*, 155–187. www.kvkk.gov.tr/SharedFolderServer/CMSFiles/0cd33e96-77cf-4989-b29b-d331af6a463f.pdf

Best Practice Guidelines on Personal Data Protection in the Banking Sector. www.kvkk.gov.tr/SharedFolderServer/CMSFiles/12236bad-8de1-4c94-aad6-bb93f53271fb.pdf

By-Law on Data Controllers' Registry. www.kvkk.gov.tr/Icerik/5442/VERI-SORUMLULARI-SICILI-HAKKINDA-YONETMELIK

By-Law on Erasure, Destruction, and Anonymisation of Personal Data. https://mevzuat.gov.tr/mevzuat?MevzuatNo=24038&MevzuatTur=7&MevzuatTertip=5

Communiqué on the Principles and Procedures for Requests to the Data Controller. www.resmigazete.gov.tr/eskiler/2018/03/20180310-6.htm

Communiqué on Principles and Procedures to be Followed in Fulfilment of the Obligation to Inform. https://kvkk.gov.tr/Icerik/5443/AYDINLATMA-YUKUMLULUGUNUN-YERINE-GETIRILMESINDE-UYULACAK-USUL-VE-ESASLAR-HAKKINDA-TEBLIG

Ekmekçi, Ö., & Yücedağ, N., Akkanat-Öztürk, E. B., & Aşıkoğlu, Ş.İ. (2024). *Kişisel Verilerin Korunması Hukuku*. Istanbul: Onikilevha Yayınevi.

Ersoy, Ç. (2022). Temel Kavramlar. *Kişisel Verilerin Korunmasına Akademik Bakış*, 103–133. www.kvkk.gov.tr/SharedFolderServer/CMSFiles/0cd33e96-77cf-4989-b29b-d331af6a463f.pdf

Guidelines on Deepfake. https://kvkk.gov.tr/SharedFolderServer/CMSFiles/703442e0-690c-4618-91c3-83e7583170ca.pdf

Guidelines on Personal Data Security (Technical and Administrative Measures). www.kvkk.gov.tr/SharedFolderServer/CMSFiles/7512d0d4-f345-41cb-bc5b-8d5cf125e3a1.pdf

Guidelines on the Processing of Biometric Data. www.kvkk.gov.tr/SharedFolderServer/CMSFiles/bd06f5f4-e8cc-487e-abe1-d32dc18e2d7e.pdf

Guidelines on the Processing of Genetic Data. https://kvkk.gov.tr/SharedFolderServer/CMSFiles/703442e0-690c-4618-91c3-83e7583170ca.pdf

Guidelines on the Processing of the Republic of Turkey Identification Numbers. https://kvkk.gov.tr/SharedFolderServer/CMSFiles/a828de56-b2b2-43bf-b77d-cc05de5b2c84.pdf

Guidelines on the Protecting Privacy in Mobile Applications. https://kvkk.gov.tr/SharedFolderServer/CMSFiles/8ba209bb-fa93-4479-84f0-dd55aac97a0f.pdf

Guidelines on the Protection of Personal Data in Political Elections.
https://kvkk.gov.tr/SharedFolderServer/CMSFiles/a4622d77-624b-4105-8064-14933319abc1.pdf

Guidelines on the Right to be Forgotten – Evaluation of the Right to be Forgotten Specific to Search Engines. www.kvkk.gov.tr/SharedFolderServer/CMSFiles/11b6fd99-d42a-45b1-a009-21f2d36ded21.pdf

Guidelines on the Use of Cookies. www.kvkk.gov.tr/SharedFolderServer/CMSFiles/fb193dbb-b159-4221-8a7b-3addc083d33f.pdf

Recommendations on the Protection of Personal Data in the Field of Artificial Intelligence. www.kvkk.gov.tr/SharedFolderServer/CMSFiles/7512d0d4-f345-41cb-bc5b-8d5cf125e3a1.pdf

Yücedağ, N. (2022). Kişisel Verilerin Korunması Kanunu Kapsamında Genel İlkeler. *Kişisel Verilerin Korunmasına Akademik Bakış*, 135–153. www.kvkk.gov.tr/SharedFolderServer/CMSFiles/0cd33e96-77cf-4989-b29b-d331af6a463f.pdf

11 Competition and Antitrust Regulation for Digital Platforms in Türkiye

Zeynep Ayata

Introduction

Digital markets exhibit unique dynamics and characteristics. Competition law tools designed for and implemented in traditional markets are not always suitable or sufficient to safeguard effective competition in digital markets. Global case law from competition authorities has demonstrated that norms prohibiting the abuse of dominance are necessary and useful to some extent, but they often fall short for various reasons. First, digital markets and platforms grow and operate swiftly while intervention is either slow or limited. Furthermore, information asymmetry is more profound in digital markets, making the potential effects more harmful. Certain parties, especially end-users, require better protection. Certain types of conduct are more frequent or impactful in digital markets, necessitating new tools. Therefore, while existing norms allow for intervention, most competition authorities have turned to ex ante regulation specifically designed for digital markets. The Turkish Competition Council (TCC) has proposed an amendment to Article 6 of the Turkish Competition Act (TCA) prohibiting the abuse of a dominant position. This initiative is rooted in the TCC's case law in digital markets. Despite a limited time frame, the authority has adopted several decisions sanctioning the conduct of digital platforms as abusive. It has also resorted to interim measures on many occasions. This experience clearly indicates that new norms and preemptive tools may be necessary for intervention in digital markets. This chapter examines the evolution of competition law implementation in digital markets in Türkiye. The first section will analyze in detail emblematic decisions that reveal the TCC's approach to digital platforms and their abusive conduct. The second section will briefly present the TCC's important findings in sector inquiries regarding digital markets. The final section will examine the proposed amendment to the TCA and draw parallels to the case law of the TCC in digital markets.

Turkish Competition Council's Case Law in Digital Markets

The TCC has scrutinized digital markets over the last five years. Although this is a short period, there have been a significant number of cases, and the

DOI: 10.4324/9781032692937-11

Council has had the opportunity to develop a stance regarding various types of conduct pertinent to digital markets. This section presents an overview of this case law, which seems to have had an important effect on the regulatory choices of the TCC in the proposed amendment to Article 6 of the TCA.

Self-Preferencing

Self-preferencing is a form of discrimination that has become topical with the rise of digital platforms. Most large platforms have one core service and several related service platforms. They often use the data collected by the core service platform (which holds a very large dataset) as a leverage tool in a related market. This practice is qualified as self-preferencing when they use their core platforms' algorithms to discriminate against other providers of the related service (Ibanez Colomo, 2020). Thus, it is a specific technique whereby data collected on the dominant platform is transformed to another platform to create a significant competitive advantage (Graef, 2019). The TCC has found in a series of decisions that Google had abused its dominant position and infringed Article 6 of TCA through self-preferencing. In three decisions adopted in two consecutive years, the TCA has established that Google, which held 90% of the search engine market, had used its dominant position to favor its products in vertical or related markets. These decisions have clearly shown that, according to the TCC, self-preferencing constitutes anti-competitive behavior in digital markets, and this approach has been reflected in the proposed amendment to Article 6 of TCA.

In its first decision against Google, the TCC investigated whether Google's placement of shopping services in its search engine is anti-competitive. This conduct has been scrutinized by many competition authorities and courts globally. The practice relates to the placement of shopping services relevant to the search word/words entered into the search engine by the user. Google's main site displays several shopping services at the top of the page when showing results for a search. In many markets, including Türkiye, Google places its shopping services first/foremost, subsequently listing its competitors' services. The practice makes competitors' services less visible or even less accessible. In its Google Shopping decision (20/10/19–69) of February 13, 2020, the TCC asserted that although users do not pay in money for services provided by search engines such as Google, they pay in data and time spent on the website or application (TCC, Google Shopping, 2020). Therefore, there are consumer welfare concerns in these markets, and competition authorities must ensure effective competition and protect incentives to innovate. When dominant undertakings such as Google favor their services in the market they dominate, it may have exclusionary effects in vertical or related markets. Thus, the TCC concluded Google's self-preferencing for shopping services hindered users' ability to compare and choose, impeding effective competition with potential exclusionary effects on competitors.

The second decision against Google regarded Adwords, the undertaking's advertising system that helps businesses promote their products and services, increasing their website's visibility and traffic. In its Google Adwords decision (20–49/675–296) of November 21, 2020, the TCC held that Adwords appearance at the top of the search results page without any clear indication that it is a paid advertisement system constituted self-preferencing (TCC, Google Adwords, 2020). According to the TCC, non-advertised organic results appear below Adwords and thus become less visible because of Google's prioritization. Thus, service providers are forced to opt for and pay for Google Adwords to secure the visibility of their websites. Dependency on Google's paid services is increased. End-users (consumers) are also misled by Google's practice as they are unable to distinguish between advertised and non-advertised results. This conduct creates a barrier to entry and growth of content-providing websites, impeding users' ability to objectively compare and choose better services.

In a third decision, the TCC investigated Google's local search service. When users search for a certain type of service providers, for example, restaurants, cinemas etc., within a particular location, Google's search engine lists matching results. The same service is also provided by other local providers such as Neredekal or Trivago. The TCC qualifies this service as vertical regarding Google's main search engine service. Thus, Google becomes a service provider to other local search service providers in the market for a general search engine while Google's Local Unit and Google Hotel Ads compete with them in the lower market. Similar to previous cases, Google prioritized its own local search sites in the results, leading local competitors to get less visibility and visits. In its Google Local Search decision (21–20/248–105) of February 8, 2021, the TCC held that Google, thanks to its dominant position in the general search engine market, is the distributor of traffic, and its self-preference practices can avert users from visiting other sites, leading them to choose or stay on Google's own services in other markets. (TCC, Google Local Search, 2021). This conduct constitutes an infringement of Article 6 of TCA, as it distorts competition in the vertical market of local search by limiting users' comparison ability and choice.

Another significant decision in terms of self-preferencing and the use of algorithms for creating an artificial advantage was the DSM Grup Danışmanlık (hereinafter referred to as Trendyol) decision (23–11/177–54) of February 27, 2023, which was closed with the platform's commitments (TCC, Trendyol, 2023). Trendyol, holding a dominant position in the multi-category e-marketplace market, was using the data it had been collecting in this market on Dolap, its secondhand clothing sales platform. Trendyol committed to not sharing information on surfing (including viewing of pages, visibility data, and click data), purchasing, and the content of purchases on Trendyol. Through this commitment, Trendyol aimed to address the concern that it was using data collected to increase visibility and use of Dolap. The platform also committed to not using data on sellers and users collected by

Trendyol in any category of search algorithm (search, product suggestion, and the determination of suggest product sets) used in Dolap. The competition law concern here was that Trendyol was using the data collected on its dominant platform to improve suggestions and, therefore, the user experience on another platform. It was agreed that the self-preferencing, contrary to Article 6 of the TCA, would cease after the commitments.

Most-Favored Customer

Most-favored customer clauses (MFC) are another practice that has gained importance with the rise of digital markets. An MFC clause is a contract condition by which the provider is obliged to give the dominant platform the best sales conditions in terms of price and contract etc., offered to other customers. Thus, if the provider gives a special price to one of its customers, they will have to match that price for the dominant platform. This practice evidently allows the dominant platform to offer the best price and terms to their end users. The practice becomes a competition law concern as competitors are unable to create an advantage by lowering prices or offering better sales conditions (Ezrachi, 2015).

One of the most impactful investigations in Türkiye in digital markets was the TCC's Yemek Sepeti decision (21–05/64–28) of January 28, 2021, which was resolved with Yemek Sepeti's commitments (TCC, Yemek Sepeti, 2021). The investigation concerned a dominant online food delivery service platform Yemek Sepeti's imposition of an MFC clause on its business users. The clause required business customers, that is, food and meal suppliers of Yemek Sepeti, to give the dominant platform the lowest price they were offering on the market. In its investigations, the TCC found that Yemek Sepeti had been practicing a narrow MFC covering not only prices offered on the market but also the content of menus, promotions, delivery destinations etc., thus "limiting consumer welfare" (Yemek Sepeti, paragraph 7) regarding not only prices but also choice and variety.

Furthermore, Yemek Sepeti set its own minimum amount per order, which proved to be below the profitable rate for many restaurants. However, if the suppliers frequently refused to accept the order due to a low amount in the basket, Yemek Sepeti would warn and impose sanctions. Additionally, restaurants would be forced to accept low amount orders from Yemek Sepeti during busy hours over higher amount orders from other channels as they are dependent on Yemek Sepeti. According to the TCC's analysis, had the suppliers been free to determine the minimum amount per order, they would have set it higher to avoid transport-related costs and losses. Yemek Sepeti's low minimum amount requirement increased restaurants' costs while reducing their profits, and the damage thereof was not incurred by the dominant platform. This condition was not imposed mostly on individual restaurants rather than chains, and the TCC argued that such small individual restaurants would be a target for new entrants, and thus Yemek Sepeti's condition would foreclose the market. Furthermore, even if the condition was not applicable to all restaurants, it had the potential to affect the entire market.

Several months after the TCC's decision to start an investigation, Yemek Sepeti offered commitments that addressed all foreclosure effects raised by the TCC. Yemek Sepeti offered to annul narrow MFC clauses with individual restaurants within the first three months and with chain restaurants within the second three months of the notification of the reasoned opinion of the TCC. Furthermore, Yemek Sepeti offered to revoke the requirement for a minimum amount per order within a week. The investigation was closed with the TCC's acceptance of Yemek Sepeti's commitments in accordance with Article 43 of the TCA.

Another decision in which the TCC had the opportunity to examine the effects of MFC clauses was the D-Market (Hepsiburada) decision (21–22/266–116) of April 15, 2012 (TCC, Hepsiburada, 2012). This decision concerned Anka Mobile, which was the sole distributor of mobile device accessories of the brand Spigen, and Hepsiburada, an e-commerce platform. The TCC found that Anka Mobil had been aiming to prevent suppliers from selling at lower prices on other platforms than Hepsiburada through an MFC clause. The suppliers could thus be deterred from working with platforms that would charge lower commission rates than Hepsiburada. What is interesting about this decision is that D-Market or Anka were not found to have a dominant position in the market. As a matter of fact, the TCC carried out the investigations based on allegations under Article 4 of the TCA prohibiting anti-competitive agreements. Respectively, the TCC made an exemption analysis under Article 5 of the TCA and the Block Exemption Regulation 2002/2 for Vertical Agreements and found that the agreement between Hepsiburada and suppliers would benefit from an exemption as the MFC clause did not have any "practical effects in the market" (D-market, paragraph 77). As Hepsiburada's market share was lower than the 40% threshold determined in the Regulation, the agreement fulfilled the criteria set in the Regulation, and the TCC found that the MFC clause could benefit from an exemption, and there was no violation of Article 4 in this respect. This analysis of the TCC is significant as it expressly confirms that MFC clauses are not a per se violation of competition law, and anti-competitive effects in the market must be proven to assert a violation of the TCA.

Access to Data and Data Portability

Access to data and the aggregation of data is one of the most significant elements of market power in digital markets (Just, 2018). Large platforms' capacity to collect and store data has allowed them to build datasets that are rapidly growing (OECD, 2020). Some of this data is provided directly by the end users of the platform. However, a significant quantity of data relates to information about the end user, such as the location of the user or visits to other websites on the same device. This data is then analyzed to create a new set of data, which allows platforms to build profiles on a countless number of commercial and end users. This data is a crucial element of quality competition between platforms, as this profiling is then used to improve user experience, product suggestions etc. For this reason, access to data and data portability has been an important concern for competition authorities.

The first significant decision of the TCC concerning access to data and data portability was the Nadirkitap decision (22–15/273) of April 7, 2022 (TCC, Nadirkitap, 2022). Nadirkitap was an intermediary website for the sale of secondhand books. The website refused to give sales information collected by the platform to secondhand book providers. According to the TCC, the market for firsthand and secondhand books are not substitutable for the supply side or the demand side. Furthermore, online sales of secondhand books constitute a separate product market from offline sales, as it offers many advantages, such as accessibility, low cost, and so on. Accordingly, Nadirkitap was found to have a dominant position in the rather narrow market for platform services for the sale of secondhand books defined by the TCC.

Nadirkitap collected information such as the name, author, and publication date of the books sold on the website. Aggregated sets of such data were held by the platform and were stored as datasets. The TCC did not qualify these datasets as original datasets that would be protected by the Intellectual and Artistic Property Act, which meant that the datasets would not benefit from the protection provided thereof. The platform's argument, according to which it would have exclusive intellectual property rights over the datasets, could not be accepted.

Nadirkitap's refusal to provide information contained in the datasets, therefore, had to be examined in terms of its effects on market competition. The TCC's survey of existing practices in the market revealed that competitors accepted the providers' right to access product information collected by their platforms. Furthermore, their contracts with the suppliers did not legally or practically prevent the use of such data by the sellers and thus did not constitute an impediment to data portability. Nadirkitap, on the other hand, limited access to data and its portability to other platforms. According to the TCC, this behavior inhibited suppliers' possibility to sell through other platforms by increasing switching costs. Although there were no concrete findings establishing the suppliers' search for alternative platforms, the TCC argues that the practice had the potential to foreclose the market significantly. Overall, the refusal to provide access to data had the potential to obstruct competitors' activities and raise barriers to entry in the relevant market.

The matter of data portability was also raised by the complainants in the Trendyol case. The platform argued that there had not been a request by the users for the provision of such data, and that a case of refusal, therefore, did not exist. Nevertheless, to dismiss any such concern, Trendyol committed to providing several categories of data, such as product information, product visuals, product brand, and so on, to sellers upon request. The platform asserted that all relevant product data would be transportable after this commitment.

The TCC has recently adopted another decision concerning data portability (Sahibinden decision 21–46/655-M of 30.09.2021). The reasoned opinion for this decision was not yet published as of January 15, 2024, and the information provided here is thus based on the brief published by the TCC. In this decision, Sahibinden, a platform that held a dominant position in the market for online real estate sale and rental activities and vehicle sale activities, was found to have violated Article 6 of the TCA by refusing to allow commercial users to transfer their data to other competitor platforms. The TCC decided that this practice was an exclusionary conduct restricting the activities of the dominant platform's competitors.

Data Privacy and Protection

Data privacy and the protection of personal data have also been under the radar of competition authorities. The relationship between data protection and competition law is fragile at best, as the former is regulated under data protection laws and often falls under the jurisdiction of another authority. However, there have been some decisions throughout Europe where competition authorities have also scrutinized data protection and violation of rules thereof as a matter of competition law. The implementation of data protection law is clearly not within the competence of competition authorities. However, there have been suggestions that the implementation of competition law rules can complement data privacy rules and thus strengthen the protection of individuals (Kuenzler, 2022).

The TCC's approach to the use of data and the interaction of data privacy and competition law can be seen in the Meta (previously named Facebook) decision (22–48/706–299) of October 20, 2022 (TCC, Meta, 2022). In January 2021, WhatsApp users received a notification stating that terms of use and privacy policy would be updated in February and that users who do not accept these new terms would no longer be able to use the service. With this update, Meta Inc. would share the personal data of WhatsApp users with Facebook Inc. The TCC not only decided to start an investigation but also immediately issued an injunction order as it considered that the new terms would cause irreparable damage. The investigation revealed that WhatsApp and Meta Inc. had actually been synchronizing and transferring data since 2016 based on the Privacy Terms implemented by WhatsApp. In addition, the transfer in question also entailed sharing data collected in WhatsApp with other Meta Inc. companies. The investigation was thus extended to all companies owned by Meta Inc.

First, the TCC found that Meta was dominant in personal social networking services, consumer communication services, and online display advertising services markets. As for the possible violation of Article 6 of the TCA, that is, an abuse of dominance, the TCC considered both exploitative and exclusionary practices. According to the TCC, users were not sufficiently informed regarding data collection and combination, and their consent to WhatsApp's use of their data was not obtained based on free will. Furthermore, since it is almost impossible for users to opt out of Meta's services and privacy terms, they are forced to give consent and continue using the platform despite decreasing privacy protection. This led to an increase in the power of the platform in terms of the collection of data, which was a result of the "disproportionate" strength of the platform regarding users (Meta, paragraph 395). However, the TCC concluded that although this practice may potentially be seen as exploitative conduct, it is primarily a matter of data protection and consumer protection law. The difficulty in providing a measurement or an analysis for evaluating the level or quality of data protection creates another problem for competition law analysis. The question could thus be resolved under data protection rules, which provide more appropriate tools. The TCC therefore chose not to examine further potential exploitative abuses and to analyze instead the exclusionary effects of privacy terms.

The TCC thus examined the impact of Meta's data merging on Meta's own dataset and, in particular, whether a dataset of this nature could also be created by its competitors. The TCC determined that it was almost impossible for rival enterprises operating in the online display advertising market to create a dataset that is equal or close to a dataset that can compete with Meta's. It concluded that Meta's data volume and quality constitute a barrier to entry that is difficult to overcome, and that over time, especially due to the feedback loops, Meta's position is further strengthened, and it becomes an even more insurmountable obstacle for potential new entrants entering the market. Furthermore, the TCC advanced that Meta was "indispensable, and often the only advertising channel" for advertisers (Meta, paragraph 451). It also found that Meta's combination of data obtained from different sources, including third parties, further strengthened its indispensable nature. Advertisers were less likely to choose a rival platform in the market which created a lock-in effect and deterred new entry. This foreclosure in the market would in turn increase costs which would be potentially incurred by the consumers.

The TCC then examined the exclusionary effects of Meta's behavior in the social networks market. The TCC concluded that exclusionary effects in this market were twofold. First, undertakings that do not have data of comparable size and quality cannot provide a sufficiently personalized experience for their users which would lead consumers to choose Meta. Furthermore, personal profiles created by Meta are not portable which further strengthens the lock-in effect. Thus, even if they are not satisfied with the experience offered by Facebook, users are unlikely to leave. Meta's data policy thus reduces consumer welfare. Second, undertakings that are active in the online advertising market also operate in the social networking market. If their access to advertisers is limited due to Meta's data combination or preference for Meta, there would also be less demand for advertising in their social networks reducing their overall income. The same effect would also deter potential entrants as they would fear not having sufficient demand for advertisement. If there is insufficient entry or competition in the market, consumers would have less choice, and costs and prices would increase. According to the TCC, this would give further power to Meta and would ultimately reduce consumer welfare. Overall, Meta's data collection, use, and most importantly, privacy policy and data combination between its various companies would have harmful exclusionary effects in the market.

The TCC thus found that by combining data collected through Facebook, Instagram, and WhatsApp, Meta had restricted competition in the social network and online advertising markets, and its exclusionary conduct was harmful to its competitors as it foreclosed the market. It also ordered Meta to adopt the necessary measures to desist from such practices within one month after the notification of the reasoned decision. On January 10, 2024, the TCC published a decision according to which Meta had failed to offer satisfactory remedies to ensure effective competition in the market. The decision also imposed an additional fine on Meta for lack of compliance.

Exclusivity

Exclusivity becomes an important competition law concern in digital markets when combined with strong network effects held by the dominant platform. Indeed, in digital markets, when a tipping point is reached, the market may shift altogether toward a single platform, creating a quasi-monopoly situation (Petit, 2020). Strong network effects may be due to the structure of the market (Khan, 2017). However, it may also be strengthened by the dominant platform's conduct in lower/upper or related markets. If legally or practically, undertakings in the lower/upper market or related markets deal exclusively with the dominant platform, it may create such a tipping point. Exclusivity agreements or practices may, therefore, constitute an exclusionary abuse whereby one platform dominates the entire market.

The TCC has also dealt with the question of exclusivity in digital markets. In the Çiçek Sepeti decision (21–20/250–106) of April 8, 2021, the TCC examined how the dominant platform practically created exclusivity through various cogent practices (TCC, Çiçek Sepeti, 2021). Çiçek Sepeti was a platform dominant in the online sale of flowers. The platform pressured its dealers into not working with other platforms, thereby becoming the exclusive intermediary service provider in the market. In particular, Çiçek Sepeti verbally warned dealers against working with other platforms, imposed high selling targets on special days (such as holidays), and set quantity requirements for orders. As a result, dealers were deterred from working with other platforms and were practically forced to deal exclusively with Çiçek Sepeti. The platform offered three main commitments which were accepted by the TCC for the closure of the case. Çiçek Sepeti committed to explicitly notifying dealers and providing written clarification stating that they are free to work with any platform of their choosing and to insert a clause in their existing and future contracts establishing that dealers have no formal or practical obligation to work exclusively with Çiçek Sepeti. The platform also committed to determining supply quantities on special days through negotiation and mutual agreement with dealers. The platform would not have the right to terminate their contract with dealers if no such agreement was reached.

Creating practical exclusivity was also examined in the Sahibinden decision. The TCA stated in its brief that in addition to restrictions on data portability (explained earlier), the platform included non-compete clauses in its contracts with commercial users advertising real estate rentals and sales and vehicle sales. These two practices led to practical exclusivity whereby commercial users were deterred from also using other platforms for their advertisements. The TCC imposed a fine on the platform for infringement of Article 6 of the TCA by foreclosing the market and adopted structural remedies ordering the platform to retract non-compete clauses and to establish the necessary infrastructure that would allow free and efficient data portability without delay upon request by users.

Turkish Competition Council's Sector Inquiries in Digital Markets

The Turkish Competition Authority (TCA) has conducted two sector inquiries relevant to digital markets: the e-marketplace platforms sector inquiry and the online advertisement sector inquiry. The final report of the former was published in April 2022 while only a preliminary version of the report for the latter has been presented. The reports not only contain factual findings of the TCA for these activities but also provide a good indication of how the authority views existing practices in terms of competition. This section will, therefore, briefly display the key elements of these reports.

The E-Marketplace Platforms Sector Inquiry Report

The e-marketplace platforms sector inquiry final report published in 2022 contains a comprehensive analysis of the structure of e-marketplace platforms (TCC, 2022). The TCA examines three main competitive problems: cross-platform competition (vertical practices such as MFN terms, exclusivity, and non-competition terms), intra-platform competition (such as self-preservation and discrimination practices and high pricing strategies of platforms), and consumer concerns.

On the matter of cross-platform competition, the report states that ensuring effective competition is of primary importance and draws attention to limitations brought by gatekeeper undertakings. In this context, it indicates that network effects created by such undertakings strengthen their power and restrict competitors' ability to grow in the sector. The TCA predicates that anti-competitive behavior by such undertakings has the potential to completely eliminate inter-platform competition in the market.

Another issue addressed in the report within the context of cross-platform competition is limitations on data portability. Among the conducts that may restrict data portability, the report lists most-favored customer clauses and exclusivity conditions. Furthermore, the report asserts that gatekeeper undertakings may gain significant advantages through the collection of data from sellers and users, which may become a barrier to entry for potential entrants. Limitations on access to data and portability of data would also have exclusionary effects on existing competitors.

Concerning intra-platform competition, the report raises the issue of the emergence of e-marketplaces, which have a dual role of both seller and competitor of third-party sellers within their platforms. In these cases, the fact that the e-marketplace has asymmetric bargaining power against third-party sellers becomes the main competitive concern. The dominant e-marketplace has the opportunity to unilaterally determine the commercial conditions applicable to sellers while competing with them for the same service provision or product. The report states that when the platform undertakes such a dual role, self-preferencing in the form of prioritizing its own products in listings and rankings could constitute an abuse. Platforms should, therefore, provide easy and transparent access to data in clear and understandable language to ensure effective competition.

The prominent concern addressed in the report in terms of consumer harm and protection is the common belief among consumers that the services they receive from e-marketplaces are free of charge. This common misconception fails to recognize that consumers, in fact, pay for these services by providing data. This lack of awareness makes users vulnerable to abuses by the e-marketplaces, especially in the context of listings, rankings, and product reviews provided by the platform. According to the report, the primary aim within this scope should be the protection of consumers against excessive data collection and the violation of privacy. Platforms should thus be encouraged to adopt consumer policies based on objective criteria, openness, transparency, easy accessibility, and adaptability to consumer preferences.

The Online Advertisement Sector Inquiry

In April 2023, the TCC published its preliminary report on the online advertisement sector inquiry, which was launched in 2021 to evaluate local and global developments in the online advertising sector and to identify behavioral and structural competition law concerns (TCC, 2023). The report states that as of 2021, online advertising has become the largest type of advertising, exceeding the share of traditional advertising in advertising expenditures. Online advertising offers many benefits, allowing advertisers to efficiently track the results of their marketing strategies with digital tools across different online channels, such as search engines, social media, or applications. These fall under the umbrella of "online advertising," forming part of different advertising strategies with various purposes.

The report identifies three categories of online advertising: search-based advertising, display advertising, and listing advertising. It evaluates these categories through sub-categories such as mobile advertising, video advertising, social media advertising, and ad advertising. According to the preliminary findings, the most significant advertising segment with the highest share of expenditure is display advertising. Social media advertising is noted for providing extensive consumer data, including users' preferences and connections, for targeted advertising applications. However, a considerable number of users are reportedly unaware of the risks associated with the use of their personal data, creating significant privacy concerns in the sector. The report emphasizes the importance of striking a balance between the benefits and harms of targeted advertising for social welfare.

The report highlights potential competition law concerns arising from the conflicting interests of vertically integrated platform providers who serve both publishers and advertisers. It mentions potentially harmful practices such as self-preferencing and leverage effects. Transparency issues are also identified, with advertisers and publishers lacking sufficient information about the supply chain, the complexity of auctions in the advertisement technology supply chain affecting stakeholders, and concerns about whether advertisement tech providers prevent the evaluation of their service performance by independent parties.

Digital platforms play a crucial role for news publishers in delivering news content to readers, making them an essential commercial partner. The report suggests that this dependence may force news publishers to unconditionally accept the terms offered by platforms, potentially causing them to lose their advertising-based income. Additionally, the report emphasizes the significance of access to data, stating that platforms should not prevent third-party service providers from accessing user data to avoid restricting competition.

Regulation of Digital Markets in Türkiye: Proposed Amendment to the Turkish Competition Act

In 2022, the Turkish Competition Council (TCC) initiated the process of amending Article 6 of the Turkish Competition Act (TCA) to establish general rules and prohibit specific conduct relevant to digital markets. Notably, the TCA has adopted a participatory approach for the proposal, engaging in consultations with relevant stakeholders. As of January 2024, the proposed amendment has not been brought before the General Assembly. The information presented in this chapter is based on the publicly available proposal from October 2022. This section aims to explore the general terms of the proposed amendment and examine specific provisions that align with the case law analyzed earlier.

Grounds for the Proposed Amendment

It should first be noted that, as explained in the first section, the TCC has, through various tools, interfered in digital markets over the past five years. Fines imposed in infringement decisions exceed six billion Turkish Liras. In the report accompanying the proposed amendment, the TCC states that ongoing and closed investigations have shown recurring and rather specific infringements that may be found in digital markets. As such, the TCC emphasizes self-preferencing, exclusivity practices, most-favored customer clauses, and data-related concerns. The TCC also draws attention to the global trend of regulating digital markets through new legislation or amendments to legislation in force. The Digital Markets Act (DMA) adopted in the EU is an example of the former, and the amendments to Article 19 of the German Competition Act are an example of the latter. There are also ongoing reports and legislative initiation processes in many countries, such as the United States and the United Kingdom. The most significant element of these legislation and initiatives is perhaps the fact that many competition authorities have turned to ex ante regulations. This tendency is often justified by the velocity of conduct and growth in digital markets, which allegedly often leads to irreparable harm. The TCC has, as explained in the previous section, conducted sector inquiries to identify problems occurring in digital markets and policy needs. These reports have also shown that legislation has to be complemented for better compliance of digital actors.

It should also be noted that the TCC has resorted to interim measures for several investigations in the context of digital markets. Meta and Trendyol decisions, accounted for in previous sections, are examples where such measures were deemed necessary for preventing irreparable harm. This approach is also justified by the velocity and the vast spread of harm caused by anti-competitive conduct in digital markets. It is certainly true that existing tools are sufficient for finding infringements and imposing fines. However, they are perhaps not sufficient to prevent serious harm to a considerable number of consumers. This argument is often cited as a justification for ex ante regulations, and the interim measures adopted by the TCC could be proof of such a necessity.

According to the proposed amendments' first article, the overarching aim is to prevent certain platforms from abusing their market power and to ensure a "fair and competitive market structure" (Article 1 of the proposed amendment to the TCA). The preamble of the proposed legislation indicates that platforms with such important market power may cause irreparable competition law concerns in relevant markets. The tools provided in the amendment will thus allow for the competitive market structure to be maintained and inhibit harm to consumer and social welfare. The preamble does not define the essence or the scope of a fair and competitive market. However, as will be explained further in this section, the proposed provisions seem to focus particularly on preventing barriers to entry and foreclosure of the market. It may thus be inferred that fair and competitive markets are distorted mostly through foreclosure effects, which will be preempted by the new ex ante tools.

Scope of the Proposed Amendment

The proposed legislation introduces Amendment 6/A to Article 6 of the TCA, establishing certain obligations and prohibitions for undertakings with significant market power. These are platforms that have achieved a specific scale in one or more core platform services, exerting a notable influence over commercial users' activities and access to end users, and have sustained this market power. Once adopted, the proposed amendment will be followed by secondary legislation that sets quantitative and qualitative thresholds for designating platforms with such market power.

Article 6/A applies exclusively to these platforms, imposing new rules in addition to those already applicable. The enforcement of various prohibitions and duties raises concerns of overregulation and potential hindrance to innovation and growth. However, a detailed examination of the procedural rules outlined in the proposed amendment indicates that the provisions of Article 6/A will primarily and foremost apply to undertakings with significant market power. It can thus be presumed that existing prohibitions under Article 6 will only be applicable to conduct not regulated under Article 6/A (Sanlı & Doğan, 2023). If this approach is adopted in the implementation, concerns of overregulation and dual burden may be alleviated to some extent.

Regarding the geographical scope, Article 2 of the proposed amendment specifies that the new rules will apply to platforms providing core platform services to end users established or resident in Türkiye. This provision can be interpreted as being in parallel with the principle of effect entrenched in Turkish competition law with Article 2 of the TCA. If there are end users in Türkiye purchasing services from the platform, there would be an affected market, fulfilling the general principle of effect. After the proposed amendment, with an addendum to Article 15 of the TCA, platforms providing at least one core service in Türkiye will have an obligation to have the necessary technical and administrative infrastructure to allow for inspections by the TCC. Thus, even if the platform is not established in Türkiye, they would practically have to hold offices where the TCA official would conduct dawn raids.

The proposed amendment also introduces several new concepts to the TCA, in addition to the definition of platforms with significant market power. These concepts are considered new and specific to digital markets. The main concern is that these elements may not necessarily be covered by traditional definitions of competition law, potentially creating loopholes that counter the implementation of new tools. As such, the amendment defines concepts such as non-public data, end users, core platform services, online intermediary services, online search engine services, online social network services, video sharing platform services, calling services independent from a (phone) number, operating systems, web browsers, virtual assistants, cloud computing services, online advertisement services, commercial users, and ancillary services.

Obligations and Prohibitions Introduced by the Amendment

The proposed amendment has an implementation logic that is similar to the DMA's do's and don'ts list. As a matter of fact, the proposed Article 6/A will establish certain obligations (do's) and prohibitions (don'ts) for designated platforms that have important market power. However, unlike the DMA, each platform will have different duties and interdictions assigned within the provided measures (explained further in the following subsection); thus the system will be, to a certain extent, more flexible and tailor-made.

As the case law demonstrates, there are key concerns that arise in digital markets. Although there are certain types of conduct that are often associated with digital platforms, infringements found in digital markets are similar to those in traditional markets in terms of their effects. In the case of implementation thus far in Türkiye, especially in light of the TCC's Meta decision, it can be asserted that sanctioned conducts have exclusionary effects. Obligations and prohibitions introduced in the proposed amendment will, therefore, be adopted to preempt such exclusionary conduct.

Prohibition of Self-Preferencing

The proposed Article 6/A (a) stipulates that platforms with important market power "shall not discriminate against goods of commercial users in the ranking, screening, indexing, or other terms in comparison with its own goods or services and shall ensure that the relevant terms are fair and transparent." This provision prohibits self-preferencing, which the TCC had sanctioned in three decisions regarding Google and partially in the Trendyol decision. In all decisions, the platform had used the data collected in the dominant market for a service provided in the relevant market. Platforms that may be qualified as gatekeepers can easily use their power, strength, and scale of their networks in related markets at low cost. The data can be used to improve the experience of end users and would thus lead to a significant advantage over their competitors in the related market. Existing competitors would have to incur very high costs to collect such data. Potential competitors could be deferred from entering the market as they would not be able to compete with the data already accumulated and the built network of the incumbent. Thus, self-preferencing can have exclusionary effects and could also limit potential competition. The proposed amendment aims to prohibit such conduct and also imposes an obligation to use fair and transparent terms for ranking and similar tools.

Most-Favored Customer

Article 6/A (f) of the draft amendment stipulates that platforms with very important market power cannot prevent commercial users "from offering different prices or conditions for goods or services when working with competing undertakings." This provision establishes a prohibition of most-favored customer clauses. In the Yemek Sepeti decision, the TCC had sanctioned the most-favored customer clause as anti-competitive conduct that prevented commercial users from offering lower or different prices on different platforms. This provision ensures that commercial users can sell at lower prices than those offered on the dominant platform, thereby protecting smaller competing platforms that provide the same service. This prohibition would not only maintain choice for the end consumers but could also invigorate price competition.

Access to Data and Data Portability

Access to data and data portability is a competition law concern that the TCC had the opportunity to consider in the Nadirkitap and Trendyol decisions. In these cases, the TCC has clearly indicated that limiting or preventing access to data can have significant foreclosure effects and raise barriers to entry. Commercial users should, therefore, be allowed to access data that is crucial for their activities and should also be allowed to transfer them to other platforms and especially their own sales channels. There are several provisions in the proposed amendment that aim to ensure effective access to data and data portability. Paragraphs (g), (h), and (i) of the proposed Article 6/A establish prohibitions that would eliminate or restrict commercial users' effective access to data and end users or professional users' right to transfer their data. Furthermore, the proposed article also establishes that the use of data must be transparent and that professional users should have access to their data efficiently, continuously, in real time, and free of charge. As for rules applicable to access to personal data of end-users, the proposed article refers to the Data Protection Act.

Data Protection and Privacy

Protection and privacy of personal data were the central issues in the TCC's Meta decision. Unlike other jurisdictions, the TCC has found that Meta's combination of data constituted an exclusionary abuse. Accordingly, it would be able to combine vast quantities of personal data and thus offer a more personalized and better service than its competitors who would not have access to such data. Article 6/A (g) (1) prohibits such a combination of data by platforms that have an important market power. The proposed provision states that unless it is necessary for the execution of a contract with the end user, the platform cannot combine data collected from other services or third parties and cannot use this data for other services such as online targeted advertisement. This prohibition would thus prevent platforms from gaining unfair advantages by combining and using data that would not be accessible to existing and potential competitors.

Exclusivity

Article 6/A (f) also includes a prohibition that aims to prevent platforms from creating exclusivity conditions by restricting commercial users' access to other sales channels. This concern was addressed by the TCC in the Çiçek Sepeti decision where the platform verbally warned its dealers against working with other service providers and set requirements for the quantity of sales, which practically led dealers to work exclusively with the platform. The proposed amendment states that platforms

> cannot restrict commercial users from working with competing undertakings, from making offers to end users on the platform or through other channels for the same products or services, from making contracts with end users, from advertising their own goods or services through these channels, or from using certain services through different channels.

This provision aims to ensure that professional users are allowed to use many and several channels for their sales and that platforms with an important market power cannot force them to use their channel exclusively.

Procedural Aspects and Sanctions

According to article 8/A of the proposed amendment, undertakings that exceed the thresholds determined by secondary legislation for the designation of platforms with very important market power will have to notify the TCC within 30 days. After notification, or by complaint or ex officio, the TCC will determine whether the undertaking qualifies as such a platform. Perhaps, more importantly, by the same decision, the TCC will also decide which obligations and prohibitions will be applicable to the designated platform. Unlike the DMA, each platform will have a different set of duties to fulfill depending on their market position, the type of service they provide etc. Therefore, not all undertakings will have the same obligations, leading to a more diverse but probably more flexible and adaptive implementation. The TCC will determine the time limit within which the undertaking would have to comply with its obligations, which cannot be longer than 90 days. This decision will be valid for a period of three years and will be automatically renewed unless the undertaking appeals to the TCC within 90 days.

If an undertaking violates the proposed article 6/A, the fine of 10% of annual turnover determined in article 16 of the TCA will be doubled. Thus, a much higher sanction for violations of articles 4, 6, and 7 is provided for noncompliance with obligations under 6/A. On the other hand, designated platforms will be subject to a fine of 0.05% of annual turnover per day for not establishing the necessary infrastructure provided in the proposed article 15. Furthermore, these undertakings will also be subject to the existing fine of 0.5% of annual turnover per day for obstructing inspections under article 15/2 of the TCA.

Conclusion

The Turkish Competition Council (TCC) has rapidly developed its analysis and approach to digital markets, addressing various types of conduct in a relatively short period. Following the global trend, the TCC has deemed self-preferencing by gatekeeper platforms as abusive, recognizing its potential to foreclose related markets. Scrutiny has been applied to the use of algorithms for discrimination, emphasizing the importance of establishing fair terms for professional users and competitors. Exclusivity practices, including Most-Favored Customer (MFC) clauses and terms creating exclusive relations, have been found to risk excluding smaller competitors and hindering market competition. The TCC has also delved into data-related issues, touching upon collection, privacy, and portability. Viewing data as a form of payment and essential for professional users' activities and end-users' privacy, the TCC underscores the significance of access to data and data portability to prevent incumbents from foreclosing the market through the control of extensive datasets. While acknowledging that the privacy of personal data falls under data protection rules, the TCC recognizes that the use and combination of personal data can lead to exclusionary effects in the market, constituting an abuse. In addition to its case law, the TCC has conducted sector inquiries into digital markets, providing policy implications. The proposed amendment to the Turkish Competition Act aligns with these findings and approaches, proposing ex ante regulation for platforms with very important market power. The prohibitions and obligations outlined in the amendment cover all competition concerns identified in case law and sector inquiries, indicating that the lessons learned have contributed to shaping effective policy measures.

References

Ezrachi, A. (2015). The competitive effects of parity clauses on online commerce, *European Competition Law Journal*, *11*(2), 488–519.

Graef, I. (2019). Differentiated treatment in platform-to- business relations: EU competition law and economic dependence, *Yearbook of European Law*, *38*(1), 448–499.

Ibanez Colomo, P. (2020). Self-preferencing: Yet another epithet in need of limiting principles, *World Competition*, *43*(4), 417–446.

Just, N. (2018). Governing online platforms: Competition policy in times of platformization, *Telecommunications Policy*, *42*(5), 386–394.

Khan, M. L. (2017). Amazon's antitrust paradox, *The Yale Law Journal*, *126*(3), 710–805.
Kuenzler, A. (2022). What competition law can do for data privacy (and vice versa), *Computer Law & Security Review*, 47, 1–17.
OECD. (2020). *Big data*. Retrieved January 10, 2024, from https://one.oecd.org/document/DAF/COMP/M(2016)2/ANN4/FINAL/en/pdf
Petit, N. (2020). *Big tech & the digital economy*, Oxford: Oxford University Press.
Sanlı, K. C., & Doğan, C. (2023). *Rekabet politikası açısından dijital piyasaların Ddüzenlenmesi: E-ticaret Kanunu ve Rekabet Kanunu değişkliği taslağı*, On İki Levha.
Turkish Competition Council (TCC). (2022). *The e-marketplace platforms sector inquiry report*. Retrieved January 10, 2024 from www.rekabet.gov.tr/Dosya/sektor-raporlari/e-pazaryeri-si-raporu-pdf-20220425105139595-pdf
Turkish Competition Council (TCC). (2023). Retrieved January 10, 2024 from www.rekabet.gov.tr/Dosya/cevrimici-reklamcilik-on-raporu-20231009170548088.pdf
Turkish Competition Council Decisions. *Çiçek Sepeti*, 21–20/250–106, 08 April 2021.
Turkish Competition Council Decisions. *DSM Grup Danışmanlık* (*Trendyol*), 23–11/177–54, 27 February 2023.
Turkish Competition Council Decisions. *Google Adwords*, 20–49/675–296, 21 November 2020.
Turkish Competition Council Decisions. *Google Local Search*, 21–20/248–105, 08 February 2021.
Turkish Competition Council Decisions. *Google Shopping*, 20/10/19–69, 13 February 2020.
Turkish Competition Council Decisions. *Hepsiburada*, 21–22/266–116, 15 April, 2012.
Turkish Competition Council Decisions. *Meta* (previously named Facebook), 22–48/706–299, 20 October 2022.
Turkish Competition Council Decisions. <cite lang="id">*Nadirkitap*, 22–15/273, 07 April 2022.
Turkish Competition Council Decisions. *Sahibinden*, 21–46/655-M of 30 September 2021.
Turkish Competition Council Decisions. *Yemek Sepeti*, 21–05/64–28, 28 January 2021.

12 Regulation of Digital Platforms in Turkish Law

The E-Commerce Law and the Draft Competition Law

Kerem Cem Sanli and Cihan Doğan

Introduction

The problem of monopolization caused by digital platforms has been one of the most discussed issues in competition law doctrine in recent years. The argument that economic characteristics of digital platforms, such as network externalities, economies of scale and scope, big data, and consumer indifference, pave the way for entrenched market power in digital markets is gaining increasing traction in scholarly discourse and among enforcement agencies. Thus, the optimistic approach predominant in the early 2010s, which posited that e-commerce would enhance competition in the marketplace, is now experiencing a partial reversal owing to the monopolistic positions held by certain digital platforms. Competition law investigations initiated against Google, Amazon, and Meta in various legal systems could be regarded as hallmarks of this new tendency.

However, it is now claimed that competition law intervention alone cannot solve the economic concentration problems associated with these markets and that specific regulations must be implemented. Competition law's perceived inadequacy stems from various factors, including delays in intervention, stringent evidentiary standards, legal uncertainties associated with market definition and interpretation of the term abuse, and shortcomings in legal remedies. Therefore, in many jurisdictions, policymakers are now considering enacting new laws that include ex ante regulations. Several countries, including the United States, the United Kingdom, and Australia, are currently in the process of preparing laws while the EU, Japan, and Germany have already enacted new regulations. In the EU, *Google*, *Microsoft*, *Meta,* and *Apple* have already been identified as gatekeepers and are being subjected to new rules (European Commission, 2023).

Turkey is perhaps one of the earliest countries to participate in this global trend, which advocates the necessity of regulating digital platforms in the name of competition policy. In a very short period, two draft regulations were prepared, one by the Ministry of Commerce and the other by the Competition Authority ("TCA"). The first of these, the Law numbered 7416 which amended the E-Commerce Law numbered 6563, was adopted by the

DOI: 10.4324/9781032692937-12

Legislature in 2022 ("the E-Commerce Law" or "Law") (The Law on the Amendment of the Law on the Regulation of Electronic Commerce, 2022). The other, the Draft Amendment to the Law on the Protection of Competition ("the Draft") is expected to be enacted in 2024 (Republic of Türkiye Presidential Directorate of Strategy and Budget, 2023). In general, this legislative activity has been influenced by comparative law and in particular by the Digital Markets Act of the European Union law ("DMA") (Regulation 2022/1925). The aim of these regulations is to curb the monopolistic power of digital platforms and promote fair competition in these markets.

In this chapter, we will explain the fundamentals of digital platform regulation in Turkish law. Herein, we will delve into both the Draft and the Law, exploring the basic characteristics of the regulation and the obligations it sets forth. It should be noted that since it is currently in force, the focus will be mainly on the E-Commerce Law. Moreover, unlike other similar regulations, the Law includes several unorthodox provisions, making it worthy of examination from a comparative law perspective. Before exploring these topics, we commence our analysis by examining the economic rationales behind the regulation of digital platforms, followed by a brief analysis on the challenges associated with applying competition law to digital platforms.

Economic Justification of Entrenched Market Power in Digital Markets

Platforms, in essence, create value by connecting two or more economic units and enabling exchanges. The primary functions of platforms are reducing transaction costs and creating value (Doğan, 2021, p. 23 et. seq.). The economic structure of digital markets, where platforms operate, is significantly different from traditional markets as digital platforms exhibit economic characteristics such as network externalities, economies of scale and scope. Besides, platforms can collect, store, and process huge volumes of data. All these characteristics fundamentally impact the competitive structure of the markets.

Network externality refers to the increase in the value of a product that occurs due to an increase in the number of users consuming that product. For example, for digital platforms, as the number of users using a social network increases, the value of that network increases. Increase in the number of users makes the network more attractive to other users. From competition policy perspective, the value created by network externalities often increases the concentration level of a given market, which creates barriers to entry for potential competitors. This is especially the case in the presence of high switching costs and economies of scale and scope.

There are two types of network externalities: direct and indirect. Direct network externality occurs when the value of a product or service increases as more people use it. For example, social networks like WhatsApp or Facebook become more valuable to users as the number of users on the platform increases. Indirect network externality occurs when two or more customer groups use a network to exchange value. To put it another way, indirect network effects occur in cases where the benefit of a use depends on the number of users belonging to another customer group. For example, an increase in the number of consumers using an online marketplace platform will render the platform more valuable for business users. This is also the case for consumers. An increase in the number of business users in an online marketplace platform will increase the value of the platform for consumers, as consumers will have more choices. In such a case, the indirect network effect is reciprocal and positive for both customer groups.

There are two additional economic characteristics associated with network externalities. The first one is the feedback loop, where, for example, an increase in the number of consumers using the online marketplace platform leads to an increase in the number of business users due to positive indirect network effects, which in turn increase the number of consumers. The feedback loops not only enhance market power but also significantly increase the negative impact of anti-competitive behaviors. The second one is the consequential necessity of incorporating both customer groups into the platform to enter the market. By establishing a network on the platform, the demand on this network must be balanced in a way that creates welfare for both customer groups while establishing a platform. This is because, in the absence of a customer group (e.g. business users) to which the platform provides service, other customer groups (e.g. consumers) will not have an incentive to use the platform. For example, an online food ordering platform that hosts only restaurants cannot survive on the market, and it is also impossible for an online marketplace platform that includes only consumers (and no business users) to conduct commercial activities.

Other than network externalities, there are significant economies of scale and scope across digital platforms. Economies of scale occur when average cost decreases as output increases, typically in markets requiring high fixed costs. Economies of scope involve reducing production costs by producing different products. For platforms which typically have high fixed and sunk costs, serving additional customers becomes relatively inexpensive. Additionally, entering new markets is comparatively low-cost for platforms. These economic advantages contribute to the market power of platforms and increase the concentration level in markets where platforms operate. To the extent that these features provide cost advantages to incumbent platforms, they can act as barriers-to-entry for new entrants.

Third and last, digital platforms can access a significant amount of data. The amount and variety of data held by platforms can be used to develop new services and increase the quality and variety of existing products thereby making substantial contributions to consumer welfare. Data enables platforms to better estimate consumer preferences and offer goods and services in line with these preferences. However, it is certainly possible that data can be used for anti-competitive purposes. For example, data can be used in some scenarios to allow the platform to gain an unfair advantage over competitors. In particular, hybrid platforms can exclude their competitors at the retail level by sharing the data they collect with an internal retail business unit, giving the retail business unit an advantage over its competitors (i.e. business users of the platform). There is also a data-driven network effect. An undertaking operating in the market can further expand its dataset as it operates. Undertakings that lack access to data may face challenges when trying to enter the market.

To sum up, while digital platforms offer considerable efficiency, notably in the reduction of transaction costs, their business model could have adverse implications for competition in the markets. The economic characteristics of digital platforms can enhance market power and thus lead to market concentration. The same economic characteristics also enable these platforms to maintain their market power effectively through anti-competitive actions such as self-preferencing and tying. These outcomes prevent the expected benefits of competition to materialize in these markets.

Application of Competition Law to Digital Platforms

Competition law is the primary tool to deal with the problems arising from market concentration. Concordantly, competition authorities worldwide, including the TCA, have been conducting numerous sector inquiries and investigations targeting digital markets, resulting in the imposition of drastic administrative sanctions and also behavioral remedies on digital platforms. Despite these efforts, which have been hardened in the last couple of years, doubts remain as to whether competition law can effectively address competition policy concerns in digital markets (Sanli & Doğan, 2023, p. 23 et seq.).

One of the main reasons for these doubts stem from the fact that competition laws are applied ex post. The investigation is typically launched only after the harm to competition has occurred, which is very hard to reverse once it is materialized. Investigations may last for a long period and exacerbate the problem, especially in these quickly evolving markets. Parallel to this, competition authorities must meet stringent conditions of proof to successfully conclude an investigation. Investigating platform behavior necessitates defining markets which is a complicated task for two-sided platforms, establishing dominance and identifying anti-competitive effects. Moreover, traditional measures of market power, like market share, may not be a reliable proxy for assessing market power in digital markets due to the two-sided nature of the platform. Furthermore, proving negative market impact and addressing behaviors beyond existing theories of harm also poses challenges and leads to legal uncertainty about how to specifically identify unlawful practices by these platforms. Another notable consideration concerns sanctions. While administrative fines serve as a primary deterrent in competition law, their effectiveness may be limited in the context of platforms. Moreover, prioritizing measures to address violations over fines becomes crucial for digital platforms, considering asymmetric access to information, which may bring into question the competence of competition authorities.

Due to these (and other) factors, there is a growing view that digital platforms exceeding certain financial thresholds should be regulated through well-defined "ex ante" obligations without undermining legal certainty. Accordingly, legislative deliberations are underway in several countries, with new laws being enacted in some jurisdictions. The best example is undoubtedly the DMA enacted by the EU. It is aimed at regulating digital platforms with significant market power (=gatekeepers) and primarily seeks to address the monopoly power of certain platforms in the digital market space.

Competition Law Amendment Draft

The first example of digital platform regulation is the draft amendment to the Competition Law ("Draft"), expected to be enacted in 2024. The Draft has been prepared by the Competition Authority and introduces significant changes to the existing Competition Act, in particular to Article 6, which governs abuse of dominance. It should be stated from the outset that the Draft is built upon a framework that considerably differs from conventional competition law principles. Digital platforms offering essential services are subject to specific obligations if they hold significant market power ("SMP"), which will be ascertained based on various quantitative criteria through secondary legislation. The main feature of these obligations, which are clearly inspired by competition policy, is that they are applied regardless of their impact on the market. Another aspect of the Draft is that obligations are not absolute in the sense that not all of them will be automatically enforced. Platforms that meet the quantitative criteria will notify the TCA, and the obligations to be enforced will be decided by the TCA after receiving the notification.

What specific amendments are envisioned in the Draft?

First, the Draft assumes that competition law is insufficient to solve the concentration problem in digital markets. The Draft justifies the necessity for ex ante regulation of digital markets due to difficulties in defining the market, determining market power, identifying behavior subject to infringement, and enforcement of effective remedies. It is also acknowledged that competition problems associated with digital markets go beyond the limits of conventional theories of harm. Illustrative examples include behaviors such as self-preferencing, obstruction of interoperability and data portability and excessive data accumulation.

Second, the Draft includes an amendment to the article outlining the objectives of the Competition Act. The aim of preventing abusive behavior by undertaking with SMP in platform services and fostering a fair and contestable market structure is added to the Draft. The reference to "fairness" and "contestability" introduces a novel concept to Competition Act, the specifics of which are to be determined through practice. Also, the scope of the Competition Act has been expanded to include the actions of digital platforms that operate globally and are not based in Turkey.

Third, new definitions are added to the Draft. These definitions mostly relate to the scope of the core platform services which is undoubtedly one of the most important concepts of the Draft. Undertakings with SMP are defined as undertakings that operate at a certain scale and with access to end users or have a significant impact on the activities of business users in terms of one or more core platform services and have the power to maintain this impact in an established and permanent manner. The quantitative criteria of SMP will be determined by secondary legislation.

Fourth, the Draft sets out numerous obligations applicable to platforms with SMP. Explaining all the obligations is beyond the scope of this chapter, but they can be categorized into different groups based on the competition problem underlying each obligation. For instance, some of the obligations aim to remedy information asymmetry between a platform and its business users. Accordingly, platforms are compelled to be more transparent vis-a-vis business users and provide information concerning their services, especially with respect to advertising. Some obligations seek to address the issue of interoperability and oblige platforms to provide service to rivals and complementary service providers. Others aim to achieve multi-homing by prohibiting exclusivity and most-favored nation ("MFN") clauses. There are also data-based obligations that aim to foster the dissemination of data. Although there are differences, these obligations are mainly influenced by the DMA and partly by the German Competition Law.

Fifth, the Draft has instituted a procedural framework necessitating reciprocal engagement between the platform and the TCA. This process commences with the platform's application to TCA and informing the TCA that the undertaking is exceeding the thresholds that will be determined within the secondary legislation. Upon this application, TCA decides whether the undertaking has SMP and, if so, determines the obligations that will be applied to the undertaking. The platform with SMP must comply within a six-month period. In case of violation of the obligations, it is envisaged that ordinary inquiry procedures under the Competition Act will be followed.

Regulating digital platforms with ex ante obligations also has its pitfalls, especially considering the innovative nature of these markets. Ex ante regulations, characterized by their inflexibility and intrusive nature, can generate social costs in the form of Type I errors. In that regard, enforcing certain obligations such as the prohibition of discrimination and data portability, poses considerable challenges. The Draft, in its present state, lacks completeness, necessitating comprehensive secondary regulations for numerous matters. Similarly, the procedural rules overlook certain scenarios and exhibit shortcomings in this regard. Despite these limitations, the Draft can be considered the result of a successful and scientific study, particularly when compared to the E-Commerce Law.

E-Commerce Law

General Characteristics of the Law

Until the 2022 amendment, the E-Commerce Law served as a consumer protection statute that endeavored to foster a secure legal environment for consumer e-commerce transaction engagement. The 2022 Amendment, on the other hand, addresses the problem of monopolization caused by platforms and focuses on competition policy goals. In this sense, the Amendment has completely changed the character of the Law. The Law, along with its secondary legislation (Regulation on Electronic Commerce Intermediary Service Providers and Electronic Commerce Service Providers, 2022), effectively enshrines regulations for two interconnected domains: addressing unfair commercial practices and preventing monopolistic behavior.

Unfair commercial practice rules are concerned with contractual relations between business users and platforms. The Law presupposes that digital platforms have asymmetric economic power that undermines the balance of interests between the platform and business users. Accordingly, it imposes certain mandatory obligations to alleviate the imbalance of interests between the platform and the business users, as in the case of the P2B Regulation (Regulation 2019/1150). These rules can be characterized as a specific version of the regulation of standard term contracts, as we observe in the law of obligations. Since these provisions only indirectly relate to competition policy, they do not constitute our primary focus (Sanli & Doğan, 2023, pp. 111–112; Kaya, 2022).

Undoubtedly, the primary focus of the Law lies in competition policy objectives. The preamble of the Law explicitly mentions the fostering of fair competition in digital markets. Accordingly, the Law imposes obligations on platforms based on their economic size, and at first glance, the obligations seem to be in line with competition policy objectives. The obligations, such as data portability and access to data requirements, are intended to reduce the economic power resulting from big data. Others aim to provide *multi-homing* and thereby foster inter-platform competition. Meanwhile, other obligations aim to prevent the leveraging of monopoly power into adjacent markets. However, upon closer scrutiny, there are some obligations in the provisions of the Law that can hardly be correlated with competition policy, and therefore, it is probably the case that other policy objectives play a role as well. We discuss this issue in detail here.[1]

An essential feature of these obligations is their application *ipso facto*, without the need for a decision by an administrative authority. This is in contrast with the Draft Competition Law, which requires both a designation decision and a determination decision outlining specific obligations for the platform in question. Conversely, under the Law, once certain financial thresholds are exceeded, all relevant obligations automatically apply. Further, obligations are enforced without consideration for the behavior's market impact or any economic justification. Essentially, the specific circumstances of the case are disregarded. In this sense, the Law represents one of the strictest forms of ex ante regulation.

Scope of Application of the Law

The Law is enacted to address the monopolization problem associated with digital platforms and is thus applicable to digital platforms. A digital platform is referred to as an Electronic Commerce Intermediary Service Provider ("ECISP"), and the Law provides a definition of this term. ECISP is defined as "an intermediary service provider that allows making contracts or placing orders for the supply of goods or services of electronic commerce service providers in the electronic commerce marketplace". According to this definition, only transaction platforms are included within the scope of the Law. Non-transaction platforms such as advertisement platforms do not qualify as ECISP and are therefore not subject to the Law (Sanli, 2023, p. 1712 et seq.). The disparate treatment of non-transactional platforms lacks justification, which runs counter to the objectives of competition policy, given the higher risk of monopolization tendency associated with non-transaction platforms.

The Law also defines business users of the platforms. They are designated as "Electronic Commerce Service Providers" ("ECSP") and defined very broadly. Any person who provides goods and services, regardless of whether in an online marketplace or an online environment, is defined as ECSP. At first glance, the definition seems reasonable as it governs the relations between platforms and business users. However, when other provisions are considered, it is understood that the Law imposes certain obligations not only on platforms but also on business users according to their economic size. The obligations herein (data portability, exclusivity, license fee etc.) are also analogous to the obligations stipulated for the platforms. Considering this, it is presupposed that not only platforms but also ECSPs tend to monopolize. However, this assertion is subject to scrutiny. To our knowledge, there is neither evidence of monopolization in the markets where ECSPs operate nor any scientific study indicating such a tendency. Therefore, these obligations appear to be puzzling.

Certain industries are made exempt from the scope of the Law. For instance, travel agencies, airlines, private pensions, banks, insurance companies, financial leasing, and factoring companies will not be subject to the obligations outlined in the Law, even if they function as platforms. Aside from the policy rationale behind these exceptions, which is inadequately addressed in the Law, the relevant article intricately governs the exceptions by merely referring to certain Laws without explicitly elucidating them. This poses challenges for delineating the scope of the exceptions.

Financial Threshold System

The financial threshold system serves as a pivotal concept in the Law. The legislation outlines three distinct financial thresholds which trigger relevant obligations upon being exceeded. These thresholds are determined based on the concept of "net transaction value", which refers to the combined value of commercial transactions conducted on the platform in Turkish Lira. Consequently, the Law does not consider the platform's income or profits from its intermediary services as a proxy for determining the obligations.

There are several issues with this system. First, it's unclear why the Law prescribes three separate thresholds. While market power may vary in degree, the concepts of dominance or gatekeeper status are binary, meaning they either exist or they do not. As a result, platform regulations in other jurisdictions typically employ a single threshold. If it's argued that there could be multiple degrees of market power, then there should be a solid economic justification for this proposition.

Second, it's unclear why the thresholds are based on net transaction value rather than other metrics that more accurately indicate market power, such as turnover and/or the number of users.

Third, it is not easily comprehensible why the obligations assigned to different thresholds are tailored to the platforms that exceed those thresholds. For instance, a medium-sized platform may face restrictions on data usage while a large-sized platform may be subject to restrictions on discounts and advertising budgets. Conversely, a very large-sized platform may face bans on certain activities like financial services. What rationale or scientific study underpins the assignment of these obligations to the specified financial thresholds? There is no persuasive reasoning for these regulations.

Fourth, net transaction value is calculated annually. As the platform expands, it may surpass a higher threshold the following year. Considering this likelihood, activity restrictions related to financial or cargo services imposed on very large platforms essentially amount to a de facto ban on large-sized platforms as well. This is because there always exists a possibility that even a large-sized (or medium-sized) platform will grow and exceed the upper financial threshold in subsequent years. Evidently, the risk of potential divestment from that business line in the future dissuades investment in it, serving as an entry barrier for all platforms.

Fifth, financial thresholds are applied regardless of the specific market context. As a result, platforms may find themselves subject to obligations even when entering new markets. Given the significance of cross-platform competition in this industry, it's evident that this outcome is not well-suited.

Based on the reasons outlined here, we firmly believe that the legitimacy of the financial threshold system as delineated in the Law is highly contentious. The issues associated with this system, which form the cornerstone of the Law, have the potential to undermine the effectiveness of the obligations, regardless of their substance.

Competition Policy-Oriented Obligations for Digital Platforms

The legislation encompasses a diverse array of obligations and prohibitions, some of which may not be directly relevant to competition policy. Hence, in this analysis, we will concentrate solely on those obligations that we deem critical from a competition policy perspective. Furthermore, the Law dictates that certain obligations designed for platforms will be also applicable to ECSPs by analogy. However, given the absence of rational justification for the obligations imposed on ECSPs, we will refrain from exploring them in further detail.

Obligations Applicable to all Platforms: Private Label Prohibition

The Law includes various obligations that are applied regardless of financial threshold. While some of these obligations may be correlated with competition policy, we will focus solely on the private label ("PL") prohibition. According to the Law, platforms are prohibited from selling their PL products on their marketplace. However, platforms are permitted to sell their private label products through different sales channels. Nevertheless, the Law prohibits providing access to or advertising between the marketplace and other sales channels.

The purpose of this prohibition appears to be to prevent conflicts of interest that may arise between the platform and business users. When the platform offers its PL for sale on the same platform, it effectively becomes a competitor with ECSPs who also operate and interact as platform's customers. This situation may incentivize the platform to prioritize its own PL over ECSP, for example, in search rankings. By imposing a ban on the sale of PL products, the Law aims to address the problems associated with self-preferencing.

It is important to emphasize that this prohibition applies regardless of market power. Therefore, even a newly entered platform is restricted from selling its own PL on its marketplace. However, in such instances, given the absence of market power, there is no competition issue, as this is unlikely to significantly disadvantage online sellers. Furthermore, PL products play a role in enhancing product diversity and fostering quality and price competition within and across platforms. The prevalence of these products in the retail sector underscores these benefits. Hence, a prohibition independent of market power ultimately results in a loss of consumer welfare.

Furthermore, it is possible to address this concern with less intrusive remedies, such as separating the private label unit from core platform services and limiting data sharing. Notably, the Law incorporates a provision restricting the utilization of data, thereby targeting this issue. Another paradoxical situation regarding the PL ban is this: the Law allows the platform to be a direct seller. However, similar competitive concerns (self-preferencing) may also be present in this case. Enabling the platform to act as a seller essentially disincentivizes the platform from generating value through brand investment. Therefore, a ban on PL products is not only unnecessary and disproportionate but also contradictory.

Obligations for Medium-Sized Platforms

DATA USAGE RESTRICTION FOR HYBRID PLATFORMS

The Law prohibits platforms from utilizing data acquired from ECSPs and consumers in direct competition with ECSPs, particularly targeting hybrid platforms to mitigate conflicts of interest in the downstream market. This restriction mandates that the gathered data can be employed only for intermediary services. While it's reasonable for the Law to regulate data usage to avoid competition with ECSPs, confining its utilization solely to intermediary services appears overly restrictive. Data represents a valuable asset that could contribute to various economic activities beyond mere intermediary services. Furthermore, the concept of intermediary services remains somewhat vague.

The secondary regulation aims to bring clarity to the matter. Platforms can use publicly available data freely without any restriction. This exception makes sense as this type of data doesn't confer a competitive advantage over ECSP. Second, the regulation permits the use of data for both provision and enhancement of intermediary services. Particularly noteworthy is the exception for the development of intermediary services, which effectively broadens the scope of permissible data usage. Despite these provisions, there's a concern that the wording of these obligations may still be overly restrictive.

OBLIGATIONS ON DATA PORTABILITY AND ACCESS TO DATA

Medium-sized platforms are obligated to provide technical infrastructure for ECSPs to transport the data obtained from their sales and to provide free and effective access to raw and/or processed data. These obligations, although governed by the same provision, pertain to distinct issues and should be analyzed separately. In fact, the Draft and the DMA address these obligations in different provisions. Data portability allows ECSPs to transfer their valuable data to other platforms. This makes it easier for ECSP to operate on multiple platforms (multi-homing) and increases cross-platform competition.

Conversely, data access enables ECSPs to make informed decisions by leveraging a broader array of data sources. This not only improves their economic position vis-à-vis platforms but also enhances efficiency. It is inevitable that this obligation will have a distributional effect. Proper ownership of data eliminates or at least redistributes the costs that business users would otherwise incur for access to this data in the absence of this provision.

ACCESS RESTRICTIONS BETWEEN DIFFERENT E-COMMERCE ENVIRONMENTS

The Law prohibits medium-sized platforms from allowing users to access different e-commerce environments and from promoting each other within these environments unless these various e-commerce platforms are included in a net transaction value calculation. For example, if a company operates multiple e-commerce platforms in different markets, consumers are not given the option to easily switch or visit other platforms. The policy rationale behind this prohibition is related to leveraging theory. It is likely assumed that as a platform reaches a certain economic size, it can use its economic power as leverage to gain advantages in adjacent markets and disrupt competitive conditions in those markets.

The prohibition outlined raises several issues. To begin with, the conditions under which it applies lack clarity. If different e-commerce platforms are owned by the same company, they are included in a net transaction value calculation. Hence, the prohibition does not apply. If platforms are owned by different companies within the same economic whole, it is likely that they will be counted in the same net transaction value. Hence, again, the prohibition will not apply. Therefore, the Law's application on this point remains ambiguous.

More importantly, the economic rationale behind the prohibition appears flawed. First, a medium-sized transaction platform may lack market power, which renders the prohibition unnecessary. Second, the prohibition disregards potential economic benefits stemming from economies of scale and scope. Even in cases where the platform wields market power, the prohibition could lead to social costs. Third, inter-platform competition is a vital aspect of digital markets. However, this prohibition erects barriers to entry and stifles crucial competitive pressures. Ultimately, it seems the prohibition may inadvertently hinder rather than promote competition and consumer welfare in e-commerce environments.

Obligations for Large-Sized Platforms

ADVERTISING AND DISCOUNT BUDGET RESTRICTIONS

The Law imposes restrictions on the discount and advertising budgets of large-sized platforms. Given the uniform approach in determining these limitations, it's useful to explain this obligation under the same heading. The Law employs the same calculation method: for net transaction value up to 45 billion Turkish liras, 2% of this value is allocated. For values exceeding 45 billion liras, 0.3% of the portion above the threshold is permitted. These two values are then summed separately to form the total discount budget. Consequently, the advertising and discount budget maximums are equivalent for the platform.

Both advertising and discount activities are deemed pro-competitive and socially beneficial. Therefore, the question is this: why are these socially beneficial activities restricted? The Law appears to presume that these actions, if implemented by large-sized platforms, can become excessive and result in anti-competitive effects in the markets. The preamble of the provision refers to excessive advertisement and predatory pricing as a rationale for these restrictions.

Let's first look at the advertisement restriction. The rationale posits that platforms engage in excessive advertising, leading to the exclusion of competitors who cannot match such a scale of advertising. Consequently, it is argued that advertisement raises rival costs and therefore can be anti-competitive. However, it is essential to note that these propositions, while seemingly coherent, lack empirical grounding. To the best of our knowledge, there exists no scientific study demonstrating a direct correlation between advertising intensity and weakened competition in e-commerce. Moreover, the ambiguity in the provision's wording exacerbates the issue. The Law defines advertising broadly, making it challenging to ascertain which actions fall within its scope and are therefore subject to limitations. While secondary regulations aim to provide clarity, there remains a notable risk of legal certainty. Efforts to mitigate this risk are crucial to ensure fair and consistent application of the Law in practice. Perhaps, the most important point is that advertisement is considered socially beneficial because it informs consumers and increase competition. Consequently, while the restriction may result in a decrease in welfare, its potential for yielding commensurate benefits remains uncertain.

The situation concerning discount budget restriction is not different. From a competition policy perspective, it is more difficult to rationalize the discount budget. Initially, it is crucial to delineate the provision's scope. This provision encompasses a broad spectrum of economic benefits classified as discounts, limiting not only consumer discounts but also those extended to sellers. Additionally, the Law also regulates the allocation of rebates, such as by prohibiting the use of all rebates within a specific time frame, rendering it exceptionally intrusive. The expansive definition of discounts engenders practical uncertainty. Simple price differentiations, such as transient variations in seller commissions, could spark debates over whether a distinct tariff or a discount was applied.

From the policy perspective, there is no doubt that discounts provide a clear and direct benefit to consumers and therefore, limiting the budgets will increase prices and both consumers and sellers will lose. Does budget limitation provide any benefit? The Law operates under the assumption that discounts provided by major platforms constitute predatory pricing. However, there is no scientific study demonstrating predatory pricing in these markets. Even if such pricing exists, competition Law intervention can address this issue effectively. Furthermore, since the discount budget limitation is not a cost-based provision, it lacks the capacity to prevent predatory pricing. Moreover, discounts offer substantial advantages, particularly when penetrating new markets. Constraining discount budgets, irrespective of any market share threshold, will diminish a platform's capacity to offer discounts during market entry, thereby curtailing overall entry and stifling competition. Therefore, we think that this restriction is anti-competitive in nature and will certainly result in social cost.

MFN, NON-COMPETITION, AND SUPPLY RESTRICTIONS

The article 2/2(c) of the Law imposes several prohibitions on large-sized platforms in a somewhat complicated manner. Among these prohibitions, three will be underscored here. The first one is the non-competition clause. The platform is barred from either legally or practically preventing sellers from participating on rival platforms. Exclusive agreements with sellers are prohibited, rendering such arrangements null and void. Sellers retain the freedom to operate across any platform of their choosing. This provision facilitates multi-homing, thereby fostering effective competition among platforms.

The second prohibition concerns parity clauses, commonly known as MFN clauses (Sanli & Doğan, 2022; Sümer Özdemir, 2023). The Law unequivocally prohibits such clauses, irrespective of their form. Consequently, any provisions within agreements between a platform and ECSP ensuring the platform receives the most favorable prices and conditions will be deemed prohibited and void. Within this framework, ECSPs are afforded the freedom to offer products and services across different channels at prices and conditions of their choosing. As widely acknowledged, especially broad MFN clauses can create and increase barriers to entry, particularly in the presence of market power of the platform. Therefore, despite the relatively strict nature of this prohibition, it has the potential to foster cross-platform competition while safeguarding the commercial interests of ECSPs.

The third restriction entails that the platform is proscribed from coercing ECSPs to procure goods or services from any specific entity. Naturally, platforms can recommend that ECSPs buy goods and services from certain suppliers. The Law prohibits only coercive acts. In particular, the prohibition governs the tying of ancillary services offered by the group companies of the platform, such as cargo, payment, and insurance. Hence, a platform cannot stipulate the receipt of these services exclusively from itself. The prohibition on tying restricts the platform from leveraging its economic advantage to the detriment of third-party service providers, particularly with respect to complementary services. This provision has the potential to promote fair and vigorous competition in the domain of complementary services.

Obligations for Very Large-Sized Platforms

RESTRICTIONS ON THE PROVISION OF FINANCIAL SERVICES

Three distinct activity restrictions have been implemented for very large-sized platforms. Two of these pertain to the financial services offered within the marketplace. First, banks, financial leasing companies, factoring and other financial companies operating within the same economic whole of the platform (i.e. group company) are restricted from providing services to customers via the marketplace. Basically, platforms are barred from entering the financial services sector. However, credit card payments and other payment transactions regulated under Law No. 5464 are exempt from this prohibition. The second limitation on financial services concerns the provision of payment services, albeit articulated in a complex manner. In summary, platforms are prohibited from accepting electronic money issued by electronic money institutions established in accordance with Law No. 6493 and from offering payment tools within their own restricted networks.

Two rationales can be posited to justify these restrictions. First, the economic position of a very large-sized platform confers it with a significant advantage in offering financial services within the marketplace. Consequently, if the platform were to provide these complementary services, it would present formidable challenges for third-party service providers attempting to compete. For instance, as the platform's proprietary payment instrument gains widespread acceptance, alternative payment instruments, including electronic money, which may serve as full or limited substitutes, would struggle to compete effectively.

Second, platforms that attain a certain scale benefit from advantages such as a sizable customer base, access to extensive data, technological superiority, and economies of scale. These advantages could potentially disrupt competition within the financial services market. Hence, there exists a risk of competitive harm based on leverage theory.

Two primary issues arise with this provision. First, through less intrusive measures such as banning tying, imposing data sharing limitations, and prohibiting self-prioritization, a level playing field can be established between third-party financial service providers and the platform. Consequently, the outright prohibition of the platform from providing financial services appears disproportionate. Moreover, this prohibition restricts consumers (and business users) from accessing innovative technological services that platforms could introduce to these markets, thus limiting potential competition and resulting in a loss of welfare. The legislature appears to have overlooked these potential benefits and instead prioritized mitigation of the concentration risk that may emerge in the medium-to-long term.

RESTRICTIONS ON THE PROVISION OF LOGISTICS SERVICES TO THIRD PARTIES

The Law imposes constraints on very large-sized platforms offering cargo services, notably restricting them from extending these services to third parties beyond their marketplace. Consequently, the Law permits very large-sized platforms to provide cargo services exclusively within their own marketplace. However, it prohibits these platforms from entering the cargo transportation market as independent carriers.

Interestingly, the nature of the limitations on financial services discussed earlier is very different from this provision on cargo. While the provision allowing very large-sized platforms to offer cargo services within their own marketplace may raise competition concerns due to their asymmetric position and data advantage over ECSPs, extending these services to third parties does not pose any such issues, as far as current state of the knowledge indicates. On the contrary, a very large-sized platform's entry into the cargo market is expected to enhance competition and benefit consumers. Leveraging their access to data-enabled and technological capabilities, platforms can offer higher quality and innovative products in the cargo market. However, the Law imposes legal barriers to entry, leaving it open to criticism from a competition policy perspective.

THE OBLIGATION TO SEPARATE THE LISTING PLATFORMS FROM TRANSACTION PLATFORMS

The final obligation imposed on very large-sized platforms pertains to the unbundling of listing services. The Law prohibits listing (advertisement) platforms and transaction platforms from reaching buyers through the same online environment. Mere separation is insufficient; there must also be no access or promotion between the two channels. These access restrictions are also reciprocal. Once again, the potential economic justification is leveraging. The legislature posited that a platform could readily leverage its economic influence from one market, such as intermediary services, to another market, such as listing services. The perceived "unfair" advantages resulting from this transfer of power were deemed likely to disrupt competitive conditions in the latter market. Consequently, the legislation prohibits the transfer of power between these markets.

This prohibition raises several concerns. Initially, it is unclear why listing platforms are treated separately from trading platforms. Both listing and transaction platforms pose similar competition concerns, with listing platforms often experiencing more noticeable concentration. Consequently, it becomes challenging to justify the seclusion of advertising platforms and to explain the prohibition of transition between these markets. Preserving competition in these markets necessitates the unfettered entry of trading platforms. However, this restriction creates barriers to entry. Furthermore, in instances where advertising and discount restrictions are in place, imposing such an obligation appears disproportionate. Hence, the provision is susceptible to criticism from a competition policy perspective.

License Fee

The Law requires platforms to acquire a license for their operation, with the sole condition being an annual financial commitment. It can be argued that this licensing fee is not directly related to competition policy. However, when one considers the method of determining the license fee, its structure seems to be employed as a competition policy tool. The license fees are determined based on the scale of the platforms, with the fee rate increasing almost exponentially as the platform expands. An intriguing aspect is that the license fee imposed on larger platforms is notably high and significantly disparate from the fees required of smaller platforms. For instance, suppose there's a platform operating with a net transaction value ranging between 15 billion and 30 billion Turkish lira. In this scenario, the platform is required to pay a license fee amounting to 0.03% of its transaction value. On the other hand, if the platform's net transaction value exceeds 97.5 billion Turkish lira, it must pay a license fee of 25% for the surplus amount.

This provision aims at maintaining an equilibrium between the competitive positions of large and smaller platforms through the determination of license fees. The imposition of higher fees on very large platforms causes their operational costs to escalate, thereby fostering a favorable operating environment for smaller platforms due to the resulting asymmetry in costs. Similar sentiments are echoed in the rationale provided within the article.

The economic ramifications of this stipulation are evident, presenting perhaps the most challenging obligation to justify from a competition policy standpoint. The imposition of license fees will inevitably raise the operational costs of platforms, particularly the larger ones, consequently leading to price hikes. Moreover, platforms may pivot toward products with higher commission rates but lower value or even lean toward direct selling. However, more critically, this provision erects barriers to economic expansion and dampens incentives for competition. By levying fees based on net transaction value, profitability is undermined, rendering the growth trajectory of platforms economically untenable. Consequently, although smaller platforms will benefit from the license fee requirement, this dynamic will adversely impact platforms' impetus for investment and innovation, essentially constituting a structural intervention in the market.

Conclusion

The issue of monopolization originating from digital platforms is increasingly acknowledged to transcend the boundaries of competition law alone. Countries gradually are turning to regulatory frameworks to address this concern. Regulatory approaches offer distinct advantages over traditional competition law tools, providing clearer rules and enabling swifter ex ante interventions. Nonetheless, it's imperative to acknowledge that regulation is not without its drawbacks. The lack of comprehensive information on the economic impacts of market behavior presents risks, especially concerning Type I errors associated with ex ante rules. Additionally, excessively intrusive and inflexible regulations may result in social costs, particularly within rapidly evolving markets where innovation is of utmost importance. Hence, the continuing discourse on the choice between regulation and competition law emphasizes the necessity for careful deliberation on the potential ramifications.

Turkey stands out as one of the nations that opted for regulation relatively early in its legislative approach. Despite the vigorous and effective enforcement policy of the TCA against digital platforms, legislators have chosen to address the issue through regulation. In fact, two laws have been prepared, and one of them, the Law has been enacted. However, given the contentious nature of this issue, it might have been wiser to adopt a more cautious legislative stance, observing the implementation of existing law like the DMA and deriving insights for preparing a tailored legal regulation. Furthermore, the "Brussels effect" presents another factor that potentially diminishes the urgency for regulation. Global platforms could possibly have invested in compliance not only within the borders of EU but in Turkey as well.

Given the current legislative choice, the question shifts from whether the regulation is premature to whether the existing legislation aligns with the objective of fostering competition. In our assessment, the current regulatory framework appears overly intrusive and carries the risk of stifling economic growth and innovation. Provisions such as PL bans, license fees, and discount budget limitations seem to target economic size rather than address anti-competitive behavior. Consequently, there appears to be a pressing need for revision in the Law. Another concern is the risk of addressing the same issues with two separate laws. While the Draft has yet to be enacted, its potential implementation in its current form poses a risk of overregulation. Should the decision be made to regulate digital platforms, it is imperative that it be accomplished by a unified law that is informed by scientific studies and comparative law.

Note

1 See, for example, D/1/a, D/3.

References

Doğan, C. (2021). *Rekabet Hukuku ve İktisadı Bağlamında Dijital Platformlar*. Istanbul: On İki Levha Yayınevi.

European Commission. (2023, September 6). *Digital markets act: Commission designates six gatekeepers* [Press release]. https://ec.europa.eu/commission/presscorner/detail/en/ip_23_4328

Kaya, M. B. (2022). *European union P2B regulation: Fair and transparent platform rules for intermediary service providers and search engines*. Istanbul: On İki Levha Yayınevi.

The Law on the Amendment of the Law on the Regulation of Electronic Commerce, No. 7416. (2022). www.resmigazete.gov.tr/eskiler/2022/07/20220707-2.htm

Regulation 2019/1150. *Regulation (EU) 2019/1150 of the European parliament and of the council of 20 June 2019 on promoting fairness and transparency for business users of online intermediation service*. https://eur-lex.europa.eu/legal-content/EN/TXT/PDF/?uri=CELEX:32019R1150

Regulation 2022/1925. *Regulation (EU) No 2022/1925 of the European parliament and of the council of 14 September 2022 on competitive and fair markets in the digital sector and amending directives (EU) 2019/1937 and (EU) 2020/1828 (digital markets act)*. https://eur-lex.europa.eu/legal-content/EN/TXT/?uri=celex%3A32022R1925

Regulation on Electronic Commerce Intermediary Service Provider and Electronic Commerce Service Providers. (2022). www.resmigazete.gov.tr/eskiler/2022/12/20221229-5.htm

Republic of Türkiye Presidential Directorate of Strategy and Budget. (2023). *2024–2026 medium-term program*. www.sbb.gov.tr/wp-content/uploads/2023/09/Orta-Vadeli-Program_2024-2026.pdf

Sanli, K. C. (2023). Elektronik Ticaretin Düzenlenmesi Hakkında Kanun'da 7416 Sayılı Kanun ile Yapılan Değişikliklerin Rekabet Politikası Açısından Değerlendirilmesi I: Kanun'daki Temel Kavramlar ve Haksız Ticari Uygulamalar. *Legal Hukuk Dergisi*, *21*(245), 1709–1749.

Sanli, K. C., & Doğan, C. (2022). Rekabet Hukuku ve İktisadı Bağlamında Dar Platform EKM Koşulları. *İstanbul Hukuk Mecmuası*, 80(1), 117–152.

Sanli, K. C., & Doğan, C. (2023). *Rekabet Politikası Açısından Dijital Piyasaların Düzenlenmesi: E-ticaret Kanunu ve Rekabet Kanunu Değişiklik Taslağı*. Istanbul: On İki Levha Yayınevi.

Sümer Özdemir, N. (2023). En Çok Kayrılan Müşteri Şartlarının Rekabete Etkileri -Dar EKM Şartlarına Özel Bakış-. *Türkiye Adalet Akademisi Dergisi*, 395–434.

13 Regulation of FinTech and Crypto Assets

Pınar Çağlayan Aksoy

Introduction

FinTech, short for financial technology, refers to the use of technological tools to enhance financial services and products. In 2018, the term was introduced in the Merriam-Webster online dictionary as "products and companies that employ newly developed digital and online technologies in the banking and financial services industries. In the same stance, FinTech can also describe a business that uses or creates such technologies" (Merriam-Webster).

The Financial Stability Board defines FinTech as "technologically enabled innovation in financial services that could result in new business models, applications, processes or products with an associated material effect on financial markets and institutions and the provision of financial services" (Financial Stability Board, n.d.). The term encompasses companies that use technology-based systems to directly provide innovative and cheaper financial services and traditional financial businesses using technological tools to reshape financial services (Stamegna & Karakas, 2019).

FinTech services and products include peer-to-peer lending, online payments, digital wallets, electronic money, crypto assets, and automated or robo-investment advice. They rely on several technologies, such as artificial intelligence (AI), blockchain, big data, the Internet of Things, and cloud computing (Clifford Chance, 2017).

The provision of certain financial products and services, such as initiating payments, opening accounts, and granting loans, depended on physical contracts that required finalization with a wet signature during face-to-face meetings between the customer and the bank representative. However, the global crisis of 2007–2008 led to questioning of the existing financial system (Rekabet Kurumu, 2021). FinTech rose from the ashes of this crisis; it has the potential to broaden access to financial services, elevate the quality of customer interactions, and minimize financial expenses. Compared to traditional financial services and products, these new financial services are cost-effective, innovative, accessible, and customer-friendly:

> If today we can receive banking services via smartphones and devices regardless of time or place, if we can apply for a loan via SMS, if we

DOI: 10.4324/9781032692937-13

> can easily change the bank from which we receive service, or if we do not pay exorbitant prices for money transfers, we owe this to financial technology.
>
> (Kocaoğlu Ulbrich, 2023)

FinTech allows for replacing traditional contracts with electronic ones concluded with digital identity verification methods. These developments are especially important for the unbanked population.

Initially, FinTech companies or financial services that benefited from FinTech solutions were exposed to little or no regulation compared to traditional financial institutions, but this has rapidly changed. Many experts have rightfully stated that the FinTech sector is difficult to regulate since it covers a broad range of activities and business models that do not fully fall within the scope of regulated financial institutions. It is also a challenge that the sector operates cross-border (Kocaoğlu Ulbrich, 2019). However, regulatory ambiguity has started limiting the development of the FinTech ecosystem (Rupeika-Apoga & Wendt, 2022), which is why regulators around the globe have begun to make efforts to provide legal clarity. Türkiye is one of the countries that have enacted regulations on many FinTech sectors. This chapter focuses primarily on how Türkiye's regulatory framework for FinTech and crypto assets compares on a global scale.

This chapter unfolds as follows:

I first explain the current situation in Türkiye surrounding the FinTech ecosystem by mentioning key developments in recent years – the transformation of payment and electronic money services and banking and the increasing recognition of digital assets, crypto asset service providers (CASPs), and coin offerings.

One should not overlook the fact that finance is a heavily regulated sector. Therefore, I focus on the regulatory framework surrounding these developments by specifically examining the licensing and registration requirements for CASPs and FinTech companies such as payment and e-money institutions. This often proves difficult since no single piece of legislation covers all aspects of FinTech and crypto assets in Türkiye. Similarly, a single authority responsible for regulating and supervising FinTech activities does not yet exist in the country. The laws concerning capital markets, taxation, data, and consumer protection apply in the FinTech realm.

I analyze the key laws and regulations and the regulatory and supervisory bodies overseeing FinTech and crypto assets in Türkiye. Over the past three years, a series of regulations have come into force in Türkiye to bolster FinTech companies, encourage the digitalization of banks, and pave the way for open banking. I also address the role of the Financial Crimes Investigation Board (FCIB) and other relevant bodies in enforcing anti-money laundering (AML) and know-your-customer (KYC) regulations. I explore how the Central Bank of the Republic of Türkiye (CBRT) and the Capital Markets Board (CMB) have approached crypto assets, stablecoins, and central bank digital currencies.

While detailing the current situation in Türkiye, I compare it with global trends. I discuss the possible prospects that can bring a balanced approach and ensure consumer protection while fostering innovation and economic growth and mitigating risks while fostering technology. We specifically focus on the possible sandboxes and expected regulations on CASPs and digital banking.

The FinTech Landscape in Türkiye

Background

The use of technology in finance is not new in Türkiye. The first credit card was issued in the country in 1968 by Setur A.Ş., an affiliate of the Koç Group, after gaining authority from the Diners Club (Tuğay & Başgül, 2007). The first electronic POS terminal in Türkiye commenced services in 1991. Türkiye was one of the first countries in Europe to use contactless credit cards. Today, the Turkish credit card market is one of the largest in Europe, taking into account the number of credit cards and POS machines. Nearly half of the transactions made with credit cards are installment purchases (Karakaya, 2022).

Like other countries, in Türkiye, the concept of FinTech gained importance after the global economic crisis in 2008. The advent of FinTech in the country occurred with the regulation on payment services and electronic money institutions (Altınsoy Arık, 2022) that came into force in 2013 (Law on Payment and Securities Settlement Systems, Payment Services and Electronic Money Institutions-Law No. 6493). This legislation was enacted through the collaboration of the CBRT and the Banking Regulation and Supervision Agency (BRSA). When this law became effective, the licensing of organizations providing payment services and/or electronic money services commenced, and payment services were no longer under the sole auspices of banks.

According to a report published in 2022 by the Finance Office of the Presidency of the Republic of Türkiye, the country has a vibrant FinTech ecosystem, especially in the fields of payment, banking, and cryptocurrency (Cumhurbaşkanlığı Finans Ofisi, 2022), and 2022 is considered a landmark for the Turkish FinTech ecosystem: the first digital bank was granted permission, the Regulation on the Operating Principles of Digital Banks and Service Model Banking was enacted, open banking started to be applied, payment and electronic money institutions were included in the FAST system, and the first payment transaction was realized in the Digital Turkish Lira network. After a record-breaking year for investments in FinTech companies in 2022, three million USD were invested in five FinTech companies as of April 2023 (Türkiye Fintek Görünümü, 2023b).

According to data from September 2023, there are 126 passive and 656 active FinTech companies in Türkiye. Based on the sectors, payments take the lead, followed by banking technologies, and blockchain and crypto assets come in third (Cumhurbaşkanlığı Finans Ofisi, 2023). The 12th Development

Plan (2024–2028), published by the Presidency of Türkiye, reports that the digitalization process and the working mechanisms of FinTech companies transform financial markets by increasing efficiency. This plan also reveals the expectation that blockchain-based digital currency will be increasingly (Cumhurbaşkanlığı Strateji ve Bütçe Başkanlığı, 2023).

The İstanbul Finance Center (IFC) deserves special attention when focusing on the FinTech landscape in Türkiye. IFC Law No. 7412 was published in the Official Gazette of the Republic of Türkiye on June 28, 2022, aiming to ensure the effective functioning of the financial ecosystem and making sure it becomes a hub with a special status like other global finance centers. The IFC brings together public and private sector banks, asset management companies, brokerage firms, insurance companies, and professional service companies with Turkish and international financial institutions. The IFC project includes the offices of the CBRT, BRSA, CMB, Borsa Istanbul, Türkiye Sigorta, Ziraat Bank, Halkbank, Vakıfbank, and İŞ REIC. As a leading global FinTech center, the IFC will host a regulation-testing environment (sandbox) on payment systems. Additionally, FinTech companies in Türkiye will be actively supported by the Finance and Technology Base operating as part of the IFC. The FinTech firms hosted by the IFC will be provided access to the critical payment systems operated by the CBRT and the relevant public databases (İstanbul Finans Merkezi, 2023). In the 12th Development Plan, it is stated that to make Türkiye a global financial center and safe harbor for international capital, steps will be taken to develop capital markets, strengthen the FinTech ecosystem, reinforce the institutional structure of participation finance, and improve the regulatory infrastructure (Cumhurbaşkanlığı Strateji ve Bütçe Başkanlığı, 2023).

Main Players

The growth of the FinTech industry raises many issues regarding the scope of regulations in the financial sector. It is difficult to determine which FinTech applications and services require regulation. Yet another challenge is determining the relationship of FinTech with existing financial institutions and the rules surrounding these institutions; another important point is deciding which governmental bodies and institutions have the authority to regulate and supervise FinTech companies (Altınsoy Arık, 2022). In Türkiye, the primary ministries monitoring the FinTech ecosystem are the Ministry of Treasury and Finance and the Ministry of Trade.

The CBRT is the main regulatory body responsible for monetary and exchange rate policies. It supervises the payment ecosystem in Türkiye, performing its activities under Law No. 1211. In the FinTech realm, where payment and digital wallet services are provided, the CBRT promotes the efficiency and security of payment systems.

The BRSA plays an important role in licensing banks, financial institutions, and FinTech companies to ensure the stability and integrity of the financial system.

The CMB is the regulatory body in Türkiye that monitors and regulates capital markets and related financial services. It monitors companies involved in crowdfunding, peer-to-peer lending, and robo-advice to ensure they comply with capital market regulations and protect investor interests.

The Information and Communication Technologies Authority (ICTA) and the Data Protection Authority (DPA) are also involved in FinTech activities. These entities oversee the telecommunications and information technology sectors and data protection and privacy, respectively. For instance, foreign FinTech service providers that process the personal data of persons residing in Türkiye fall under the application of the Law on Protection of Personal Data (Law No. 6698), which means that even if these companies have no physical or legal presence in Türkiye, they must register with the Personal Data Protection Board as a data controller. Moreover, foreign firms must notify the board of data breaches while processing information linked to a Turkish citizen.

The FCIB is the government authority that focuses on anti-money laundering (AML) and combating the financing of terrorism (CFT). FinTech companies, payment service providers, CASPs, and crowdfunding platforms must pay attention to AML/CFT regulations and are required to report suspicious transactions to the FCIB.

The Turkish Competition Authority (TCA) also monitors the FinTech sector closely. A report prepared by the TCA underlined that "The developments in the field of FinTech raise not only concerns about financial stability, but also concerns about the competitive structure of financial markets" (Rekabet Kurumu, 2021). In 2022, several important amendments were made to the Communiqué Concerning the Mergers and Acquisitions (M&A) Calling for the Authorization of the Competition Board (No. 2010/4 ("Communiqué") with the Communiqué No. 2022/2 issued by the TCA. The amended communiqué defines technology enterprises as "enterprises or related assets operating in the fields of digital platforms, software and game software, financial technologies, biotechnology, pharmacology, agricultural chemicals and health technologies." Accordingly, the M&A transactions of technology enterprises will be subject to approval under certain conditions.

Payments and Banking in the FinTech Era

Within the scope of the FinTech movement, there have also been developments in the fields of banking law and regulations (Kocaoğlu Ulbrich, 2019). After the growth of FinTech, banking legislation is no longer limited to banking, payment, and consumer protection regulations. Many issues, such as data security, electronic signatures, remote transactions, digital identity, cyber security, and algorithm applications, fall within the scope of FinTech law (Kocaoğlu Ulbrich, 2023).

The FinTech regulations in Türkiye are constantly shifting and often scattered. The main legislation (Law no. 6492) underwent a comprehensive and impactful alteration on October 7, 2023, that significantly reshaped the entire FinTech landscape. In this section of the chapter, we will elucidate the present regulatory framework in Türkiye concerning specific areas within payments and banking, considering their ongoing development due to increasing digitalization.

Payment and Payment Systems

Law No. 6493 on Payment and Securities Settlement Systems, Payment Services and Electronic Money Institutions, dated 2013, lays down the main rules for electronic money and payment systems. In Türkiye, payment systems previously regulated by different pieces of legislation, and payment services, payment service providers, and electronic money services not previously subject to any legislation were regulated together for the first time (MASAK, 2021). The law was revised on November 22, 2019 to keep up with the developments in the FinTech ecosystem. One of the major changes was that supervisory and regulatory authority over payment service providers changed from the BRSA to the CBRT.

Three regulations were enacted based on Law No 6493: the Regulation on Payment Services and Electronic Money Issuance and Payment Service Providers (2021), the Regulation on the Production and Use of TR QR Codes in Payment Services (2020), and the Regulation on the Disuse of Crypto Assets in Payments (2021). A related communiqué also exists – the Communiqué on Information Systems of Payment and Electronic Money Institutions and Data Sharing Services of Payment Service Providers in the Field of Payment Services. It is important to note that The Regulation Amending the Regulation on Payment Services and Electronic Money Issuance and Payment Service Providers, prepared by the CBRT, was published in the Official Gazette on October 7, 2023. These pieces of legislation, which build on Law No. 6493, show the central importance of this law for the FinTech ecosystem.

Electronic money and payment institutions perform only part of the activity of banks related to payment intermediation, issuance of electronic money, and issuance of prepaid cards. Any amount collected by electronic money and payment institutions is not under the state guarantee provided by the Savings Deposit Insurance Fund of Türkiye (Perçin, 2023). The CBRT and independent audit institutions audit electronic money and payment institutions. The Public Oversight Accounting and Auditing Standards Authority granted a decision on December 28, 2023 that includes payment and e-money institutions in the group of public interest institutions, signifying that payment and e-money institutions will be subject to stricter monitoring and inspections by the CBRT. The aim is to prevent financial abuse and fraud and render the financial system more transparent and reliable, resulting in increased consumer security.

Law No. 6493 defines the concept of a "payment system." In addition, the framework of the payment system and the necessary conditions to become a system operator, the operating permit process, and the measures to be taken, along with the supervision of the systems, are determined through this law. Moreover, the concept of payment service is defined, and activities that do not fall within the scope of payment service are outlined.

According to Law no. 6493, "e-money" is defined as

> monetary value that is issued equivalent the funds accepted by the electronic money issuer institution, stored electronically and used to provide the payment transactions defined in the Law and accepted as a means of payment by real and legal persons other than the electronic money issuer institution.

Electronic money institutions are defined as legal entities with the authority to issue electronic money within the scope of this particular law.

The main fields of activity of e-money and payment institutions include paying bills by payment service providers using bank infrastructures and/or creating their own infrastructures, making domestic/international money transfers based on a payment account, mobile payment, money transfers with no link to a payment account, operation of the payment account, issuance and acceptance of the payment instrument, presenting account information at financial institutions, initiating payment services from accounts in different financial institutions, and providing digital wallet services (Perçin, 2023).

In this context, no difference exists between an electronic money institution and a payment institution in terms of activities such as providing physical POS and/or virtual POS services, mediating money transfers, or mediating the payment of bills. The main difference between electronic money and payment institutions is that while the former can issue electronic money in return for the funds it collects, the latter cannot. As a result, issuing prepaid cards, which is one electronic money issuance method, can be initiated only by electronic money institutions. Moreover, pursuant to Article 13 of Law No. 6493, since electronic money institutions can also provide payment services as payment service providers, it is possible that all activities of payment institutions can be carried out by electronic money institutions, provided that they obtain the necessary permissions (Perçin, 2023).

Payment and electronic money institutions may provide payment services within the scope of the operating license issued by the CBRT. The bank issues a license if an institution fulfills the criteria in Article 14 (for payment institutions) and Article 18 (for e-money institutions). Both types of institutions need to be established as joint-stock companies. In addition, these firms must abide by the condition that those holding 10% or more of the capital shares and having control must meet the conditions required for bank founders in the Banking Law. E-money and payment institutions are also subject to regulations regarding financial crimes, protection of consumers, electronic commerce, taxation, and professional principles.

According to Article 13(2) of Law No. 6493, a payment service can be offered by only payment service providers. Payment service providers under Turkish law are banks, e-money institutions, payment institutions, and the Post and Telegraph Organization Joint Stock Company (PTT), which is the country's national post office.

According to Law No. 6493's Article 18, only banks, e-money institutions, and the PTT can issue e-money. Banks and the PTT do not need to obtain an operating license from the CBRT since they have direct authority to issue e-money.

According to data retrieved from the CBRT's website, as of November 2023, there were 53 e-money institutions in operation, and all are authorized to issue electronic money in accordance with Article 18 of Law No. 6493. In addition, they can offer other payment services specified in accordance with Article 12 of Law No. 6493. As previously mentioned, as of January 2024, there were 26 payment institutions in existence.

As a final note about payment and e-money systems, the Payment and Electronic Money Institutions Association of Türkiye, founded in 2019, should be mentioned. This body is a professional organization in the nature of a public institution but formed as a legal entity. Payment and electronic money institutions operating in Türkiye are obliged to be members of this association within the scope of Additional Article 1 of Law No. 6493.

Open Banking

The concept of open banking has existed for quite some time, especially in the United Kingdom, but it became a regulatory reality with PSD2 (Payment Services Directive) in Europe in 2015. In the process of open banking, "account information service providers (AISPs) and payment initiation service providers (PISPs) offer (or enable other parties to provide) value added services to users by accessing – upon user request – their account data held by banks and other payment account providers". Open banking is a reliable and secure service model that helps provide better banking and financial opportunities to users by sharing their financial data with third-party institutions such as banks and service providers. Better banking and financial opportunities mean decreased costs and increased effectiveness, competitiveness, and innovation, which increase financial inclusion (Gürses, 2023a). The system operates through application programming interfaces (API) (Canko & Tümer, 2023) and allows third parties to access user data based on their consent.

In Türkiye, the European path was followed regarding the regulation of open banking. The concept of open banking services is defined in Article 3 of the Regulation on Banks' Information Systems and Electronic Banking Services. Accordingly, open banking services refer to the electronic distribution channel through which customers or parties acting on behalf of customers can perform banking transactions or instruct the bank to carry out their banking transactions by remotely accessing the financial services offered by the bank through methods such as API, web services, and file transfer protocols. The same regulation also introduces customer authentication, security, and data protection measures in line with PSD2 in Europe (Şahin & Cantürk, 2020).

Currently, in Türkiye, the "payment initiation service" and "account information service" models are prominent. These concepts are defined in the amendments introduced to Law No. 6493 in 2019. According to Article 12(f), a payment initiation service is defined as a payment order initiation service offered for a payment account in another payment service provider – at the request of the payment service user. Article 12(g) states that an account information service presents consolidated information regarding one or more payment accounts of the payment service user on online platforms, provided that the payment service user's consent is obtained.

According to the legislation, there are two types of payment service providers: the Account Information Service Provider and the Payment Initiation Service Provider. The payment service provider providing one or both of these services based on the required permissions is called an Authorized Payment Service Provider, and the payment service provider that possesses a payment account is the Account Servicing Payment Service Provider. Banks, e-money institutions, payment institutions, and the PTT are legally considered account servicing payment service providers.

According to Article 14/A-2 of Law No. 6493, the authority to determine the procedures and principles regarding open banking services is given to the CBRT, and the relevant regulation set was enacted by the bank in December 2021. The sub-regulations include the Regulation on Payment Services and Electronic Money Issuance and Payment Providers, the Communiqué on Information Systems of Payment and Electronic Money Institutions, and Data Sharing Services in the Field of Payment Services Providers and its annexes.

The CBRT launched open banking services in the field of payments with an official announcement in December 2022. The bank stated that open banking was an important component of the digital economy roadmap of the Liraization Strategy. Banks in Türkiye began to offer services through the Open Banking Gateway (GATE-GEÇİT) infrastructure, developed by the Interbank Card Center (BKM), and provide standard open banking transactions to all parties (TCMB, 2022).

Account servicing payment service providers are obligated to provide data sharing services to account information service providers and payment initiation service providers through the GEÇİT infrastructure. The parties tasked with opening communication in payment initiation services are the payment initiation service providers and account servicing payment service providers. In the case of account information services occurring, the parties involved are account information service providers and account servicing payment service providers. The connection between account servicing payment service providers, GEÇİT, and account information service providers/payment initiation service providers will be maintained end-to-end in a secure manner. In the provision of these services, strong customer authentication is required.

On April 30, 2023, the CBRT published the Guide on Data Sharing Services in Payment Services. This is a guiding document created for all stakeholders on issues such as whether some frequently encountered business models in the field of payments require an operating permit for payment initiation and account information services; it also concerns the licensing and technical certification process (TCMB, 2023).

With the amendments of October 7, 2023, the payment service providers authorized for open banking services can provide qualified services to natural persons, including individual budget management, bill management, account verification, and payment reminders. Moreover, some uncertainties that had existed in practice have been overcome with regard to whether or not several transactions constituted payment initiation services.

Digital Wallets

The state of digital (virtual) wallets has been uncertain in Türkiye for some time. The CBRT prepared a guideline in September 2022 titled Guide on Associating Business Models Offered in the Field of Payments with Payment Service Types. The Guideline stated that the provision of digital wallet services depended on permission given from the CBRT as a payment institution.

On October 7, 2023, with the Regulation Amending the Regulation on Payment Services and Electronic Money Issuance and Payment Service Providers, the concept of "digital wallet" was defined for the first time in Turkish law. Accordingly, a digital wallet is defined as a payment instrument that stores information about the payment account or payment instrument defined by the customer, something that is offered as an electronic device, online service, or application, and a service allowing the customer to carry out payment transactions using the information regarding the payment account or payment instrument defined by the customer. The definition of this type of wallet is rather wide-ranging and includes "staged wallets" and "pass-through wallets" (Canpolat, 2023). A "staged wallet" is a business model managed by entities with electronic money licenses. Conversely, a "pass-through wallet" operates by tokenizing an established payment method and refrains from retaining funds. In the case of business models like the pass-through wallet, recognized as an open banking service by the CBRT, obtaining a payment order initiation service license is mandatory (Cantürk, 2023).

Digital wallet services can be mainly provided by payment service providers holding an operating license exclusive to issuing payment instruments, that is, payment institutions, e-money institutions, banks, and the PTT. It is mandatory that the operating licenses of payment service providers cover the issuance of the payment instruments.

TR Karekod, FAST, and KOLAS

Work within the scope of the TR QR code is carried out by the CBRT and the BKM. The Regulation on the Production and Use of TR QR Codes in Payment Services prepared by the CBRT came into force on August 21, 2020. Thus, a standard was set for using this technology, which facilitates contactless transactions. The TR QR code is the standard QR code used in payment services in Türkiye.

The TR QR Code Regulation determines the principles regarding the production and use of TR QR codes in payment services. To produce a TR QR code, a QR code generator code must first be obtained by request to the BKM. To use a TR QR code in certain payment systems and payment services, it is obligatory to comply with the technical principles and rules prepared by the CBRT, which were put into effect in May 2022 (Türkiye Cumhuriyet Merkez Bankası, 2022a).

The FAST (Instant and Continuous Transfer of Funds) system is the instant payment system recently implemented by the CBRT. In FAST, payments can be transferred to the counterparty account 24/7 and instantaneously. The parties involved are instantly informed by their banks about the payment status. FAST is used for payments between customers of different financial institutions.

A press release about the Participation of Payment and Electronic Money Institutions in the FAST system was published on December 26, 2022 announcing that through the FAST solution provided by the CBRT, it would be possible to instantly send payments in Turkish lira to an account in another bank 24 hours a day, seven days a week. Twenty-four banks initially joined the FAST system, and the number of financial institutions that have since joined the FAST system is 26.

Payment service providers specified in Article 13 of Law No. 6493 can participate in the FAST system. To increase the scope and comprehensiveness of this payment system, payment and e-money institutions that meet the requirements can join FAST as of 2023 (TCMB, 2022). It is also now possible to make FAST payments with QR codes in workplaces and e-commerce sites where TR QR codes are valid.

With the introduction of the Easy Address Identification (KOLAS) system, long IBAN numbers have been replaced by personal information, such as a phone number, a national ID number, or an email address. Therefore, it is now possible in Türkiye to use ID numbers, telephone numbers, and email addresses instead of IBANs to effectuate fund transfers and payments. There is no need to register in the system to send money via KOLAS. However, to receive money, registration with a mobile phone or email address is mandatory.

These advancements strive to attain economic digitization by transitioning currency and payments into the digital realm.

Remote Customer Acquisition

Remote customer acquisition means carrying out identity verification and contracting processes in a digital environment with electronic communication devices, eliminating the necessity for physical presence. To establish and perform the contractual relationship, the customer's declaration of intent must be initiated by sending the contract digitally to the customer.

Starting in 2020, many changes have occurred in the relevant legislation in Türkiye so that banks and FinTech companies can create contracts through digital methods without dealing with customers face-to-face. With the communiqués and amendments prepared by entities such as the FCIB, CMB, and BRSA, regulations that complement each other and enable progress in remote customer acquisition have emerged. Gradually, banks, payment and e-money institutions, brokerage firms, and portfolio management organizations have been included in the scope of remote customer acquisition.

The year 2023 has been an important one in this regard. With the Regulation Amending the Regulation on Measures to Prevent Laundering Proceeds of Crime and Financing of Terrorism, published in the Official Gazette on April 5, 2023, it has become possible for banks, payment and electronic money institutions, and other financial organizations to accept customers through remote identification in legal entities registered in the trade registry. For legal entities to be subject to remote customer acquisition, an amendment had to be made to Communiqué No. 19, dated May 1, 2021, published by the FCIB. The last piece of the puzzle allowing for the Digital Customer Acquisition for FinTechs was completed with Communiqué No. 25, published on November 4, 2023. Thus, a method was established for payment and electronic money institutions to acquire customers remotely within the framework of both CBRT and FCIB legislation.

Digital Banking and Service Model Banking

The Regulation on the Operating Principles of Digital Banks and Service Model Banking (ROPDBSMB), issued by the BRSA, entered into force on January 1, 2022. This regulation defines the operating principles of digital banks and lays down additional conditions required for the establishment and operating permits of digital banks. The regulation also includes service model banking.

Digital Banking

Digital banks are organizations that offer only banking services electronically rather than through physical branches. Digital banks that receive operating permission within the scope of the aforementioned regulation can operate without physical branches – except for mandatory customer relations offices. Digital banks cannot open branches even if they wanted to. They offer their services distantly via internet banking, mobile banking, open banking, ATMs, and kiosks (Perçin, 2023). Thus, these banks can reach a wider audience and offer customers a more practical, accessible, and user-oriented banking experience. Digital banking also reduces costs.

According to Article 3 of the ROPDBSMB, digital banks are credit institutions offering services through electronic banking service distribution channels instead of physical branches. According to Law No. 5411, three types of banks exist in Türkiye: deposit banks, development and investment banks, and participation banks. Deposit banks and participation banks are regarded as credit institutions. According to the ROPDBSMB, digital banks are defined as credit institutions. Accordingly, digital banks in Türkiye can be established as deposit banks or participation banks. In other words, a digital bank cannot be established as a development and investment bank, as this type of bank does not fall within the definition of a credit institution.

Digital banks must exhibit solid financial capabilities. In the Regulation mentioned earlier, to obtain a digital bank-operating permit, unlike traditional banks, the minimum paid-in capital lower limit is determined as one billion Turkish liras instead of 30 million Turkish liras. Fully licensed digital banks should perform all the activities that credit institutions can perform. Digital banks with limited licenses are subject to activity restrictions, and their customer portfolios must consist of only individual and SME customers within the scope of activity restrictions (Cumhurbaşkanlığı Finans Ofisi, 2023). Thus, digital banks must focus solely on consumers and SMEs. Considering these provisions, it is envisaged that the products and services offered by digital banks will appeal to target audiences such as students, homemakers, young people under 18, and SMEs (Perçin, 2023).

It should also be noted that if digital banks increase their paid-in capital amounts to 2.5 billion Turkish liras, the activity limitations specified in the Regulation can be removed entirely or with an appropriate transition plan. Therefore, digital banks can carry out all banking activities that other credit institutions can perform within the framework of the relevant legislation. Apart from these, the general conditions for traditional and digital banks are similar in terms of establishment permits, operating permits, and the qualifications required for their founders (Kolcuoğlu, 2023).

There are several laws soon to be implemented in Türkiye regarding digital banking. However, the ROPDBSMB lays down the fundamental provisions. Some can be applied to digital banking in Banking Law No. 5411 – the Regulation on Information Systems and Electronic Banking Services of Banks – that came into force in 2020, in the Regulation on Remote Identification Methods to be Used by Banks, and in the Establishment of Contracts in the Electronic Environment, effective as of 2021.

In 2022, the first digital bank establishment permit was granted, and four institutions in Türkiye received licenses to establish digital banks. The BRSA has decided to establish six digital banks and grant an operating permit to one digital bank since April 2022. Thus, many banking transactions such as EFT, money transfers, money transfer transactions, bill payments, the purchasing of foreign exchange, selling transactions, stock and fund buying and selling, account opening transactions, and credit card and loan applications can be carried out using digital banking channels in Türkiye. Digital banks are obliged to comply with all legislative provisions credit institutions are obliged to follow.

Service Model Banking (Banking as a Service-BaaS)

Service model banking is based on the understanding that customers can benefit from banking products and services wherever and whenever they need without regular online access to their bank. Thus, when customers want to access any banking product or service, they will not have to enter a bank's mobile application or log in to the internet branch. Customers will be able to access the banking products and services they need directly, either directly from their current interlocutor or through a third party in cooperation with their current interlocutor (Perçin, 2023).

With service model banking, banking services are offered via mobile application or through an internet environment of third-party organizations (interface provider) using the bank's (service bank) infrastructure. It should be noted that service banking is not banking in the literal sense. Bank products and services are still offered by the bank, but third parties act as intermediaries. In this context, a support service relationship is established between the interface provider and the service bank. According to the ROPDBSMB, service model banking is a service model in which customers can perform banking transactions through the service bank by directly connecting with a system of "service banks" through "open banking services" through the interface offered by the interface providers. Service model banking is based on the technical infrastructure of open banking services (Perçin, 2023).

According to the ROPDBSMB, all banking products and services can be offered through interface providers within the scope of service model banking. This model allows interface developers to offer new banking products and services through banking infrastructure. The service bank has the authority to decide which banking services interface providers can provide. Interface providers are jointly responsible with the service bank for all security measures.

ROPDBSMB Article 13 states that interface providers must reside in Türkiye to benefit from service bank provisions. For this reason, a bank established in Türkiye cannot conduct service model banking through an interface provider based abroad. In Türkiye, the interface provider's ability to serve as a support service organization to the service bank is subject to the permission of the BRSA. A bank cannot serve as an interface provider. The Regulation Amending the Regulation on Payment Services and Electronic Money Issuance and Payment Service Providers, enacted by the CBRT, clarifies that electronic money institutions and payment institutions can provide services as interface providers within the scope of the ROPDBSMB.

Robo-Advice

Traditional asset management and financial consultancy services are carried out manually under human supervision, creating disadvantages for banks, such as increased costs and decreased efficiency in planning processes. In addition, criteria such as minimum account opening limits and high commission fees requested by banks for asset management services prevent access to an increased potential customer base.

Robo-advice is a popular and innovative application of the FinTech ecosystem where finance and AI intersect. Predictive AI systems have already been deployed in the financial industry across various functions, such as advanced analytics and automation for error and fraud detection, know-your-customer checks, and audit and compliance. AI adoption in financial services has expanded with the emergence of generative AI (GenAI) (UK Finance, 2023). This new form of AI improves efficiency through process automation and customer experience and helps detect and prevent fraud. Several Turkish FinTech companies are already active and benefit from these technologies, using them to understand customer habits better and create personalized financial advice (Baştuğ, 2024).

Robo-advice uses algorithms based on modern financial theories with minimum human interference (Demirdöğen, 2019). These applications make automated investment recommendations and provide automatic portfolio allocation through these algorithms. Thanks to machine learning, algorithms analyze users' various characteristics, measure their risk profile, and recommend an appropriate asset distribution. Using robo-advisory methods, financial institutions automate their asset management and financial advisory service processes, provide services to a large customer base, and gain efficiency in processes by minimizing human-caused errors. GenAI has the potential to allow investment advisors to enhance their robo-advice with differentiated recommendations produced in a fast, efficient, and customized manner and delivered in a human-like conversational manner tailored to each client (OECD, 2023).

Robo-advice, examples of which have been observed globally since 2008, has started to be implemented in Türkiye in recent years. In 2017, the number of people benefiting from robo-advisory totaled 1.5 million, but this number increased to 3.1 million in 2018 (Kaymak, 2019). Investment consultancy is traditionally carried out manually in Türkiye. However, there are no specific regulations, and asset management service rules can be applied by analogy. For instance, banks require a minimum account balance to provide asset management services. At present, the most important target audience for robo-advisor applications is the Private Retirement System (BES) participants in Türkiye.

Crypto Asset Transactions

In Türkiye, the use of distributed ledger technology (DLT) is not limited to cryptocurrencies. The popularity of crypto assets is ever-growing. According to data from a report prepared by KuCoin, the fifth-largest crypto exchange in the world, crypto adoption is on the rise in Türkiye. As of May 2023, over half of Turkish adults hold crypto assets. The report states that the growing number and percentage of crypto investors indicate an increasing interest in and acceptance of cryptocurrency as a hedge against inflation (KuCoin, 2023).

It is also crucial to note that the CBRT plans to introduce its Central Bank Digital Currency (CBDC), the Digital Lira, based on DLT. Moreover, in November 2023, Türkiye's Finance Minister announced plans to enact crypto asset regulations in an address to a parliamentary body shortly after. The Minister underlined the aim to improve Türkiye's standing with the Financial Action Task Force and combat money laundering (Türkiye to toughen crypto assets law for FATF "grey list" removal, 2023).

Tokenization projects, initial coin offerings (ICOs), security token offerings (STOs), Decentralized Autonomous Organizations (DAOs), and NFTs have current and potential use cases. In this section of the chapter, we explain the regulatory framework in Türkiye by focusing on crypto assets, CASPs, ICOs, STOs, and CBDCs.

Crypto Assets in General

Legal Nature of Crypto Assets

Crypto assets are divided into two main groups. The first group is coins. Coins operate on their blockchain with their own protocol (Coşkun, 2023). Bitcoin is the most famous example. All of the other coin types are known as "altcoins." Stablecoins also fall under the category of tokens. The most common stablecoin indexed to the USD is the Tether. Stablecoins need to be protected from the volatility of crypto assets and are seen as one of the central and promising use-cases of DLT.

The second group of crypto assets is tokens. According to a report prepared by the IMF, digital tokens represent one of the most promising applications of DLT. The IMF defines tokens as units designated by entries in a digital ledger that uses cryptographic techniques (Garrido, 2023). Tokens do not necessarily operate on their own blockchains. Since they are pieces of code, they can have various characteristics depending on how they are designed and programmed (Çağlayan Aksoy, 2023).

Because many different types of tokens exist, they do not have a universal classification. Various international authorities have endorsed a variety of categorizations (Çağlayan Aksoy, 2023. This depends on which criteria are taken as a basis to categorize tokens. According to their financial functions/uses, tokens generally have a tripartite distinction: security tokens (asset or investment tokens), payment tokens, and utility tokens. Depending on the fungibility of the tokens, they can be divided into two main categories, namely fungible and non-fungible tokens.

It is important to define the legal character of crypto assets (Garrido, 2023). This enables us to determine which legal rules apply to crypto asset transactions. However, this is not an easy task, as taking into account the different types of tokens and their characteristics is essential. In the realm of crypto assets, numerous inquiries arise, such as the following: are cryptocurrencies a form of currency or electronic money? Can crypto assets be classified as securities? Alternatively, can they be deemed as assets subject to property rights? Providing definitive responses to these questions is challenging as tokens exhibit varying behaviors. However, finding answers to these queries is essential to develop a regulatory framework.

According to Turkish law, cryptocurrencies do not constitute money since they are not issued by a central bank, and they are not acquired by trusting an intermediary. Money, on the other hand, is under the exclusive authority of the state that issues it – and there is a trust in the state that issues it (Çetin, 2023). According to the prevailing view, crypto assets are generally not regarded as money (Turanboy, 2019; Güçlütürk, 2020; Karamanlıoğlu, 2021; Dayanç Kuzeyli & Töremiş, 2022; Coşkun, 2023). However, the BRSA stated in 2013 that Bitcoin is a type of virtual currency (BDDK, 2013).

Crypto assets are not issued in exchange for a specific fund or in exchange for a currency. Individuals and organizations that issue crypto assets are decentralized. Hence, crypto assets cannot qualify as electronic money (Çetin, 54). In the aforementioned statement of the BRSA, it was evaluated that Bitcoin did not qualify as electronic money.

No special regulations regarding crypto assets in the Capital Markets Law and related legislation exist. However, some provisions in the Capital Markets Law may apply to crypto assets based on their function. Per Article 3(1)(ş) of the Capital Markets Law, capital market instruments consist of securities and other capital market instruments determined to be within this scope by the CMB, including investment contracts for derivative instruments. Whether crypto assets can be considered capital market instruments is significant due to three aspects. The first is that the issuance and public offering of capital market instruments and subsequent public disclosure obligations are subject to CMB regulations. Second, purchase and sale orders related to capital market instruments are considered investment services and activities in accordance with the Capital Markets Law. Third, they might fall within the scope of crimes such as information abuse, market fraud, irregular public offerings, and unauthorized capital market activity regarding capital market (Töremiş, 2021). Tokens issued as a share-like security by giving away some of the partnership rights or a crypto asset that is traded depending on the price or price change of a capital market instrument or precious metal – therefore potentially considered a derivative instrument – can be treated as a capital market instrument within the scope of the Capital Markets Law (Töremiş, 2021). According to Article 13 of the Capital Markets Law, the dematerialized issuance of capital market instruments is essential and monitored by the Central Securities Depository. For this reason, issuing security tokens via blockchain may constitute an irregular public offering in the context of the CMB (Dayanç Kuzeyli & Töremiş, 2022).

There are no specific regulations in the Turkish tax code regarding the taxation of crypto assets. To tax the income derived from a crypto asset, the asset should fall within the income categories listed in the income tax code. Due to the ambiguity surrounding the legal classification of crypto assets, assigning such income to a specific category poses a challenge. The principle of tax legality, a cornerstone in tax law, dictates that income must align with predefined categories for taxation. Consequently, income from crypto assets currently remains exempt from income tax. Introducing a new category labeled "digital assets" for taxing income derived from tokens would represent a positive regulatory step forward. However, unlike individual income tax, exchanges generate commission income in exchange for brokerage services, and the profits of exchanges organized as institutions are subject to corporate tax; additionally, the commissions these institutions earn are subject to value-added tax (VAT). While this aligns with Türkiye's current legislation, many countries do not subject these commissions to VAT, considering them financial services (Blockchain Turkey, 2021).

On a final note about crypto assets, despite the lack of tailor-made regulations on crypto assets, some decisions have been made by the Turkish courts allowing crypto assets to be seized (Kurt Konca & Selçuk, 2023). Moreover, crypto assets can be passed down to heirs by officially applying to a CASP.

The Regulation on the Disuse of Crypto Assets for Payment

There is no separate and special regulation focusing on CASPs in Türkiye. Crypto assets were defined for the first time in the CBRT's Regulation on the Disuse of Crypto Assets for Payment, dated April 16, 2021. This regulation defines crypto assets and bans their use for payment purposes.

According to Article 3(1) of this regulation, in its implementation, a crypto asset refers to an intangible asset created virtually using DLT or similar technology and distributed via digital networks but one that is not classed as fiat money, deposit money, electronic money, a payment instrument, securities, or other capital market instruments.

The acceptance of this definition as a universally applicable standard for crypto assets in Turkish law remains controversial. Some experts believe that this definition should be evaluated only within the scope of implementing the CBRT Regulation. In other words, since the definition of a "crypto asset" is included only in the CBRT Regulation, it is accepted that this definition can only be used in terms of payments (Cankat & Güçlütürk, 2021; Çetin, 2023). Therefore, this regulation does not introduce a definition of a general crypto asset that can be taken as a basis for contract law, capital markets law, or tax law (Cankat & Güçlütürk, 2021).

Usually, coins can be used as a source of payment. According to Article 3 of the aforementioned regulation, crypto assets shall not be used directly or indirectly in payments. Article 3 states that no services that involve using crypto assets directly or indirectly in payments will be provided. These provisions are criticized in the Turkish literature since Turkish law is unclear about how the scope of payments should be defined (Tevetoğlu, 2023).

Although this regulation prohibits the use of crypto assets for payments, it stipulates regulations regarding channels and collaborations in sending/withdrawing money to crypto asset platforms. According to Article 4(1), payment service providers shall not develop business models that directly or indirectly use crypto assets in the provision of payment services and the issuance of electronic money; they also cannot provide any services related to such business models. Article 4(2) further states that payment and electronic money institutions shall not intermediate the fund transfers from and to the platforms providing services linked to trading, custody, transfer, or issuance related to crypto assets. However, since these prohibitions do not cover banks and the PTT, it is possible for crypto asset exchanges and other platforms that offer buying, selling, storage, transfer, or export services of crypto assets to continue their activities with fund transfers carried out through banks and the PTT. Within the scope of these bans, business models using crypto assets, examples of which are seen in the FinTech field, have been blocked or banned (Güçlütürk & Cankat, 236).

The CMB is expected to issue a regulation to define crypto assets in the future. Türkiye's Presidential Annual Program for 2024 was released on October 25, 2023 and published in the Official Gazette of the Republic of Türkiye. It includes the objective to finalize regulations governing cryptocurrencies by the end of 2024. Article 400.5 emphasizes the intention to establish precise definitions for crypto assets, potentially subjecting them to taxation in the future. The new regulations are expected to come into effect in 2024.

Finally, no regulations focusing on stablecoins exist in Türkiye. The general financial law regulations must be observed for transactions involving stablecoins. An article thought to be aimed at stablecoins was added to the Regulation on Payment Services and Electronic Money Issuance and Payment Service Providers (Article 5). Accordingly, intangible assets that are issued only in exchange for one-to-one fiat money, created virtually and distributed over digital networks, can be issued in exchange for funds accepted by the issuing institution, stored electronically, used to carry out payment transactions, and transferred to real assets other than the issuing institution. It was stated that this would be accepted as electronic money if it is accepted as a means of payment by legal entities. Accordingly, it should be possible to issue stablecoins pegged to the Turkish lira (KPMG, 2023), and the issuance of this crypto asset is subject to e-money regulations. The funds collected in exchange for the issuance of stablecoins need to be transferred to a different account held by the banks. It would be useful if the CBRT could enact a specific regulation on the issuance of e-money in the form of stablecoins.

Crypto Asset Service Providers (CASPs)

In Türkiye, a definition of CASPs in the existing legislation does not exist. In practice, CASPs buy and sell, transfer, and keep custody of crypto assets on behalf of their customers. Despite the lack of regulation, there are numerous active cryptocurrency exchange platforms in Türkiye. The largest one is Paribu, followed by BtcTurk.

Although there is no specific regulation regarding CASPs, the concept of "crypto asset service providers" was used for the first time in Turkish law in the Regulation on Amendments to the Regulation on Measures on the Prevention of Laundering Proceeds of Crime and Financing of Terrorism, which came into force on May 1, 2021. The concept of CASP, however, is not defined in this regulation either.

In Turkish Law, "obliged entities" are determined to prevent money laundering and the financing of terrorism, ensure effectiveness in the fight against these crimes, and prevent criminal use of the financial system. Several obligations are envisaged for these obliged parties, such as KYC, suspicious transaction reporting, provision of information and documents, and retention and presentation obligations. The obliged entities are listed in Article 2(1-d) of the Law on Prevention of Laundering Proceeds of Crime and the Regulation on Measures to Prevent Money Laundering and Financing of Terrorism, Article 4(1). In this context, banks, payment institutions, e-money institutions, and financing and factoring companies are among the obligors. With the aforementioned regulation, CASPs were added to the list of obligors.

On May 4, 2021, the FCIB issued a guideline to determine the scope of the obligations of CASPs. The concept of CASP was defined in this guideline, albeit it did not serve as a legislative instrument. This was crucial since the aforementioned regulation failed to explain what a CASP entailed and, therefore, deciding which entities fell within the scope of the regulation to bear AML and CFT obligations was a challenge. The FCIB's guideline defines crypto assets based on the crypto asset definition laid down in the regulation on the disuse of crypto assets for payment services. According to the guideline, CASPs are institutions that facilitate crypto asset transactions on electronic transaction platforms. Consequently, within the scope of the principles regarding customer recognition, CASPs are obliged to determine the identities of those making transactions and or on whose behalf transactions are made; in addition, the providers must take other necessary measures before transactions are made with them or that they directly mediate.

Although this guideline provided some guidance regarding the scope of obligations, it is insufficient to conclude which entities would be regarded as crypto asset service platforms. For instance, it is still unclear whether NFT marketplaces or crypto custody service providers – or the entities that provide wallet services – fall under the scope of the CASP definition.

Since there is no generally accepted definition of a crypto asset or a CASP, reaching a conclusion on the taxation of crypto assets in Türkiye is difficult (Güngör, 2022). It is stated that establishing transparent taxation policies on crypto asset income is important in terms of bringing taxation revenues to the country's treasury (Türkiye Bankalar Birliği, 2022).

Initial Coin Offerings (ICOs) and Security Token Offerings (STOs)

An ICO is a process in which a crypto asset is designed, created, and offered to investors. In the initial phase of an ICO, crypto assets are introduced and explained through whitepapers. Whitepapers define the aim and use of the token offered, the way it was created, its technical structure, and how the offering process will be realized. They also define the rights that the investors will gain through the ICO. Whitepapers include information on the minimum amount of crypto assets needed to initiate a project (Tevetoğlu, 2021; Araalan, 2021).

Essentially, countries have focused on two main issues when enacting capital market regulations regarding crypto assets. The first is the public offering of crypto assets, and the other is the regulation of CASPs (Töremiş, 2021). In Türkiye, there are no regulations on ICOs. However, they are closely monitored by the CBRT, CMB, and BRSA.

In 2018, the CMB issued a notification warning investors against the threats posed by ICOs. The board stated that many practices aimed at raising capital using blockchain technology, known as "Cryptocurrency Sale" or "Token Sale," fell outside their regulation and supervision. The document highlights the fact that ICOs are very high-risk and speculative investments. For this reason, investors considering the purchase of digital assets needed to be aware of the risks and examine in detail what is promised in return for the digital asset to be purchased (Sermaye Piyasası Kurumu, 2018).

Central Bank Digital Currencies

Within the scope of the first phase studies of the Digital Turkish Lira Project, which is being carried out under the leadership of the CBRT, the first payment transactions on the Digital Turkish Lira Network were successfully carried out in late 2022. The CBRT stated that it would continue its narrow-scope and closed-loop pilot application tests, carried out together with technology stakeholders, in the first quarter of 2023.

At the end of 2023, the CBRT published its Digital Turkish Lira-Phase 1 Evaluation Report. In the report, the Digital Lira is defined as the digital form or version of the Turkish lira. The Digital Lira will be a digital form of banknotes rather than a payment tool. The report also highlights that the Digital Lira should be distinct from crypto assets (TCMB, 2023). This approach is in line with declarations made by the European Central Bank.

The main purposes of the Digital Lira are to expand access to financial services, make payments continuous and uninterrupted, enable access to the Digital Turkish Lira through all intermediary institutions thanks to special accounts, and facilitate the transformation between assets and Digital Turkish Lira using DLT.

The report highlights that priority will be given to studies on the economic and regulatory framework of the Digital Turkish Lira and its technological requirements. The report also mentions that in the design of the Digital Turkish Lira System, the issues required by the mandatory provisions of current Turkish law are taken into consideration. Moreover, there is a need to amend all necessary regulations, especially the CBRT's (Law No. 1211) purview to successfully circulate digital currency. However, several questions need to be addressed by Turkish lawmakers: does the Digital Turkish Lira require an additional definition? How do the rules on protecting personal data apply to the Digital Turkish Lira system? How should the risks concerning money laundering and terrorism financing be addressed – and is there a need for new tailor-made rules? How does the Digital Turkish Lira relate to existing payment systems? Is there a need to regulate cross-border transactions and the interoperability of systems? Finally, how should the Digital Turkish Lira be regulated (TCMB, 2023)?

Studies on the legal dimension of the Digital Turkish Lira show that digital identity is critical for the project. The report states that the self-sovereign identity model is used. While establishing the legal dimension of the Digital Turkish Lira, digital identity is identified as critically important. Therefore, it will be given priority. Wallet applications and relevant digital identity software in brokerage systems will also be regulated according to specific country standards.

A Glimpse into the Future

In many countries, clear and specific regulations supporting the establishment and operations of FinTech companies are lacking, making it challenging to seamlessly integrate FinTech activities into existing legal frameworks. While the absence of regulations for FinTech, or its components, does not pose a theoretical or practical barrier for unregulated FinTech companies to swiftly enter the market and start operations, it is important to note that these "unregulated" companies do not operate within a legal vacuum. They remain subject to existing regulations applicable to the scope of their activities. Until a determination is made regarding the regulatory and supervisory authority overseeing their activities, FinTech operations carry inherent risks for both the market and its participants (Kocaoğlu Ulbrich, 2019).

To integrate FinTech models and activities effectively into the banking and finance sectors, a robust legal framework is imperative. However, the rapid evolution of technology presents a challenge as regulatory bodies struggle to match this pace due to limited technological literacy. The advent of new technologies and FinTech introduces novel risks for consumers, investors, and the banking system, necessitating constant oversight. Globally, regulatory bodies face pressing concerns surrounding data security, integrity, money laundering, and terrorism financing, which directly affect consumers, investors, and the broader market. Failure to address these issues compromises both the financial stability of nations and the efficient operation of the market.

When new technologies emerge, addressing them involves several strategies: adopting a wait-and-see approach, adapting existing regulations, or devising new rules tailored to emerging challenges. This dilemma is shared by both the global FinTech sector and the crypto asset industry. While it is still unknown what the term "FinTech" encompasses, it is not surprising that lawmakers try to fit the FinTech companies into existing laws surrounding traditional financial institutions (Kocaoğlu Ulbrich, 2019). The conventional regulatory framework within traditional banking and finance, however, struggles to deal with the intricate dynamics, novel paradigms, and conflicts of interest inherent to these evolving ecosystems. A paramount necessity to safeguard the interests of FinTech companies and their clientele while ensuring a resilient marketplace within this dynamic landscape is to establish a comprehensive and coherent regulatory structure. Moreover, regulators must acknowledge the significant regulatory challenges posed by conflicting rules across different jurisdictions. Collaborative regulatory efforts are indispensable for ensuring that FinTech enterprises and regulatory bodies remain aligned with technological advancements and effectively mitigate potential risks.

Türkiye holds immense potential for and interest in FinTech. The rapid evolution of financial markets and the surging enthusiasm for FinTech highlight the importance of continual reassessment of regulatory frameworks within the financial services sector. Currently, Türkiye's regulatory landscape lacks a cohesive and robust structure specifically tailored to govern the FinTech and crypto assets ecosystem. Instead, it delineates divisions among the banking, insurance, and capital market domains. The velocity and impact of this transformative wave have led to a regulatory environment around FinTech that is fragmented, intricate, perplexing, and persistently evolving – a patchwork system striving to reconcile traditional financial paradigms with emergent concepts. Comprehending the legal framework necessitates consulting an array of laws and regulations encompassing banking, payment systems, crowdfunding, capital markets, negotiable instruments, and bank information systems. This fragmented approach poses significant hurdles for customers, end-users, and FinTech companies and start-ups (Altınsoy Arık, 2022).

In the near future, it is expected that Türkiye will enact new tailor-made laws and regulations. As mentioned in the previous section, at the top of the list of these new rules are those governing CBDCs. Regulations that ensure data security and integrity are also a priority for FinTech companies and CASPs. Along with developments in Europe, implementing robust digital identity verification solutions to strengthen security measures while simplifying authentication requires regulatory priority. In Europe, digital wallet applications include digital identity integration. If, as stated in the Digital Turkish Lira report, a digital identity integration infrastructure can be established, the scope of digital wallets will also expand.

The regulatory ambiguity surrounding crypto assets was previously seen as an attraction for investment in certain countries. However, this prevailing uncertainty has now become a catalyst for investor exodus. Globally, crypto assets are steadily securing a robust legal framework. Consequently, it becomes imperative for Türkiye to establish comprehensive regulations explicitly tailored to crypto assets, particularly concerning their definition, trading methods, and custody services. Such regulations are pivotal in cultivating trust among individual and institutional investors in the country (Baştuğ, 2024). Türkiye is presently transitioning from a stance of "wait and see" to a proactive "regulatory response" approach. In January 2024, the government announced its plans concerning the regulation of crypto assets. The government announced that crypto assets, wallets, CASPs, custody services, and platforms will be defined per international regulations. This is a very significant step since these definitions impact many different fields of law. Based on the government's statement, it is clear that one of the main monitoring bodies will be the CMB, as it will oversee the licensing of all CASPs. CASPs are likely to be exposed to obligations experienced by other financial institutions – a situation that has already been criticized because an institution is either a financial institution or not, not something in between (Tevetoğlu, 2024). The CMB will also have the authority to regulate ICOs through crowdfunding. Digital asset custody also appears to be one of the highlights of the new rules concerning crypto assets. The forthcoming regulations will be implemented as amendments and additions to the current Capital Markets Law. This circumstance suggests a departure from a comprehensive regulatory strategy, signaling an intent to effect changes by incorporating new practices into the existing legal framework.

It has been highlighted that one of the biggest hurdles needing to be overcome before the improvement of FinTech in Türkiye is the lack of a robust regulatory framework. Another problem is compliance with legal rules, which are constantly amended due to evolving needs (Altınsoy Arık, 2022). The concept of RegTech refers to practices that blend regulatory practices with technology (Kocaoğlu Ulbrich, 2019). RegTech solutions that benefit from AI, blockchain, big data analytics, and cloud computing are important in this new FinTech era. RegTech tools can help detect financial crimes, establish if industry standards are kept, or inspect whether KYC procedures are carried out according to data protection laws. The ability to adapt to new laws and regulations is an important leverage for companies to enjoy competitive advantage over FinTech firms (Aydede, 2023). RegTech solutions can streamline compliance processes, automate reporting, and enhance risk management. Consequently, FinTech companies can better understand regulatory requirements, follow amendments, adapt to any changes, and act in compliance with existing regulations. Advancements in RegTech can guarantee that FinTech companies navigate complex regulatory frameworks while maintaining operational efficiency. Adopting RegTech solutions can be crucial for institutions and organizations overseeing financial technologies in Türkiye. This could be pivotal in enhancing risk management, minimizing compliance expenses, and aligning with legal regulations. Companies that proactively embrace new obligations arising from regulations, such as KYC processes, and effectively manage risks to safeguard their licenses are likely to experience healthier growth in the fiercely competitive Fintech market (Aydede, 2023).

Conclusion

The FinTech sector in Türkiye is experiencing substantial growth, and regulatory authorities have shown an openness to innovative business and service models. It is essential to recognize that, much like the global FinTech landscape, developments in Türkiye can evolve swiftly, causing market dynamics to shift rapidly. As a result, assessments and decisions concerning this field must be regularly updated to remain relevant and effective.

In the time it took to write the current chapter, numerous amendments and updates have already been made to the regulatory framework governing FinTech in Türkiye. This highlights the dynamic nature of the industry and the continuous effort required to keep pace with its evolution. Therefore, keeping informed and adapting to these changes is paramount for all stakeholders in the Turkish FinTech ecosystem.

There have been reflections of the EU in many FinTech regulations in Turkey, and most of these regulations are still very new. For this reason, as FinTech applications develop in areas such as open banking, service model banking, digital banking, and digital wallets, regulations are expected to be shaped within the framework of their needs.

It is anticipated that the Turkish government will soon take steps toward establishing comprehensive regulations for the crypto asset ecosystem. The motivation for this impending legislation is undeniably rooted in the adoption of MiCA (Markets in Crypto Assets Regulation), which has served as a strong catalyst for Türkiye to address the regulatory framework for crypto assets.

A holistic approach to regulation is mandatory in the crypto asset ecosystem, considering the unique and evolving nature of crypto assets, which often do not fit into conventional regulatory categories. The Turkish authorities must design a regulatory framework that accommodates this complexity and answers any emerging challenges.

Among the main priorities are designing the corporate structures of platforms offering crypto asset services and licensing CASPs. These areas deserve special attention as they are fundamental for ensuring the integrity and security of the crypto asset ecosystem. Secondary legislation can then provide a more detailed structure to deal with this unique dynamic and functioning of the market.

Regulation has the power to change the competitive balance in this new and dynamic market. For this reason, legislators and regulatory bodies need to carry out regulatory activities for the harmonization of the market and keep abreast of the developments in the sector, without intervening in the market (Kocaoğlu Ulbrich, 2019). Finding a balance is the key to ensuring market growth while protecting the consumers and other market participants.

Note

The author expresses sincere gratitude to Burcu Tümer for her invaluable contributions to the chapter's revision. Special thanks are also extended to Associate Professor Dr Erkan Eren and Dr N. Nilay Dayanç Kuzeyli for their guidance and insights in shaping this chapter. The author assumes full responsibility for the content and conclusions presented herein.

References

Altınsoy Arık, R. G. (2022). *Finansal Teknolojilerde Regülasyon*. Retrieved January 4, 2024, from https://openaccess.hacettepe.edu.tr/xmlui/bitstream/handle/11655/26452/Finansal%20Teknolojilerde%20Reg%C3%BClasyon%20Y%C3%BCksek%20Lisans%20Tezi%2028062022.pdf?sequence=1&isAllowed=y

Araalan, C. (2021). Kripto Varlık İlk Arzı (ICO) Ve Konunun Türk Hukuku ve Bazı Ülke Uygulamaları Açısından Değerlendirilmesi. *Banka ve Finans Hukuku Dergisi*, *10*(40), 877–912.

Aydede, C. (2023). *Fintech Katalizörü: RegTech'in fintech'lere olan katkısı*. Retrieved January 15, 2024 from https://fintechtime.com/2023/12/fintech-katalizoru-regtechin-fintechlere-olan-katkisi/

Baştuğ, U. (2024). *Fintek Sektöründe Küresel Görünüm ve Türkiye Perspektifi*. Retrieved January 15, 2024, from www.ey.com/tr_tr/banking-capital-markets/fintech-ecosystems/fintek-sektorunde-kuresel-gorunum-ve-turkiye-perspektifi

BDDK. (2013). *Bitcoin Hakkında Basın Açıklaması*. Retrieved November 9, 2023, from www.bddk.org.tr/Duyuru/EkGetir/510?ekId=530

Blockchain Turkey. (2021). *Kripto Varliklarin Vergi – Muhasebe Ve Denetim Yönünden İncelenmesi Raporu*. https://bctr.org/dokumanlar/Kripto_Varliklarin_Vergi_Muhasebe_ve_Denetim_Yonunden_Incelenmesi.pdf

Çağlayan Aksoy, P. (2023, January 2). The applicability of property law rules for crypto assets: Considerations from civil law and common law perspectives. *Law, Innovation and Technology*, *15*(1), 185–221. https://doi.org/10.1080/17579961.2023.2184140

Cankat, R., & Güçlütürk, O. G. (2021). Gelişen Teknolojiler ve Hukuk I: Blokzincir ve Hukuk. E. E. Aksoy Retornaz & O. G. Güçlütürk (Eds.), *Güncel Gelişmeler Işığında Türk Hukukunda Kripto Varlıkların Hukuki Niteliği* (pp. 215–216). Istanbul: On İki Levha Yayıncılık.

Canko, S., & Tümer, B. (2023, June 13). *Açık Bankacılık Uygulamaları; Dünyada ve Türkiye'de Mevzuat Gelişmeleri. Hukuk Ve Bilişim Dergisi*. Retrieved November 9, 2023, from www.hukukvebilisimdergisi.com/acik-bankacilik-uygulamalari-dunyada-ve-turkiyede-mevzuat-gelismeleri/

Canpolat, Y. K. (2023, October 10). TCMB'nin Yeni Kuralları Ödeme ve Elektronik Para Sektörü İçin Neler Getiriyor? *Medium*. https://medium.com/canpolat-legal/tcmbnin-yeni-kurallar%C4%B1-%C3%B6deme-ve-elektronik-para-sekt%C3%B6r%C3%BC-i%CC%87%C3%A7in-neler-getiriyor-43cb5d9e2de3

Çetin, M. (2023, June 1). *Sermaye Piyasasi Hukuku Bakımından Kripto Varlıklar*. Oniki Levha Yayıncılık.

Clifford Chance. (2017). *European fintech regulation an overview*.Retrieved November 9, 2023, from www.cliffordchance.com/content/dam/cliffordchance/briefings/2017/04/european-fintech-regulation.pdf

Coşkun, M. E. (2023). *Hukuki Açıdan Kripto Varlıklar ve İlk Kriptopara Arzı (Initial Coin Offering)*. Istanbul: On İki Levha Yayıncılık.

Cumhurbaşkanlığı Finans Ofisi. (2022). *Türkiye Fintek Ekosistemi Durum Raporu*. Retrieved November 9, 2023, from https://www.cbfo.gov.tr/sites/default/files/2024-04/fintek-durum-raporu-2022_v0.9_digital_lowsize_ayrisayfalar-compressed.pdf

Cumhurbaşkanlığı Finans Ofisi. (2023, September 30). *Türkiye Fintek Görünümü*. Retrieved November 9, 2023, from www.cbfo.gov.tr/sites/default/files/docs/2023-07/ekran-resmi-2023-07-21-12.32.15.pdf

Cumhurbaşkanlığı Strateji ve Bütçe Başkanlığı. (2023, December 11). *On İkinci Kalkınma Planı*. Retrieved December 25, 2023, from https://www.sbb.gov.tr/wp-content/uploads/2023/12/On-Ikinci-Kalkinma-Plani_2024-2028_11122023.pdf

Dayanç Kuzeyli, N., & Töremiş, H. E. (2022, October). Kripto Varlıkların Hukuki Niteliği. *Vergi Dünyası*, *42*(94), 63–77.

Demirdöğen, Y. (2019). Fintek Ekosistemi İçin Gerekli Düzenlemeler (REGTEK). *Suleyman Demirel University Visionary Journa*, *10*(24), 311–321.

Financial Stability Board. (n.d.). *Fintech*. www.fsb.org/work-of-the-fsb/financial-innovation-and-structural-change/fintech/#:~:text=The%20FSB%20defines%20FinTech%20as,the%20provision%20of%20financial%20services

Garrido, J. M. (2023, July). Digital tokens: A legal perspective. *IMF* (WP/23/151).

Güçlütürk, O. G. (2020). Türk Hukukunda Kripto Varlıkların Para ve Elektronik Para Niteliğinin İncelenmesi. <cite lang="la">*Regesta*, *4*(3).

Güngör, A. İ. (2022, October). Kripto Varlık Ekosisteminin Düzenleme Gerektiren Kısımları: Mevcut Düzenlemeler ve Öneriler. *Vergi Dünyası*, *42*(494), 90–105.

Gürses, D. (2023a). www.adanabarosu.org.tr/uploads/haber_3/BiliAim_Komisyonu_Ekim_SayAsA_1.pdf

Gürses, D. (2023b). *Hukuki Açıdan Dijital Bankalar ve Servis Modeli Bankacılığı*. Istanbul: Oniki Levha Yayıncılık.

İstanbul Finans Merkezi. (2023). *İstanbul Finans Merkezi*. Retrieved July 7, 2024, from https://ifm.gov.tr/ana-sayfa

Karakaya, M. F. (2022). The making of a market: The relational aspects of credit card installments in Turkey. *İstanbul Üniversitesi Sosyoloji Dergisi*, *41*(2), 435–449.

Karamanlıoğlu, A. (2021, April 30). Son Gelişmeler Işığında Kripto Paraların Hukuki Niteliği ve Kripto Para Borsalarına Dair Tespit ve Öneriler. *Hukuk Bülteni*. Retrieved November 9, 2023, from https://hukukbulteni.khas.edu.tr/bulten/45

Kaymak, O. (2019). *Dijital Bankacilik Kapsamında Türkiye'de Fintech İnovasyonu Ve Uygulaması: Rusya Sektör Karşilaştirmasi*. https://guides.library.uq.edu.au/referencing/apa7/thesis

Kolcuoğlu, U. (2023). Türkiye'de Dijital Banka Çağı. *Lebib Yalkın*. Retrieved November 9, 2023, from https://lebibyalkin.com.tr/haber/turkiyede-dijital-banka-cagi

Kocaoğlu Ulbrich, E. Ş. (2023, March 9). Yeni Başlayanlar İçin Finansal Teknoloji (FinTek). *Lexpera*. Retrieved November 9, 2023, from https://blog.lexpera.com.tr/yeni-baslayanlar-icin-finansal-teknoloji-fintek/

Kocaoğlu Ulbrich, Ş. E. (2019). *Avrupa Birliği ve Türk Banka Hukuku yönünden fintek/Fintech from European Union and Turkish Banking Law perspectives* [Unpublished LL.M Thesis, Galatasaray University, Social Sciences Institute, Department of Private Law].

Konca, N. K., & Selçuk, S. (2023). Kripto Varlık Alacaklarına İlişkin Davalarda Görevli Mahkeme. *Türkiye Barolar Birliği Dergisi*, *166*, 61–100.

KPMG Perspektifinden Web 3.0. (2023, June). *KPMG*. Retrieved November 9, 2023, from https://assets.kpmg.com/content/dam/kpmg/tr/pdf/2023/06/KPMG-perspektifinden-Web3.pdf

KuCoin. (2023, August 31). *Into the cryptoverse: Türkiye'deki Kripto Kullanıcılarını Anlamak*. https://www.kucoin.com/tr/blog/more-than-half-of-Turkish-adults-invest-in-crypto-tr

MASAK. (2021, May). *Suç Gelirlerinin Aklanmasının ve Terörizmin Finansmanının Önlenmesine Dair Yükümlülüklere İlişkin Temel Esaslar*. Retrieved November 9, 2023, from https://ms.hmb.gov.tr/uploads/sites/12/2021/05/Kripto-Varlik-Hizmet-Saglayicilar-Rehberi.pdf

OECD. (2023). Generative artificial intelligence in finance. *OECD Artificial Intelligence Papers*, No. 9, OECD Publishing, Paris. https://doi.org/10.1787/ac7149cc-en

Rekabet Kurumu. (2021, December). *Ödeme Hizmetlerindeki Finansal Teknolojilere Yönelik İnceleme Raporu*. Retrieved July 1, 2024, from https://www.rekabet.gov.tr/Dosya/geneldosya/odeme-hizmetlerindeki-finansal-teknolojilere-yonelik-inceleme-raporu-pdf

Rupeika-Apoga, R., & Wendt, S. (2022, August 23). FinTech development and regulatory scrutiny: A contradiction? The case of Latvia. *Risks*, *10*(9), 167. https://doi.org/10.3390/risks10090167

Şahin, B. Ş., & Cantürk, B. C. (2020). Türkiye'deki Hukuki Altyapı ve Ödeme Hizmetleri Yönergesi 2 Bağlamında API Teknolojisi ve Açık Bankacılık. *Maliye ve Finans Yazıları*, (114), 149–148. https://doi.org/10.33203/mfy.637661

Sermaye Piyasası Kurumu. (2018, September 27). *Sermaye Piyasası Kurulu Bülteni (2018–42)*. <cite lang="id"> . Retrieved November 9, 2023, from https://spk.gov.tr/data/61e0b4db1b41c613a0d633dc/20c458af9ec636f50e86f04a02c3c89c.pdf

Stamegna, C., & Karakas, C. (2019, February 12). Fintech (financial technology) and the European union state of play and outlook. *European Parliament*. Retrieved November 9, 2023, from www.europarl.europa.eu/RegData/etudes/BRIE/2019/635513/EPRS_BRI(2019)635513_EN.pdf

Tevetoğlu, M. (2021).*Hukuki Yönleriyle Kripto Varlıklar ve Kripto Varlıkların İlk Arzı (Initial Coin Offering)* (Genişletilmiş İkinci Baskı). Istanbul: Aristo Yayıncılık.

Tevetoğlu, M. (2023, September 23). Kripto Para ile Ödeme Yapılabilir Mi? *Tevetoglu Legal*. www.tevetoglu.av.tr/tr/yayinlarimiz/kripto-para-ile-odeme-yapilabilir-mi-2023-09-23-060902

Tevetoğlu, M. (2024). *İki konu var: 1. Kripto varlık hizmet sağlayıcılar* [LinkedIn post]. LinkedIn. https://www.linkedin.com/posts/mete-teveto%C4%9Flu-4023104b_i%CC%87ki-konu-var-1-kripto-varl%C4%B1k-hizmet-sa%C4%9Flay%C4%B1c%C4%B1lar-activity-7150851711845253122-P6AG?utm_source=share&utm_medium=member_desktop

Töremiş, H. E. (2021). Kripto Varlıklar ve Sermaye Piyasasında Düzenleme İhtiyacı, *Kripto Varlıklarda Düzenleme Arayışı Çalıştayı*, 155–167. Ankara.

Tuğay, Y., & Başgül, Ö. (2007). Önemli Bir Finansman Kaynağı Olarak Kredi Kartları: Kredi Kartlarının Kart Sahiplerinin Harcamaları Üzerindeki Etkisini Belirlemeye Yönelik Burdur İlinde Bir Araştırma. *Süleyman Demirel Üniversitesi İktisadi ve İdari Bilimler Fakültesi Dergisi*, *12*(3), 215–226. https://dergipark.org.tr/tr/pub/sduiibfd/issue/20835/223248

Turanboy, A. (2019). Kripto Paraların Ortaya Çıkmaları ve Hukukî Nitelikleri. *Banka ve Ticaret Hukuku Dergisi*, *35*, 47–62.

Türkiye Bankalar Birliği. (2022). *Dijital Varlıklar Raporu*. https://www.tbb.org.tr/Content/Upload/tos/Dijital%20Varl%C4%B1klar%20Raporu.pd

Türkiye Cumhuriyet Merkez Bankası. (2022a). *Açık Bankacılık Basın Duyurusu*. www.tcmb.gov.tr/wps/wcm/connect/TR/TCMB+TR/Main+Menu/Duyurular/Basin/2022/DUY2022-48

Türkiye Cumhuriyet Merkez Bankası. (2022b). *Dijital Türk Lirası Kullanımına İlişkin Basın Duyurusu*. www.tcmb.gov.tr/wps/wcm/connect/TR/TCMB+TR/Main+Menu/Duyurular/Basin/2022/DUY2022-55

Türkiye Cumhuriyet Merkez Bankası. (2023a). *Ödeme Hizmetlerinde Veri Paylaşım Servislerine İlişkin Rehber*. Retrieved November 9, 2023, from www.tcmb.gov.tr/wps/wcm/connect/d60cc679-ce04-4941-b310-b3788b6f3540/Odeme+Hizmetlerinde+Veri+Paylasim+Servislerine+Iliskin+Rehber.pdf?MOD=AJPERES

Türkiye Cumhuriyet Merkez Bankası. (2023b). *Dijital Türk Lirası Birinci Faz Değerlendirme Raporu*. Retrieved January 15, 2024 from https://tcmb.gov.tr/wps/wcm/connect/509a3c6c-d906-4099-aa27-d1900d9227fc/Dijital+T%C3%BCrk+Liras%C4%B1+Birinci+Faz+De%C4%9Ferlendirme+Raporu.pdf?MOD=AJPERES&CACHEID=ROOTWORKSPACE-509a3c6c-d906-4099-aa27-d1900d9227fc-oO.7xaH

Türkiye to toughen crypto assets law for FATF "grey list" removal. (2023, November 1). <cite lang="ms">*Daily Sabah*. Retrieved November 9, 2023, from www.dailysabah.com/business/economy/turkiye-to-toughen-crypto-assets-law-for-fatf-grey-list-removal

UK Finance. (2023). *The impact of AI in financial services: Opportunities, risks and policy considerations*. www.ukfinance.org.uk/system/files/2023-11/The%20impact%20of%20AI%20in%20financial%20services.pdf

14 Social Media Regulation

Mehmet Bedii Kaya and Muhammed Furkan Akıncı

Introduction

Social media has always been at the epicenter of regulatory debates in Türkiye. The legal rules governing social media have undergone numerous revisions, and stricter rules have been added over time. The rulings of the Turkish Constitutional Court have also significantly shaped this subject.

The main legal framework governing the internet in Türkiye is Law No. 5651, dated 2007 and titled The Law on the Regulation of Broadcasts via Internet and Prevention of Crimes Committed Through Such Broadcasts ("Internet Law"). Türkiye has opted to control the internet primarily by preventing access to illegal content by using IP and DNS-restriction techniques. The Turkish internet infrastructure has undergone a significant upgrade to prevent access to material that has been classified unlawful by the relevant authorities. At every access point throughout Türkiye, a sophisticated and extensive deep packet inspection (DPI) system has been installed. However, as encryption methods have become more widely used – particularly with the rise of https traffic – such technologies have become less effective.

The inability of network technology to manage content has forced Türkiye to reconsider its approach to internet censorship. Türkiye has undergone a profound paradigm change in terms of internet regulation, particularly since the usage of social media has increased dramatically and become an integral component of social and economic life. To control all facets of social media in this respect, a new provision was added to the Internet Law in 2020.

The new paradigm is to resolve the issue of managing content in social media at its root. In other words, the information must be removed from its original source rather than merely restricting access to it or having its visibility reduced. There is no doubt that such a significant paradigm change necessitates the active cooperation of social media companies.

Türkiye has consistently complained that social media companies are hesitant to comply with its demands. Therefore, the new law required social media corporations to designate a local representative to establish direct communication with them. They must also respond to user requests quickly, provide

DOI: 10.4324/9781032692937-14

reports on the material they moderate, put data localization mechanisms in place, fight crime more effectively, and safeguard children and young people.

The cornerstone for implementing Türkiye's larger digital agenda is the Internet Law of 2020, that is, social media law. The new social media regulations have created a distinctive accountability framework designed to fit the Turkish policy goals. To guarantee that the legislation is being fully implemented, new sanction mechanisms have also been added to the Internet Law. If social media companies fail to fulfill their obligations, they could be subject to an advertisement ban, bandwidth throttling, joint civil liability from any illegal content, and high administrative fines.

This chapter aims to deeply scrutinize Turkish social media rules and regulations. Further, this chapter will attempt to examine the evolution of Turkish social media law, map out the institutional framework, lay down the general principles of Internet Law applicable to social media, scrutinize the new social media regime, and question the subsidiarity of such strict and intricate regulation. This chapter seeks to further the field of scholarship by offering a thorough and current analysis of Turkish social media legislation. A study of the literature is necessary because the Turkish Internet Law underwent considerable amendments in 2020 and 2021, rendering certain parts of the academic work largely outdated.

The Overall Legal Framework Governing the Internet in Türkiye

The regulation of social media and internet usage in Türkiye is governed by a comprehensive legislative framework comprising various legislations (see, for comparative analysis, Lambert, 2015). The Turkish Internet Law, formally titled The Law on the Regulation of Broadcasts via Internet and Prevention of Crimes Committed Through Such Broadcasts, was enacted in 2007 and subsequently amended in 2014 and 2020. This legislation specifically focuses on defining the obligations of various entities involved in internet operations, including content providers, hosting providers, ISPs, and social network providers. The rules encompass measures relevant to the restriction of access in specific criminal activities, protocols for the removal of infringing content, as well as the implementation of internet filtering and surveillance mechanisms.

The Turkish Data Protection Law (Law No. 6698), which came into force on April 7, 2016, was implemented with the objective of safeguarding fundamental rights and freedoms, with a specific focus on the right to privacy throughout the handling of personal data. This provision pertains to individuals whose personal information is being processed, as well as those who are responsible for carrying out such processing activities. The legal framework delineates overarching principles governing the processing of data, stipulates the requirements for processing personal data and handling sensitive categories of data, and establishes regulations pertaining to the cross-border transfer of personal data, both domestically and internationally.

Turkish Internet Law

The primary legal framework governing the internet in Türkiye is the Turkish Internet Law. Its text outlines the legal, criminal, and administrative responsibilities of entities operating on the internet, such as content providers (as stated in Article 4), hosting providers (as mentioned in Article 5), ISPs (as indicated in Article 6), public use providers (as outlined in Article 7), and social network providers (as elaborated in Additional Article 4). The inclusiveness of this extensive range guarantees that all entities engaged in online broadcasting assume accountability for their content and services (Kaya, 2010, p. 138).

Furthermore, the legislation outlines protocols for restricting access in the event of specific criminal offenses, notably during urgent situations (Articles 8 and 8/A). The aforementioned provision within the legal framework assumes a pivotal function in facilitating expeditious counteraction against cyber offenses and ensuring the protection of societal well-being (Işık, 2023, p. 207).

In addition, the framework establishes protocols for addressing instances of content infringement, with particular emphasis on violations of personal rights, as outlined in Articles 9 and 9/A. This approach facilitates the elimination of objectionable content, thereby safeguarding the rights and privacy of persons (Işık, 2023, p. 221).

Finally, the legislation includes rules pertaining to filtering techniques and internet surveillance (Article 10), which play a crucial role in the monitoring and regulation of online information with the aim of preventing illicit activity.

In its entirety, the Turkish Internet Law, particularly through its subsequent amendments, demonstrates a deliberate endeavor to strike a harmonious equilibrium between governing online material and services, safeguarding individual rights, and upholding public order. The major aim of the law, as articulated in its preamble, is to safeguard children and families from detrimental and unlawful online content. This legislation places particular emphasis on addressing various criminal activities, including but not limited to the promotion of suicide, child sexual exploitation, drug misuse, obscenity, prostitution, and gambling.

2020 Amendments to the Turkish Internet Law

The revisions to Türkiye's Internet Law No. 5651 in 2020 have sparked significant discussion, highlighting a notable change in Türkiye's control of the internet, with a special focus on social media platforms. These amendments represent a strategic shift in Türkiye's digital governance, increasingly aligning with models similar to the EU's Digital Services Act (DSA) (Zech, 2021; Turillazzi et al., 2023). The revisions have considerably broadened the scope of the law and enhanced its procedures for enforcement.

Significantly, the present legislation has expanded its scope to include a broader range of internet entities, such as content-, hosting-, and access providers, in addition to social network providers. The objective of this expansion is to reduce the occurrence of illicit online material and expand its authority to foreign businesses by requiring social network providers to have legal representation in Türkiye. Failure to adhere to these criteria results in severe penalties such as significant administrative fines and the possibility of bandwidth limiting.

One significant modification to legal practice involves the implementation of both "content removal" and "access blocking" as regulatory mechanisms. This amendment mandates that internet service providers must promptly respond, specifically within a four-hour time frame, to specific categories of content that have been identified as illegal. The need for prompt adherence to this compliance requirement is reinforced by the potential imposition of significant monetary fines and operational limitations in instances of noncompliance.

In addition, the changes have incorporated the concept of the "right to be forgotten", aligning with prevailing data protection regulations on a global scale. This particular entitlement grants individuals the ability to formally request the deletion of their personal information, with the caveat that such removal does not contradict overarching public interests. The introduction of this additional measure, albeit forward-thinking in its stance on safeguarding privacy, prompts a thoughtful examination of its possible ramifications for the freedom of speech.

Nevertheless, these legislative modifications have not been without criticism. Supporters of digital rights and the preservation of freedom of expression have expressed apprehensions, positing that these proposed modifications may heighten governmental supervision of online material, thus infringing upon the principles of unrestricted communication and, perhaps, resulting in a manifestation of digital censorship. The concerns expressed are further magnified because of the expeditious nature of the legislative procedures and the gravity of the sanctions imposed, emphasizing the possibility of a "chilling effect" on the freedom of online expression and digital rights. In light of the regulatory modifications, a number of notable social media corporations have acquiesced to the legal requirements by creating legal entities within the borders of Türkiye. Prominent among these platforms are Pinterest, Facebook, YouTube, TikTok, and Twitter.

2022 Amendments With Law No. 7418

The recent modifications to Turkish legislation in 2022, particularly under Law No. 7418, represent a noteworthy advancement in the realm of social media governance within Türkiye. The modifications, specifically in Articles 29, 30, 31, and subsequent provisions, signify a deliberate endeavor by the Turkish government to tackle the escalating apprehensions over the dissemination of false information and the regulation of digital content.

The inclusion of Article 29 in the Turkish Penal Code (No. 5237) represents a significant amendment that imposes penalties for the intentional dissemination of false material that has the potential to impact national security, public order, and public health. The primary objective of this legislation is to mitigate the dissemination of false or misleading information that has the capacity to incite public turmoil or anxiety. The legal system mandates a custodial term ranging from one to three years for such transgressions, with more severe consequences if the conduct is perpetrated while concealing one's identity or as a component of an organized endeavor. This serves as a direct reaction to the difficulties presented by the swift distribution of information via social media platforms.

Article 30 serves as a supplementary provision to the Criminal Procedure Law (No. 5271) by introducing the inclusion of the offense of disseminating deceptive information within the established legal framework. The integration described here represents a more comprehensive legal strategy for addressing misinformation, enhancing the capacity of the judicial system to properly address such instances.

The revisions implemented in Article 31, specifically in relation to Law No. 5651 which applies to the regulation of online broadcasts and the prevention of crimes committed through such broadcasts, are of significant importance. These modifications impose substantial obligations on internet service providers and social network platforms, requiring them to uphold a technical framework for communicating content removal or determining access bans. This stipulation highlights the government's objective to ensure that these platforms are held responsible for the content they distribute or provide a medium for.

Moreover, these revisions institute rigorous compliance obligations for social network providers, particularly those operating from foreign jurisdictions. It is anticipated that, as a result, these foreign providers will designate delegates within the borders of Türkiye, guarantee transparency in the management of material, and collaborate with the relevant Turkish authorities. The emphasis on social networks originating from other countries underscores the worldwide scope of digital platforms and the difficulties that national governments encounter in overseeing content that surpasses regional limits.

Turkish Data Protection Law

The interplay between rules governing social media and the Turkish Data Protection Law (Law No: 6698) is complex and has substantial implications for the functioning of social media platforms in Türkiye. The enactment of the Turkish Data Protection Law in 2016 marked a significant milestone for Türkiye because it represented the country's first comprehensive legislation designed to govern the handling of personal data. This declaration is in accordance with the constitutional amendment of 2010, which formally recognized the right to personal data protection as an inherent individual right. The mentioned legislation includes the right to receive information and obtain access to, correct, and erase personal data while also guaranteeing that personal data are used for appropriate objectives.

According to this legislation, the processing of personal data is permissible solely upon obtaining explicit agreement from the individual to whom the data pertain or in cases where such processing is authorized by other applicable legal provisions. Social media networks bear a substantial responsibility to ensure that they obtain explicit consent from users regarding their data processing activities. The legislation additionally outlines specific protocols and fundamental principles pertaining to the handling of data, including provisions for the removal, eradication, or anonymization of data; the creation of a register comprising data controllers; and instructions for fulfilling responsibilities to provide users with relevant information.

The primary supervisory and regulatory entity responsible for enforcing the Data Protection Law is the Turkish Data Protection Authority ("TDPA"). The functions of this entity encompass the undertaking of investigations pertaining to alleged infringements, the resolution of complaints concerning data protection rights, the upkeep of a registry containing information on data controllers, and the imposition of administrative penalties for breaches of the law.

Social media platforms are required to adhere to rigorous laws concerning the management of user data as a result of this legislation. It is imperative for them to guarantee the transparency of data processing; acquire explicit consent from users; and adhere to users' rights to access, amend, or delete their data. In addition, it is imperative for social media platforms to promptly address inquiries made by the TDPA and adhere to the established legal protocols, which encompass data protection regulations tailored to sectors such as telecommunications and banking.

In essence, the Turkish Data Protection Law sets out a comprehensive framework related to the protection of personal data, which has a direct impact on social media sites that operate under the jurisdiction of Türkiye. To adhere to legal requirements, these platforms are required to effectively deal with the complex requirements of this legislation. This entails ensuring compliance in several aspects such as the handling, retention, and safeguarding of user data, as well as appropriately addressing user inquiries and adhering to regulatory supervision.

The Institutional Framework of the Internet

In Türkiye, the governance of the internet is characterized by a complex institutional architecture that incorporates multiple bodies and entities, each fulfilling certain roles in accordance with the country's internet legislation. At the core of this architectural framework lie crucial regulatory entities, namely BTK and TDPA. These organizations bear the responsibility of adopting and enforcing legal norms, overseeing online content regulation, and safeguarding data protection and privacy. The framework additionally delineates the responsibilities of diverse online service providers, such as social network providers, in upholding a secure and compliant digital environment.

Introduction to the Institutions

Internet governance in Türkiye is characterized by a well-developed institutional framework, wherein each body has a specific responsibility in ensuring a controlled and secure digital environment. The presence of regulatory authorities and organizations plays a crucial role in supervising the various aspects of internet usage and administration within Türkiye.

BTK is positioned at the forefront of this framework and serves as the primary governing entity responsible for overseeing telecommunications and internet services in Türkiye. The obligations of the BTK are broad in scope, including activities such as the regulation of online content and the enforcement of adherence to national standards. However, the role of BTK encompasses more than enforcement alone – it also includes the promotion of internet safety and security, positioning it as a significant participant in the digital domain.

TDPA operates in parallel to the BTK. The significance of this entity is within the domain of safeguarding data, with a specific emphasis on ensuring the confidentiality and integrity of individuals' personal information within the digital environment. TDPA plays a crucial role in ensuring that internet businesses, especially prominent social media platforms, adhere to legal and ethical requirements when collecting and processing personal data. The focal point of personal data governance is its prioritization of user consent and data protection.

In addition to the primary regulating authorities, the Turkish legal system plays a crucial role in the implementation of internet legislation. The system assumes a pivotal function within decision-making procedures pertaining to the removal of information, the banning of access, and the interpretation of legislation in delicate domains such as censorship, freedom of speech, and individual liberties.

Social media providers play a defined and significant function within the internet governance framework of Türkiye. These providers are formally acknowledged as entities that are subject to regulation. They provide platforms that enable users to engage in social interaction by creating, viewing, and sharing material. However, in addition to their function of promoting online communication, these platforms now bear substantial duties in accordance with the regulatory norms of Türkiye. Their categorization as regulated enterprises necessitates that social network providers adhere to national internet rules to ensure compliance with both their operational practices and the information uploaded on their platforms. This obligation signifies a notable transition in their role, establishing them not just as enablers of digital engagement but also as crucial participants in maintaining the legal and ethical norms of digital material within the country.

The Access Providers Association occupies a unique and crucial role within this framework. The primary objective of this organization is to effectively oversee and streamline the duties and functions of access providers throughout Türkiye. The association functions as a central coordinating entity, responsible for overseeing the adherence of access providers to statutory mandates and established standards. The function of ISPs is crucial in upholding the infrastructure necessary for uninterrupted and regulated internet connectivity, making them a pivotal element within the broader framework of internet regulation in a given nation.

The comprehensive network comprises a varied range of institutions, including regulatory bodies such as the BTK and TDPA, judicial authorities, and specific organizations like social network providers and The Access Providers Association. This network is designed to facilitate efficient governance across all facets of internet operation, encompassing content management and data protection, hence providing a foundational structure for the digital framework of Türkiye.

The Information Technologies and Communication Authority (BTK)

According to the Turkish Internet Law and other related legislation, BTK plays a crucial role in overseeing Türkiye's communications and online infrastructure. BTK was first formed under Law No. 4502 and was given additional authority by Law No. 5809 – the Electronic Communications Law (ECL) – which goes beyond simple regulation to promote competition, innovation, and security in the telecommunications industry. The responsibilities of this regulating entity, as prescribed by the ECL, encompass the preservation of competition within the sector, safeguarding the interests of stakeholders, facilitating the resolution of disputes among operators, and monitoring progress and advancements within the sector. BTK is also in charge of radio equipment licensing, spectrum management, and maintaining national security in electronic communications. Furthermore, it executes standards and resolutions that align with prevailing global conventions, thereby assuming a prominent position within the realm of international telecommunications.

The Turkish Internet Law grants the BTK a multidimensional authoritative function, encompassing regulatory and enforcement responsibilities inside the digital domain. The principal objective, as outlined in legislation, is to build a secure and lawful digital environment, with a particular focus on protecting children and families from harmful and unlawful online information.

The BTK is responsible for the prohibition of illicit online activities and dissemination of unauthorized materials. These tasks involve the coordination of multiple institutions, such as ministries, law enforcement agencies, and ISPs, to efficiently address unlawful actions on the internet and promote a more secure online environment, as stipulated in Article 4 of the Turkish

Internet Law. Additionally, the BTK is responsible for monitoring internet content to detect and respond to illicit activities conducted online. This entails the establishment of parameters and approaches for overseeing online transmissions, as well as implementing measures to restrict access upon the detection of illicit material. Such responsibilities are bestowed by Articles 5, 6, and 7 of the Law.

One of the key roles of BTK entails the establishment of standards and protocols for the filtration and restriction of internet material. Article 10 outlines the provisions for permitting local operators and administrators to utilize designated systems, as well as establishing standards for hardware and software in public internet services with the purpose of filtering and monitoring. Moreover, the mission of BTK encompasses international collaboration, involving interactions with worldwide entities in the field of informatics and the internet. Global collaboration plays a crucial role in facilitating policy formulation, standardization, and the exchange of best practices within the realm of internet governance and safety.

The BTK actively assists law enforcement agencies in their efforts to mitigate the dissemination and commercialization of products that contain content pertaining to the offenses outlined in the Turkish Internet Law. This entails offering technical support and facilitating collaboration to enforce the legislative stipulations pertaining to internet safety and security, as highlighted in Article 8.

The Turkish Data Protection Authority

Turkish Data Protection Act (KVKK) has established the Turkish Data Protection Authority (TDPA) as the principal regulatory entity tasked with the responsibility of safeguarding personal data within Türkiye. The organization and structure of the TDPA are delineated in accordance with the legislative provisions it establishes for data protection and the processing of personal data (for in-depth anaysis, see Çekin et al., 2023, p. 81) (Tan, 2018).

The primary function of the TDPA is to supervise and ensure compliance with the terms of the KVKK. This encompasses the monitoring of adherence to data protection regulations, the investigation of infractions, and the implementation of penalties as deemed necessary. The Authority additionally offers recommendations pertaining to data protection issues, enhances public consciousness regarding data rights and obligations, and engages in collaborative efforts with international data protection entities.

Moreover, the TDPA possesses the authority to issue legally enforceable resolutions pertaining to matters of data protection, carry out audits, and propose amendments to legislation and policies to enhance the efficacy of data protection measures. The role of the Authority is of utmost importance in maintaining a delicate equilibrium between the privacy rights of individuals and the lawful data processing requirements of entities operating in both the public and private domains, as stipulated by Turkish legislation.

The Access Providers Association

The Access Providers Association, as stipulated in the Turkish Internet Law, assumes a pivotal role in the oversight and administration of Internet content and accessibility within Türkiye. The Association, which operates as a privately owned legal entity, bears the responsibility of overseeing the enforcement of judgments pertaining to the removal of content and the barring of access, excluding those falling under the purview of Articles 8 and 8/A of the legislation. The operational processes and principles of the Association are regulated by a statute that mandates approval from the BTK, which is responsible for internet regulation.

The Association comprises all internet service providers who have been duly approved under the Electronic Communication Law, as well as other operators who offer internet access services. This composition emphasizes its complete function in overseeing internet access across diverse service providers. The responsibility for implementing access blocking decisions mostly lies with the access providers, as assigned by the Association. The suppliers are obligated to provide the essential hardware and software required for the execution of these decisions.

Furthermore, the Association possesses the jurisdiction to raise objections to judgments that it perceives as being against legislation, thus demonstrating a component of supervisory and regulatory adherence. The financial framework of the organization is sustained through the collection of fees from its members, contributions from donors, and other revenues generated from its operations. The fees are determined by the net sales of the members, and the Association's law provides detailed information regarding the payment intervals and conditions.

Nonmembers of the Association are barred from operating as ISPs, highlighting the comprehensive and obligatory nature of the Association within the Turkish internet industry. The Association possesses the capacity to communicate decisions pertaining to the removal of content and the barring of access to the email addresses of pertinent content or hosting providers (Kaya, 2021, p. 60).

The Technical Infrastructure of the Internet in Türkiye

There is a robust legislative structure in Türkiye that governs the regulation of ISPs, comprising the Internet Law and various rules issued by the BTK.

ISPs are required to obtain a blanket permit from BTK before they may begin serving customers. The regulatory framework pertaining to the granting of operation certificates to access and hosting providers by the BTK is outlined in the "Regulation governing the Principles and Procedures for Granting Operation Certificates to Access and Hosting Providers by the Telecommunications Authority". Licenses may be issued for an infinite duration or for a specified period, and both domestic and international economic operators have the potential to become ISPs if they satisfy the requisite conditions. It is worth mentioning that ISPs are required to be members of the Access Providers Association, and failure to comply with this requirement may lead to substantial financial penalties (Kaya, 2010, p. 21).

The liability system pertaining to ISPs, as outlined in the Internet Law, is characterized by a notably permissive approach. ISPs are not obligated to proactively monitor their systems for illicit activities. However, they are mandated to restrict access to unlawful content upon receiving notification of its presence. The present system is based on the E-Commerce Directive of the EU, with a particular focus on implementing a notice-and-takedown mechanism. ISPs are required by law to publicly disclose and regularly update identifiable information for the purpose of legal notifications (see, for a recent discussion, Grassie, 2017).

The limitation of access to illicit content constitutes a fundamental component of Türkiye's internet strategy. ISPs play a critical role in this context because they are obligated to restrict access to illicit content upon receiving notification. The techniques employed for restriction have undergone development, commencing with the utilization of DNS- and IP-based restrictions and subsequently transitioning toward more precise approaches such as URL restrictions and DPI. DPI, nonetheless, encounters difficulties in effectively filtering encrypted traffic, such as from websites that utilize the HTTPS protocol. ISPs are now obligated to assume the financial responsibility associated with the installation of essential software and hardware required for the purpose of restricting access to illicit information. It is important to note that the argument of technological infeasibility can no longer serve as a viable justification because recent amendments to the Internet Law have addressed this concern.

The Internet Law encompasses a wide array of court and administrative penalties that are imposed on ISPs if they fail to execute rulings or collaborate with administrative entities. Significantly, the European Court of Human Rights has issued rulings against Türkiye in cases pertaining to the imposition of limitations on the accessibility of platforms such as YouTube and Twitter. These rulings underscore the profound implications of these restrictions on the fundamental right to freedom of speech.

The Internet Law delineates additional obligations, including emergency limits, safeguarding personal rights, bypassing access tools, retaining traffic data, obligatory cooperation with the BTK, and the implementation of filtering measures in accordance with the Safe Internet Service. ISPs may incur significant financial penalties for failing to adhere to regulations and requirements in certain specific domains. The regulatory framework presented herein underscores the intricate equilibrium between rights and obligations within the domain of internet regulation in Türkiye (Kaya, 2010, p. 75).

Moreover, there exists a significant interaction between Internet Law and Intellectual Property Law, namely in relation to the issue of copyright infringement in the online domain. ISPs actively participate in this domain by complying with obligatory notice-and-takedown protocols, thereby safeguarding the rights of authors and other stakeholders associated with intellectual property rights (Kaya, 2010, p. 24, 2021, p. 70).

In brief, the technical framework of the internet in Türkiye is distinguished by a rigorous regulatory atmosphere, which necessitates the adherence of ISPs to diverse operational, content management, and legal collaboration obligations. These obligations are supervised by the BTK and pertinent legislation frameworks.

Social Media Regulation

Before delving into the regulatory aspects pertaining to social media, it is imperative to acknowledge the importance and complexities of this topic within the framework of our progressively digitized society. Social media, a crucial component of contemporary communication and media consumption, presents unique challenges in regard to its regulation and governance (for comparative analysis, see Vranaki, 2022; Tan, 2018). This section aims to examine how Türkiye effectively addresses these challenges by utilizing its legal framework, with a particular emphasis on the Internet Law and its implications for individuals using social media platforms. Additionally, it will analyze the delicate equilibrium between freedom of expression and professional ethics, as well as the specific regulations that govern public officials and influencers. The intricate and multifaceted characteristics of social media require a nuanced regulatory strategy that effectively navigates the delicate equilibrium between individual liberties and communal concerns while also accounting for the ever-changing nature of the digital communication landscape.

The Internet Law and Its Application to Social Media Platforms

The Internet Law establishes the fundamental legal framework for governing internet content in Türkiye. A primary element of this legislation pertains to its emphasis on addressing offenses perpetrated via digital platforms. This comprises a spectrum of transgressions, spanning from the dissemination of propaganda on behalf of terrorist organizations to violations against individual rights. Under this legislation, the BTK is granted the power to enforce monitoring and content-filtering mechanisms. The procedures have been devised with the intention of limiting the availability of websites and content that have been categorized as illegal according to Turkish legislation. The broad reach of the law enables the surveillance of a diverse range of online activity, rendering it a crucial instrument in Türkiye's digital governance (Işık, 2023, p. 39).

Building upon the fundamental principles of the Internet Law, it is imperative to examine the modifications introduced by Additional Article 4, which specifically addresses the governance of social network providers. This particular provision assumes significance due to the increasing significance of social media platforms in modern-day communication. This amendment highlights the Turkish government's commitment to ensure that digital platforms – especially those operating outside of Türkiye – adhere to a regulatory framework that is in accordance with national legal requirements and societal values.

In accordance with the legislation, overseas social network companies that have a substantial number of users from Türkiye are required to designate a representative located within the country. The representative, serving as a vital intermediary, is responsible for ensuring adherence to Turkish rules and facilitating direct correspondence with the relevant authorities. To subject worldwide social networks to more stringent regulatory oversight, it is necessary for providers experiencing significant user traffic to create a legal business within Türkiye.

To ensure compliance with these standards, Additional Article 4 provides a system of sanctions that encompass significant administrative fines as well as harsh measures such as the restriction of advertisement contracts and bandwidth throttling. The punitive measures not only demonstrate the Turkish government's commitment to enforcing compliance but also exemplify the expanding jurisdiction of legislation in governing digital material.

Additionally, the amendment requires social network providers to provide comprehensive biannual reports. The objective of these reports is to improve openness and accountability in the digital domain by providing comprehensive information on many topics such as content management, user applications, algorithms, and advertising rules.

The legislation also prioritizes the protection of user data security and the safety of children. To ensure data protection and legal accessibility, it is mandated that providers keep user data inside the borders of Türkiye. Furthermore, it is important to note that the legislation imposes child protection protocols, highlighting the increasing concerns regarding the well-being of susceptible users within the digital realm.

Ultimately, the legislation places significant emphasis on the crucial aspects of legal collaboration and openness. To address internet-related crimes and provide a secure and lawful digital environment, it is imperative for social network providers to engage in cooperation with Turkish authorities and comply with court rulings pertaining to content control. This underscores the government's dedication to upholding the principles of safety and legality within the online sphere.

In essence, the inclusion of Additional Article 4 in the Internet Law signifies a notable broadening of Türkiye's stance on the control of social media platforms. The amendment seeks to improve legal adherence, safeguard users, and promote transparency by implementing rigorous criteria and penalties for social network providers, particularly those operating internationally. This initiative is designed to tackle the distinct obstacles presented by the ever-changing realm of digital communication.

Specific Regulations for Public Officials Using Social Media

The regulation of social media usage by public officials in Türkiye, such as judges, prosecutors, and other government employees, is a matter of considerable importance. One key aspect of this issue involves striking a balance between maintaining professional etiquette and upholding the fundamental right to freedom of expression.

A ruling made by the Turkish Constitutional Court, as documented in Application No. 2018/36354 and dated 18/10/2022, offers significant scholarly perspective on this equilibrium. The individual in question, who works as an engineer for the water and sewage administration of the metropolitan municipality, faced disciplinary action due to a social media post whereby they expressed criticism toward the appointments made to fill positions that became vacant as a result of ongoing investigations. The aforementioned statement was perceived as derogatory toward the integrity of the public sector, resulting in an official inquiry into the matter and subsequent punitive measures being taken against the individual in question. Nevertheless, the court determined that the disciplinary measure contravened the applicant's constitutional right to freedom of expression, underscoring the imperative of conducting comprehensive, precise, and personalized assessments in similar instances.

The court underscored the importance of public officials being cognizant of the impact their words have on their professional roles and responsibilities even when expressing personal beliefs outside the scope of their official duties. When assessing the potential impact of a public official's social media activity on their perceived integrity and trustworthiness, it is important to take into account the contextual factors surrounding their statements and if they have exploited any privileges associated with their public position. The court additionally emphasized the significance of evaluating whether such manifestations impede the uninterrupted provision, efficacy, or productivity of public services, and whether disciplinary measures align with a requisite societal necessity and are commensurate with the extent of influence on the public function.

To enhance the comprehensiveness of the regulatory framework, the Public Officials Ethics Committee has developed a set of guidelines titled "Social Media Ethical Principles" to provide direction to public officials on their behavior on online platforms. These principles underscore the need to maintain neutrality, particularly in conversations pertaining to public policies, wherein officials are required to refrain from engaging in behaviors that may be interpreted as compromising their impartiality. Individuals are recommended to refrain from engaging in discriminatory behaviors that are rooted in language, race, or political ideologies. Furthermore, these standards emphasize the significance of preserving the reputation of the organizations they are associated with. This necessitates a meticulous evaluation of the potential ramifications of individuals' personal social media engagement inside their professional domain, ensuring that their statements are consistent with empirical evidence and do not distort their professional responsibilities.

The principles also emphasize the significance of avoiding conflicts of interest, especially in scenarios where the utilization of social media by a public figure may be interpreted as self-serving or generating a sense of partiality. Furthermore, the significance of utilizing social media in a productive manner throughout official working hours is emphasized, with a focus on ensuring that such engagements do not impede the execution of professional responsibilities. Officials are expected to disseminate precise and up-to-date information, refraining from perpetuating disinformation or sharing anything that may involve violence or explicit sexual material.

Adherence to human rights is an additional fundamental component of these rules. Public authorities are mandated to refrain from engaging in any conduct that may encroach upon the rights of individuals, including avoiding the use of intolerant language or engaging in behaviors that could potentially be interpreted as discriminatory. Moreover, it is crucial to highlight the significance of exercising responsibility when utilizing institutional social media platforms. These accounts should be administered with utmost professionalism, refraining from pursuing personal or political interests, and prioritizing the preservation of confidentiality and information security.

The prevailing policy for the utilization of social media within the Turkish public administration centers around the endeavor to strike a harmonious equilibrium between the professional obligations and personal self-expression of public officials. The standard practice generally restricts the dissemination of secret institutional information on personal social media platforms, thereby ensuring the preservation of confidentiality and ethical conduct. Furthermore, these policies encompass strategies aimed at guaranteeing that the utilization of social media does not hinder work efficiency or the fulfillment of organizational objectives. The management of personal online activities and professional obligations is frequently achieved by implementing regulated access to social media platforms, particularly for individuals who lack authorization to handle official ministry accounts. This measure aims to mitigate potential conflicts that may arise between personal online engagements and professional responsibilities. This approach exemplifies a collective dedication to upholding a harmonious equilibrium between personal liberties and the requisites of professionalism and security within the realm of public service positions.

Legal Framework for Social Media Influencers and Content Providers

In the dynamic digital environment of Türkiye, there has been a notable increase in the extent and organization of regulations pertaining to social media influencers and content providers (Goanta & Ranchordás, 2020). The adoption of the "Guideline on Commercial Advertising and Unfair Commercial Practices by Social Media Influencers" by the Board of Advertisement via principal decision No. 2021/2, on May 4, 2021, marks a noteworthy advancement in the realm of Turkish digital marketing legislation. The guideline in question is substantiated by significant legal instruments such as the Law on Consumer Protection No. 6502 and the Regulation on Commercial Advertising and Unfair Commercial Practices. It offers comprehensive instructions for various parties involved, including individual influencers, advertising agencies, and media organizations. The provided statement establishes precise definitions for the terms "social media" and "social media influencers" within a legally enforceable framework, thereby establishing explicit guidelines for adherence to regulatory requirements.

The legislative framework in question mandates the use of transparent and discernible advertising content, explicitly forbidding covert product placement on social media sites. There is a requirement for influencers to reveal any commercial affiliations in their posts, using appropriate phrases and formats tailored to various digital platforms, including video-sharing sites, social networking platforms, and podcasting services. The purpose of these regulations is to enhance the consumer's ability to identify promotional content, hence providing protection against misleading marketing techniques.

Furthermore, the framework enforces rigorous requirements on both influencers and advertisers. To maintain ethical advertising practices, influencers are obligated to comply with certain requirements that encompass refraining from making deceptive health assertions and possessing firsthand familiarity with the endorsed merchandise. The obligation to inform influencers about these criteria and ensure their compliance lies with advertisers.

Concurrently, the growing significance of social media influencers in Türkiye is acknowledged within the realm of digital marketing. Originally regarded as a means of enjoyment or personal gratification, the practice of influencing has undergone a significant transformation, emerging as a lucrative commercial enterprise. Considering their capacity to influence and shape human behavior, influencers have become the focus of regulatory measures akin to those imposed on conventional business entities. This evolutionary process is in accordance with prevailing worldwide patterns, wherein European national courts have initiated the establishment of regulations pertaining to social media advertising.

In relation to tax liabilities, the tax legislation in Türkiye categorizes the revenue generated from influencer engagements as commercial income. The revenue generated by advertising serves as a direct contributor to the sales and overall financial performance of the advertising organization. In accordance with Turkish legislation, influencers actively participate in ongoing and structured endeavors through the utilization of many instruments and platforms, thereby fulfilling the requirements for being subject to income taxation. Presidential Decree no. 476, which was announced in 2019, reinforces the tax responsibilities associated with internet advertising, specifically encompassing the actions conducted by individuals known as social media influencers.

In summary, the regulatory measures implemented by Türkiye with regard to social media influencers and content providers can be characterized as both progressive and comprehensive. The safeguarding of consumer interests is not the sole purpose, but, rather, an additional benefit, of digital marketing techniques. Moreover, these practices contribute to the reinforcement of credibility and trustworthiness in the field, aligning with a wider international movement toward increased accountability and transparency in the realm of online advertising.

Conclusion

The regulatory framework around social media in Türkiye has seen a notable transformation, characterized by substantial shifts that demonstrate the country's flexible stance toward governing the internet. Prior to recent revisions, the legal framework concerning the internet in Türkiye mostly centered on the regulation of online material accessibility by means of IP- and DNS restriction methods. The foundation of internet regulation since 2007 has been the Law on the Regulation of Broadcasts via Internet and Prevention of Crimes Committed via Such Broadcasts, upon which this strategy is based.

Nevertheless, the growing complexity of encryption techniques and the significance of social media in socioeconomic spheres called for a fundamental change in approach. The implementation of the 2020 amendment to the Internet Law, which marked a pivotal moment, mandated that social media corporations create a domestic presence within the borders of Türkiye. This requirement not only enabled the establishment of direct contact channels between users and these organizations but also placed additional obligations on them. These obligations include promptly addressing user inquiries, generating moderation reports, adopting methods for localizing data, and strengthening safeguards for minors.

The alterations indicate a transition from a responsive to a proactive regulatory system. Prior to the implementation of these regulations, the authorities predominantly employed a strategy of access restriction as a means to curtail usage of social media platforms. In contrast, the existing protocol entails direct interaction with social media platforms through their respective local representatives. This move places a strong emphasis on collaboration and accountability, hence shifting the responsibility to social media platforms to adhere to Türkiye's regulatory framework.

These achievements exemplify Türkiye's dedication to adapting its internet legislation to tackle the current issues presented by the digital era. There has been a transition in emphasis from only limiting material to adopting a comprehensive strategy that encompasses the protection of individual rights, the promotion of transparency, and the establishment of responsible practices in the realm of social media. This transition encompasses not just a modification to regulations but also serves as an embodiment of Türkiye's comprehensive digital strategy, aiming to strike a delicate equilibrium between internet freedom and the needs of society and national security.

Data Availability Statement

Data sharing is not applicable to this chapter as no new data were created or analyzed in this book.

References

Çekin, M. S., Berktaş, A. E., & Akıncı, M. F. (2023). *Veri Hukuku*. Istanbul: On İki Levha Yayıncılık.

Goanta, C., & Ranchordás, S. (2020). *The regulation of social media influencers*. Cheltenham: Edward Elgar Publishing.

Grassie, G. (2017). Control of content on social media – Technology as judge, jury and executioner? *Journal of Intellectual Property Law & Practice*, 533–534. https://doi.org/10.1093/jiplp/jpx117

Işık, A. (2023). *İnternet Aktörleri ve Egemenliğin Değişen Boyutları*. Istanbul: On İki Levha Yayıncılık.

Kaya, M. B. (2010). *Teknik ve Hukuki Boyutlarıyla İnternete Erişimin Engellenmesi*. Istanbul: On İki Levha Yayıncılık.

Kaya, M. B. (2021). *İnternet Hukuku*. Istanbul: On İki Levha Yayıncılık.

Lambert, P. (2015). *International handbook of social media laws*. West Sussex: Bloomsbury Publishing.

Tan, C. (2018). *Regulating content on social media: Copyright, terms of service and technological features*. London: UCL Press.

Turillazzi, A., Taddeo, M., Floridi, L., & Casolari, F. (2023). The digital services act: An analysis of its ethical, legal, and social implications. *Law, Innovation and Technology*, 83–106. https://doi.org/10.1080/17579961.2023.2184136

Vranaki, A. (2022). *Regulating social network sites data protection, copyright and power*. Cheltenham: Edward Elgar Publishing.

Zech, H. (2021). General and specific monitoring obligations in the digital services act. In H. Richter, M. Straub, & E. Tuchtfeld (Eds.), *To break up or regulate big tech? Avenues to constrain private power in the DSA/DMA package*. Max Planck Institute for Innovation & Competition Research Paper No. 21–25, https://doi.org/10.17176/20210902-113002-0

Index

Note: Page numbers in *italic* indicate a figure and page numbers in **bold** indicate a table on the corresponding page.